D0780077

Practical Tortoise Raising

Practical Tortoise Raising

and Other Philosophical Essays

Simon Blackburn

UNIVERSITY PRESS

OXFORD
UNIVERSITY PRESS

Great Clarendon Street, Oxford OX2 6DP

Oxford University Press is a department of the University of Oxford.
It furthers the University's objective of excellence in research, scholarship,
and education by publishing worldwide in

Oxford New York

Auckland Cape Town Dar es Salaam Hong Kong Karachi
Kuala Lumpur Madrid Melbourne Mexico City Nairobi
New Delhi Shanghai Taipei Toronto

With offices in

Argentina Austria Brazil Chile Czech Republic France Greece
Guatemala Hungary Italy Japan Poland Portugal Singapore
South Korea Switzerland Thailand Turkey Ukraine Vietnam

Oxford is a registered trade mark of Oxford University Press
in the UK and in certain other countries

Published in the United States
by Oxford University Press Inc., New York

British Library Cataloguing in Publication Data
Data available

Library of Congress Cataloging in Publication Data
Library of Congress Control Number: 2010927210

Typeset by Laserwords Private Limited, Chennai, India
Printed in Great Britain
on acid-free paper by
Clays Ltd, St Ives plc

ISBN 978-0-19-954805-7

10 9 8 7 6 5 4 3 2 1

Preface

The papers collected in this volume have been published before. They are reprinted here with minimal editorial changes, but sometimes with postscripts saying how I now regard issues, or wish that I had expressed myself. In the case of the most recent papers, there has been no time for this process yet to take place. The division between those centred upon practical reasoning, and those with a more semantic or metaphysical focus, might be useful, but it should not be thought particularly important, since I have always found it easy to ignore that borderline, and a number of papers could easily have found themselves on either side of it.

As its title indicated, the previous collection of my papers, *Essays in Quasi-Realism*, had a definite focus, although it also contained papers that had little to do with that focus. Insofar as this collection has an equivalent centre of gravity, it is probably best thought of as pragmatism. At the time of the previous collection I suspect I had not fully absorbed the deflationary theory of truth, nor had I obtained my current view of the relation between the expressive theory of ethics defended in that volume, and those modern approaches to the theory of meaning that fly under the banner of pragmatism. This volume does something, I hope, to rectify those omissions, with some essays directly concerned with pragmatism, and others largely directed to the implications of deflationism. The collection therefore concentrates less on the virtues and vicissitudes of 'quasi-realism' itself, although I have allowed myself to take notice of reactions to that position that seemed to me sufficiently interesting to repay attention. But I would rather the collection be seen as a pot-pourri of diverse interests and problems. I am not single-minded enough, or vain enough, to devote an entire professional life to defending any one position with which, for better or worse, I tend to be identified. Nevertheless I fear that the old Adam raises its head occasionally, and those who believe it should be buried once and for all may have to search for bigger silver bullets, sharper stakes, or more deserted crossroads. But some of the papers, especially in the first section, while of some use in sectarian battles about expressivism, bring in much wider issues and are to that extent self-standing. Others, as I say, have little or nothing to do with that issue.

SWB

Cambridge, February 2010

Acknowledgements

The following essays in this volume are reprinted with permission:

'Circles, Finks, Smells, and Biconditionals', first published in James Tomberlin, ed., *Philosophical Perspectives*, vol. 7, *Language and Logic*. Copyright © by Ridgeview Publishing Co., Atascadero, CA. Reprinted by permission of Ridgeview Publishing Company.

'Dilemmas: Dithering, Plumping, and Grief', first published in Gene Mason, ed., *Moral Dilemmas and Moral Theory* (Oxford: Oxford University Press, 1996). Reprinted by permission of Oxford University Press.

'Group Minds and Expressive Harm', first published in *Maryland Law Review* 60.3 (2001): 467–92. Reprinted by permission of *Maryland Law Review*.

'Julius Caesar and George Berkeley Play Leapfro', first published in Cynthia MacDonald and Graham MacDonald, eds, *McDowell and His Critics* (Oxford: Blackwell, 2006). Reprinted by permission of John Wiley & Sons Ltd.

'Must We Weep for Sentimentalism?', first published in J. Dreier, ed., *Contemporary Ethics* (Oxford: Blackwell, 2005). Reprinted by permission of John Wiley & Sons Ltd.

'Perspectives, Fictions, Errors, Play', first published in Brian Leiter and Neil Sinhababu, eds, *Nietzsche and Morality* (Oxford: Oxford University Press, 2007). Reprinted by permission of Oxford University Press.

'Practical Tortoise Raising', first published in *Mind* 104 (1995): 695–711. Reprinted by permission of the editors of *Mind* and Oxford University Press.

'Success Semantics', first published in H. Mellor and H. Lillehammer, eds, *Ramsey's Legacy* (Oxford: Clarendon Press, 2005). Reprinted by permission of Oxford University Press.

'The Absolute Conception: Putnam vs. Williams', first published in Daniel Calcutt, ed., *Reading Bernard Williams* (London: Routledge, 2008), pp. 9–13. Reprinted by permission.

'The Majesty of Reason', first published in *Philosophy* 85.1 (2010): 5–27, © Royal Institute of Philosophy, published by Cambridge University Press, reproduced with permission.

'The Steps from Doing to Saying', first published in *Proceedings of the Aristotelian Society* 2010. Reprinted courtesy of the Editors of the Aristotelian Society, © 2010.

'Through Thick and Thin', first published in *Proceedings of the Aristotelian Society Supplementary Volume* 66 (1992): 285–99. Reprinted by courtesy of the Editors of the Aristotelian Society, © 1992.

'Trust, Cooperation, and Human Psychology', first published in Valerie Braithwaite and Margaret Levi, eds, *Trust and Governance*, © 1998 Russell Sage Foundation, 112 East 64th Street, New York, N.Y. 10021. Reprinted with permission.

'Truth, Beauty, and Goodness', first published in Russ Shafer Landau, ed., *Oxford Studies in Metaethics*, vol. 4 (Oxford: Oxford University Press, 2009). Reprinted by permission of Oxford University Press.

'Wittgenstein's Irrealism', first published in Rudolf Haller and Johannes Brandl, eds, *Wittgenstein: Towards a Re-evaluation* (Vienna: Hölder-Pichler-Tempsky, 1990). Reprinted by permission of the Österreichische Ludwig Wittgenstein Gesellschaft, Kirchberg, Austria.

Contents

Introduction

Practical thought has always struck me as an ideal laboratory in which to perform experiments with notions like representation, truth, reason, and assertion. These notions, so bland and familiar when we navigate the middle-sized dry goods that make up the philosopher's friendliest environment, are apt to sound strange and to blur somewhat when we turn to less familiar topics, and amongst these, values and norms rank high, alongside other well-known suspects such as abstract objects, possible worlds, and intentional relations. It is, of course, quite possible to try to soothe away any such suspicion, urging that with a proper account of representation and the others, values and the rest no more deserve to be objects of puzzle or inquiry than anything else. But puzzles are tenacious things, and in this case I believe rightly.

For in the everyday we are content with our abilities, guaranteed by smoothly running sensory capacities, to put ourselves into situations where what we say is going to co-vary causally with how things stand. This is what our senses and our cognitive functions together enable us to do in respect of middle-sized dry goods and their familiar, perceptible properties. These make up the physical environment into which we are each thrown at birth. But we have no such confidence in causal co-variation in other cases. These then attract attention precisely because it can seem a miracle that we should know anything about them, for how, in Kantian terms, can concepts get a grip when intuition fails?

From 1984, when I published *Spreading the Word*, I became known for a particular approach to some of the issues raised in the last paragraph. This went under the unappealing name of 'quasi-realism' although in essay 9 in this volume I explain that I now regard that title with something of the embarrassment that ought to afflict parents who call their children things like 'Honeymoon' or 'Sheetrock'. I no longer think that in the relevant areas there is a position called 'realism' which it is worth using as a bearing, and I think it was unfortunate to suggest that if there were, the right position would be to speak 'as if' it were true. However, the task that was indicated by that title still exists, for there is still a route to be traversed when we try to understand what we say in terms of what we are doing when we say it. A functional pluralist still has to confront the smooth propositional surface of ordinary discourse and thought: the fact that, as Wittgenstein said, 'the clothing of our language makes everything alike'. This can be a technical task, which I christen the task of crossing Frege's abyss. The technical part comes in showing how propositional operations, such as negation, conditionalization, disjunction, or quantification, interact with linguistic expressions (sentences) whose primary function is identified in terms of actions performed in expressing commitments with them, when those commitments are thought of in practical rather than descriptive terms.

The topic has been extensively discussed in a long literature, and the technical issues no longer galvanize me. So the papers in this volume are generally not about that. I no longer think of the predicates involved in evaluation or in offering modal judgements, for instance, as semantically different from others. But this is only because semantic categories are too coarse-grained to do the necessary work: they lull us into remaining 'unconscious of the prodigious diversity of all the everyday language-games' (Wittgenstein). Instead, in essay 2 I explain how I take deflationism to suggest a simple way of avoiding them, but happily without giving any ground to the critics of expressivism. Semantics tells us only where we have ended up; my explanatory interest is in suggesting why and how we have ended up where we did. This brings in wider questions of functional pluralism, of pragmatism, of philosophy of mind, and of the nature of practical reasoning, and these are the topics addressed here.

Explanation is frowned upon in some circles. Twenty years ago, at a conference celebrating Wittgenstein's centenary, I read the paper reprinted here as essay 11 pointing out that Wittgenstein cannot conceivably be read as hostile to the kind of journey from doing to saying that interests me. Wittgenstein may have doubted whether philosophy gives explanations. But he never doubted that it was possible to obtain an *übersichtliche Darstellung* or perspicuous representation of puzzling areas of discourse—a view from where the questions that plague us stop doing so. Ideally, our difficulties could no longer be expressed. They would be revealed as the creatures of our misunderstandings of our own language. I find this ambition perfectly congenial, and I hope it is visible in some of the papers included here.

Reflecting on the journey these papers illustrate, I find that I have become ever more suspicious of a kind of inflated rationalism or logicism. Too much confidence in notions like that of a concept or rule blinds us to the subtleties with which we conduct our practical, and therefore our linguistic, lives. To the inflated logicist, using language is like boarding a tram which then shunts you willy-nilly to set destinations fixedly foretold by the itinerary available when you boarded. Whereas I see it more in terms of sailing or climbing, where any number of contextually variable factors, not to mention personal skills or inadequacies or interactions, may alter where you end up. From this perspective, inflated logicism is like trying to understand ballroom dancing in terms of a tram timetable. I even have the temerity to apply this stance to the logician's darling topic, vagueness, in the addendum to essay 7, but I am conscious that much more needs to be said.

I
Practical Philosophy and Ethics

1

Practical Tortoise Raising

In 1895 Lewis Carroll wrote his famous *Mind* article, 'What the Tortoise Said to Achilles'. The problem he raised can succinctly be put like this: can logic make the mind move? Or, less enigmatically, how do we describe what is wrong with the tortoise's argument that, however many premises Achilles has him accept, he always has space to refrain from drawing the conclusion?

In this paper I am not so much concerned with movements of the mind, as movements of the will. But my question bears a similarity to that of the tortoise. I want to ask whether the will is under the control of fact and reason, combined. And I shall try to show that there is always something else, something that is not under the control of fact and reason, which has to be given as a brute extra, if deliberation is ever to end by determining the will. This is, of course, a Humean conclusion, and the only novelty comes in the way I wish to argue it. For I believe that many philosophers think, erroneously, that Hume relies on a naive and outdated conception of facts, or an even more naive and outdated conception of reason, in order to put passion on their throne. My tortoise defends Hume: what we do with our premises is not itself construed as acceptance of a premise.

As it stands the project is only described metaphorically. Presumably everything, including movement of the will, is under the control of facts in some sense, for even if they are only facts about our physiology or chemistry, still, they make us move. I am interested of course, only in cognitive control, or control by the apprehension of fact and reason.

Day I

Achilles, then, had overtaken the tortoise and was sitting comfortably on its back. 'You see,' he said, 'the distances were constantly diminishing, and so—'

'But if they had been constantly increasing?' the tortoise interrupted, 'how then? . . . Well now, would you like to hear of a race-course, that most people fancy they can get to the end of in two or three steps, while it really consists of an infinite number of distances, each one longer than the previous one? . . . Let us take a little bit of an argument for acting:'

(P) I would prefer eating lettuce to eating souvlaki.
(B) The moment of decision is at hand.
(Z) Let me choose to eat lettuce rather than souvlaki!

'Well,' continued the tortoise, 'there is no question of accepting (Z) as true, but there may be a question of accepting it. Let us agree that accepting (Z) amounts to actually doing whatever is involved in choosing lettuce rather than souvlaki. We accept (Z) only if the will is determined, and an intention is formed. Are we to suppose that if we accept (P) and (B), then we must accept (Z)?'

'Wait a minute,' said Achilles, 'I don't want to rush you. It occurs to me that some philosophers make a distinction between what you prefer and what you think you ought to prefer, or would prefer if you were ideally placed, for a tortoise. Perhaps this affects the issue.'

'If you like,' said the tortoise. 'I too hate this modern fad for rushing past anything like that. Let us put it in:'

(P) I would prefer eating lettuce to eating souvlaki.
(M) I think it is right to prefer lettuce to souvlaki.
(B) The moment of decision is at hand.
(Z) Let me choose to eat lettuce rather than souvlaki!

'That's better!' said Achilles. 'That certainly wraps it up for (Z). Surely you must accept (Z) if all those are true!'

'I don't quite know,' said the tortoise sadly. 'Sometimes, well, I am not sure how important rightness is. I certainly get these urges to do what I think is wrong, don't you know. I am really quite good at what you Greeks keep calling akrasia; in fact I rather enjoy it.'

'Good heavens,' replied Achilles sternly yet compassionately. 'If there is one thing modern moral philosophy will tell you, it is that any such behaviour is quite irrational. The norms of reason are foundations for the norms of ethics.'

'And we don't want to be unreasonable, do we?' said the tortoise. 'In fact, we had better add it, just to make sure.'

(RM) I think it is rational to do what I think is right.

'There we are,' announced Achilles in triumph. 'Reason prevails!'

'Well, that is certainly a change,' said the tortoise, 'and yet sometimes, well, I am not sure how important rationality is. I certainly get these urges to act against reason, don't you know. I am really quite good at that kind of akrasia; in fact I rather enjoy it.'

'Holy Apollo!' exclaimed Achilles. 'Do you mean you have been reading the Romantics, so many millennia before their time? Are you in favour of short-termism and spontaneity, and against prudence and economics? Or is it something else?'

'I don't know,' said the tortoise, 'but perhaps you can explain to me: must I be rational?'

'Oh, certainly,' said Achilles, 'you must if . . . well, if you want to be rational, you know.'

'I love hypothetical imperatives,' said the tortoise, 'but I am not sure this one is going to help. Still, we could make sure that rationality and ethics pull together, if you like,' he conceded helpfully.

(MR) I think it right to do what I think is rational.

'Hmmm,' said Achilles. 'I hadn't expected to put that in, but it is terribly decent of you to let me. And now at last we are home and dry!'

'Only,' said the tortoise apologetically, 'I get so terribly confused. We had to add (M) and I can't help wondering that although I am sure it is right to do what is rational, these fits of akrasia still afflict me so chronically. I must have been badly brought up,' he added bashfully.

Achilles frowned as he replaced his pencil with a new one. 'I think that is probably a bit morbid,' he said. 'Surely in general you prefer to do what is right and rational?' 'Perhaps we should add it,' encouraged the tortoise:

(P') I prefer to do what I think it right and rational to do.

'And now,' said Achilles in triumph again, 'we really are getting somewhere. The last time I talked with you, a century ago, you made me keep adding different premises! But now there is simply nothing more to add!' And he did a little dance.

'I love the way you move yourself,' said the tortoise, sitting comfortably. 'All I admit is that I prefer to do what is right and rational. But then, after all, I preferred lettuce to souvlaki. And we had to add a bit to that, didn't we?' he laughed, modestly.

'Sacred Zeno!' expostulated Achilles. 'You are not going to make me add another round, are you? I can see it coming: you need that it is right to prefer to do what you think it is right and rational to do, and so on and so on. You really are the most stubborn animal.'

'Well, I am a bit careful,' confessed the tortoise. 'And I don't really know that I am all that confident that it is right and rational to prefer to do what I think it is right and rational to do. After all, many people are wrong and stupid in preferring to do what they think it is right and rational to do. I wouldn't want to act while I am worried in case I am like them!'

But great Achilles had flown to the libraries to collect some volumes on the Theory of Rational Choice. Munching some lettuce, the tortoise awaited his return.

Day II

'You know,' resumed Achilles, 'this whole business is off on the wrong foot. We have been talking as if there is a gap between preference and actual choice. Whereas I now read that in the best circles it is done to believe in the theory of revealed preference. Which means we read your preference back from your choice. It is not an antecedent state whose apprehension determines choices—I admit that yesterday's conversation made that idea puzzling—but simply a logical construct from the choices you make!'

'Pardon me,' said the tortoise. 'I must have misunderstood something. Don't these economists and game theorists get paid for giving advice—advice about what to do?'

'Absolutely,' said Achilles. 'They are very rich and regarded as very good at it.'

'Tell me more,' said the tortoise admiringly.

'Well,' responded Achilles, putting on his lecturer's gown, 'it seems to go like this.

'The reasoning behind talking of revealed preference comes in two parts.[1] In the bad old days, it goes, it was thought that "utility" will be a Benthamite, empirical quantity which happened to be the object of desire, or ought to be the object of desire. But utilities so conceived prove both empirically and philosophically bogus, as indeed Bentham might have learned from Bishop Butler.[2] It is neither true nor useful as an approximation that people or tortoises act so as to maximize the intensity or duration of some state of themselves. They do not even always act with their own interests in mind, where these interests are construed as states of themselves. Rather, we see them as having an interest in some object when that object figures in their decision making. But objects here include states that are not states of the subject: the survival of the whales, or the relief of the famine, or the death of the blasphemer, or the success of a friend. Indeed, notoriously, unless this is so, the life resulting is apt to be unenviable and the selfishness is self-defeating. So let us instead reverse the equation: utilities are no longer empirically given, but are simply constructs from mathematically tractable ways of handling preferences. That is, given very weak assumptions an agent with an ordering of preferences over each of some set of options can be represented as if she had attached measurable "values", called utilities, to those options. The provision of a scale is similar in principle to that of providing numerical measures for weights, given only the results from a balance. A balance is an empirical determination of when one object weighs at least as much as another. The results of tests for whether one object is at least as heavy as another can be presented numerically, with the numbers representing "weights" of the objects in the set. An element has at least as great a weight as another if and only if the other does not outweigh it, which is to tip the balance against it.[3]

'So if we have pairwise preferences across choices in a set, we can represent their utilities numerically. But what corresponds to the empirical results from the balance, telling us when choice a is preferred to choice b? The orthodox answer amongst economists and game theorists is to accept the theory of revealed preferences. This was initially defended in the work of the economist Samuelson, and holds that preferences themselves are not

---

[1] A forceful recent presentation by a leading practitioner is Binmore 1994. See also Kreps 1990: 26, Dawes 1988: 154ff.

[2] Butler 1953: esp. Sermons I and XI.

[3] The classic presentation is von Neumann and Morgenstern 1944.

antecedent psychological states that happen to control (most) decisions. Rather, true preferences are those that are revealed by decisions.[4] It is, after all, a truism that to know what you or anyone else wants, see what you or anyone else chooses, or would choose given suitable options. To know that you prefer oil to butter, you see whether you choose it, at least when nothing further hangs on the decision. The theory of revealed preferences is perhaps less popular among philosopher than economists. But we shall see below good reason for accepting it, for there is really no other candidate for the necessary empirical test. Putting the two foundation stones together then, we have:

> (Util) A utility function is defined such that the utility of a is at least as great as b if and only if a is weakly preferred to b (i.e. preferred to b, or at least as much as b). Such a function can be defined over a set of options if preference satisfies two consistency conditions: for all outcomes a, b either a is weakly preferred to b, or b to a (totality), and if a is weakly preferred to b, and b to c, then a is weakly preferred to c (transitivity).

> (Revpref) Choice behaviour is primitive. If a player makes choices, then he is making choices as though he were equipped with a preference relation which has that choice preferred to others. An eligible agent is always interpretable as though he were seeking to further a preference.

'In a nutshell, the first part of the approach makes utilities "logical constructions" out of preferences, while the second makes preferences logical constructions out of actual choices.[5]

'To whom do (Util) and (Revpref) apply? To anyone with consistent, transitive preferences over a set of options. I shall call such persons eligible persons (it is vital not to confuse the issue by calling them rational, as is frequently done). An ineligible person would be someone who cannot be interpreted in terms of utilities, just as a balance that cannot weigh some element in a set, or that weighs a > b, and b > c, but c > a, cannot deliver a set of weights defined over the set. It is of the utmost importance, then, to realize that there are not two sorts of players in a prisoners' dilemma, or other

---

[4] Samuelson 1947.

[5] To avoid misunderstanding, I should add that in a full discussion belief would have to be introduced as a variable. I am really only repeating the methodology of F. P. Ramsey. In the text as it stands belief is taken pretty much for granted but this was not intended to make it invisible. Patrick Shaw laments its absence in Shaw 1996.

game-theoretic structure, the eligible ones and the ineligible ones. "Ineligible" refers not to a kind of player, but to someone who cannot be interpreted as playing at all. An ineligible player is like someone who approaches chess by knocking over the board. It is, however, often a matter of judgement whether someone who appears to be ineligible through having intransitive preferences is so really, or is best interpreted as having redefined the options in front of her, but this is not our concern in what follows.

'Of course, both (Util) and (Revpref) have not gone uncriticized. Amartya Sen, for example, introduces notions of sympathy (having your welfare affected by the position of others) and an individual's commitments (conceived of as standing outside, and even in opposition to their own welfare) as independent pressures on action.[6] He points out that preference, in the economics literature, has two liaisons: one is with choice, but the other is with welfare. That is, increased preference satisfaction is supposed to increase welfare, and he denies that a notion of preference based on (Revpref) can fulfil this second condition. For people may behave as if they had certain preferences (those are the preferences we would read back from their behaviour) when their welfare, or even their expected welfare, would be better served if they behaved differently. Sen also believes that this undermines the authority of an approach based on (Util). And if it does so, it also undermines (Revpref), since if because of sympathy or commitment an agent acts against his preferences (what he would really like to do, if only the situation allowed it), then of course his action will not be revealing those preferences.

'The orthodox game theorist's response is that their framework is quite elastic enough to encompass whatever motivations we believe to exist. As I have already sketched, there is no need to deny that a player may care about other things than their own interests, real or perceived, or their own welfare as opposed to that of others. In the apt phrase of David Gauthier, "it is not interests in the self, that take oneself as object, but interests of the self, held by oneself as subject, that provide the basis for rational choice and action."[7] Choice is the upshot of whatever the player cares about, and as I have sketched, utility derives from choice.[8] So it is wrong to criticize

---

[6] Sen 1982, esp. the essays collected in Part I.   [7] Gauthier 1986: 7.

[8] It is very easy to forget this. Binmore, for example, describes *homo economicus* as someone whose 'concern is with his own self-interest, *broadly conceived*' (1994: 19). But this is wrong: *homo economicus* need not be concerned with himself at all, under any conception of his own interests.

either axiom by reminding ourselves of the heterogeneous nature of desire. Rather, we must simply be careful to build any apparently "exogenous" or external independent desires into the payoffs represented in the choice situation.

'The same caveats apply if we start to contrast preference with principle or with conscience. There is certainly a vernacular distinction here, for we talk of being obliged to do what we do not prefer to do. But the concepts defined by our two axioms do not match this distinction, and are not refuted by it. Rather, preference, revealed by choice, may include the preference for acting on any specific principle: the preference to keep a promise, or keep a vow to God, or to avoid the gaze of the man within, or the preference to do one's bit, the preference for being the man who bought the Brooklyn Bridge rather than the man who sold it, or even the preference to try to live up to our better selves. The better way to describe the "conflict" between a narrow sense of preference and what happens when principle is introduced is to say that sometimes we are obliged to do what we would not otherwise have preferred to do; but this leaves it open that now, in the presence of the obligation, our preference is actually that we conform to the requirements of obligation or duty. The counterfactual preference, that we would have had, had we not made the promise or felt obliged to cooperate, or whatever it is, is not our all-things-considered preference.'

'Splendid, absolutely splendid,' interrupted the tortoise, a little sharply. 'But now tell me how this translates into advice, for this is what we were hoping to find.'

'Well,' said Achilles, confidently, 'consider the familiar prisoners' dilemma.'

		A	
		Hawk	Dove
	Hawk	1,1	0,3
B			
	Dove	3,0	2,2

'Each player acts independently, causally, of the other, and each knows the other's utilities. Now, looking at this the game theorist can advise you to be a hawk. For whatever your opponent does, you do better by playing hawk. Yet this advice has been contested, and indeed some people think it is rational to play dove.'

'Well, well,' said the tortoise. 'If the advice has been contested, then it must be significant advice! But tell me, to whom does it apply exactly?'

'As we have explained,' said Achilles huffily, 'to anyone eligible, and who is presented with the game.'

'*Timeo Danaos et dona ferentes*,' said the tortoise, smugly. 'Tell me, what would happen if I didn't follow the advice to choose hawk? Wouldn't I reveal a preference for being a dove?'

'Well, yes,' admitted Achilles, somewhat impatiently.

'And if that is so,' continued the tortoise imperturbably, 'how does it happen that these little figures you have in the boxes are the right ones? I mean, I can see how they might represent money or years in prison or something, but the game theorist is surely not telling me that it is rational to care only about money or years in prison. I thought these figures represented the sum total of my preferences. But since these are revealed by choice, if I play dove, then they cannot be right.'

'Explain to me,' said Achilles, tottering slightly.

Here, the tortoise paused to put on the lecturer's gown. 'Suppose a player makes the dove choice. Then he preferred one or both of the options in which he acts as a dove to the others; by (Revpref) we must construct a utility function in accordance with that preference, and hence he was not actually in a prisoners' dilemma. In the terms often used, his decision problem cannot have been accurately "modelled" by presenting him as if he were in a prisoners' dilemma. For a prisoners' dilemma is defined so that the hawkish utilities outrank the doveish ones, and that in turn simply means that the hawkish options are the ones that get chosen. The conclusion ought to read that it is a tautology that an eligible player will necessarily choose hawk in the prisoners' dilemma.'

'Aha,' said Achilles, 'it is not quite as simple as that. For in such strategic problems, we have to consider the other player's likely choice. Imagine, if you will, the poor agent lurching towards a choice, and knowing that on the other side of a mirror, as it were, but quite independently, his twin is doing the same. It will be better all round if they plump for dove, in spite of the way that such a choice is dominated. Mightn't they each do so?'

'Oh, well,' replied the tortoise, 'if they know that it is a real twin, who will magically do exactly the same as they do, then the upshots are restricted to the symmetric ones, and playing dove dominates. But in real situations they don't know this, and they might do anything. If they have a minute to choose, then recalling what their twin is doing they might change their mind once in the first thirty seconds, again in the next fifteen seconds, again in half the remaining time, and so on. It would be like one of those lamps going on and off ever more quickly. I seem to remember you once modelled your running on just such a contraption,' he said, nostalgically remembering his first foray into philosophy, more than two thousand years earlier. 'Heaven knows where they end. All I am saying is that if they do go haywire, as well they might, and plump for dove, then if anything they reveal different preferences, and hence expected utilities, from the ones on show.

'For example,' continued the tortoise, 'when on p. 27 of his book Binmore stresses that "it is tautological that *homo economicus* maximizes all the time", we might think that this is peculiar to that kind of *homo*, or equally to *testudo economicus*, whom we then may or may not want to imitate. Whereas in the light of (Util) and (Revpref), it is tautological that any eligible agent maximizes all the time. And in interpreting this it is well to remember the extremely weak imposition that consistency involves: only that you have transitive preferences over the entire set of options in play. In particular, consistency does not entail any particular attitude towards risk, or towards other people, or towards action on principle. Nor does it entail constancy, or consistency over time, which means making the same choice on later occasions as you made on earlier ones.[9]

'More importantly, it is to be remembered that inconsistent players are of no interest. For if a player is genuinely inconsistent, in any way that matters to the game, then we will be unable to construct a function from preferences to utilities. In such a case we cannot say what the utilities of the agent are under different choices, and the interpretation of him as in a prisoners' dilemma, or any other kind of specific decision-theoretic problem, collapses. So in fact the tautology applies across the board: it is tautological than any player who can be interpreted as being in a prisoners'

---

[9] Why should it? Preferring butter today and oil tomorrow may be the key to a healthy diet. Change of preference is often good strategy, in poker, or in real and metaphorical battles. Some men find fickle inconstant women especially charming, in which case these are genetically successful traits.

dilemma chooses the dominant strategy. There exists no theory about non-eligible players, so the restriction to eligible players is insignificant.'

'Surely the game theorists know all this?' queried Achilles.

'Well,' said the tortoise, shaking his head mournfully, 'they tend to be forthright about the official framework in some places, but more coy when they are offering all that richly paid advice. For example, Binmore frequently describes himself as arguing against those who think that strongly dominated choices are rational (1994: 174); he sometimes describes his opponents as supposing that "out of equilibrium play can be sustained in the long run" (175), and by contrast presents himself as the realistic, Hobbesian man who is hard-headed enough to know that eventually if we can get more for ourselves, we will be tempted to do so. Theorists such as Gauthier, who think it is sometimes rational to choose the dominated strategy, are particular targets.'

'But isn't that as it should be?' said Achilles, fumbling a little.

'Well, I think it should be clear,' replied the tortoise, 'that these attitudes are thoroughly incoherent. It is not that out of equilibrium play cannot be sustained in the long run, or needs psychologies that we have not got, or is the private preserve of benighted and irrational bleeding-heart Kantians, but that it cannot happen at all. In out of equilibrium play in the prisoners' dilemma, an agent chooses the dominated strategy. But by (Util) and (Revpref) this is impossible: if an agent chooses a strategy, then this shows that the utility attached to it is higher than that attaching to any other strategy over which it was chosen.'[10]

---

[10] The point here is resisted by Shaw 1996, with a distinction between the action that an agent prefers (playing hawk or playing dove) and the outcome, that is, which of the four boxes he or she ends up in. But I think the distinction does not do the work he wishes. Here is another way of appreciating the tortoise's analysis of the situation. Let us distinguish between the empirical game, with payoffs described in terms of years in prison, dollars, and so forth, and the theoretical game, described in terms of agent's preferences and (thence, and interchangeably by (Util)) utilities. An agent faced with the *empirical* matrix is in a *theoretical* prisoners' dilemma only if $<3,0>$ is preferred to $<2,2>$ is preferred to $<1,1>$ is preferred to $<0,3>$. Adam's first preference is that he play hawk, and Eve dove. His second is that both play dove, third that both play hawk, and fourth that Eve plays hawk while he plays dove. Eve's are the same as applied to her, that is, she prefers most her playing hawk and Adam playing dove and so on down. So Adam's best outcome is her worst, and vice versa. They each rank $<H,H>$ third, and $<D,D>$ second. Their choices are thought of at this stage as made independently, and in ignorance of the other's choice.

What will Adam do, understanding this to be the situation? He will play hawk. Here is the proof. Adam knows that either Eve plays hawk, or she plays dove, and which she plays is independent of anything he does. Suppose she plays hawk. Then Adam is better off playing hawk: he gets his third

'Hmmm,' said Achilles. 'And yet, hasn't the enterprise of bringing rational weight to bear against selfishness made the prisoner's dilemma the central parable of modern political theory? How can that be so if you are right?'

'Oh, it has nothing to do with rationality,' said the tortoise, 'or even being good. The same point applies even if you want to be bad,' and he shuddered slightly, which is hard for a tortoise.

'Explain,' said Achilles wonderingly.

'Well, take blackmail,' said the tortoise. 'We can think of it in extended form in terms of a sequence of plays, one in succession by each of two players, Adam and Eve. At each node the player has to play one of two options, hawk or dove. In the following diagram, plays succeed each other in time. Hawkish behaviour is to the right, and doveish to the left. Adam's payoffs are described first. We are assuming as usual that each of Adam and Eve's payoffs is known to themselves, and to the other.

'We can draw the choices thus:

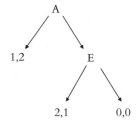

'The story is that before the game starts Eve has committed an indiscretion. If Adam does nothing (doveish) he has 1 unit and Eve 2. If he blackmails Eve (hawkish) and she submits (doveish) he takes one of Eve's units. But if

---

preference instead of his fourth and worst. Suppose she plays dove. Then Adam is better off playing hawk: he gets his first preference instead of his second. Playing hawk therefore has greater utility than playing dove for Adam. Mathematically its greater expected utility than playing dove is the sum:

(3rd − 4th)(Prob. Eve plays hawk) + (1st − 2nd)(Prob. Eve plays dove)

where '3rd', etc., represent the utility of the third, etc., upshots. Here the increased utility of 3rd over 4th is multiplied by the probability of Eve playing hawk, and the increased utility of 1st over 2nd multiplied by the probability of Eve playing dove. We know this expression is positive, since otherwise we would have got the rankings wrong. Knowing it is positive, we can only interpret Adam as being in this situation if he chooses the hawk option. If he were to choose the other, then by (Revpref) and (Util) dove is outranking hawk, in which case his preferences (meaning, of course, the sum total of his concerns) are not as described.

she does not submit (hawkish) she blows the gaff on him, revealing him as a blackmailer, but also revealing her own indiscretion, leaving them both worse off, in the 0,0 finale.[11]

'Orthodox decision theory has us reason as follows. In blackmail, eligible Eve will not play the final hawkish option. For doing so represents simple loss. Eligible Adam knows that this is so. Hence he plays hawk, and since she then plays dove, his blackmail is successful.

'Suppose, now, that Adam knows in advance that this is the matrix. Then he knows in advance that eligible Eve will not choose to be a hawk when it comes to her turn. For it would be a contradiction (by (Util) and (Revpref)) for Eve to choose 0 units of utility when she can have 1. So eligible Eve will play dove, and eligible Adam will play hawk. For, once more, it would be a contradiction for Adam to play dove when he could play hawk, leaving him with 1 instead of 2. So Adam does not face a choice: once he knows the matrix, he knows what is going to happen.

'Now remember that expert game theorists endorse both (Util) and (Revpref), and Binmore, for example, implies that all the rest of their kind do so as well.[12] He believes that the "advantages of the methodology in clarifying the underlying logic are overwhelming". What this means is that the game theorist takes care of any facts about psychologies at the modelling stage.[13] We have successfully modelled a set of players only when they have no interests (nothing they care about) that are unrepresented in the game's payoff structure. Often persons with other elements in their psychologies will not be in such games when others are.

'So what Eve needs to be is someone who is not modelled correctly as being in this game. In short, she needs to present herself as being vengeful and proud, disinclined to submit to blackmail, preferring her own financial ruin and that of Adam to the feeling of having been done down by him.

---

[11] I have changed the presentation and numbers slightly from the paper as it appeared in *Mind* purely for the sake of exposition.

[12] Actually, I think he is wrong about this, at least as far as the founding fathers are concerned. Von Neumann and Morgenstern, for instance, write that 'we shall therefore assume that the aim of all participants in the economic system is money, or equivalently a single monetary commodity' (1944: 2.2.1). Harsanyi 1977 contrasts the pursuit of 'self interest and individual values' with the 'rational pursuit of the interests of society as a whole', and sees games as modelling the former interest. The point is that in such approaches, an empirically given aim or type of aim is contrasted with concerns deriving from a person's overall inclinations or concerns. Of course, any resultant advice is then hypothetical in form: if you want to maximize only these specific concerns, act as follows.

[13] See esp. Binmore 1994: 162.

Should she know she will face such situations regularly, she needs to cultivate a nice public vicious streak. Of course, if she hasn't done that in advance, or had it done for her in a good school, she will be a plausible target for blackmail, poor thing.'

'Good lord, or rather Zeus,' said Achilles, correcting himself quickly. 'I suppose people like Gauthier would have to say that it is rational to be vicious.' And he shuddered in his turn. 'Let me try to sort it out. It certainly qualifies what we might have thought was meant by calling a strategy rational, or indeed calling the situation a game that calls for choices and strategies. We might have thought that if we talk of a game, and someone tells us that a particular strategy is rational, then we can interpret that as tantamount to giving us permission to follow it, or if it is uniquely rational, telling us to follow it. You do not in deliberation draw up two lists; one of what to do in given circumstances, and the other of what it is rational to do in the same circumstances.[14] But in game theory as it is now being conceived, nothing can be translated into advice. For suppose we are "advised" to follow the dominant strategy. This is null advice, equivalent to: behave so that a tautology is true of you. So if we don't follow the advice, then our choice reveals that it wasn't that game. But if it wasn't that game then the advice was inapplicable, and if the advice was inapplicable, then there was no point in following it in any event, for the game theorist had failed to model the situation properly. As Wittgenstein might have said, anything could accord with the advice, and that means that no advice was given. The economists' slogan "Maximize!" turns out not to be an injunction at all, for nothing could count as failing to follow it.[15] So the promise that we can learn something about rationality by these means collapses. Or, if we prefer it, the idea that the notion of rationality gains any purchase here is refuted. It is inevitable that so-called countertheoretical actions do not reveal the irrationality of the players, but the inadequacy of this application of the theory.'

'You always did catch up fast,' said the tortoise admiringly. 'And it also suggests that the question is not so much one of whether it is rational for Eve to be vicious, as whether she has been educated so that she and her

[14] Unless 'rational' is being used in an irrelevant, restricted sense in which what is rational contrasts with spontaneous or emotionally satisfying.

[15] Gauthier 1986: 27 points out the futility of this injunction on similar grounds. But his own views are not disentangled from the problem.

peers thrive in the situations in which they will be put. Some have, some haven't,' he added sententiously, and sat down, which is also quite difficult for a tortoise, and ate some more lettuce.

Day III

'Look,' said Achilles, forlornly contemplating his bonfire of books on the Theory of Rational Choice, 'decision making is at least under the control of fact and reason in another way. There will come after us one greater than us, who will show that it is a dictate of pure practical reason that we treat everyone as an end in themself. And his name shall be called Immanuel. But let's not start on that,' he added hurriedly.

'And every tortoise, I hope,' added the tortoise.

'If they are rational,' assured Achilles, muttering something under his breath.

'Tell me,' said the tortoise, 'it sounds nice and impartial. Must I be impartial?' he asked, innocently.

'Absolutely,' said Achilles piously. 'Even Hume, whom you somewhat resemble, realizes that we have to take up a common point of view. In a conversation with anyone else about what to do, there is a point where we must cease speaking the language of self-love, and correct our sentiments by invoking common standards, whereby we judge things and persons as they affect those surrounding them.'

'And the penalty if we don't?' asked the tortoise.

'Well, practical reasoning could not go forward,' said Achilles, 'and we would lose the benefits of cooperation, or of putting the first person plural in place of the first person singular.[16] We couldn't even row boats together.'

'We wouldn't want that,' said the tortoise sociably. 'But I remember a couple of days ago we thrashed out wants and preferences, and I am afraid I remained unmoved, if you remember. So what is new?'

'Kant improves upon Hume,' said Achilles enthusiastically. 'He shows how pure practical reason dictates respect for the law. For impartiality, fairness, and all that. All sorts of good things,' he finished lamely.

---

[16] Postema 1995.

'It sounds appetizing,' agreed the tortoise, 'but tell me about this dictation and this respect. What is my awful fate if I find this respect is not actually dictated?'

'Well, if you don't respect the law,' said Achilles, 'you will not be free, not an autonomous self-governing tortoise.'

'And I expect at least you are going to tell me that I wouldn't want to be anything else,' chimed in the tortoise, 'but that is not going to get us much further, is it? Presumably you really would like to tell me that it is contrary to reason not to respect the law, thereby achieving freedom and self-respect. And I doubt if I am going to believe you. For I believe that Kant will one day tell us that

The real morality of actions, their merit or guilt, even that of our own conduct, thus remains entirely hidden from us. Our imputations can refer only to the empirical character. How much of this character is ascribable to the pure effect of freedom, how much to mere nature, that is, to faults of temperament for which there is no responsibility, or to its happy constitution, can never be determined.[17]

'And I am afraid my own self-respect as a just and caring tortoise is not beholden to any such murky transcendental facts. And,' he added dropping his voice a little, 'I rather doubt whether your self-respect as a hero is, either.'

'But you are a just and fair and compassionate tortoise,' reminded Achilles.

'You're too kind,' said the tortoise, blushing modestly. 'But it is true. You will know how Adam Smith writes that

The jurisdiction of the man within, is founded altogether in the desire of praise-worthiness, and in the aversion to blame-worthiness; in the desire of possessing those qualities, and performing those actions, which we love and admire in other people; and in the dread of possessing those qualities, and performing those actions, which we hate and despise in other people.[18]

'Well, the same goes for the tortoise within,' he added helpfully.

'But it is not rational,' wailed Achilles, beating his head on the tortoise's shell.

'Just as well,' said the tortoise, 'given where that leaves us. And it is lucky my shell is so solid.'

[17] Kant 1963: A551/B579, p. 475.   [18] Smith 1976: III.2, 33.

Day IV

'Listen,' began Achilles, his locks dishevelled by what appeared to have been a sleepless night. 'At least you respect means–ends reasoning, do you not? And quite possibly there exists argument that if you do that then you cannot remain unmoved in other ways. Once you have some musts then you have to allow others.'

'Respect means–ends reasoning?' queried the tortoise. 'Explain to me what you mean.'

'Well, suppose you want some of that lettuce across the road. And you apprehend that the only way to get it is to cross the road, since lettuce is even less likely to move than you are. In other words, you know that if you want the lettuce, you must cross the road. So it follows that you conceive yourself under a necessity to cross the road. There would then be a kind of inconsistency in not crossing the road.'

'I think I only know one kind of inconsistency,' said the tortoise. 'The kind that goes p & ~p. Do you mean I am contradicting myself? It doesn't feel as if I am.'

'But don't you agree that if you want the lettuce you must cross the road? And you want the lettuce (and the moment of decision is at hand) . . . so you must cross the road.'

'By modus ponens,' said the tortoise, a nasty glint coming into his eye.

'Grrr,' said Achilles warningly.

'All right,' said the tortoise, backing off relatively hastily, 'but it isn't even modus ponens, is it? I mean, if I want a million pounds I must buy a lottery ticket, and I do want a million pounds, but I don't see that I must buy a lottery ticket. It is one of those off-colour conditionals where musts and oughts make the conclusion non-detachable. And in fact, I am not going to buy a lottery ticket,' he concluded with a flourish.

'Aha,' replied Achilles, 'that must mean you want something else more, such as avoiding lotteries or sitting still.'

'I rather think we are back in the world of (Revpref),' said the tortoise. 'Of course I recognize that if I am to get what I want, I must adopt the only means available. If I am to get the lettuce I must cross the road, and wanting the lettuce as I do I expect in time to cross the road. If I don't do so, we might agree that I really didn't want the lettuce all that much, or perhaps that I wanted something else more. Maybe I just didn't want to cross the road. No harm in that,' he concluded smugly.

'You make it sound a kind of accident if you choose the means to the end,' complained Achilles. 'Whereas I am trying to show that reason enjoins the choice! To coin a phrase, it is an a priori principle constitutive of practical rationality!'

'Not an accident, and not that, whatever it is,' said the tortoise. 'Naturally, some difficult radical interpretation has to be done. If I prefer lettuce to starvation, and recognize crossing the road as the only means to lettuce, yet act as if I prefer the joint outcome <starvation, sit still> to <lettuce, cross the road>, then we will cast around for other objects of concern to explain my choice. And equally obviously tortoises of a race that does not choose necessary means to ends will fail to achieve their ends; assuming their ends include satisfying their needs, then they will die out rather rapidly. I expect that is why I may be about to cross the road. On the other hand, tortoises who rush around buying lottery tickets may not do all that well either. The race is not always to the swift,' he mused.

'But wouldn't you call a fellow tortoise who persistently failed to adapt means to ends unreasonable? Don't there have to be authoritative, instrumental norms?' fumed Achilles.[19]

'Oh, I call lots of people unreasonable,' said the tortoise. 'People who get angry too quickly or eat too much so that they can get sick and lose weight, or who enter dwarf-throwing competitions. It doesn't signify very much, except that their behaviour doesn't make sense to me, or even that I disapprove of them. But as for norms, yes, indeed I am glad I am not the kind of tortoise who constantly fails to adopt means to ends. I am not sure I am ever going to meet any who do so fail, both because it is so hard to identify them, and because we agreed that they will have died out pretty quickly. But if I did, well, I am sure they would really arouse my passions—good-for-nothing, useless animals, every last tortoise of them,' he said with a frown.

'At least I can agree to that,' replied Achilles, sadly.

---

[19] This way of putting it is that of Hampton 1995: 66. In the same issue of *Hume Studies* Elijah Milgram thinks that Hume was, implausibly, a sceptic about practical reasoning (Milgram 1995). The tortoise suggests that we have no coherent concept of anything of which Hume was implausibly sceptical.

'Why so sad?' asked the tortoise, caringly.

'Nothing,' said Achilles. 'It is just that I thought I had a different thought, and now I think I didn't.'

Day V

'But look,' said Achilles, 'you have resisted all the arguments I could muster. And yet I notice that this pile of lettuce has steadily shrunk. So what is going on?'

'Oh, didn't I tell you?' said the tortoise, pausing surprised in mid-mouthful. 'I have an absolute passion for the stuff. In fact, I scarcely ever resist it. Would you like some too?'

POSTSCRIPT

This paper was written for a conference at Glasgow University to celebrate the centenary of Lewis Carroll's great paper 'What the Tortoise Said to Achilles', which first appeared in *Mind* in 1895. I was grateful for the invitation, but it was also a particular pleasure to me that *Mind* decided to publish my own contribution as a separate paper. I must apologize to any avid readers of my own work that I subsequently made use of material from Day II in chapter 6 of *Ruling Passions* (Blackburn 1998). However, since so far as I am aware neither exposure has had any influence on the tyranny of rationalism and for that matter rational choice theory, I do not feel so guilty about reprinting it here.

There is more about detachment and practical conditionals in essay 15.

2

Truth, Beauty, and Goodness

> TROILUS. What's aught but as 'tis valued?
> HECTOR. But value dwells not in particular will.
> It holds his estimate and dignity
> As well wherein 'tis precious of itself
> As in the prizer. 'Tis mad idolatry
> To make the service greater than the god;
> And the will dotes that is inclinable
> To what infectiously itself affects,
> Without some image of th' affected merit.
>
> Shakespeare, *Troilus and Cressida*, II.ii.51[1]

I

Far be it from me to grudge writers their thrill as they hymn the awful intransigence of reasons and values and duties: their shining self-sufficiency, their necessity, their indifference to human wishes and desires. Our values and duties are as impervious to human mess and failure as the stars in the heavens or the rigid commands of logic and mathematics. Kant's poetical flights in this vein ought to appeal to us, and it often seems that many people who think of themselves as theorists of ethics or of normativity in general find it centrally important to assert that these flights appeal to them (examples include Nagel 1970, Scanlon 1998, Dancy 2000, Shafer-Landau 2003, Parfit 1997, Raz 2003). They appeal to me as well, as they should to any Humean expressivist.

---

[1] I am grateful to Professor Jonathan Bate for bringing this quotation to my notice.

This last clause may surprise people. Many accept that the Euthyphro question splits those who believe that we discover or detect value from those who believe that we create or confer it. People pull their heroes into one side or another of the fray. Hume and other sentimentalists and expressivists are regularly vilified by those of a more objectivist frame of mind as standing on the wrong side of this issue, committing the mad idolatry of elevating our sentiments above the merits to which they properly respond. Furthermore, Humeans think our sentiments are responsible for our values, say critics, but just think what that implies about cases in which we have different sentiments! You don't have to go far out into logical space to find scenarios in which anything goes, and this upsets people. But it is not only Humeans who are so pilloried: even some Kantians stand alongside them. For the issue is a *casus belli* between Kantian constructivists, such as Christine Korsgaard, and purer Kantian spirits such as Jerry Cohen, and more recently, Rae Langton (Korsgaard 1996; Langton 2007: 157). And even when the Euthyphro question is not explicitly in the foreground of writers' minds, it can be detected in the motivation or rationale for things that are. What fuels the chase after 'objectivity' or 'rational constraint' except a need to find something *there* to which we are bound to answer, beyond the self-propelling forces of the will and desire? Indeed, the whole debate between so-called 'externalists' in the theory of value, and their 'internalist' opponents, hinges on Euthyphronic thought experiments and intuition pumps. If, as I shall argue, these are misconducted and useless, a great deal of modern theory of ethics falls with them. Almost all the sacred texts of 'normativity' turn out to contain no more than platitudes at their hearts, and the theory of ethics has been drawn into the blindest of alleys.

The leading thought experiment in answering the Euthyphro question is Moore's isolation test (Moore 1903: 83). Does beauty lie in the eye of the beholder? Yes, say those who think we create or confer value (Troilus, pro Euthyphro). No, say those who hold that we detect or respond to it (Hector, pro Socrates). Let us think further, following Moore. Consider then a possible world: a lifeless, formless waste of filth and slime. Since it is lifeless there are no beholders. Now, ask yourself: is this world ugly? If you are honest, you will admit that it is. Yet there is nobody beholding it! Hence ugliness cannot lie in the eye of the beholder. A slight variation of the case might have persons in the world who love filth and slime, and frolic rejoicing in it. They find it beautiful, but is it? Of course not: the whole thing doesn't bear contemplating. It remains ugly, and they are disgusting, like flies feeding on carrion. But compare a paradise of trees and streams, meadows and hills, waving grass and fluffy clouds, again with nobody there. Isn't it beautiful? Of course it is. So beauty, like ugliness, does not depend on the eye of the beholder. Detectors win, as Socrates held. As with beauty, so with reasons and norms, values and duties.

You do not have to be very far into philosophy to suspect that there is something fishy here. I do not think it is a particular boast to say that I vividly remember suspecting there was something fishy when I first read *Principia Ethica*, before I had dreamed of doing philosophy as an undergraduate. I would now put it like this: but look, you have just given your own verdict on Moore's worlds. You contemplated a heap of filth and slime, and of course, repelled, you pronounced it ugly. You contemplated the meadows and trees and found them beautiful. But it is your own repulsion or pleasure that you are voicing. So how could that possibly make the Detector's case? For all that the case shows is that the ugliness continues to lie in the eye of the beholder, or in this case your own eye, or the eye of Moore's reader, the subject imagining the fortunately unwitnessed slime and filth, and similarly the sadly unseen trees and meadows.

There is a puzzle here. This beginner's reply is obviously correct. There is something fishy about Moore's isolation test. But can we explain further what it is?

Evidently, it is this. The battle between Creators and Detectors is presented as one about *dependency*. 'Does value (or normativity—all the points I am about to make apply equally to them both) depend on our conferring it, or on something independent to which we are fortunately receptive?' And scientifically there is a way to assess dependencies—Mill's method. You specify, either experimentally or in thought, a scenario in which the elements are varied, and see, either in the experimental set-up, or by imagining the scenario if it is a thought experiment, what comes and goes with them. This is exactly what Moore does. He has us consider the scenario, but remove or vary the spectators. And we are still repulsed or attracted. We find the ugliness or beauty still there—after all, to find something repulsive or attractive we do not normally have to look to see if someone else is spectating it!

If it were a question of assessing ordinary dependencies, Moore's argument would not be fishy. Mill's method is the correct method to use if we are in the business of assessing dependencies. When it gives a verdict it establishes what I shall call Mill Moore or MM dependency. But Moore's argument is fishy, and the moral to draw is that as theorists of the nature of ethics, we should not here be in the business of urging or denying MM dependencies at all. But this needs further explanation.

We should agree that there is only one way of assessing propositions of the form 'the value of X depends upon Y' and it is, indeed, Moore's way or Mill's way. We must contemplate the scenario in which Y is varied and see whether as a result X varies. But as the beginner suspects, we will necessarily be 'standing within' as we do this, or in other words, deploying our own evaluative sensibilities. This is in itself a perfectly good thing to do, and it needs stressing that there are perfectly good questions of this kind, *for first-order ethicists*. Does the wrongness of lying depend upon its consequences? Does the value of cheerfulness lie in the benefit to its possessor, or to those around him? Set up the scenario and rotate the variables, and you may get an answer. Your answer will be a verdict on whether in such-and-such a scenario, X remains valuable, or good, or bad, or obligatory, or whatever it was. Such is the business of the first-order ethicist, trying to chart the standards for things. Well-brought-up ethicists say things with which we should agree when they do this. Less lucky ones, or ones who know less or who have less sensitive imaginations, or coarser or misdirected sentiments, do not.

Hume used a nice earthy test of this kind against Wollaston, who had apparently claimed that the vice of bad actions lay in their tendency to engender false conclusions in persons who are aware of them. Hume points out that if he conducts himself improperly with his neighbour's wife, his action remains just as reprehensible even if he takes the precaution of closing the shutters, so that his lewd behaviour 'perfectly concealed, would have had no tendency to produce any false conclusion' (Hume 1978: III.i.1).

But what about the metaethicist, trying to understand the Place of Value in the World as a whole? Can't she use MM dependencies as a guide? No. She might set out doing so, but she will then have to stand or fall with the isolation test. When Korsgaard, for instance, writes about our autonomous acts of choice or willing 'conferring' value on things she opens herself to the Socratic, Moorean response, voiced by Langton, who asks us to think of scenarios in which nobody and no God blesses the spontaneous act of good will (Korsgaard 1996: Lecture IV; Langton 2007). This answers the question, 'Does our autonomous act of blessing things confer value?' and it answers it, Langton rightly asserts, as Kant would, but against Korsgaard. For if you rotate the scenarios, the MM test will give it that the selfless act of duty has its value in a way that has *nothing* to do with anyone autonomously blessing it, just as Hume's imagined behaviour with his neighbour's wife remains off-colour, even when nobody could be misled by it. Even in the desert where nobody is there with a blessing, the selfless act of duty still shines like a jewel, all alone, having 'full worth in itself' (Langton 2007: 185, quoting Kant). That's Socrates's verdict, Moore's, Kant's, Langton's, Hector's, mine, and I hope the reader's as well.

Unfortunately, however, as far as understanding the nature of ethics goes, this edifying piece of moralizing does not get us anywhere. For the puzzled beginner is going to insist that although that is indeed our verdict, as we think about this selfless act of duty, nevertheless, in the words that Nagel found so threatening, perhaps that's just us. We cannot pretend to escape from using our own sensibility as we use it. And we are all at least moderately well brought up, after all.[2] Of course what we are valuing is not our own sentiment or our own will, as Hector seemed to think, but the object and its properties, things that are 'just there anyway'—but we only value them, because our eyes and ears tell us of things that attract us and that we admire: things that 'enkindle' us, to use the lovely word with which Troilus subsequently replies.

The situation here is parallel to the dialectic when idealists advance claims of mind dependency, and the common-sense, Moorean, opponent advances scenarios of mind-free prehistorical landscapes with their volcanoes and dinosaurs in occupation, and events and causal happenings. But there is nobody about. So the idealist loses if he tries to import dependencies into the empirical world. The MM test rejects any such dependency. As a result, many people think we can reject any tincture of idealism, and those whose spokesman is Philonous lose (Berkeley 1988). We are Detectors not

---

[2] There is a scholarly question, then, whether Moore lays a glove on Sidgwick or not. In the passage that Moore quotes at 1903: 81, Sidgwick says, 'we can find nothing that, on reflection, appears to possess this quality of goodness out of relation to human existence, or at least to some consciousness or feeling.' If Sidgwick is doing first-order ethics, Moore makes a case against him; if he is talking about the nature of valuation and its explanation, the beginner is right and Moore misses his point. Sidgwick's unclarity also bedevils Hector in the scene quoted in the epigraph.

Creators. But Berkeley, or Philonous, knowing that this is how we think and how we are going to go on thinking, replies that while indeed this is so, still at some level we must recognize that these are just 'our ideas', or, this is just us.

The test for MM dependency in the philosophy of mathematics always yields a Socratic verdict, going against Euthyphro. Where p is some arbitrary mathematical truth, the truth that p does not depend on anything within the causal order, anything either human or divine. There is nothing you can vary or alter and watch the truth of p do the same, since p just sails on inviolate, and must do so, since it is necessarily true. Does this force Platonism or something similar upon us? If it did, it would still be our Platonism: just us. But we should go more slowly. Wittgenstein says that nothing in these MM claims stymies, let alone refutes, the view that the foundation of the language game lies in our 'stream of life', in something that it takes a philosophical anthropology or ethnology to uncover (1953: II.xi, p. 226).

There is, however, a wrong way to proceed, which is to invoke an alleged distinction between an 'internal' MM dependency claim, and an 'external' or 'transcendental' one. True, someone may say, when we give verdicts on imagined scenarios, the test goes against Euthyphro. But that is because we confine ourselves to an internal reading. But there is also an *external* reading, and it is here that the philosophy must lie. *Externally* or *transcendentally*, do values depend on Creation, or do we Discover them? Moore can be patronized (here, as in the case of knowledge) as having thought to answer a difficult and deep external question with a trivial internal MM dependency.

But that requires there to be an external question of dependency. However it may be in the general case of idealism, in ethics how is it to be framed? Suppose we don metaethical clothing, and ask in what we hope to be an upper-case, metaethical tone of voice, 'Do Values as such depend on our Sentiments or our Wills as such?' We still have to answer by considering examples. So, for instance, does the value of the selfless act of benevolence depend on our sentiments, or does the awfulness of unmotivated cruelty depend on our willing to avoid it, or does . . .? And now the claim is that we can hear these as *other* than requests for first-order MM dependency tests. But we cannot. We can only run the test one more time, and we will again get the Socratic verdict. There is no external question of *dependency*.

We might be tempted to think that there must be one, that people must be dragged willy-nilly into the halls of metaphysics. But this would only be so if we ignore expressivism. If we think expressivism is false, we might believe in a normative or evaluative 'truth condition', a fact, or ontologically heavy 'truth-maker', an environmentally pressing real law or chunk of glowing normativity which might indeed have its own strange pattern of comings and goings and its own dependencies, or its own magical immunity to contingent fact. But according to expressivism, our activities of evaluation invoke no such mysteries, so there is no external question of dependency either.

Does this mean that we cannot 'stand outside' at all? Wittgenstein certainly did not think so. 'If we look at things from an ethnological point of view, does that mean we are saying that philosophy is ethnology? No, it only means that we are taking up a position right outside so as to be able to see things *more objectively*' (Wittgenstein 1980: 37). He thought the deep, ethnological stance does reveal something. It even reveals a claim of dependency, but a benign one. It reveals that *our* valuations depend in their different ways on our form or stream of life, on our activities, on our practices, or even our feelings. In mathematics, it tells us that our practice depends upon such-and-such contingencies in our lives, or answers such-and-such needs, or could have been abandoned or varied under such-and-such circumstances. But that never gives us that 'had things been otherwise, 2 + 2 would not have been 4'. This investigation never issues in a false dependency claim. It would only give us—and this is an ordinary enough claim, not a transcendental one—that had things been otherwise, we would not have been talking about numbers at all.

This means that idealists, or sympathizers with Euthyphro, must be careful how to express themselves. In earlier works I used to talk of the 'projection' of sentiments, although I realized that this, too, can raise suspicion that it falls foul of an MM test. I hope that I always took care to say that it did not because, as described above, when it is a question of valuation, any MM test merely shows us contouring our first-order ethics, and projectivists have no problem with our contouring our first-order ethics as well-brought-up persons should. We project our sentiments by valuing things in the way we do in the words we do. But we do not indulge a first-order ethics in which the disvalue, say, of wanton cruelty depends on someone disvaluing it. It only depends on the things that make cruelty abhorrent, which are primarily the distress to its victims, and sometimes, secondarily, the perpetrator's pleasure in that distress.

Although I stand by all this, I now think the precaution was not strong enough, and the only right course may be to avoid talk of projecting, just as Kantian constructivists may do better to avoid talk of conferring (or constructing) values. For me, this leaves us with enough to say, although I must leave it to Kantian constructivists to work out how much it leaves them. It is quite hard to interpret, but it is possible, I believe, that Korsgaard intends the conferral of value to live *within* the first-order justification of things, in which case the MM test will clearly show her to be at odds with Kant, and at odds with Socrates, Moore, Cohen, Langton, and myself. Her constructivism would not remain at the level of an explanation of our evaluating and moralizing propensities, but would seep through into a very un-Kantian doctrine about justification. The casual notion of the 'source of normativity' itself encourages this confusion, and many writers have fallen headlong into it (I discuss two more examples in essay 6).

So I now believe that the better course is to say what needs to be said about the expressions to which we are led, and to avoid the dangerous metaphors. Here, on the one hand, we are with likes and dislikes, sources of joy and pain, set in a social world, with limited but real sympathies, and limited but real needs to cooperate with each other. Here, on the other hand, is our language of valuation. Is it intelligible that beings of the kind we sketch should develop language of the kind we have, with its inputs, inferential rules, and outputs as we have them? Do we have to invoke divine sparks, skyhooks, faculties of intuition, cognitive powers beyond anything given by the five senses and general intelligence, to close the gap? Do we have to invoke 'response-dependent' truth conditions, whereby we are to be represented as 'really' talking about ourselves, and thereby 'making the service greater than the god'? Or can we make the evolution intelligible just by thinking of what we had to do, and therefore did? My hope, following Hume, is that we can do the latter. And what is quite certain is that nothing mysterious arrived with the Euthyphronic phenomena. The MM test shows only how and why we value things, not what it is to do so, why we do so, or what is required to understand our doing so. Metaethics must entirely avoid it.

If we are to discourage talk of construction and projection, how should we pursue any project of 'naturalizing' ethics, or fitting it into the world of nature, which includes ourselves? Largely, it depends on where the shoe pinches. If, for instance, we think that a puzzling 'normativity' arises with very basic psychological phenomena, such as a capacity for intentional thought or intentional behaviour, we will have to start a long way back indeed. If we are happy with those, and think that their cousinship with anything seriously normative is sufficiently slight—for after all, animals perceive and act—we can start by taking those capacities for granted (this is what Hume does). My own contribution to the project is to allow us at least elementary psychological capacities, and then to ask: what would we lose if, for instance, we had only a simple language of commands, or a simple language of overt ejaculations or expressions of like or dislike, or desire or aversion? If there are things we would miss out, in the sense of discussions we need to have, or elements of our repertoires in choosing and planning that we would thereby lose, then the promise is that we can close the gap—that we have developed no more than we need, and nothing mysterious or unjustifiable happened in the evolution.

Does Berkeley gain a parallel space in which to operate, or is he tied to a 'transcendental' method of doubtful value? His problem is to find a compelling starting point, without situating his agents, even considered purely in respect of their conscious lives, in a common-sense external world from the beginning. It is only if he can motivate us to start with a stream of 'ideas', thought of as self-standing mental possessions, and then imagine ourselves being faced with the task of bringing order and control into the shifting kaleidoscope, that anything like his idealism can emerge. But this starting point is not compelling, and many would say it is entirely fanciful. To have the stream of ideas, presented as temporally ordered, the agent must be already fully placed in an external world. That, at least, is how the majority of contemporary philosophers see it.

But the theory of ethics is less ambitious, and more hospitable to stripped-down, basic starting points (hence the allure of state-of-nature, evolutionary stories about ethics, whereas evolutionary stories about perception must start much further back down the tree of life). One advantage of thinking of it this way is that there is no necessary competition with other thinkers who find other building blocks important and other aspects of the phenomena puzzling. We should not aspire to a complete story all in one small compass, but to one 'perspicuous representation' amongst others, a small contribution to smoothing the path, and removing any residual bewilderment at the fact that we end up doing what we do. In the rest of this paper I shall add one building block to this project.

II

Following Quine, deflationists and disquotationalists about truth like to say that the truth predicate is a 'device of generalization'. Nobody, so far as I know, has explicitly followed up the corresponding suggestion about the goodness predicate, although experimentally I floated the comparison some time back (Blackburn 1998: 75–6). Yet as I shall show, the parallels are striking. To highlight them I do not have to defend, or wish to defend, deflationism in all its detail.

Somewhat arbitrarily, I shall use the term 'truth predicate' equally to refer to the predicate 'is true' and the sequence of words 'it is true that . . .' as prefix to propositions. I shall be talking mainly of the latter construction, but nothing hinges on that in what follows. Then the idea behind saying that the truth predicate is such a device is well known. We start with the transparency of truth: the Frege–Ramsey idea that there is a direct, logical, equivalence between asserting a proposition and asserting that the proposition is true. We might add, with Paul Horwich, that the disposition to assent to any example of the schema 'it is true that p iff p', or perhaps more cautiously, to any non-pathological instance of it, is the core of our understanding of truth. In other words, corresponding to the schema, there is such a disposition. If you have this disposition, then you can qualify as a fully fledged user of the truth predicate (Horwich 1990).

Familiarly, however, this foundation stone of the theory of truth needs to be built upon. By itself the foundational schema leaves it mysterious why we talk in terms of truth at all. Why have such a term, if we can say what we want without it? Why is it not redundant, as the old name for deflationism implied? The well-known answer is that the truth predicate enables us to generalize, or slightly more accurately, enables us to quantify and to refer indirectly. So consider:

John said something true at breakfast.
Nothing Bush said is true.

If our repertoire is finite, then we can approximate to each of these with simple lists. Suppose $p_1 \ldots p_n$ exhaust the things that we can say, then we can offer:

(At breakfast John said p_1 & p_1) v $\ldots$ v (At breakfast John said p_n & p_n)
If Bush said (p_1 then $\neg p_1$) & $\ldots$ & (if Bush said p_n then $\neg p_n$)

These have the right implications. If John said something true at breakfast and the only thing he said was p_j then we can deduce that p_j, or equivalently, that p_j is true. And they are implied as they should be: if p_j and John said p_j at breakfast, then the disjunction follows: John said something true.

More impressive generalizations, such as 'Whenever p is true and if p then q is true, q is true', can be treated the same way, conjoining all the finite number of instances of the form. Even in the finite world, these disjunctions and conjunctions are only approximations, of course, since they do not offer a closure condition. But that too makes no use of the truth predicate: it only needs to tell us that $p_1 \ldots p_n$ are all the propositions (in the domain or relevant context) that there are, all the things that can be said or thought.

If we move to the real world with its indefinite or infinite number of things to say, direct paraphrase in terms of a list is not possible. But the right inferential dispositions can still exist. Given the first statement, that John said something true at breakfast, then we become ready, given a list of what John actually said at breakfast, to infer the disjunction of those propositions. And given the second, then we become ready, on learning a list of what Bush said, to infer a conjunction of their negations. Our firm assent to 'Whenever p is true and if p then q is true, q is true' corresponds to an inferential disposition in just the same way. Our actual state is a little more complex than this suggests, for assent to the premise that John said something true, or Bush said nothing true, is itself likely to be defeasible. We might be 'given' the second, for example, but on learning that Bush said that Canada is a country to the north of the United States not be inclined to infer the negation of that, but to backtrack on what we were 'given'. But that is familiar territory: our readiness ties us to the tree of alternatives, either to accept that Canada is not a country to the north of the United States, or to reject what we were initially given. And that is a dispositional state.

Other contexts in which we use the truth predicate are given essentially the same treatment. Consider, for example, norms and injunctions: 'Find out what is true before opening your mouth about an issue,' or, slightly more stiffly, 'Aim to believe only what is true.' These generalize over schemata such as, 'Find out whether p before asserting whether p,' or, 'Aim to believe p only if p'—and both of these are schemata for many excellent pieces of advice. We can detect whether someone is successfully following such advice by being on the alert for particular instances: he may have asserted that Cedric has fallen out with Sally before finding out whether Cedric had fallen out with Sally; or recklessly convinced himself that his money was safe when it was not. The more he avoids being like that the better he is following the advice. Some people are better at this than others.

The idea smoothly accounts for the appearance of truth in explanation. Why are we successful in computing trajectories in accordance with Newton's laws of motion? Because those laws are (near enough) true. We might accept this without knowing what Newton's laws of motion say. But the acceptance gives us a disposition, such that when we learn that one of them says that force is mass times acceleration, we suppose that we are successful in computing trajectories on the supposition that force is mass times acceleration because (near enough) it is. And conversely, if we accept explanations having this form often enough, we become disposed to wrap them up in the generalization that we are more often successful in acting on scientific assertions when they are (near enough) true.

Although it is standard to sum all this up, in deflationist writing, by saying that the truth predicate is a device of generalization, we might more accurately express the result by saying that the truth predicate, together with the correlated notion of a proposition, make up devices of generalization and indirect reference. It is one thing to accept or reject particular sayings one by one, but another thing to be able to generate these states of readiness, generalizing or referring indirectly in a domain of things that are said and thought. We want to generalize and to refer indirectly, and we need both the notion of a proposition and the notion of truth to do so. My own view is that this should blunt the metaphysical barbs aimed at the notion of a proposition, just as it blunts the barbs aimed by doubters and deniers at the notion of truth. But this is not an axe I need to grind for what follows. Nor do I want to take sides on whether Horwich's version of deflationism is less or more preferable than, for instance, a prosentential version, locating the truth predicate as a kind of anaphoric device (Grover, Camp, and Belnap

1975).[3] It should not be described as an anaphoric device of *back* reference to an expressed assertion or sentence, since we can be told that John said three true things without the things having been previously located. But if we think in terms of deferred reference, we get a similar theory.

On these accounts, what is someone told by the assertion that John said three true things at breakfast? The hearer is, as it were, put into a waiting state by the information, a state that will only be completed when the proposition or propositions that John asserted come to light. It is an informational state, in itself: it could be used, for instance, as evidence about John's character, or his recovery from a state in which he could do nothing but talk random nonsense or tell fairy stories. But it is in a good sense incomplete. 'What John said was true' is not unlike 'I like the way you do that' heard from the next-door hotel room. In the absence of further information enabling us to know or to guess what the speaker was referring to by 'that', there is something incomplete about such an episode. In Kaplan's account (Kaplan 1978), we know the character but not the content of the remark. And yet a kind of content has surely been conveyed: assuming the speaker is sincere and serious we can infer other contentful propositions—that one person was doing something and the other liked it, for instance. I shall talk in what follows of a *deferred content* in order to focus on this combination of something being said, and yet more being needed to complete our informational state.

How can all this be applied to the 'good' predicate?

Suppose we had only the simple language discussed in my *Spreading the Word* (Blackburn 1984c: ch. 6), reflecting the underlying practical role of ethical assertion. The language has an expressive device with which to voice endorsement or approval (hooray!) and one with which to voice rejection (boo!). And to simplify, let us suppose that the things we endorse or reject are all of them doings: actions performed or omitted by agents. When we hooray a doing, we must be given a reference to what was done, and the operator attaches to that: hooray for Cedric helping Annie to find her book; boo to Johnny for pulling Katie's hair. In this simple model, nuances in our actual ethical attitudes are ignored, but they could be added. For instance, the difference between rejecting what John did

---

[3] The benefits of a prosentential version in this connection have been urged upon me by Geoff Sayre-McCord.

as not altogether admirable, and rejecting it as out and out wrong, is not registered. The difference between approving of something selfishly, and approving of it from the common point of view, is not there yet. Similarly, there is as yet no room for the attributive use of the term, as when we talk about 'good tennis match' or 'good from the farmer's point of view'. But once we have endorsement and rejection, we can also expect graded valuations, valuations within one dimension or another, and evaluations qua one thing or another. These and other refinements can be added as we imagine the difference, for instance, between regretting that someone does something, and actually being disposed to forbid it or to set in place emotional or social sanctions against it. In any case, we could do a great deal with this primitive language, just as a great deal of ethics can be shown in practice, and voiced in simple injunctions and ejaculations.

But we would be limited, in the way that without the notions of a proposition and a truth predicate we would be limited. Without those notions, in the truth case, I can say:

At breakfast John said that pigs fly, but pigs do not fly.

But not:

John said something untrue at breakfast.

So in the ethical case, I could say:

At breakfast John hit Katie, and boo! to that.

But not:

John did something bad at breakfast.

This last sentence does not mean, 'John did something at breakfast, and boo! to that.' We are not saying that John was at fault for acting at all, but rather, there is something in particular he did fit to excite condemnation. A good way of seeing this point is to imagine not a language with explicit 'boo!' and 'hooray!' devices, but one that achieves the same effect through intonation. 'At breakfast, John hit Katie' could be said in a particularly grave or falling tone of voice, indicating condemnation or rejection. But if we were confined to saying 'John did something at breakfast' with the same tone, we would be construed, again, as simply condemning John for acting at all.[4]

With a device for deferred indirect reference to hand, we can extend our repertoire, and we will be understood in exactly the parallel way to how we are when we deploy the truth predicate. So, instead of saying, 'John did such-and-such, and hooray! for that & John did thus-and-so, and hooray! for that, and . . . and that's all John did,' we can sum it up by saying that everything John did was good. Instead of listing (John hit Kay & boo! to that) v (John stole Katie's apple & boo! to that) . . ., which requires being able to enumerate all John's possible doings, we say that John did something bad. Once more, this does not mean that John did something and it was bad to do so, but rather John did something *which* it was bad to do. Again, we have a deferred content, which puts us in the same waiting state or state of readiness: if John's doings come to light, we expect to reject at least one of them, and our state carries the commitment that if we find them all quite acceptable, we must reject what we were told. This is just as with the truth predicate, where if we have been told that John said something true, then if John's sayings come to light we expect to be able to assent to at least one of them, and we are committed to rejecting what we have been told if we do not do so.

So the arrival of quantification, in this case over doings, and the use of the good predicate (and of course the bad predicate), together expand our repertoire just as the arrival of propositions, as a class over which we can quantify, and the truth predicate, together expand our repertoire.

The case of the truth predicate is aided by two things. There is a canonical presentation of a proposition, in the use of a sentence expressing it. There is no similar canonical presentation of an action, although we are familiar with more or less helpful descriptions of what was done. And then there is the syntactic similarity between the semantically basic p and the equivalent 'p is true'. That is, where the sentence expressing p stands in a sentence frame, so will the equivalent. So, in the truth case we can simply use the basic schema 'p is true iff p' to introduce the relevant dispositions. In the case of ethical expression, it is not quite so simple. In the ethics case we cannot use 'd is good iff hooray! for d' as a basic schema, since 'hooray!

[4] I am grateful to Jamie Dreier for suggesting this way of putting the point at the Madison metaethics conference in 2008. I discuss intonation and prosody in connection with so-called 'thick' concepts in essay 7.

for d' cannot generally be substituted by sayings that will stand on one side of a conditional.

However, from the present perspective the difference is superficial, since we can introduce the relevant basic dispositions just as easily. The understanding of the truth predicate, deflationists say, is fundamentally possession of the disposition to assent to every non-pathological instance of the schema.[5] Similarly, the understanding of the goodness predicate is fundamentally possession of the disposition to assent to any instance of the form 'd is good' when and only when you are disposed to endorse d, and to any instance of the form 'd is bad' when and only when you are disposed to reject d.

It should be noted that this does *not* introduce the basic disposition that identifies understanding as the disposition to obey the injunction: 'hooray! for d if and only if d is good.' For people may understand the good predicate well enough although, unhappily, they are not too disposed to follow *that* injunction. This will be so wherever they have defective standards. This is parallel to the fact that the basic disposition that corresponds to understanding the truth predicate is not that you are disposed to assert p whenever p is true. For people who are largely and widely mistaken may still have grasped the notion of truth. The disposition ties assent to the proposition in terms of good when you are disposed to hooray! things, regardless of whether you do both just when you should or not, and in this parallels the disposition which gives understanding of the truth predicate.

Deflationism gives us an understanding of the norms associated with truth. And as with the norms surrounding truth, so with those surrounding goodness. 'Do d only if d is good' is no doubt excellent advice, and we will suppose an agent to be acting in accord with it if whenever he does d we are disposed to endorse d. Similarly with 'admire only what is good', or 'do not even feel tempted to what is bad', and the other golden mantras of the moralist.

Explanation by means of deferred content follows on as well. Compare 'John turned out intelligent because his parents told him many true things' with 'John turned out honest because his parents brought him up well'.

---

[5] Like Horwich, I bypass complexity arising from the pathological semantic paradoxes with this disclaimer.

When we assent to the first we most likely have in mind a vague set of propositions $p_1 \ldots p_n$ which his parents told him, and where we ourselves are disposed to think that $p_1 \ldots p_n$, and also think that John turned out intelligent because he was told $p_1 \ldots p_n$. In the same way, when we assent to the second we most likely have in mind various things $d_1 \ldots d_n$ his parents probably did, and which we are disposed to endorse, and again suppose that because of those John turned out honest. However, these are only first approximations. In the truth case we can imagine someone who accepts that John turned out intelligent because his parents told him many true things, but who has no idea what these may have been (the deferential peasant applauding the young scholar's Oxford career, perhaps). But deflationism can parse the thought that there are truths which we ourselves do not know, that is, instances of the schema 'p & I do not know whether p'. Instances of this do not get said, on pain of Moore's paradox, but we can nevertheless happily understand that instances of it may describe our current position. There is no further difficulty about supposing there to be unknown instances of the schema 'I do not know whether p & John turned out intelligent because his parents told him p and p'.

And then the same remedy applies to the rare, morally modest, commentator on the obscure parental forces behind John's goodness, who would not himself essay a view about which things his parents are likely to have done to bring about the happy result. Moral deflationism can parse the thought that there are good deeds of which we know nothing, and even good deeds which we ourselves do not recognize to be good.[6]

In the more common case, where one has a range of instances in mind, each case, of course, shares the same risk that the audience misunderstands which intended range of propositions, or range of actions, it is. You may say the first, having in mind the science that Cedric's parents taught him, but be heard by someone who casts around for religious doctrines they must have been inculcating. And similarly you may say the second, having in mind the examples of honesty and kindness his parents illustrated, but be heard by some Evangelical who casts around for frivolous religious observances they must have followed. That is why it is usually better to cash out the deferred content. Instead of saying that John turned out honest because his parents brought him up well, we go into detail: his parents

---

[6] For more on moral fallibilism, see Blackburn 2009.

brought him up with respect and love, and a firm tendency to steer him back onto the straight and narrow if he ever said that p when he apparently did not believe it. Hooray for doing those things! We descend from the generalization when his parents' specific goodness comes into question. It was not because of their obsessive religious observances—which our Evangelical unfortunately calls good—that John turned out well. The essential point is that there is no environmental property, the goodness of the doings, which is necessary to the explanations, any more than in the truth case.

The parallel has another set of interesting consequences. Having devoted a book to the property of Goodness, Moore, like Sidgwick before him, was left with almost nothing to say about it: it was known only by the theological *via negativa*—unanalysable, only known by intuition, bearing a mysterious and *sui generis* relationship of supervenience to other properties, magnetically connected with the will, and so on (Moore 1903; Sidgwick 1874: I.3.§1). We can now see that Moore's ear for the phenomena was perfect, but the error, into which he is drearily followed by contemporary intuitionists, lay in pitching the whole inquiry in a misleading metaphysical key. As a device of generalization, the good predicate will indeed resist analysis, resist any account of empirical or causal access, and bear a relation of supervenience to other properties. It will consort with necessity, but not with a prioricity. Expressivists who follow the quasi-realist route of explaining the phenomena of ethics have noticed these properties before. But it is nice to be able to pull them together.

So: the magnetic property of Goodness, that so excited and repelled John Mackie (see Mackie 1977: 38–42), becomes no more than the fact that you do not call things good unless you are also disposed to endorse them. Supervenience becomes the requirement that you endorse things in the light of their other properties: one of the very few, and perhaps the only, constitutive requirement on practices of evaluation. Any *fundamental* principle or standard connecting the properties of things to their being good will, if acceptable to me, be deemed necessary by me, because I will apply the same standards to any possible scenario. It will not be a priori because, however lovable it may be, it will be intelligibly deniable. Goodness resists analysis, because no empirical predicate can serve the same logical function. And there is no question of empirical or causal access to goodness, because there is no robust or thick substantive property there to access. As with truth, we can *say* that there is a property there, if properties are just the semantic projection of predicates. But there is no topic there, no residual mystery, therefore, about how we get our hooks into it or why we should want to do so.

Everything said about the good should also be said about reason. We talk about reason in the abstract simply as a way of thinking about what is good in the way of guided movements of the mind and movements of the will. It would often be good that people's minds and wills should move in various ways even if they are too ignorant to be able so to move, or too limited in other ways to feel any inclination to do so. Someone seeking reasons for a conclusion or an action is looking for facts in the light of which it would be good to move to the conclusion or the action. Some fail to find reasons that are there; others fail to be moved by them as they should. It would often be good if people were better, in this respect as in others. That is all the admired and much discussed 'externalism' of reason amounts to, and again it cannot act as any kind of pivot on which substantial philosophical issues rise or fall (see also essay 15).

The view will differ from naturalism of the Cornell variety, since the understanding of ethics is not fundamentally an ability to identify one or another natural property or cluster of natural properties. It is the ability to endorse or reject various courses of action. If the Cornell realists have hit upon the right natural properties to privilege or endorse, then good ethicists will have their attention focused on those. Others will not, since some people have woeful standards. But they do not thereby forfeit their status in the game, as they ought to if reference to the Cornell cluster of natural properties were the semantic entry ticket. People with misguided standards commend and reject, love and hate, like the rest of us. That is why it is so important to convert or combat them.

The parallel theory works elegantly and harmoniously in aesthetics, not only vindicating Austin's recommendation that philosophers should think less about the good and the beautiful, and more about the dainty and the dumpy, but also helping us to interpret Kant's dark views about judgement (and perhaps doing something to unify the two senses of judgement as on the one hand assent to the truth, and on the other appreciation of the beautiful). Kant held that there was no rule or concept determining the beautiful, for otherwise free creative activity would be merely mechanical. So, how is it that if we are told in advance that John made two beautiful sketches before breakfast, we will have been told *something* in spite of there being no rule or concept in play delineating the *kind* of thing that John did? Well, there are individual objects of disinterested sensory pleasure, stimulated by the harmonious free play of our imaginative powers, which we may expect (Kant says, 'demand') that everyone shares. Accepting what we are told, we are put into a state that would be consummated or completed if a free play of our cognitive and imaginative powers brings us disinterested pleasure, upon our contemplating John's two sketches. If it does not, we may worry about our own sensibilities on this occasion, or reject what we were told. If we hold that beauty is important, we hold that such occasions are worth seeking out and cherishing. We will suppose that someone takes pleasure in what is beautiful insofar as we do share his sensibility. Beauty is magnetic because pleasure is.

It is standard to supplement deflationism about truth with something like a use theory of meaning (Horwich 1995) or an inferential role semantics or game-theoretic semantics (Brandom 1994). The point is that the very notion of a proposition or an assertion itself needs locating within some kind of social space, such as the activities of giving and receiving reasons, making inferences, conducting observations, and acting in the light of what we think. The idea, in Brandom's terms, is to understand *saying* in terms of *doing* (Brandom 2008). The current proposal fits directly into such a program: indeed, as has been emphasized by Huw Price (Price 2004), the more general program can be seen as a generalization of it across yet wider areas of discourse (see also essay 9).

Nobody supposes that 'John said something true at breakfast' is 'expressive' as opposed to 'descriptive'. Deferred content is still content. Similarly, I now think, the semantic epicycles that expressivism brought to the table can be elegantly avoided. By using evaluative language we say things. What we say is explained in deflationary terms, subject to the fundamental acceptance disposition that you may sincerely say that a doing was good when you are inclined to applaud or approve it. That is the part that expressivism gets absolutely right and that marks a departure from other approaches. But the norms and inference patterns that then govern the use of the vocabulary are exactly the same as those governing other kinds of sayings. There is no need for logical or semantic epicycles, any more than there is with the truth predicate. The package I am presenting here shares with quasi-realism the aim of 'explaining and justifying' the propositional surface of our moral and evaluative lives. But its way of doing this is slightly different. It derives propositionality from function more directly and with less commitment to any kind of contrast with description or representation. You may even say, if you like that kind of language, that 'X is good' is true if and only if X is good—but remember first to explain the practices of evaluation in different terms.

Past all the phantoms that have haunted the last century of ethical theory we can see, clearly enough, what is involved in loving and choosing, admiring and rejecting, insisting and forbidding, erecting and policing boundaries to behaviour, encouraging and discouraging. We see it without doing metaphysics and without opening the door to anything deserving the name. We thereby gain what Wittgenstein wanted, a 'perspicuous representation' of what we are doing when we voice these things. In the beginning was the deed, and it is these deeds that give us the substance of all our evaluative and normative repertoires. We can call the overall package pragmatism, or expressivism, or non-descriptive functionalism, or just Wittgensteinianism if we like. In any event, it is the path to conquering those three majestic and magnetic philosophical summits: truth, beauty, and goodness.

3

Dilemmas: Dithering, Plumping, and Grief

I

At the risk of lowering the tone, I am not going to start in concentration camps, the French resistance, or the hard world of Greek tragedy. I am going to start in the supermarket, and by introducing a distinction. Let us call a *quandary* any situation in which there are a number of alternatives, of which you must adopt one and only one, but where you do not know which one to adopt. You do now know what to do. It is undeniable that there are quandaries. One spends a lot of time in supermarkets in a quandary. Buridan's ass was in a quandary. Now we can distinguish between an *objective* and a *subjective* or *agent's* quandary. An objective quandary is one where one does not know what to do, and there is no fact that would provide a reason that settles what to do: even a God's-eye view would not reveal that one alternative beats the others. For instance, one is undecided about which can of beans of the same price to buy, but, in fact, although packaged differently, they are of the same manufacture. There simply exists nothing that, if known, would provide a reason to settle the matter in favour of one can or the other. Suppose we say that some events vindicate a decision if, once they are known, the events make it apparent that the decision was uniquely the right one, and that events undermine a decision if they do the reverse. Then a quandary is objective if nothing would either vindicate or undermine either decision. A subjective quandary, or agent's quandary, on the other hand, is one in which one does not know anything that settles the matter, but in which there may be such a fact. It is because one fears that the beans inside one can may be vastly better than those inside the other that one dithers, and even if in fact they are just the same, one can be in an agent's quandary. We can notice in passing that an objective quandary as I have defined it need not be objective all the way down. A quandary will only be an objective quandary because of contingent profiles of preference and indifference.[1] If the packaging mattered—if your partner is made sick by blue cans, for example—then there would not be an objective quandary, although if you do not know this you may still be in an agent's quandary. Agent's quandaries typically feel bad partly because we fear that the quandary actually is not objective. We think that there is a right answer, again, contingently upon the profiles of interest and desire in the offing, but we don't know what it is.

I now define a *stable agent's quandary* as one in which one does not know anything that settles the choice in favour of one alternative, and also where no practical investigation or further exercise of thought or imagination can reasonably be expected to alter this. The beans case is one. (You may say that one could buy both cans, and taste the beans in both, thereby effecting a ranking unless the beans are in fact identical or equal in point of taste. But if buying both is an option, the case is not a quandary at all. A quandary only exists where just one option is possible, not both.) Whether an investigation is practical will typically depend on its cost, as opposed to the likely benefit of discovering an objective ranking. There may exist no further possible investigation, or its costs may be too great. In either case, the quandary is irremediable. You are in a stable agent's quandary in the supermarket because your available strategy is pretty much confined to just looking, and what you see does not rank the alternatives. Perhaps some neutron bombardment would provide information to rank the beans in one can above those in the other, but even if it were possible, it would certainly not be worth it to bring the equipment into the store. In such a case then we can be pretty sure that an agent's quandary is stable, even if we suspect that it is not objective. That is, we can be pretty sure that in the long run one can would prove to have been a better buy than the other.

The supermarket provides a clear case of a stable agent's quandary. But it is unusual in this. For in wider contexts it is very hard to know whether further investigation, or further exercises of thought or imagination, will not discover an asymmetry resolving the quandary. Two cars may strike us as equally attractive, but we may fear that there is some practical test

---

[1] I am not here entering on any grand debate about the objectivity of ethics, or the existence of Kantian reasons that have a life independent of agents' desires. I am simply pointing out that not all reasons have that kind of grand, superlunary independence.

for ranking them, if only we could think what it is. Here too there is an objective/subjective distinction. There may indeed be a test, but if there is no effective way of knowing what it is, then the quandary is stable. Perhaps one car has hidden under its carpet a service record showing that it is a complete lemon, but if there is no way of suspecting this, it cannot help resolve the issue. The quandary remains stable. But the judgement that a quandary is stable is in general defeasible, and this has consequences for our behaviour. For because of this defeasibility, quandaries typically do not *feel* stable. It typically feels as if there must be one simple investigation, or exercise of thought or imagination, that will provide the decisive reason for just one side. This is what we fear. But we might nonetheless know that the fear is irrational. It may really be quite predictable that the quandary is stable. One might offer the advice to someone never to treat a quandary as stable: always go on looking for the elusive decision procedure. This would be bad advice, fit only for Buridan's ass. But we are sometimes prone to behave as if it were good advice. Our dithering takes the form of running again and again at the issue, as if some secret ranking will reveal itself, long after we ought to know that it will not. And after a decision has been made we agonize over whether there were practicable tests that we didn't consider, so that we could have done more to remove the quandary. Sometimes such reflections will be merely neurotic, but sometimes not. I come back to this later.

There is a different notion of stability worth mentioning. Some quandaries have what I shall call a great deal of *inertia*. It is not just that one is in a quandary, but that even if some fact came along to favour one side, one would still be in a quandary. One is agonizing over which car to choose, and it will not settle the issue if the salesman offers you $1 to choose car A. Or even $10 or $20, although it might if he offered $1,000. The reason is that if weighty considerations are at stake, small incentives seem irrelevant. Some asymmetries may be inappropriate and even insulting. If you are torn between marrying A and B, it does not help if your parents, who prefer A, say they will throw in a holiday in Martinique if you choose to marry A. The amount of inertia in a quandary will affect the difficulty of solving it: there may be practical strategies for finding some asymmetry helping A against B, but none for finding a sufficiently important asymmetry to prevent one still being in a quandary. One of the problems with serious moral quandaries is that they have so much inertia that any asymmetries we are likely to establish between the two possible courses of action will seem inadequate to solving them.

Once an agent's quandary is perceived as stable, both common sense and high theory tell us how to handle it. The agent has to *plump* for one alternative. I say 'plump' deliberately, because saying that you have to choose carries a bad implicature. Choice is a process that invokes reasons. But the reasoning is all in *before* the case is describable as a stable agent's quandary. It is because the reasoning leaves no ranking of alternatives, and because this is seen to be irremediable, that there is nothing left to do but plump. Common sense tells us that this is so. It is because Buridan's ass could not plump that it lived up to its name. Theory tells us the same. Reasons fail to rank the alternatives and practicable investigation is expected to fail to do so as well. But a quandary was defined so that just one alternative had to be taken: in other words, there is a cost or other embargo attached to refusing to act at all, which makes refusing worse than plumping.

Plumping sounds light-hearted, and some of the writings on moral dilemmas—which we have not reached yet, of course—speak of it with disdain, as if one were to recommend that great Agamemnon toss a coin. But as I use the term, plumping can be done with a heavy heart, and under a heavy umbrella of doom, as one convinces oneself that the alternative one did not plump for will prove to have been the right one in time. In fact, it is often very unpleasant to have to plump, precisely because we would have liked reasons to determine a choice, and we fear that with hindsight one will see that they would have, if one had investigated, thought, or imagined better. In a situation in which you have to plump, it is true that as far as making the choice goes you *might as well* toss a coin. If the advice to toss a coin sounds unserious, inadequate to the gravity of some choice, this is, I believe, a cultural matter. Notice that the most serious quandaries, in which plumping for one side or another is almost unbearable, are often solved by drawing lots. Cards and straws have a history of deciding volunteers and victims, so they have a fateful gravity that coins, used mainly in sporting events, perhaps lack. Agamemnon might not be inclined to toss a coin, but a suitably solemn ritual of turning up a fateful card might be a good deal more appropriate.

Once we have a stable agent's quandary, then, we have to plump. Assuming, for the moment, that moral dilemmas are at least stable agent's quandaries, there is then something odd about one thought people some-times have. This is that there exists the possibility of rational strategies for solving dilemmas. But there can be no rational strategy for solving a stable agent's quandary, except plumping. To repeat: the exercise of reasoning went on *before* the situation was so identified. Once it is accepted to be a stable agent's quandary, no further rational strategy is possible, except one that makes the process of plumping as painless as possible. There is, I agree, room for strategy and imagination in doing this. As I have said, knowing that you have to plump is typically an unpleasant state for most of us, so anything that hastens the event is good. On the other hand, there may be people who enjoy wallowing in indecision, and for them delay may be desirable. In the case of a very serious quandary we do not want to be hurried too much, although we also do not want to be debilitated by inaction, which may, of course, have other costs. Common-sense practical rationality therefore knows that there is a time to dither, and a time to plump. Both come after the time to reason. They come when we are in a stable agent's quandary. But the real use of straws and cards suggests that in some cases plumping may be so traumatic that we need some kind of shelter, enabling us to see the matter as fated or decided by forces outside our control. In very serious cases we may have to tell ourselves a story afterwards that makes our plumping an adequately dignified event. There may be need for grief, and for therapy for those who have had to plump.

Suppose now we imagine an attempt to codify practical rationality, at least as it applies to someone with my profile of preferences and priorities. The code should contain decision-theoretic lore, and might give me advice to take with me when shopping: never spend more than one minute working out calculations like whether a pint at 48 cents is better than 12 fluid ounces at 35 cents; do not spend time dwelling on cholesterol, because doing so causes hypertension; try not to think of how the food got there; and so on. This might be good advice for me, in the simple sense that by following it I avoid needless dissatisfactions and satisfy more preferences. Of course, I don't need such a code, because I shop by *phronesis* rather than by consciously following norms. This is partly because I am practised at being a good enough trustee of my own interests, partly because I do not have to justify my decisions to others. But we can imagine such a code, with norms determining how I should act at various choice points. Ought I to expect the code to remove altogether the need to plump? Of course not. Saving miracles, the code cannot possibly foresee the stable agent's quandaries I shall meet. All it can do is give me advice on how to act once a situation is so identified: how much time to spend dithering, how to plump. It will be *after* using the code that a situation is identified as a quandary. The code has then done its work, except insofar as it contains advice on how quickly to plump, whether to shelter from the responsibility (toss a coin, ask your spouse which one to buy), and so on.

Leaving opportunities for plumping is not the same as containing conflicting advice. A code might do that, in the strong sense: never buy the cheapest brand; always buy the cheapest brand. This is a clear defect. More interesting is inconsistency in the weak sense of containing advice that, given a contingency, counsels conflicting action: never buy the cheapest brand; always buy the brand that Mother recommends. Good advice, until Mother recommends what is in fact the cheapest brand. An occasion on which this happens is one in which *these* bits of the code leave one in a quandary. But it does not follow that one is in a quandary *tout court*: there may be other factors that sway the choice decisively. If there are not, one will have to plump, and we have seen that it would be silly to promote as an ideal a code that never left you having to do this.

It is not silly to promote as an ideal a code that cannot give rise to inconsistent advice, whatever the contingencies, but the form it takes needs some thought. Provided Mother seldom recommends the cheapest, each piece of advice might save me much dissatisfaction; perhaps it is better to have them in a simple form than have them hedged against the remote case, especially if there is no practicable way of seeing what might on occasion resolve the conflict. On the other hand, if we need to know where we stand, a code would do well to anticipate contingencies in which its advice conflicts with itself. A building code, for example, will not be defensible if it mandates one depth of footing for slopes and a different one for clay soils, even if (luckily) nobody ever starts to build a house on sloping clay. Might it be tolerable to have weakly conflicting norms or mandates, but qualified in a general way? The code would be headed by a rubric: remember that each piece of advice is to be thought of as hedged. There is a *ceteris paribus* clause, and other things are not equal if a weak inconsistency has arisen. Although we want this protection against weak inconsistency, we would not want it if, as a result, what ought to be swift choices become laborious. I return to this in the moral case below, when we consider requirements.

A final point before we turn to higher ground. Plumping resolves the merely practical quandaries I have talked about. But it need not resolve them without leaving a residue, akin to the residue that Sartre (1946) and Williams (1966) first highlighted in ethical cases. First, it can be hard to turn one's back on a choice made by plumping. Many people no sooner plump than they suffer a strong sense that they are bound to have made the wrong choice. The other car would have been better, this one will turn out to be a lemon. As we have already mentioned, people can believe, irrationally, that it was their fault that plumping became necessary: 'If only I knew more about cars,' they think, 'I would have been able to spot the crucial reason for preferring one to the other.' They can doubt whether the situation was really a stable quandary: 'If only I had taken it for one more test drive,' they think, 'the crucial evidence would have been apparent.' A full set of norms for plumping would tell us to what extent these reflections make sense, and to what extent they are neurotic.

Second, in some cases the residue involves something like reparation: making it up to some proponent of the side for which you did not plump. Suppose each of two friends offers me the use of her chain saw. It doesn't matter which I take, so I plump for Alice's. I then owe it to Bertha to make some friendly overture to show that I took her offer seriously, that I had no particular preference for Alice, and so on. Notice, however, that this might be so even if the situation never put me in a quandary. Perhaps it was easier for me to pick up Alice's chain saw, but I still owe Bertha some soothing noises. At the very least I have to show that I appreciated the offer. This is important, because it is sometimes argued that the need for reparation or apology to a side whose interests are not met after a dilemma shows that a genuine requirement has been violated. Here I simply point out that the phenomenon is more widespread, for similar apology and even reparation may be in order when no requirements have been violated, and even when no quandary ever existed. In fact, this issue of proper residue is quite independent of whether the situation is ever a quandary in moral cases as well, as we shall see below.

Third, some fortunate people may be able to contour themselves around the consequences of plumping in such a way that, in retrospect, the decision can seem to have been the only right one. They can think that the choice revealed their real preference. Having plumped for the Ferrari rather than the Plymouth, I live up to the role, so that after a time I cannot understand how I was ever at all drawn to the Plymouth in the first place. Some people are better at this than others. In spite of Sartre, we should not think that everybody can do it all the time. Nor should we always recommend it, although it may often be good advice, to ward off useless regret. If we admire it, we are admiring a lack of understanding of our past selves, and this seems to me to be a pity. Worse, as we shall see below, it may create intolerance of those who plumped the other way.

To sum up so far: We have seen the unproblematic, inevitable nature of stable agent's quandaries. We have seen that no codification of practical rationality could avoid them. We have seen that there can be no strategy for resolving them, beyond one making the experience of plumping as painless as possible. We see something of the defeasible nature of the judgement that a quandary is stable, and of the residue of more or less neurotic doubt that this can leave. We have seen, finally, how a protagonist of the choice that is plumped against may be offered apology or reparation, even when no requirement of any kind has been violated.

II

It would be pleasant to be able to say that morality brings in nothing new. If we can see moral dilemmas as simply juicy examples of stable agent's quandaries, there will be nothing puzzling about them. In effect, I think this is true, but there is much to be said to make it seem plausible.

First, then, what makes a quandary a moral one? In the cases discussed so far, the reasoning has been entirely cost-benefit. The pressures on each side may have been commensurable, but balanced, as in the beans case. Or they may have involved different considerations that ended up balanced, as when choosing between cars that offer different attractive features and different drawbacks. But in either case the pressures simply work through subjective desirability. We make a quandary a moral one by adding motivations from the territory of virtue, obligation, duty, and right and wrong. We can all accept that much without having an agreed-upon theory of what delineates that territory. We may think that it gets its identity from the presence of altruistic and social motivations, or from the existence of rational demands, or from some other source entirely, while agreeing that it is only when a pressure comes from that territory that a quandary has a moral element.

Notice that there can be mixed quandaries, in which one of the factors making it a quandary is a moral one but the others are not. Much is going for the Ferrari, but it produces worse exhaust emissions than the Plymouth, and one feels under a duty not to contribute more than necessary to atmospheric pollution. Notoriously, some philosophers have suggested that as soon as a tincture of morality enters on just one side, as in this case, that settles it, so that if the agent remains in a quandary, this is because he is out of control, or is only using ethical terms in an inverted-commas sense, or is a hypocrite. This strikes me, as it has many others, as simply wrong. Nobody is out of control here, and the other diagnoses may be clearly inapplicable: it is only *because* the agent takes the moral issue seriously that he is in a quandary at all. Otherwise it would be a walkover for the Ferrari.

Mixed quandaries can be stable. There may be no practicable investigation or further exercise of thought and imagination that will enable me to rank the alternatives. This will mean that I cannot place the moral ingredient, and whatever else is working for its side, above or below the total package of considerations on the other side. I will know, of course, that if I plump for the Ferrari, I will have to put up with whatever discomfort is produced by my perception of myself as polluting more than I should. A bad conscience on that score will be a cost. A small amount of foreseeable guilt may be balanced by a large amount of foreseeable regret. In that case, as usual, I have to plump. And as usual there will be residues whichever way that is done. If the moral consideration was not impersonal but arose from the decision's effect on some identified person, reparation or apology may be in order. If the problem with the Ferrari was that it makes more noise than it ought to on starting up, I may feel obliged to make soothing remarks to my neighbour after I have plumped for it.

You may be thinking that even if mixed quandaries exist, good people would not get into them. For a good person the moral tincture would 'trump' or even 'silence' the others. If we are good, once we realize the moral objection to the Ferrari, its blandishments count as nothing. Partly this may be a matter of definition: a good person is one in whom ethical considerations trump or silence others, just as an economic person is one in whom economic considerations trump or silence others. But if it involves a recommendation that we should particularly emulate or admire people for whom there cannot be mixed quandaries, it needs a little critical attention. If their purity arms them against even seeing the blandishments of the world as blandishments, there may be costs of self-righteousness or self-pity, of limited imagination or sympathy. In this sense, there is nothing paradoxical about it being better not to be all that good.

Similarly, and perhaps more importantly, the sheer number of everyday quandaries, practical, mixed, or moral, casts doubt on one influential ethical ideal. This is the ideal of reflective equilibrium, if that is conceived of as strong enough so that the system in such equilibrium contains the rankings and principles necessary for solving all quandaries. I believe that we should not admire anything of that strength. It is not an ideal, for it would not be ideal to be equipped in advance with an algorithm preventing any choice's being seen as a stable quandary. It is essential to moral maturity that we get into stable quandaries. Being equipped in advance to award outright verdicts to one side or another is indeed to be armed against one kind of indecision, just as someone who always eats exactly the same brand of food is armed against indecision in the supermarket. But the cost is too great—the cost of limited sympathy, imagination, or sheer awareness of the possibilities that life has to offer.

Once we have mixed cases, we can play with the mix. We can add the same moral considerations to each side, or different considerations, and if we end up with a stable quandary all the remarks made so far apply. I conclude that if moral dilemmas involve something more puzzling than stable practical quandaries, it is not because of the addition of the moral to the practical. It must be because there is more to a dilemma than a quandary. What more?

The usual definition is in terms of *requirements*. It is when there is something more than a consideration or a practical pressure, or even a moral pressure, on each side that dilemmas exist. It is when there is a requirement to perform each alternative, so we can say that an agent is in a moral dilemma if he is in a moral quandary, in which there is a requirement to perform each alternative. The difference this brings is that whichever way the agent acts, he will have failed to do something that is required of him. Equivalently, we might think that he will have failed to do something that he was obliged to do or had to do.

It is not at all obvious that any situation deserves being described like this. Consider that the language of requirements is at least sometimes the language of resolution of quandary. 'What am I required to do?' is likely to be a request for an answer to a problem of choice, equivalent to asking,

'What am I to do?' Only an answer picking out a unique choice satisfies the question. To identify a requirement is then to give an outright verdict. The requirement is to do whichever wins. If no choice wins, none is required. In other words, a demand may be matched by conflicting demands, but if one of them is issued as a requirement, then in this outright sense it brooks no competition. To sidestep this outright or verdictive logic, proponents of this way of looking at quandaries may choose to define a notion of a 'non-overriding' requirement: a requirement that can in principle be matched or beaten by another, more important requirement, or matched by another equally important requirement, as it is in a case of dilemma (Sinnott-Armstrong 1988). But it is not clear that the strategy is a good one. Races can be run in the knowledge that two runners may tie, and they may be judged to be 'first equal'. But suppose a race is in the nature of a play-off, run to determine an outright winner for some purpose. We cannot then use the concept of a matched outright winner. If a putative winner is matched by another putative winner whose claims are equally good, then neither is an outright winner. You cannot say that they both are. If the notion of a requirement shares this logic, as its use in giving a verdict suggests, then the notion of a matched or beaten requirement is contradictory. Sophie and Agamemnon are not required to do either thing, and whatever they do, they will not have transgressed a requirement. They will have done something awful, but in their situation they were not required not to do that awful thing. So the question of whether there are dilemmas as opposed to quandaries now becomes the question of whether we insist that the notion of a requirement be tied to a verdictive logic, or whether we allow what I am calling matched requirements. The one choice assimilates the logic of requirements to that of 'outright winner'; the other assimilates it to that of, say, demands, where we can perfectly well contemplate matched and inconsistent demands.

The question of whether 'requirement' in English means 'outright requirement', or permits matched requirements, might seem to be an empirical and possibly indeterminate one. The issue must be whether we ought to think in terms of matched requirements—whether we miss some important facet of moral quandaries if we fail to understand them in these terms. The only arguments I know for allowing matched requirements allege that some desirable feature of our reaction to quandaries is better preserved if we think of the quandary as involving a requirement on each side. Thus Sinnott-Armstrong argues that the goal of enabling people to live better together in society is better served when people

recognize the worth and rights of others, and this is done when an agent displays regret or offers excuses, apologies or compensation after violating a moral requirement. Theories that exclude moral conflicts cannot serve this purpose as well, because they cannot justify such residue when the moral requirement was overridden. (Sinnott-Armstrong 1988: 188)

The idea is that if I see myself as having been subject to two requirements in my quandary, I will know that I have violated one, and this is *all* that justifies my display of excuses, apologies, and compensation. But I see no reason to accept this. We saw above that when I accepted Alice's chain saw rather than Bertha's, good behaviour might demand making some excuse or apology or even compensation to Bertha, yet no moral issues, let alone moral requirements, were involved. In the weighty cases in the literature, *of course* a good person is going to feel awful about the side whose claims were not met. Having decided to go to war, Sartre's hero knows that he has not done things for his mother that he could have, so he will be motivated to proffer excuses, apologies, reparation, atonement. It makes no difference whether he filters his knowledge through the category of having failed in a requirement. If it appears to make a difference, this is, I suspect, because we are illegitimately importing something from the verdictive or 'outright' sense into the supposed matching sense. In other words, some of the importance of failing to respect an outright winner is supposed to rub off onto the case in which we plump against a first equal. Or even, which is more perturbing, when we rationally choose against a beaten competitor. For on the more liberal logic, a requirement can exist even though it is obviously outmatched by a more important and demanding requirement.

Notice especially that as far as reparation and compensation go, it may make no difference whether the choice is actually the outcome of a quandary at all. A coach may never be in doubt that he has to choose Rupert rather than Cedric for the team, but if Cedric had reason to hope, invested effort in the enterprise, and so on, the coach will still recognize an obligation to talk to Cedric, compensate him for dashed hopes, or remember to give his claims some priority next time around. The coach has violated no requirement made on him by Cedric or Cedric's claims to a place, but for all that may properly feel the residual obligation.

We have seen already that all quandaries are apt to leave residues. A serious moral quandary will leave more than others. Sometimes we look askance at someone who, having had to plump for one terrible course of action rather than another, sleeps perfectly easily. Suppose we not only understand but also admire or expect a residual guilt or sense of taint or curse, as in the Sophie and Agamemnon cases. Must we then be conceiving of the matter in terms of an unmet requirement? Again, I do no think so. Agamemnon and Sophie make a choice that condemns one of their children to death. Isn't that bad enough? It is not likely to make it much worse if we say: 'P.S. You also failed to meet a moral requirement.'

Another suggestion is that seeing quandaries in terms of matched require- ments gives us a proper tolerance of persons making the other decision (Sinnott-Armstrong 1988: ch. 8). We do not have to see them as mistaken or defective. But, again, it is not apparent that this toleration is helped by conceiving the matter in terms of matched requirements. Once the situation is identified as a stable moral quandary, we know that we might as well toss a coin; we have to plump, and do so knowing that we can have no possible quarrel with those who plump the other way. It makes no difference whether we also conceptualize the issue in terms of competing matched requirements, or whether we just say that there were competing moral pressures but no requirement. The real enemy of proper toleration will be the Sartrean psychology that, having plumped, reformats its charac- ter and its view of the past so that its particular choice is thought of as the only possible one. Once that has happened, those opting the other way may get condemned. This is a reason we need to beware of that psychology.

I think, therefore, that there are no pressing reasons to insist on describing these quandaries in terms of matched requirements. Are there good reasons against doing so? Of course, there may be background reasons against thinking of morality in terms of requirements at all: reasons for thinking in terms of virtue and practical wisdom, rather than in terms of obligation or duty. But waiving that large issue, should we insist on an outright logic for the notion of a requirement? The best argument for doing so, apart from conceptual economy, is, I think, as follows. Think of morality as like the norms issued by some authority. If an authority issues outright requirements and penalties for disobedience, then well and good. But if it issues conflicting requirements with the same penalties, then things are not so good. As we saw above in the case of a building code, it seems like a defect, even an irrationality, in an authority that it should do this. If the conflict counted as no excuse, the authority would be unjust and arbitrary. A better authority would build in exception clauses, as legal codes do ('Unless a case is covered by subsection 7.35, then providing the regulations in 6.89 are met . . .'). If a morality issues conflicting, matched requirements, then it seems irrationally harsh, a taskmaster that can be feared but not really respected.

Although I sympathize with this train of thought, I do not think it speaks decisively against conceptualizing quandaries in terms of matched requirements. The harshness or injustice has already gone into the situation when it is recognized as a stable moral quandary. That is, things are already as bad as could be for Agamemnon and Sophie. It is going to be hellish whatever they do, but not because an unjust lawmaker has irrationally issued requirements that match and conflict. It is the world that has landed them in a hellish situation. If they had absorbed and internalized different moralities, they might not find the situations hellish, but it is impossible to see how this could be without their being severely defective, or scarcely human at all.[2]

The upshot is not, I think, that there is anything especially wrong about conceiving moral quandaries in terms of conflicting moral requirements. It is just that there is nothing especially helpful about doing so. English is wise to remain indeterminate over insisting on an outright logic, or allowing a matching logic, for requirements. If we allow the latter we have one set of descriptions, but if we insist on the former we can substitute others equally good. Understood properly, no ethical or intellectual consequences follow from preferring one move to the other.

That leaves me inclined to recommend sticking with the outright logic, and conceiving of moral quandaries as simply stable agent's quandaries in which moral considerations favour each alternative, or stand in the way of each alternative, equally.

III

We saw that the best possible practical reasoning, codified as ideally as we could imagine, would not ward off the possibility of stable agent's

---

[2] Sophie's case is perhaps stronger than Agamemnon's here. Some might think that Agamemnon is only tragic because he puts too much weight on kingly and military duties.

quandaries. The same will be true of that part of practical reasoning that concerns our relations with others, and situations in which we must think in terms of excuses, apologies, reparation, and even guilt and atonement: in short, moral quandaries. In moral cases, as in wider practical ones, there is a time to reason, a time to dither, a time to plump, and sometimes a time to mourn. Nevertheless, moral cases do show some interesting differences from other practical cases, and I shall conclude by mentioning some of them.

Many practical quandaries are stable but not objective. That is, there may well be a best choice, but it will only be revealed in the future, and there is no way of foreseeing which it is. On the other hand, some moral dilemmas may be objective. They are neither vindicated nor undermined by anything that happens. They may have sufficient inertia for the future not to bring in a ranking consideration. There is simply no fact, nothing in the outcome, that shows that Sophie made an outright uniquely right or an outright uniquely wrong choice. There might have been, but there need not be. The war turned out reasonably well for Agamemnon, but even if it had not, he might still look back on his quandary as having been objectively insoluble. Perhaps his unfortunate homecoming undermined his decision in our eyes, but it might not have in his.

If this is so, it might seem to make the actual experience of a quandary—its phenomenology—difficult to understand. In his quandary the agent paces the floor, asking again and again what he ought to do. Is he presupposing that there is a unique thing that he ought to do, an outright requirement? And, if so, ought he not recognize this is likely false, for not only may his quandary be predictably stable, but it may also even be objective?

The phenomenology is understandable, however, even if we know that this is a possibility. In some practical cases, it is easy to conclude that a quandary is stable: in the supermarket, our only practicable strategy of inquiry was to look at the can, and that was not going to tell us what its contents tasted like. But we saw that even in purely practical cases the judgement that the quandary is stable is defeasible, and we may not be all that ready to believe it. We fear that we have overlooked something. We fear that putting the facts a new way, or turning the issue over in one light or another, ranks the alternatives. We do not know when we have exhausted all such strategies. We may suspect that we have, but the more momentous the choice, the more we twist and turn to escape the moment when we must plump. In moral cases the same is true, and frequently more so. The divergent sources of values and obligations, our awareness that we are prone to forget and overlook things that turn out to have mattered, all stand in the way of finally believing that the quandary is stable. So we twist and turn, and even if we come to believe it, we dither. And having plumped, we wonder whether we should have, and may mourn whatever values we had to trespass against when we did so. There is nothing difficult to understand in all of this, nor does any sensible theory of ethics need to suppose that there is. In other words, I accept neither the view associated with Bernard Williams that quandaries provide an argument for moral anti-realism, nor the rival view that they provide an argument for moral realism.

Earlier I raised a question over the ambition of providing rational strategies for solving dilemmas. Dilemmas, or quandaries, arise when rational considerations have all had their turn on the floor. Stable quandaries arise when we know that giving them another turn will not help. Someone might think that this makes the situation analogous to social decision theory, so that a rational strategy according different votes to different considerations, or producing an algorithm for turning votes into a verdict, could be a useful thing to find. But this is misdirected. If considerations on one side are visibly weaker than those on the other, then there is no quandary in the first place. If they are not, then reason has had its day. Accepting that we are in a stable quandary, we can only dither and plump. There can indeed be decision-theoretic analyses of when we should accept that a quandary is stable: as we saw above, main variables will be the cost of further investigation, the cost of lost time, and the probability of a ranking emerging. We may also be aware of the long-term effects of cultivating a habit either of being too quick or too slow in accepting that a quandary is stable. We do not want people to take serious decisions too lightly or dither too long. Otherwise, it seems to me, there are only two places where there is room for rational strategy. One is finding ways to make plumping painless. The main strategy we actually use is to shelter, behind excuses, behind false consciousness that a decision was forced, or behind devices for making fate play the decisive role, as when using cards or straws or self-imposed policies of random choice. The other place for rational strategy is in dealing with post-plumping grief. We do not expect Sophie and Agamemnon to bounce back, but people can wallow in guilt, become paralysed by turning the decision over and over in their imaginations, to no purpose, and so on. I suspect that the best the philosopher can do, by way of therapy, is to go over exactly the ground we have been covering. Once you see what practical reasoning is bound to be like, what morals add, and where requirements stop, then unless you actually know in retrospect that you got it wrong, you should be able to accept yourself for making any but the most hellish decisions.

4

Group Minds and Expressive Harm

I. Preliminaries

I shall take as my only target for discussion a landmark article by Elizabeth Anderson and Richard Pildes (Anderson and Pildes 2000). Their paper touches on many issues in ethics, philosophy of law, and philosophy of language, and I shall certainly not begin to cover many of these. But I do want to highlight some central themes.

First, however, I should like to register a small discomfort with some of the language in front of us. I am not myself convinced that it helps us to think in terms of an 'expressive theory of law' or an 'expressive theory of action'. It is, presumably, uncontroversial that law expresses prohibitions and permissions and acceptance of norms, and that legal reasonings express acceptances and exclusions of factors as appropriately bearing upon practical affairs. It is uncontroversial that actions—and not only speech acts—express beliefs, attitudes, emotions, and more complex states, such as, once more, the acceptance and exclusion of factors as appropriately bearing upon practical affairs. Theory here would presumably offer an account of such things as legal standing or the structure of norms that need to be in play for a group to constitute a collective, subject to a legal order. And a full theory would include an account of what it is for a group to constitute itself as subject to a norm in the first place. It is only here that one of my own philosophical views, the doctrine in ethics or metaethics known as expressivism, might have a part to play. But neither of these enterprises is, so far as I can make out, intended in the current works promoting expressive theories of law. So we might query whether we are faced with anything as grand as an overall theory of law or theory of action.

In fact, the label seems intended to cover a number of views about one, but only one, category of harm that the law ought to recognize.[1] To hold an expressive theory of law, then, is to hold that the law ought to take note of that kind of harm, and that the law can, in principle, use it to invalidate the acts of courts and other bodies. The suggestion is that the law ought to note cases whereby a person or group can be harmed simply by virtue of the expression of an attitude or other mental state by a person or group. Anderson and Pildes give us a definition of this: 'A person suffers expressive harm when she is treated according to principles that express negative or inappropriate attitudes toward her' (2000: 1527). Here and throughout, Anderson and Pildes's discussion closely links 'goals', 'attitudes', and 'principles'. According to them, expressive theories ask, 'does performing act *A* for the sake of goal *G* express rational or morally right attitudes toward people?' (2000: 1510). Here it is the acceptance of a goal *as a reason* for action that betokens both attitude and principle. The leading illustration is that of avoiding visiting one's mother in a hospital for the sake of sparing oneself unpleasantness. Taking this as a reason for staying away from the hospital would be callous, and it is 'wrong to express such an uncaring attitude towards one's mother' (2000: 1511). Anderson and Pildes do not discuss other cases in which it is not the acceptance of a *goal* as a reason that is in question, but, for instance, acceptance of some backward-looking fact, or acceptance of some further principle. Nor do they discuss cases in which the expression of attitude is prompted not by principle but by emotion or habit. However, they offer no argument against generalizing to such examples.

More significantly, I shall argue, they do not extend their description to cover cases where attitudes seem to be expressed, but not principles of any kind. To take one of their examples, teenagers signalling to a friend by making raucous noises around a residential neighbourhood at night might reasonably be taken to express inconsiderateness towards their neighbours (2000: 1512–13). But they most obviously do this through having *failed* to consider their neighbours' interests. It is not right to think of them as acting on a principle whose subject is their neighbours' interests (such as: 'never

---

[1] At one point, Anderson and Pildes flirt with the idea of a theory that would 'account for both expressive and nonexpressive harms in ultimately expressivist terms' (2000: 1531). This strikes me as extraordinary: the harm of physical injury, for instance, has little or nothing to do with the harm of being slighted.

show any consideration for your neighbours' interests'). We might see them as acting on such a principle, for example, if they had discussed the matter in just those terms. Otherwise, the principle of their action is more clearly something like: 'when you see a friend, express unbridled joy noisily'. Since some of the cases in point are ones in which public bodies fail to notice or fail to take proper account of such matters as race and religion, it will be important for Anderson and Pildes to have a view in which such failures not only express attitudes, but also express goals and principles. Or, they could tease apart liabilities due to failure from liabilities due to the presence of goals and principles. I return to this briefly later.

Anderson and Pildes present a large portfolio of these in the course of their discussion. Although, I should say, I substantially agree with the *thrust* of their position, I have some doubts about the way they present it. Indeed, I shall shortly show that the way they present it seems to be inconsistent. So some adjustments need to be made. When those adjustments are made, I think the way is cleared for a better focus on the issue. In fact, I shall argue that less controversial resources are sufficient for doing all the work that they want to do. These resources include ideas of impermissible reasonings and harms that any theory of law would recognize without controversy.

II. The Anderson and Pildes Position

Anderson and Pildes are clear that they are *not* talking only of cases where the agent consciously intends or purposes a harm, or intends or purposes to belittle or 'stigmatize' the group so treated. Anderson and Pildes hold that people may express attitudes through acting negligently or recklessly, or through ignorance of social conventions or norms, or by acting on attitudes or assumptions of which they are unaware (2000: 1512–13). It would not, therefore, be *necessary* for a court to show conscious intention or purpose in deciding that an expressive harm has been committed.[2] Indeed, even the disavowal of an impermissible intent by a public body would not settle the issue in their favour. They could still be held to have committed the harm.

---

[2] 'It follows that people's conscious purposes and intentions, while relevant, are not the sole determinants of what their reactions express . . . Expressive theories of action hold people accountable for the public meanings of their actions' (2000: 1513).

I shall call this the 'Opacity' element of the position, signifying that the expressive harm of an action need not be transparent to its agent. A rival position, that expressive harm requires conscious intention or purpose, we can call 'Transparency'.

Anderson and Pildes are also clear that the test for expressive harm does not lie in actual consequences, such as distress to the target of some attitude.[3] This would make the issue of harm hostage to, on the one hand, the blithe insensitivity of the target, or, on the other hand, hypersensitivity, whereby distress results from actions that do not in fact express negative or inappropriate attitudes. In what follows, I shall occasionally refer to this as the 'Victim's Damage' view of harm, which Anderson and Pildes reject.

Neither does the harm need to arise from actual communication, whereby the target registers the negative or inappropriate attitude expressed and is thereby injured.[4] We can call this 'Victim's Uptake'. It is not necessary to the harm Anderson and Pildes have in mind. That harm is not a *consequence* of the action at all. The contrast they seem to have in mind is only falteringly expressed in the following sentence: 'The expressive harm is a result of acting on an unjustified expressive principle (a principle that expresses the wrong attitudes), while the nonexpressive harm is a causal consequence of the action' (2000: 1530). This is not very useful unless we know a contrast between results, on the one hand, and causal consequences, on the other, which is hardly transparent. But I take it that the drift is clear: the harm lies *in* the negativity expressed, not in its effects. We might say that the harm occurs at the time and place of the expressive act, not in virtue of anything that happens at later times or places. In this Aristotelian sense, it may be that a dead person can be harmed by later derogatory expression. It is not entirely easy to understand this, but as a first shot, a harm in this sense may be thought of as something like a diminution of status. A person's status can diminish after he or she dies, and, similarly, a person's status might be said to diminish as others treat her in the derogatory way described. But perhaps a better formulation would say that an expressive

---

[3] To convey this point, Anderson and Pildes use an analogy in which a neighbour cavalierly tosses her bottles onto your lawn. You suffer an expressive harm when treated 'according to principles that express negative or inappropriate attitudes'—in this case, your neighbours' rudeness—and not in the actual consequence of the burden and inconveniences of picking up the beer bottles (2000: 1527).

[4] Anderson and Pildes explain that a 'failure to communicate . . . can constitute a repudiation, retraction, or withholding of the acknowledgement of a valued social relationship with someone else' (2000: 1529).

harm is anything done or said to or about an object that gives a person who cares for the object reason to protest.[5] For example, a person would have reason to make an objection to someone expressing derogatory thoughts about an object for which she cares.

This view is therefore fundamentally nonconsequentialist.[6] But by the end of this essay, I shall raise doubts whether it is wise or necessary to mingle in this way the language of harm with the deontologically oriented doctrine that certain kinds of expression, by certain kinds of bodies, are impermissible in law. I shall argue that the introduction of expressive harm is an unnecessary mongrel. It is, however, a stylistic variant on something that is important.

Over the matter of Victim's Uptake, it is appropriate to issue a warning. There are many locutions that are unfortunately ambiguous at just this point. Consider the informal idea that legislators should not act in ways that 'send a message' that, say, one religion is preferable to another.[7] There is a sense in which 'send a message' is a success term, so that if the audience does not receive and understand it, you fail to send (them) a message. But there is another sense in which you send the message, just as you can send a parcel, whether the audience accepts it and understands it or not. The denial of any need for Victim's Uptake would insist on the latter reading.

Given Opacity, denial of Victim's Damage as a necessary condition of expressive harm, and a similar denial of Victim's Uptake, doubts might naturally arise about the epistemology of expressive harm. Anderson and Pildes offer us the basic ideas that '[e]xpressive theories of action hold people accountable for the public meanings of their actions', and that only 'external normative judgment' is the determinant (2000: 1513). '[T]he public meaning of an action is not even determined by shared

---

[5] This is very rough. So, for instance, we might wonder whether it is only someone who cares about the object who has this reason, or whether it should be a reason from 'the common point of view'. A full analysis at this point would need to concentrate on differences between, say, disliking something, regretting it, and objecting to it. Fortunately, not very much hangs on this in what follows.

[6] I should remark in passing that this makes their endorsement of Justice O'Connor's reasoning in *Lemon* v. *Kurtzman*, 403 U.S. 602 (1971), and *Lynch* v. *Donnelly*, 465 U.S. 668 (1984), surprising (Anderson and Pildes 2000: 1549–50). O'Connor explicitly singles out government action that has 'the effect of communicating a message of government endorsement or disapproval of religion' (Anderson and Pildes 2000: 1550, quoting *Lynch*). But it is not the effect that Anderson and Pildes want to make salient.

[7] See e.g. *Lynch*, 465 U.S. at 688 (O'Connor, J., concurring): 'Endorsement sends a message to nonadherents that they are outsiders, not full members of the political community, and an accompanying message to adherents that they are insiders, favored members of the political community.'

understandings of what the action means' (2000: 1524). Public meanings are 'socially constructed'—they are a 'result of the ways in which actions fit with (or fail to fit with) other meaningful norms and practices in the community' (2000: 1524). So, in particular, they insist that even when the agent is a legislative body, the articulated reasons of the group are not dispositive of public meaning (2000: 1526–7). Again, the expressive meaning of a norm is a 'product of interpreting the norm in the full context in which it is adopted and implemented' (2000: 1528). It is the 'external attribution of meaning' (2000: 1526). I shall call this the 'External Construction' view of expression, and it too will be salient in what follows.

   The central target of 'expressive theories of law' is not the derogatory or stigmatizing actions of individuals, but those expressed by public bodies. So Anderson and Pildes need a theory of what makes it legitimate to talk of a group as having a belief, or intention, or attitude, or goal, or principle of action. They do this by subscribing to the valuable work of Margaret Gilbert.[8] Gilbert approaches the concerted action problem as one of describing the difference between our doing things individually and our doing things together—things like conversing, or singing, or going for a walk, or digging the snow. She locates the difference in joint commitments, where each manifests a *conditional commitment* of his will, understanding that only if the others express similar commitments are all of the wills jointly committed to accept a certain goal when the time comes' (Gilbert 1989: 205). Such plural subjects are now a 'we', bound by norms of expectations and joint commitments. A group may then be attributed a belief or other propositional attitude:

When an individual believes that p, he grants the proposition that p the status of an assumption in his own private reasoning. When people jointly accept that p, they commit themselves to granting p the status of an assumption in their public reasoning, their discussions, arguments, and conversations with the relevant others in the contexts at issue.   (Gilbert 1989: 309)

Gilbert argues persuasively that this account accords with many of our intuitive judgements of group belief. In particular, she contrasts the way this approach handles the notion of the group belief with a more 'summative' account whereby a group can be said to have a belief only if a sufficient

---

[8] Anderson and Pildes 'draw heavily' on Gilbert 1989 in their discussion of expression and collective action. Anderson and Pildes 2000: 1515 n. 20.

majority of individual members of the group have the belief (1989: 308–12).
Her criterion departs so far from the 'summative' account that a group can
have and express a belief that is held by none of its members.[9]

And this seems right. A court, for instance, might express the belief that
the defendant is innocent although each member privately believes he is
guilty. It does this when enough members of the court commit themselves
to granting the guilty verdict the status of an assumption in their public
reasoning. Parallel accounts would cover group hopes, fears, principles,
goals, and attitudes.

It is important that there is nothing 'spooky' here. For all the facts about
the group mind supervene on beliefs and attitudes of the members. It is just
that those beliefs and attitudes relate in a more complex way to the upshot
than on anything like an aggregative or summative account. Anderson and
Pildes sum it up in a definition, which they accept:

A group, G, has mental state M if and only if the members of G are jointly
committed to expressing M as a body.   (Anderson and Pildes 2000: 1517)

Gilbert's own formulation is a little more complex:

A group G believes that p if and only if the members of G jointly accept that
p.   (Gilbert 1989: 306)

This in turn may be explicated thus:

The members of G *jointly accept* that p if and only if it is common knowledge in G
that the members of G individually have intentionally and openly* expressed their
willingness jointly to accept that p with the other members of G.[10]

Anderson and Pildes do not suggest any divergence from Gilbert here.
Therefore, I believe it is provisionally fair to assume that they are aligned in
their positions, although I shall eventually offer them a necessary divergence.
I shall call the view that gains full-dress expression in the last quote, 'Open
Affirmation'.

Anderson and Pildes offer not only an account of when a group has
a mental state, but also a general account of expression of such a state.

---

[9] Gilbert asserts that through negotiation, intimidation, or perhaps even coercion, a group may end
up jointly accepting a view that each member thinks is incorrect (1989: 307–8).

[10] Gilbert 1989: 306. The term 'openly' in this context means that there are no cross-purposes or
hidden glitches in the fact that everyone knows of everyone's commitments and their knowledge of
those commitments.

They offer examples where what is expressed is, in effect, something that is *indicated*, or something that is embodied and realized in the action (2000: 1506–7). When music expresses sadness, the sadness is in the music itself. When his sigh expresses his misery, he sighed, and he was miserable. It is, of course, a very difficult thing to say that the relation between the misery and the sigh makes it true that the one expresses the other. But they both have to be there. Anderson and Pildes say that '[t]he expression of a mental state brings that state into the open, for oneself and potentially for others to recognize' (2000: 1507). We can call this a 'Revelation' account of expression, whereby an action reveals something further true of the agent. On the Revelation account, what is revealed must actually exist. Only then can it be brought into the open and recognized.

There is an option here that Anderson and Pildes do not take. Expression is often more 'intensional' than this. We can say that a person can express a belief or attitude that she does not hold. She can do this by adopting appropriate means of expression that would normally, or conventionally, or customarily, or in some way be thought to indicate a mental state, although on this occasion there is no such mental state. In this sense, someone saying *p* may express a belief that he does not hold, and someone saying that *x* is wonderful may express admiration for *x*, although in fact she detests him.

III. Difficulties

But now a contradiction looms. On the face of it, Open Affirmation is inconsistent with Opacity. And thence it is inconsistent with External Construction. Open Affirmation requires awareness, whereas Opacity allows meanings that are concealed from agents, even when the agency is that of a group.

Consider the issue in the light of Open Affirmation. For a group to hold a principle—say, that race is a satisfactory reason for imposing disadvantage on a class of people—the group has to jointly accept the principle, and that means that it is common knowledge amongst them that they have 'individually and intentionally and openly' expressed willingness jointly to accept the principle. This is what is meant by Open Affirmation. It is inconsistent with the view that the group may accept, as a group, an assumption or principle of which it is unaware. On this account, there *can be no such thing* as a group *having* a belief of which it is unaware. Lack of Transparency entails that the group has no such belief, although individual members may.

Gilbert's Open Affirmation formulation is confined to *beliefs*, and we might wonder whether it is to be extended to cover mental states such as attitudes or dispositions to hold attitudes because of principles. I do not think this worry would be well directed, however, for three reasons. First, the whole thrust of Gilbert's discussion suggests that parallel common knowledge or openness clauses should govern any case of propositional attitude and not just cases of belief. Second, the principles at the centre of the discussion are usually thought of as objects of belief: people are said to believe in a principle of equality or to hold that some goal justifies some end. But, third, in the quotation above, Anderson and Pildes overtly extend the treatment to cover any mental state.

The contradiction is only immediate if we are talking of attitudes, beliefs, or goals that groups are supposed to *have*. But Anderson and Pildes might try to avert the contradiction by retreating from the Revelation concept of 'expression'. As I have said, you can only bring into the open what is there; a group can only bring into the open its belief that lesbianism should be suppressed if it believes that lesbianism should be suppressed. By Open Affirmation, therefore, this has to be common knowledge and openly affirmed among group members for it to be true.

Anderson and Pildes *could* abandon Revelation in favour of an intensional view of expression. Then, the target of External Construction need not be a belief or other state that the group has. And this would allow Opacity to govern this target (the public meaning), while Open Affirmation only governs states that they possess. But I do not think this is really open to them. For surely courts cannot be interpreted as employing such a division. This is because the intensional reading of 'expression' does not fit with an ambition of finding principles that *governed* action. Principles can govern action only if they exist, that is, if they are held by the person or group whose action is sensitive to a representation of them. A belief cannot govern the action of an agent who does not hold the belief. We must remember that the reason for External Constructivism is often the suspicion that an articulated reason is only a 'pretext' or a 'rationalization' when some other attitude or goal is actually doing the work. Anderson and Pildes cite cases that expressly state that it is the actual purpose, such as 'the purpose of discriminating against Negroes', that invalidates a law.[11] So at least a large part of the court practices they cite as supporting their position suggests that courts do conceive of themselves as looking for attitudes, principles, or goals that were present and actually governing decisions, whether wittingly or not. And then, if Revelation is retained, Open Affirmation is inconsistent with Opacity and with External Construction.

Although I have presented the contradiction starkly in this part, I think there is a way out of it. But the way out, which may indeed be the way that Anderson and Pildes would take, is best explored after we have seen reason to modify Open Affirmation in any case.

IV. Accord and Governance

Before beginning a reconstruction, we need to be firmly aware of a famous ambiguity. According to the formula quoted, expressive harm occurs when a person or group is treated 'according to principles that *communicate* negative or inappropriate attitudes toward [them]'.[12] Now a treatment may *accord* with certain principles, but not be *directed* by them. Behaviour may conform to certain norms or rules, or it may be governed by them. Kant's famous example of the distinction is the shopkeeper who gives a child the right change, in accordance with a principle of honesty, but who is actually acting out of a principle of self-interest (Kant 1997: 41, 53 [4: 397]). My polite behaviour towards a person may accord with a principle of respect, although I am actually motivated by hope of advantage.

The epistemology of accord is easier than that of government. Indeed, Kant thought that the epistemology of government, establishing, for instance, that an action was the upshot of respect for a principle of duty, was impossible: 'we can never, even by the most strenuous self-examination, get entirely behind our covert incentives, since, when moral worth is at issue, what counts is not actions, which one sees, but those inner principles of actions that one does not see' (Kant 1997: 61–2 [4: 407]).

---

[11] See e.g, Anderson and Pildes 2000: 1535 (quoting *City of Richmond* v. *United States*, 422 U.S. 358, 378 (1975)).

[12] Anderson and Pildes 2000: 1528. Anderson and Pildes refer to this subset of expressive harms as 'communicative harms' (1527).

The problem with mere accord is that the epistemology is *too* easy, leaving it alarmingly indiscriminate. That is, as the example of the shopkeeper shows, the same act may accord with a principle of respect for honesty, or accord with a principle of self-interest, or with many other principles yet again. The sentence passed on a criminal might accord with a principle of disrespect, being the very sentence one might have wanted in order to demean or stigmatize him, but it might also accord with principles of justice. The former fact could not properly be used to strike down the sentence absent further argument—for instance, that the sentence was passed *because of* disrespect for the defendant. If no further argument were required, then in effect we would be saying that if an act is that which would have resulted from *some* principle expressing negative attitude, then it is impermissible. But then, any act at all will stand condemned. My drinking coffee at eleven o'clock *accords* with the principle of either drinking coffee or hurling racial abuse at eleven o'clock. But it wasn't *directed* by the latter principle.[13]

An act may accord with a principle in this sense if the agent acted 'as if' holding that principle. The problem is that any act *could* be the upshot of any number of different principles, just as any conclusion could be the result of reasoning from any number of different premises. This problem seems endemic to the area. Consider, for instance, Justice O'Connor's concern that the state not ally itself with particular religions.[14] An act may be the act expected of, and in that sense allied with, the operations of many different principles, including ones abhorrent to its agent. The fact that a judgement is 'what you would have got' if the state had a goal of supporting Christianity as opposed to Islam is no more proof of the presence of that goal than the fact that my behaviour is 'what you would have got' if I had the principle of drinking coffee or hurling racial abuse proves the presence of that principle.

The indeterminacy here parallels a well-known problem in the philosophy of language: the so-called rule-following considerations. Any pattern of answers to any series of questions—for instance, to give the result of

---

[13] The example is deliberately artificial. Even so, the principle *could* be that which directs my coffee-drinking, if, for instance, I listen to Voices, and the Voices told me either to drink a coffee or hurl racial abuse, and fortunately coffee was to hand.

[14] See *Lynch* v. *Donnelly*, 465 U.S. 668, 687–94 (1984) (O'Connor, J., concurring) (discussing and applying a state endorsement test).

adding two numbers—is compatible with indefinitely many interpreta-tions of which rule the subject was following. If we think the subject was following a unique rule, we apparently cannot say that it, and it alone, was 'manifest' in the pattern of answers, for many other rules would have given exactly the same pattern.

If the problem with the 'accord' reading is that it lets in too much, the problem with the 'government' reading is that the epistemology becomes, at least, very difficult. Even if it is not impossible, as Kant held, we seem to enter an epistemological wilderness, the desert of hermeneutics. Does the External Construction view give us a chart across the wilderness?

A preliminary suspicion that it does not arises from the very phrasing in terms of attempt to discover 'the public meaning' of an action. The problem is that in contested cases, there is no such thing as 'the' public meaning—there is only the different interpretations different groups put upon whatever was done. In their anxiety to avoid what I call 'Victim's Uptake', Anderson and Pildes may have forgotten that the actions of a body may mean different things to different people. Similarly, those meanings may change over time. So, for instance, the language in a work by Mark Twain may have expressed unexceptionable, even liberal and progressive, attitudes towards race in the middle of the nineteenth century, but such language is interpreted by many today as racist and unacceptable. If it is a question of Mark Twain's mindset, then the public meaning at the time is what is important. If it is a question of whether, for instance, to allow the books in the school curriculum, the contemporary meaning is more important. This, in turn, suggests that the purpose of legislative review may dictate different directions of the court's gaze.

V. Group Goals

At stake here are serious issues of legislative practice. If we sympathize with Open Affirmation and must have a Revelation account of expression, then any doctrine of expressive harm has very limited application. A reasoning body would have to have made clear in its actual recorded reasonings that an impermissible purpose or impermissible principle governed their deliberations. For otherwise, there would be no evidence for common knowledge and openness among the members of the body. The scope of review and repeal would be extremely limited. If, on the other hand, we keep Open Affirmation, but deny the Revelation condition on expression, admitting that a body can express a principle that it does not hold, then the scope for creative reinterpretation becomes wide indeed. Remembering Opacity, and the denial of Victim's Uptake, and Victim's Damage, it becomes alarmingly possible that External Constructivism, like modern literary criticism, takes us towards a landscape where anything goes.

Anderson and Pildes defend themselves against scepticism about finding public meaning derived from public choice theorists (2000: 1521–3). But they do not consider an allied range of arguments. Some of the difficulties of reading back from actions to principles, in social groups, are illustrated by the following fascinating kind of case, highlighted by Philip Pettit and Wlodek Rabinowicz.[15] Imagine a three-member board deliberating on the publication of a paper in a journal that they control. They have reduced the question to three elements. To publish the paper, they must find that it is original, that the topic is important, and that it is presented in a scholarly manner. We suppose that there are three members of the board, A, B, and C, and individually they hold the following views:

Member	Original?	Important?	Scholarly?	Verdict/C
A	Y	Y	N	N
B	Y	N	Y	N
C	N	Y	Y	N
Verdict/P	Y	Y	Y	

Here the board might reach one of two verdicts. If the members are asked to vote on a conclusion (verdict/C, or what Pettit and Rabinowicz call conclusion-driven reasoning or voting), they each reject the paper. If they are asked to vote separately on each premise (verdict/P or what Pettit and Rabinowicz call premise-driven reasoning), then each premise will gain a majority, and the paper will be accepted. So a different verdict results depending on which procedure is adopted (yet no member of the board is inconsistent).

---

[15] Pettit and Rabinowicz 2001. My discussion of Pettit and Rabinowicz's work here, and throughout this essay, is based upon an early draft of their article.

The dilemma of which procedure to adopt generalizes to cases with any number of premises and any number of members of the group. All it requires is the following: that there is a conclusion to be decided on a conjunction of independent premises, so that the conclusion is to be accepted if the premises are; that each member makes a judgement on the premises and on the conclusion; that there is a majority in favour of each premise, but a different majority for each; that the intersection of those majorities supports the conclusion; and that the intersection of the majorities is itself not a majority. In the case illustrated, the intersection of the majorities is null, as nobody supports the conclusion outright.

The same structure arises if a decision requires only that a group accepts one of a disjunction of premises. Suppose the paper should be published if it meets any of three criteria: it must be original, or it must be useful to students, or it must be a valuable summation of the state of the art for scholars. Now we have:

Member	Original?	Useful?	Summation?	Verdict/C
A	Y	N	N	Y
B	N	Y	N	Y
C	N	N	Y	Y
Verdict/P	N	N	N	

Here the paper is rejected if the vote is taken on each criterion. But it is accepted if each member is asked whether it should be accepted.

Pettit and Rabinowicz argue convincingly that organized groups should impose the discipline of reason on themselves at the collective level. This means that they ought to find out what 'we' think about each premise, and then what 'we' think about the conclusion, based upon what we have already accepted. In this first case, this means that the paper was to be accepted; in the second case it is rejected, although each member of the board believes there is a decisive reason that determines acceptance. The core of Pettit and Rabinowicz's argument concerns groups that have specific goals and that recognize the need to present themselves as 'credible promoters' of those goals. This will require fidelity to past judgements and fidelity to consistency and coherence in a pattern of judgements. A group allowing majority voting on each issue as it comes up, with no regard to previously established commitment, will easily fall into contradiction.

If a group does let itself establish only a verdict/C, then it may be impossible to infer back anything about its attitude towards the elements of the case necessary to support verdict/C. Consider the first conjunctive case. The disgruntled writer might suppose, given the verdict, that 'they' didn't consider the paper original or that 'they' didn't think it was scholarly. But two out of the three thought each of these things. Or, consider the disjunctive case. Here, if the verdict/C is communicated, the delighted scholar may suppose that 'they' considered the paper original, or useful to students, or a good summation for the scholar. But in each case, there is no sufficient reason to say 'they' did. An aggregative story would say that 'they' thought the reverse of each of these things, of course. And Open Affirmation would force us to denial: in the absence of deliberation and discursive reasoning on each of the premises, we cannot say *anything* about the premises the group accepted in delivering its verdict/C. There is no state of acceptance that meets the condition of Open Affirmation. So any proposition of the form 'the group accepted premise —' is false. And in this case this seems correct. There is no public commitment.

Now imagine that our author is aggrieved and, turning his back on Open Affirmation, resorts to an External Construction hermeneutic. Supposes the paper was on Derrida, and he says that the verdict accorded with the principle that work on Derrida is not important, or that the rejection 'sends a message' that work on Derrida is unimportant, or has the 'public meaning' that this is so. There are things he can say in support of this. He can say that the verdict is what you would have expected had the committee accepted that work on Derrida is not important. The second is more normative: the verdict is one that would 'make sense', or predictably be the verdict of rational agents who in fact hold that work on Derrida is not important.

Although these things can be said, they should not be accepted. For in the case described, there are the other interpretations about which exactly the same can be said. The verdict equally 'sends a message' that the author's paper is not scholarly, although work on Derrida is important, or the message that his work on Derrida is not original, although it is scholarly and on an important writer. Yet none of these views would actually have commanded a committee majority or have gained assent had it been put to a vote.

In other words, these structures suggest that when only verdict/C is on the table, the process of extracting a 'public meaning', sending a message according to some hidden principle, is too indeterminate to be respectable. There is no such thing as 'the principle that best justifies' their verdict, for instance, since any of many different combinations of belief equally yields the verdict.

In their discussion, Pettit and Rabinowicz advance, as reasons for collectives to adopt 'premise-driven' reasoning procedures, that these are ways to guard against partially hidden agendas. These procedures bring out into the open the collective opinion of the group. And once the collective opinion of the group has been settled—for instance, by accepting the result of a declaration or by a voting procedure—then, as a plural or collective agent there is nothing more to be said. 'We' have spoken—regardless of the private opinions or agendas of the agents making up the group.

Yet someone might go in for External Constructivism, even when a group has submitted itself to the discipline of public reason. Even if it makes manifest its own reasoning procedures, coming to a verdict/P we can open yet further interpretive space. For example, suppose the committee accepted that originality is a proper member of the set of premises. Then we can ask what 'message' this decision sends, and, treating it as a conclusion, think of principles in accordance with which such a conclusion follows. The same hermeneutic indeterminacy follows.

We could have made the same point in terms of goals. If, instead of premises necessary for a verdict, we construct the example in terms of institutional goals, we can again get the structure whereby a majority accepts each goal, but their conclusion-driven decision favours an action that accords with none of them. Or we could get cases where an action suggests a goal that, in fact, could not command group assent. Again, it will be very dangerous to infer back goals, and principles allowing courses of action to be pursued for the sake of goals, simply from raw decision making. In the absence of a process of information exchange and certification, there are too many 'as ifs' around—too many principles, any of which might equally or justifiably be advanced as the very one with which action accorded.

In the light of all this, it seems to me very difficult to control an External Constructivist approach to the 'public meaning' of group decisions. When a group has not submitted itself collectively to a discipline of reason, wide indeterminacies open up. And when a group has committed itself to the discipline of reason as a collective body, any attempt to get behind their overt acceptances and to conjure hidden principles 'in accordance with which' they were acting enters a similar hermeneutic desert. So the argument of this section suggest that it is wise to stick with Open Affirmation.

VI. More on Commitments

But let us reconsider. Open Affirmation, as it stands, looks to be too restrictive. Surely there should be some respectable cases in which a group that has not given open affirmation to a belief or principle may be said to have committed themselves to it.

One kind of case would arise from deductive closure. If a group has openly affirmed each of several premises, then we would reasonably hold them committed to the conclusion of those premises, even if they had never explicitly considered the conclusion. A similar kind of case would come from the explicit extraction of principles of inference that were 'implicit' in their reasonings.[16] The first quotation I gave from Gilbert is certainly consistent with these extensions of Open Affirmation (see above, p. 70). For in that, she talks only of people 'committing' themselves to things, and it is often reasonable to say that people have committed themselves to beliefs or principles, perhaps unwittingly and certainly without open affirmation required in the second Gilbert formulation (above, p. 70). In this sense we commit ourselves to a principle of uniformity of nature when we reason from past to future. A group who argue 'A, so B' commit themselves to the conditional 'if A, then B'.

This is what I had in mind as an escape route from the contradiction of section III. It enables us to back away from Open Affirmation—the second Gilbert account—in favour of a less overt conception of 'Commitment'. In the formulation I quoted, Anderson and Pildes offered 'joint commitment' (2000: 1574), which certainly sounds more like Gilbert's Open Affirmation

---

[16] These principles might be purely formal, but they might include 'material' conditionals and generalizations. A public body saying in one breath that all As are B, in the following breath that all Cs are D, and in the third breath inferring that all As are D, could be said to be committed to the view that all Bs are C.

criterion. But they may have intended the first, which accords better with External Construction.

These relaxations of Open Affirmation do not, I think, get us very far by themselves. The interpretive method they do allow is simply that of the logician. But they suggest at least one kind of formula that may be of more use than the dangerously lax formulae of 'according with' goals or principles. As a first shot, the formula they suggest is that in which a joint affirmation simply *could not* have been made without the belief necessary for making sense of the inference, or *could not* have been held had not the further implicit belief also been held. Then I should gloss 'could not have been held without a belief' in the following principle, which I shall call 'Credibility':

> A group may be said to have been committed to a belief (goal, principle) if there is no way—no credible way—that the group could rationally sustain their open affirmations were they not also prepared to stand by the belief (goal, principle).

The proof would be that there is no way to make sense of the explicit statements of the body, unless they were also committed to the implicit principle or premise teased out this way.

Credibility is obviously more exacting than formulations in terms of actions 'according with' principles. It is also more exacting than a 'best explanation' criterion. The problem with those was that where a number of interpretations are in play, even the 'best' may fall far short of making the others incredible, even by quite low standards of credibility. If there are nine hypotheses in play, one with a probability of 0.2 and the others with a probability of 0.1, the first is the 'best'. But it is far from incredible—in fact, it is more probable than not—that something else was going on. Of course, standards of what is credible may vary here as elsewhere. It will require judgement to say which interpretations of a body's doings are too far-fetched to be credible.

To see the formulation in action, consider a corporate case, such as the recent Microsoft case.[17] Suppose the question is whether some corporation intended to drive competitors out of business by abusing its

---

[17] See generally *United States* v. *Microsoft Corp.*, 97 F. Supp. 2d 59 (D.D.C. 2000) (final judgment and order); 87 F. Supp. 2d 30 (D.D.C. 2000) (district court holding); 84 F. Supp. 2d 9 (D.D.C. 1999) (findings of fact).

monopoly power. Unless prosecutors are lucky, they will be unlikely to find open affirmations of this intention, of Gilbert's kind. But they may find decisions, and whole patterns of decisions, of which there is not a credible way of making sense without supposing the corporation to have had this intent. They may find evidence of what Durkheim considered a mark of the 'group mind'—namely, a coercive culture organized around an understood implicit commitment to the intention in question.

Consider another example. Suppose a club makes an open affirmation to bar from membership all those living south of the river. And suppose the only salient common factor is that those living north of the river are white, and those living south of the river are black. Even though the issue was never raised (never breathed, one might say), Credibility could sustain the view that this decision was racially motivated. For it may be that nobody in their right mind would suppose that geographic relationship to the river per se had a bearing on any of the club's goals. There *might* be a legitimate purpose—a club might have the goal of serving a local function, like a football club, for example—but if all the candidates are sufficiently far-fetched, Credibility will sustain the racist interpretation.

Credibility is not favourable to wild interpretational stabs in the dark. The aggrieved author may say that the journal intends to refuse papers on Derrida. But even if in fact they have taken no papers on Derrida, Credibility will not sustain the charge for exactly the reasons displayed above. There are too many equally credible competitors. For this reason it may not deliver all the verdicts that Anderson and Pildes would want to support. For example, consider the case of a town council that happed to be Christian allowing land to be used for Christmas symbols.[18] It seems to me that there may well be other ways of making sense of their decision, without imputing any purpose or intention to promote Christianity and to demean other religions. They may simply hold only some principle of continuing a tradition that a majority of townspeople want to continue, for instance, and if that dominated their overt affirmations, Credibility will offer no purchase for a conspiracy theory in which concealed purposes are unmasked.

Credibility does well, I believe, in a case such as that of flying the Confederate flag over public buildings. There might, say, be three contenders for the purpose or principle that explains a state doing this. The purpose may

---

[18] Cf. *Lynch* v. *Donnelly*, 465 U.S. 668 (1984) (analysing a factually similar scenario).

be to honour a way of life that enslaved black people. Or, the purpose may be to honour the goal of dissolving the union of the states. Or, the purpose may be to signal remembrance of the dead. Suppose the first two purposes are deemed constitutionally impermissible, but the third is not. Then Credibility requires that we discover that one or the other of the first two is the state purpose. This may not be as difficult as it sounds, if, for instance, substitute symbols of memorials to the dead, which carry no risk of the impermissible interpretation, have been publicly rejected, or not even considered. If this kind of reasoning rules out the legitimate purpose, then the only interpretations that remain require one or the other of the impermissible purposes, and therefore imply illegitimate intent.[19]

Where Credibility is satisfied, we can, if we like, talk of public meaning. I do not think this phrase adds anything to simply talking of commitments without which the agents' actions could not, rationally have occurred. But along with a number of philosophers, I am sceptical of the full 'Gricean' panoply of intentions that have been thought necessary for meaning.[20] I prefer to remember the original, core notion of natural meaning from which Grice departed, and to work with the idea that one thing means another if it is a sure enough indication of it. The principle of Credibility accords with exactly that core notion. Hence, it legitimizes a sense of public meaning that does not require Open Affirmation.

VII. Principles and Failures

However, although we now open a category of public meanings determined via Credibility, I actually do not think that these are what we need to concentrate upon. The reason has to do with the element of *failure* that I mentioned at the beginning. Consider two cases: the teenagers that scream round the neighbourhood inconsiderately, and the INS treating immigrants demeaningly. Is it sensible to look for goals and principles expressed in these actions?

---

[19] There is an interesting piece of logic at this point. In this case, we may be sure that a disjunction (illegitimate purpose A or illegitimate purpose B) is certified by Credibility, although neither disjunction is. It would be interesting to compare this with court practice where other examples of the same structure arise.

[20] For a forceful statement of scepticism, see Horwich 1998: 19–20.

There *could* have been open affirmations, of Gilbert's kind. The teenagers might have gone into a huddle and agreed to do whatever they could to show the neighbours how little they cared about them. The INS could have assented in a meeting to a policy of displaying contempt of, or hostility towards, those who hold green cards. In the case where no such reasons came out for open affirmation, the most natural thing to say is only that these actions express *failures* and *absences*. The relevant bodies simply did not take into account some things that by some standard or another we believe they *ought* to have taken into account. The teenagers *should* have recognized their actions to be inconsiderate, and the INS *should* have recognized its actions to be demeaning.

I do not set much store by an ontological difference, as it were, between failure and flawed intent, or between omissions and commissions. To fail to reply to someone's invitation is to slight them. As Anderson and Pildes say, a failure occurring when a particular response is demanded can itself be an action: a manifestation of disrespect or a stigmatization.[21] Let me then concentrate upon the one example of the INS. Suppose we say that reasonable efficiency in dealing with legitimate inquiries and needs is demanded of government organizations. Hence, its grotesque failures to implement such standards convicts the INS, and ultimately Congress, of failure of respect—that is, contempt of, or hostility towards, green card holders.[22]

We have here a large class of cases that depart from Open Affirmation. To make the above interpretation of the INS, we do not have to find

---

[21] See above, n. 4.

[22] Obviously this requires detail. It is not hard to find. To give one example, it is a general civil right that one not be punished twice for the same crime, nor be punished without trial. See U.S. Const. art. III, § 2, cl. 3 ('The Trial of all Crimes, except in Cases of Impeachment, shall be by Jury . . .'); U.S. Const. amend. V ('No person shall be . . . subject for the same offence to be twice put in jeopardy of life or limb . . .'). Since 1996, however, it seems that neither provision has applied to 'alien residents' living in the United States. In 1996, Congress adopted the Antiterrorism and Effective Death Penalty Act of 1996, which was intended to give government agents greater authority to detain and deport alien terrorists. See Pub. L. No. 104–32, 110 Stat. 1216 (codified as amended in scattered sections of 8, 18, and 42 U.S.C. (2000)). While Congress's intentions in passing this law may have been noble, the effects of the law have been disastrous: Immigration and Naturalization officials now use this law to 'detain and deport noncitizens because they have previously been convicted of a crime, no matter how long ago or how minor. Among those being detained are lawful permanent residents—those who have lived in the country for at least seven years, have married American citizens or have children who are citizens.' Lena Williams, 'A Law Aimed at Terrorists Hits Legal Immigrants', *New York Times*, 17 July 1996, A1. This has effectively denied to alien residents the constitutional rights enjoyed by American citizens.

open affirmation of Gilbert's kind. The ur-phenomenon is a failure, or lack of care. And it seems as though Credibility gives us a determinate interpretation.

The reason Credibility gives us this result is that we are not going so far as to attribute any goal, purpose, or principle to the INS. There need be no one goal visible in the individual decisions that make up the ethos. Failure to publish rules is just bungling; failure to make appointments is lack of secretarial funding; failure to ensure elementary civil rights is Congressional error, and so on. The same is true of the teenagers. Their failure is a sure indication of disrespect, not because a principle of disrespect was ever openly affirmed, but just because they could not have acted as they did had they respected the neighbours.[23]

Why are these cases free of the alarming indeterminacies that opened up above? Because we are stopping short of introducing principles with which acts accord as candidates for 'public meaning'. We say instead that the teenagers' behaviour could not have occurred without them having neglected the interests of the neighbours. The INS could not behave as it does, did it not disregard interests that it ought to protect. The behaviours are not, to repeat, a sure indication of any goals or principles or beliefs that the agents have. A judgement of negligence is not hostage to what people actually thought, but only to what they did not think.

VIII. Do We Need Expressive Harm?

The verdicts that might be made on this account have the form, 'such-and-such a body should not have acted as it did, because it could not have done as it did without failure to respect some norm.' Now this is, surely, a common and uncontroversial form of judgement in law. A court may have its verdict struck down, for instance, because it failed to respect some norm of trial procedure. A court that failed to take into account required evidence could not have acted as it did without so failing; a court that

---

[23] Of course, such a judgement is defeasible, given a context that makes other explanations credible. They might have believed that it was New Year's Eve and all the adults were partying like them, for instance. There are, of course, very difficult issues connecting pure failure with responsibility. But in the kinds of cases that Anderson and Pildes consider, a doctrine of 'strict liability' would seem appropriate. We are not so concerned with groups' responsibilities as with whether to strike out their decisions.

failed to abide by exclusionary rules could not have acted as it did without breaking those rules.

The 'failure to abide by a norm' formula relates in an interesting way to the idea that we ought to find an impermissible commitment in order to reject the reasonings of a group. A norm *may* have the form of striking out as impermissible a purpose, goal, or form of reasoning—for instance, taking racial classification as relevant in some context. And then it takes the cautious interpretive strategy I have described to determine whether an impermissible goal, purpose, or form of reasoning indeed animated the group making the decision. But a norm may more directly forbid various kinds of negligence or trespass in reasoning procedures. And these do not require finding hidden meanings, purposes, or goals. So the effect of my proposal may be to expand the kinds of cases with which we should be concerned.

The core appeal would be in the first place to an impermissible failure—a failure to abide by some constitutionally obligatory standard, or a failure to take account of aspects of things that it was obligated to take into account. It is this that convicts the teenagers, the INS, or perhaps even the insensitive town council that allows only Christian symbols on the common ground. Just as their goals or principles do not enter in, neither do harms arising in virtue of the expression of imputed meanings. These are short-circuited by direct concentration on failure to meet obligatory standards.

This view does justice to two elements that Anderson and Pildes highlight in the actual practice of the law. The first is the nonconsequential direction of the court's gaze. Asking whether the agent failed to accord with some obligatory norm is not asking about the consequences of their actions. The teenagers' failure is just that, regardless of whether they actually wake any sleepers. Just as certain protections can be regarded as upholding 'rights against rules', others uphold 'rights against normative trespasses': omissions or commissions in the deliberative process of bodies that trespass against constitutional or other requirements.

Once this is said, however, it seems to make unnecessary the mongrel doctrine of expressive harm. The norm against which the group trespasses may indeed be a norm that is there precisely to defend people in general against harm. But the harm here will be *ordinary* injury, loss, or diminution of well-being, rather than any *sui generis* expressive harm. A rule against accepting public reasonings that fail to respect people's equal political standing can be justified consequentially, in terms of ordinary harms, and then the failure of a group so to reason is a self-standing, determinable matter. If this is so, we have the familiar combination of consequentialism and deontology that is found across the law. The speed limit is there to prevent public harm, but the policeman and the court do not have to prove actual harm or even increased risk of harm on each occasion on which the rule is enforced.

This is a structure of 'indirect consequentialism' in which the rules are justified by the consequences, and cases are decided on the rules. The second point of accord with court practice is that such an approach better explains some writing that might appear to be expressivist. Consider Paul Brest, for example, on the Equal Protection Clause, talking of harms resulting from race-dependent decisions:

Often, the most obvious harm is the denial of the opportunity to secure a desired benefit—a job, a night's lodging at a motel, a vote. But this does not completely describe the consequences of race-dependent decisionmaking. Decisions based on assumptions of intrinsic worth and selective indifference inflict psychological injury by stigmatizing their victims as inferior. Moreover, because acts of discrimination tend to occur in pervasive patterns, their victims suffer especially frustrating, cumulative and debilitating injuries. (Brest 1976: 8)

This does not require the mongrel doctrine. It is reasoning that any classical utilitarian could accept. This is especially so when we have become sensitive to the idea that self-worth, including the Hegelian reflection of worth from the eyes of others, is an ineliminable and central component of well-being. The same remarks apply to those decisions that hinged on formulations whereby a message may harm 'a person's standing in the political community'.[24] We should admit that this does not make the issue hinge on whether *actual* harm to standing occurred, but without for a moment supposing that 'frustrating, cumulative, and debilitating injuries' have nothing to do with it. The median is that such a message is of a kind that is *apt* to harm, just as in recklessness and negligence in general. And then an indirect consequentialist reading becomes apposite.

Consequences sometimes lie a long way from principles—so far that some philosophers will suppose they do nothing to support their authority.

---

[24] *Lynch* v. *Donnelly*, 465 U.S. 668, 687 (1984) (O'Connor, J., concurring), quoted in Anderson and Pildes 2000: 1547.

I do not want to prejudge this hard question of moral theory. In one kind of case, a state decision governing finance was struck down as 'inconsistent with the very idea of political union, even a limited federal union'.[25] In these cases, a state's purpose in passing some law is deemed to be protectionist, and the protectionist principle is cited as impermissible. It is not expressly stated that the principle is consequentially harmful. But it is inconsistent with another principle (of political union between the states) that, in this context, is taken as sacrosanct. This leaves open whether the sacrosanct nature of the background principle is itself justified on consequentialist grounds.

A similar silence about the status of the background principle may arise when we consider equal concern and respect for all persons (or at least, all citizens) under the law. This is treated as a sacrosanct principle. Where reasonings are struck down as flouting it, there need be no judgement as to the status of the principle itself. It may ultimately be justified on consequentialist grounds, or on some doctrine of natural rights, or on Kantian or contractualist grounds, or elsewhere yet. What is salient, however, is that where judgement is *silent* on the status of such background principles, it is also *silent* about expressive harms. What it is not silent about are impermissible trespasses against compulsory norms.

My formulation of the notion of expressive harm made it something to which an agent who cared for its object had reason to object. A person who cares for another has reason to object if another expresses hurtful or demeaning attitudes towards them, regardless of the actual consequences. On the indirect consequentialist account, the application of this requires finding that the attitudes or principles expressed are apt to cause more ordinary kinds of harm. In most cases, of course, we could go so far as to say that this is their function: a demeaning remark is there *for* causing harm. In other cases, the attitudes or principles may be impermissible on more 'deontological' grounds, existing quite regardless of aptitude to cause harm. To repeat, for the purpose of this essay, I do not have to solve for how wide this latter class may be.

The salient point is that in either event, on this analysis, the legal judgements involved are not different from those the law must make

---

[25] Regan 1986: 1113, quoted in Anderson and Pildes 2000: 1554 . Anderson and Pildes cite additional material from Regan but the cited material does not talk of expressive harms, only of legitimate purposes; see their 2000: 1554 nn. 139–41.

over most of its domain. The law looks to the kinds of principle or kinds of reasoning behind a collective's decision. I have suggested that we tighten the idea of External Construction at this point by using the principle I called Credibility. If it finds that the reasonings and principles are impermissible—either because they are apt to cause tangible harms, or because they are inconsistent with fundamental norms of justice, equality, or our understanding of what is owed to people—the law can strike out the decision. The law may or may not then choose to adopt the language of expressive harm, provided that the underlying logic is clear. This would, as it were, be window dressing, and like most window dressing, it carries the risk that style is mistaken for substance.

Of course, it would be presumptuous of me to offer this as a panacea for all the difficult cases. First, the judgement whether a group could have behaved as it did had it not trespassed against a norm will remain a judgement, and difficult cases will remain difficult. All that a proposal like mine could hope to do is to clear the way for a view of the principles that ought to determine judgement in such cases. Second, however, without further analysis, it remains a speculation whether a substantial proportion of the cases in which doctrines of expressive harm have been invoked would solve themselves in this interpretatively much clearer way. But from the philosophical sidelines, it looks to me as though they would.

POSTSCRIPT

This paper bears its marks as a contribution to a conference on a specialized topic in legal philosophy. Notwithstanding, it seems to me that some of the issues it raises have a more general application when we think of group action and especially the interpretation of groups in intentional terms. For that reason it seemed worth including, especially as the admirable *Maryland Law Review* is probably not on many philosophers' reading lists. Rewriting it to remove the lingering aroma of a conference would have changed the essay unrecognizably, so I have opted to let it stand with minimal alteration.

5

Trust, Cooperation, and Human Psychology

Trust and cooperation concern everyone. A search in the major journals database under the two words gives results from journals of architecture, dentistry, economics, education, law, and music, as well as politics, psychology, and philosophy. Why philosophy? It may not at first be clear what specifically philosophical questions such concepts raise. In thinking about them we seem to be in the domain of the social psychologist who can do empirical research on the existence of trust, or the economist who can measure its effects, for instance on the costs of making various transactions. But there are deep currents in the modern world that suggest that there is something surprising, unnatural, and in need of explanation about cooperative relations, in a way in which there is nothing surprising or difficult to understand about adversarial relations. Part of this, of course, is the legacy of a century of the mutual interaction of popular Darwinism, with its metaphors of competition and struggle, and neoclassical economics, with its model of the self-interested consumer. But part is the result of a certain conception of rationality. This conception may, indeed, only grow in the soil of the Darwinian ideology, but it then exerts its own authority. At its most bare, it is characterized as follows:

1. Actors pursue goals
2. These goals reflect the actor's perceived self-interest
3. Behaviour results from a process that involves, or functions as if it entails, conscious choice
4. The individual is the basic agent in society
5. Actors have preferences that are consistent and stable

6. If given options, actors will choose the alternative with the highest expected utility

7. Actors possess extensive information on both the available alternatives and the likely consequences of their choices. (Monroe 1995: 2)

There is room for debate about what these mean, of course. Number (6), for example, can veer critically between being substantial and false or being true but a tautology, a piece of book-keeping for interpreting an agent within the grid of maximizing expected utility, whatever their actual concerns. But it is not clear how it expresses a substantial truth (see essay 1, above). But at face value, what is intended is indeed a conception of the rational agent as both entirely forward-looking, and entirely self-interested. If such agents look back, it is only to make strategic calculations for the future. If they forgo immediate advantage, it is only for the sake of deferred gains in the future. If they pay regard to the interests of others, it is so that the others will with increased probability benefit them, some time in the future. Henceforth, when I talk of rational actor theory, it is this full-blown interpretation that I have in mind.

It is, I think, a remarkable fact, and a fact for philosophers, that this paradigm still dominates the social sciences. We have been through a quarter of a century when the humanities have been swept above all by a sense of untranslatability, of difference, of incommensurability, and a resulting politics of identity has developed devoted to stressing and celebrating the different cognitive and emotional contours of different people, whether in different groups or of different genders. For many people it is a serious issue whether we understand each other well enough so that women can be taught by men, or vice versa, or people of one ethnic background by people of another. Yet amidst all this difference, the paradigm of *homo economicus* still reigns supreme. It provides the spectacles through which diversity itself is brought into universal view.

It is a philosophical task to uncover the presuppositions on which this view depends. In this paper I wish to clear some of the ground for such a task, first by reflecting on what it is for a disposition to trust to be embedded in a human psychology. As we shall see, trust is easier to understand than cooperation. But it may enable us to draw some morals for the analysis of social and political cooperation, perhaps rather different from those standardly drawn from reflection on non-cooperative situations.

1. The Austere Basis of Trust

First of all, what is our concept of trust, and what are its principal divisions? I think the obvious point of entry is a tripartite relationship: one person trusts another to do something—'X trusts Y to do Z.' This allows, rightly, that one might trust one person to do things that one would not trust another to do. And it allows, equally rightly, that one might trust a person to do some things but not others: one can trust Vronsky to pay his gambling debts, but not to keep his hands off one's wife, for instance.

The tripartite formula allows for expansion. There are cases where Y refers not to another person, but to an institution, or a government, or possibly even to an inanimate thing, for we talk, for example, of trusting the rope to bear our weight, or trusting the old car to keep going for a while. We even trust to luck, rather too often in some cases. It is also possible, antecedently, that X need not be a person. One insurance company, for instance, may trust its policy holders more than a rival does. We do not always talk of trusting someone *to do* something, but also of trusting people *with* things and people. Sometimes the equivalence is fairly obvious. If I trust you with my child, it means that I trust you to do a fairly wide but reasonably well-understood range of things, and not to do various others. But sometimes the context is less clear, and there is scope for misunderstanding. If we talk just of whether we trust the government, for instance, we may easily get at cross-purposes. I may trust the government to collect its revenues without trusting it to spend them wisely.

We can also speak not only of trusting someone to do something, but to do it in a certain way, or we can trust someone to be in a certain state: to be at home, or to be cheerful at the party, for instance. So although we start with the simple tripartite form, we should approach it with more than half an eye on the various expansions that we might want to accommodate. If any analysis rules out these expansions, or is forced to talk about 'different senses' of the term, that will be a cost.

There is one expansion that is absolutely critical. We must bring into view cases where we trust someone or some corporate entity not so much to do a certain thing, Z, but to act *from* a certain motivation, whatever they do. In Kantian terms, we might trust someone to act on certain 'maxims', and not to act on others. In more sentimentalist terms (in the sense of Hutcheson, Hume, or Smith) I may trust someone to be, for instance, revolted by some fact, or I may trust them to recoil from some project. I shall speak simply of trusting someone to act from a *concern*, where 'concern' is a very broad, portmanteau term, covering any of the factors that influence an agent. A concern influences an agent when, if she is aware of it, her practical reasoning takes it into account. The measure of this will be her stronger disposition to seek or avoid the object of concern. Here we may not have a particular action Z in mind. We might trust, say, a guru to act out of wisdom and benevolence, whilst we don't know what his wisdom and benevolence will lead him to do. We may even look forward to being surprised.[1]

Although the interests of the rational actor, *homo economicus*, are always forward-looking, concerns by contrast may be backward-looking (she was kind to me when I was ill, so I can't just leave her in the lurch), or even keyed neither to the past nor the future, but purely derived from our conception of our role ('they're my children, so I have to look after them'). They may even be purely counterfactual ('imagine what someone would say if they saw me do that'). This point becomes extremely important, so let me dwell on it for a minute. Nobody sane denies that on the surface we have such susceptibilities, and that they can influence us. The proponents of the rational actor have to say either that when we have them, we are irrational, or that when we have them, they are a kind of disguise for an underlying calculus of self-interest (in the neo-Darwinian version popularized by Richard Dawkins (1976), a disguise for an unconscious calculus of genetic advantage). Thus apparent altruism is diagnosed as disguised expectation of reciprocal advantage; apparent trustworthiness is diagnosed as disguised desire to reap the benefits of appearing trustworthy, and so on.

Now, the first option, claiming that agents with plural sensibilities are irrational, is surely completely untenable. 'Rational' is an endorsement. It claims that being some way, and only being that way, makes sense (Gibbard 1990). But why should anyone think that it doesn't make sense to think in terms of the past, or what one's role demands, or what people would think if they knew what one was doing—and all regardless of whatever light the

---

[1] I thank Keith Lehrer for drawing my attention to this case.

past casts on the future? Furthermore, it is well known that it is only if we have the various susceptibilities that we can solve the problem of collective action, and there is nothing attractive, let alone normatively compelling, in the psychology of any proto-human agents who cannot manage that (Olson 1963; Hardin 1982; Kraus 1993). I return to this later.

So let us turn to the second option: the superficial thoughts disguise the rational actor below. My immediate point is that the second horn is importantly unmotivated. Talk of an unconscious calculus suggests that the surface disguises the 'real' psychology underneath. But there is no reason to think that. Even if we like adaptive evolutionary stories, according to which the surface psychology is as it is because it benefits the individuals who have it, this gives no reason to deny that this *is* the psychology, and it is the beginning and end of it as well. The mother who cares for her baby may be like that because it is an adaptation to be like that. That is, either single individuals, or groups of individuals, who were programmed not to be like that would have lost out in the evolutionary struggle to people who are like that, and this explains why we are. But it does not follow, and there is not the slightest reason for believing, that the evolutionary advantage is *implemented* anywhere in the individual's psychology. The mother does not think, at some deep unconscious level, that it will benefit her, or her genes, if she looks after her baby (after all, she might know that the former is not true, if she is sacrificing herself for the baby in some obvious way, and she might be quite unable to think the latter, since the concept of a gene is hardly common property). She only has to think that it will benefit the baby, and this is what she does think, period.

What then is true when X trusts Y to do Z? The neutral core on which to build is simply that X relies on Y to do Z. This is all that there is to it when, for instance, I trust the rope to bear my weight. I rely on it to do so, and show this by climbing on it. As Holton (1994) has stressed, it may even be that I do not fully believe that the rope will bear my weight. All that seems necessary is that I incorporate the supposition that it will bear my weight into my actions or plans for the future. I can do this while lacking at least some of the dispositions that would be part of really *believing* that the rope will bear my weight, and a fortiori without being certain that it will do so. This lack of confidence would be shown, for instance, by my eagerness to use another aid as soon as I can do so, or my relief at getting into the position where I no longer have to rely on it. 'Relying on the rope' is a matter of acting or planning for action rather than one of being confident or believing. So I may have no option but to rely on the rope, or trust myself to it. Similarly, in a large range of social circumstances, I may have no option but to trust the post office, or my insurance company, or the government, at least with respect to some actions and policies.

So why do we rely upon people to do some things and not others? Again, the fundamental case is where it is just what they always do. We may rely upon birds to fly south in winter, and to return in the spring. It is said that the people of Königsberg trusted Kant to provide the time for them by taking his walk every afternoon at exactly the same hour, and their reliance was justified because this is what he always did. But bare inductive cases are rare. Once Kant understands that the people have this reliance, it could in turn act as a motive to keep up his habit. He might begin to feel that he ought to take his walk on the dot, just because they rely on him to do so. In my terms, the other people's expectation would have become one of his concerns. It might be, even if he regrets getting accidentally into such a position. And a less benevolent person might take no account of their reliance, not allowing it to influence him in any way, whilst a mischievous person might even regard it as good fun to let them down.

Once civil society is up and running, there are devices for shoring up the stability of Kant's habit, making it independent of his benevolence at the moment. Kant can *promise* the townspeople to take his walk on time, or he can *contract* with them to do so for a consideration. These performances are ones designed to make him more reliable, for this is the essential function of the practices of promising and contracting. I return to this below.

If Kant reneges on a promise or contract, then moral emotions come into play. But at the first level, when we just rely on him because it is what he always does, then a failure need not justify any such reaction. I may, for instance, rely on a child to perform some errand, perhaps as part of an overall project of practising her in the ways of trusting and being trusted, although even if she fails through intention or recklessness or a variety of *mens rea*. I can't feel resentment or indignation or anger—I might just feel a bit stupid for having treated her as more mature than she is, for example. The moral reaction would be possible, but inappropriate, and I need not be disposed to it.

To sum up, then: reliance on Y to do Z may be sustained by a variety of causes or reasons, but the simple case is just that Z is what they do.

It is not necessary that Y knows of the reliance; not necessary that Y is motivated by such knowledge; not necessary that Y feels altruistic or bound by principle, or any other particular concern. Their own psychological state is not necessarily implicated, although frequently it will be beliefs about that state that justify the other party's reliance.

So far we have been talking of reliance rather than trust. But by keeping the core concept extremely general, we are able to say that children become trusting and trustworthy by practice. We rely on them in little things, reward them when the reliance is well placed, and success builds on success until a habit is generated. When it has done so, the mere fact that she is being relied upon becomes a concern of the child. She finds it difficult or impossible to let someone down, and finds it confusing and flattening to be let down in turn. What is practised is just reliability and what is discovered is the importance people put on it. It is important to this process that a decision to trust can be made in advance, before there is a long history of trustworthiness

The austere basis of trust, I am suggesting, is just reliance. This of course does not imply cooperation, because it does not imply the mutual awareness or common knowledge that are necessarily involved in cooperating with someone.

2. Backward Concerns and Forward Goals

When I rely on other people it may be because I have little option, or it may be because I have reason to be confident in them. Technologists of trust can work both ends. When people join a regiment or a cult, they are systematically, even brutally, stripped of their other resources, and so put in a position where they have nowhere else to turn. They are made vulnerable, and then their loyalty to the regiment or the cult is built upon it being their only lifeline: if they cannot rely on their fellows for various things, then they cannot rely on anyone or anything. But in a decent childhood, although the child is completely vulnerable, if life is moderately stable she is constantly given reason to rely on her parents and those who care for her to do a whole variety of things she needs.

Reliance may be merely inductively based, as in the Kant case. But humans behave differently from one another. The child can rely on her mother to feed her, but not a passing stranger. So we need communication.

Just as a bird or a monkey can signal a danger to other birds and monkeys, so we can signal a future action of our own. And if things go well, there is a high correlation between people giving such signals and then acting as signalled, and this too is an inductive reliability that we can learn to depend upon.

Here we have the essence not only of devices such as giving promises, or writing contracts, but also for that matter of putting on uniforms or otherwise displaying the roles we are acting in. I do not think there is a general term covering what I have in mind, so I shall say that by displaying to others that we are prepared to perform some action, so that they may rely upon us, we submit to what I shall call *typecasting*. Being typecast I shall define as being put, either voluntarily or not, and either truly or not, into a class whose performance statistics for doing a certain kind of thing or acting from a certain kind of concern are better than average, or indeed anything up to perfect. If you are typecast it is as if you have announced what you will do, or what concerns will motivate you. What is the advantage of being typecast? A person who is typecast is in a state in which the audience has more reason to rely upon him to perform some action than it would have reason to rely upon anyone at random to do so. For an audience it is obviously often a benefit when people can be typecast, for it allows more refined and reliable predictions about their future behaviour. But also consider the matter from the standpoint of the agent. Getting typecast is a matter of a relationship to the expectations of others. As such it may be either a cost or a benefit to the agent. It will be a benefit if the audience's reliance on the agent to do something is likely to prompt them to behave in a way that is advantageous to the agent. So, for instance getting typecast as friendly (likely to perform friendly actions and avoid aggressive ones) is advantageous to the agent if an audience who so casts him is more likely to behave in a friendly manner than if he is not so regarded. So even amongst animals it can be advantageous to be able to give a submissive signal, or an aggressive one, precisely when the reaction to such signals brings more good than when no signal is given.

In human beings, once a basic inductive correlation exists, we can rapidly ascend the kind of hierarchies of psychological state made familiar by Grice (1957) and Lewis (1969). We can signal our future actions intentionally, and we can intend that the audience recognize our intent. And of course once devices for signalling future action are under intentional control, they can be exploited in a variety of ways, leading to stratagems of deception.

But for the moment we will stay with cases where everything is above board: where there is no failure of the 'common knowledge' condition.

Now suppose an audience A needs to be able to rely upon agent B to do something C. Then A can ask how much it will cost to ensure that B is in a class of agents, β, such that members of β frequently, or invariably, or almost invariably, do C (i.e. actions corresponding to C). A can typically get B into such a class in a variety of ways. She can cajole, or threaten harm, or promise reward. In other words, she can work on B's other concerns, trying to align them with performance of C. In turn, if it is to B's benefit to be relied upon, that is, to be typecast as someone who does C, B may be willing to work reciprocally on A in order to persuade A to typecast him, and if it is not to his benefit, he may only be willing to be put in the performing class β if in turn A pays him. Why might it be to B's benefit to be typecast? As we have seen, because if you have a definite expectation of me, you may modify your own behaviour in ways that are mutually advantageous.

Suppose, now, you have made no signal, but I decide to rely upon you to perform a task and I communicate that I do so. This may become a concern of yours. You may be motivated by my trust in your doing so, and perform accordingly. If I hadn't trusted you to do it, and told you that I was doing so, perhaps you would not have done it. If I know that this is a causal chain that is very likely to be in place, there comes to be an element of self-fulfilment about my trust: given that I trust you, and communicate this, I can be sure that my trust will not be misplaced. A part of the mechanism may be showing that I trust you, and part of your mechanism for assuring me that the trust is not misplaced will be to announce that I can trust you. Mutual reassurances have this point, and this is confirmed rather than refuted by the fact that one of the first things a fraudster may want to do is to announce that you can trust him.

Now normativity, or the notions associated with obligation and duty, enter. People are *supposed* to find it salient that they are being relied upon by others. If someone communicates to me that they expect me to do something, then, other things being equal, that is supposed to influence my decision. It is supposed to be a concern. In the simplest case I may be subject to criticism and penalty if I do not do what they expect. And if I have played a role in creating that expectation, encouraging typecasting, then the criticism and penalties are likely to be all the greater. This is no more surprising than that I become a nuisance and liable to be treated as such if I give signals that are usually correlated with some state, such as the arrival of a predator, when in fact this state is lacking. It is thus that the normative practices of promise and contract come to life.

Of course, it is a contingent fact whether getting someone into the high performance class β in any particular way actually works. That is, although by definition the performance statistics of β are good, it may partition into those who are in it from one cause, and those who are in it from another. If I have exacted a promise from you under duress, then as well as being in the high performance class of those who have promised, you are in what may be the much lower-performing subset of the class, namely those who gave a promise reluctantly, or resent having had to give it, or who are professional diplomats, or a member of clan X hoping to get a member of clan Y to drop his guard, and these are things we have to take into account.

That 'being trusted' or still more 'having deliberately encouraged trust' sometimes motivates us is simply beyond dispute. It is one of the platitudes of human life that takes no empirical research to discover, like 'people make friends' or 'people sometimes speak languages' or 'mothers sometimes love their children'.

Notice how natural it has been to slip from the language of reliance towards the language of trust, once the mechanisms of motivation I have described come into being. This means that the discussion so far is slightly orthogonal to a claim often made in the literature. Karen Jones, for example, writes that

trust is an attitude of optimism that the goodwill and competence of another will extend to cover the domain of our interaction with her, together with the expectation that the one trusted will be directly and favourably moved by the thought that we are counting on her.   (Jones 1996: 4)

I have not wanted to be so specific. Another's goodwill is of course frequently and centrally involved in trusting them: we trust other people to care for us and our concerns, and if they know we are counting on them, we trust them to be concerned by that. And central cases—indeed, in human terms, the *best* cases of trust—are ones that might equally be called love: not only optimism, but certainty, that however vulnerable you are to another, you are at the same time perfectly safe. But I want to include other cases: I do not, for instance, want to exclude the idea of trusting someone to do something because it is their duty to do it quite regardless of whether they bear any goodwill towards me. Consider too third-party cases. One of an estranged couple may trust the other to look after the children, but not by pretending that the other bears him or her (the trusting party) any goodwill. And in institutional cases, there is typically no presumption of altruistic motivation. You trust the postman to bring you the mail, but not because you think he wishes you well. You trust him to do it because that is his job. Associated with that may be the confidence that he will believe there are penalties if he does not. But you may not even believe that this bothers him. You may just think he is conscientious, at least to the extent of thinking of himself as a postman—and delivering the mail is what postmen do. So trusting someone to do something because of goodwill towards you is only one particular case, even if it is the best case.

3. Deciding to Trust

Before approaching the richer phenomenon of cooperation, I want to take a small detour through the phenomenon of deciding to trust someone. There is nothing surprising about deciding to trust, that is, to rely upon, a rope or the post office. The more interesting phenomenon is that we can decide to trust an informant, such as one witness to some events, rather than another. This is puzzling, for it sounds very like deciding to believe one thing rather than another, and philosophers have frequently held that belief is not and cannot be directly under the control of the will. It seems important to a state being a belief state that it is open to evidence, and I cannot will evidence away, or will it to point in directions other than those in which it actually points.

There are complexities here, for we all know that beliefs are influenced by our emotions and concerns. We can also deceive ourselves, or so it seems, and we can set about courses of action with the intention that at the end we shall actually have come to believe something, although we cannot see our way to believing it now. These are what we can call Pascal cases, since the famous wager is an example. But the case of deciding to trust a witness is not straightforwardly a Pascal case. Let us put the problem in the form of a threatened contradiction:

(1) Starting from a state of agnosticism, I cannot decide directly to believe a proposition p.

(2) Starting from a state of agnosticism, I can decide to trust a witness who testifies that p.

(3) If I decide to trust a witness who testifies that p, then I believe p.

A Pascal case might seem to be of the same structure:

(1′) Starting from a state of agnosticism, I cannot decide directly to believe in God.

(2′) Starting from a state of agnosticism, I can decide to stupefy myself.

(3′) If I decide to stupefy myself, then I will believe in God.

Pascal cases are not contradictory. They show that I can adopt means with foreseeable ends that involve acquisitions of belief that I do not at present have. So should we say that the same point defuses the threat of paradox in deciding to trust a witness? Not immediately. The difference is that in Pascal cases, stupefying yourself (associating with the faithful, going through the motions) is a causal *antecedent* to belief. So (3′) represents a causal conditional; this is why I put the future tense 'will' in it. It is just a brute fact that it is effective, and indeed there may be psychologies in which it is not—people whose doubts cannot be put to sleep by these means. But in the first case it is different: trusting the witness and believing what he says are not distinct events related as means to end. There is apparently no trusting the witness without believing what he says: the two are logically related rather than causally related, which is why I put no future tense in (3).

But is the conditional logical rather than causal? We saw above that trusting the rope is not quite the same as believing that the rope is safe. So let us interpret (2) with this in mind. Discussing these cases Holton says that we can 'trust a friend to speak knowledgeably and sincerely without believing that they will' (Holton 1994: 75). The idea is that this trust, like trust in the rope, can be manifested in just some of the dispositions that would be necessary for full belief. We rely on the witness, in the same sense as we rely on the rope. It may be that, typically, full belief follows on causally, just as in the Pascal case, or any other case of coming to acquire a new belief as a result of our decisions (Holton 1994: 75–6). So the air of paradox is dispelled by backing away from belief. We may decide to rely upon a witness, but insofar as it is a decision (because his testimony does not compel conviction), we only rely *pro tem*. If we decide to trust, we decide to rely, but we don't really believe.

In some cases this may be the full story. But I think it is important that there are others. Suppose the witness has just told his (or her) version of events. I decide to trust him. This means that I trust him at least to have spoken knowledgeably and sincerely. But in turn this surely does involve *believing* him to have spoken knowledgeably and sincerely. Here, it seems to me, there is not the same gap between reliance and belief. I may rely on someone to do something, although I do not fully believe that he will. But the gap between reliance and belief only opens when things are hostage to fortune: to accidents and chances over which he, the subject, has no control. But the subject does have control over whether he speaks knowledgeably and sincerely.[2] So if I am relying on him to have done so, must I not thereby believe his version of events? And in that case, deciding to trust him does sound like deciding to believe some particular thing.

If this is right, then the witness case cannot simply be solved by interpreting it as a Pascal case. For when I decide to trust the witness to be speaking knowledgeably and sincerely, there is not a core that I genuinely believe about the witness, and another part that is hostage to fortune, and about which I may have hopes but no confidence. This is why to trust a witness to be speaking knowledgeably and sincerely seems to entail believing them: it is not a preliminary to belief but equivalent to it. And I think it is not accidental that in these cases, just as naturally as saying that we decided to trust one witness, we can also say that we *decided* to believe him or her (just as we say that the jury *preferred* to believe one side or another). We should also notice the following. Suppose trust in this case does fall short of confidence: suppose it is better described as mere 'acceptance', a state with only some of the marks of full belief. Then it would seem that the only natural concomitant would be similar 'acceptance' of the proposition to which the witness testifies: perhaps a recognition that this is the version we have to write down or the version of events with which our verdict has to accord, but without any confidence

---

[2] This is a little swift. 'Externalists' about knowledge construct cases in which someone may speak knowledgeably without knowing whether she is doing so, because an element of luck is involved in whether the situation is one in which there is indeed knowledge. But for the purpose of this paper we can safely set such examples aside: the basic and normal case is one in which a witness knows whether she did or did not perceive what she says she did.

that it is true. Now if that is the starting point, it is very obscure what so naturally takes the place of the Pascal process: the causal process supposed to turn this state into one of full belief. I don't think there is usually a chemistry that turns this kind of nominal acceptance into true belief; indeed, if we start by distinctly withholding belief from what the witness says, I think we shall end up by doing so as well. This would not be trusting the witness, but mistrusting him, and mistrust does not evaporate easily. Pascal processes are quite difficult, at least for most of us, most of the time.

So how should we conceptualize deciding to trust, or deciding to believe? What best resolves the threat of contradiction contained in (1) to (3)? I want to restore a similarity to Pascal cases by thinking about it in terms of seduction and surrender. Thus, it has often been noticed that testimony is typically infectious (Coady 1992). Arguably the default, hearing someone say something, is belief. It takes active suspicion to overcome this default. There is a philosophical issue here into which we need not go, whether this is just a fact about most of us in most circumstances, or whether it is somehow integral to sharing a language at all. Without settling that, clearly people can start off pretty sceptical about what a witness says, but let themselves be won over. As I listen, I find myself drawn to him or her, or to his or her version of events. I could resist the process, but often I don't: I allow myself to surrender to them, and to believe what they say. If we let this process happen too quickly and easily, then we are gullible, and lack judgement. The reverse is being stubborn, or even counter-suggestible. It may be wrong to think of this 'allowing oneself to surrender' as something one *decides* to do. But it happens, and it is within our control, in the sense that we can, when we are so minded, resist it.

Although I can let myself be influenced or seduced in this way, it does not follow that I can do it all by myself. I cannot succumb to the atmosphere of the party if there is no party and no atmosphere. So indeed I cannot directly and immediately decide to like an ice cream, or believe that aliens have landed in Arkansas. Neither the ice cream nor the proposition have any charms for me. But I can, or some people can, let themselves be influenced by people who are addicts of ice cream or flying saucers. This is a process within our control, and that ends up with belief or desire. For some people it may only take the briefest push for full surrender. The push might even be self-generated: sometimes people can be said to have made up their minds to believe some proposition, even without the exposure to outside testimony or other evidence. They make up a story, and the story becomes the way they take things to be.

Pascal's process took practice and a long time. I am suggesting that it is the drawn-out version of a process that can happen quite easily and take very little time. We can succumb to the witness's story even as it is being told, if it is told seductively enough. It is in this sense that we decide to trust, and equally decide to believe. 'Decide', however, is not exactly the word to stress: better is the idea of 'letting oneself believe' or 'letting oneself trust', which nods in the right way to the passive elements of the process, which it would take resistance to oppose.

We might think that even if what I have said is psychologically correct, it must be a manifestation of irrationality, and a paradox may reappear: I cannot rationally decide to believe something; trusting a witness entails believing what he said; hence I cannot rationally decide to trust a witness. The right reaction to this is to reverse it. By surrendering to a witness one is not flying in the face of evidence. One is deeming his testimony to be evidence, just by deciding that he is knowledgeable and sincere. It is exactly as if two instruments give different readings of a physical quantity, and by deciding that one instrument is functioning as it should, one would be treating one reading as evidence. Such a decision may be unfounded and irrational, but it may be quite appropriate and well judged.

Of course, some surrenders are indeed irrational: there is wishful thinking, self-deception, gullibility, and plain bad judgement. But there is also rigid thinking, unimaginative application of rules, and unwarranted scepticism. So in fact I can rationally decide to believe some things and in some circumstances. These will be circumstances in which, if someone comes along and testifies that p, it would be rational to trust him.

We might also remember that the air of paradox may partly depend upon treating belief (and trust) too much as all-or-nothing states, and forgetting the different amounts of credence that may be involved in a real case. Even while I let myself be seduced by the witness's version of events, I may still retain some self-control. I wouldn't bet my life on it. Even when I avow my belief, and avow it to myself, it may be that in truth I would not feel nearly as surprised if it turns out to be a fiction as I would have expected to be. I wouldn't be flabbergasted, as I would if it turned out that George Bush was a woman all along. Equally, my belief may be real, but surprisingly fragile: seduction is fraught, and the witness may only have to put one foot wrong to destroy the mood.

4. Cooperation

We have imagined regularities of action and motivation, and we have imagined them relied upon, and then reinforced by signals from the actor that they can be relied upon, or from the agent that they are being relied upon. And we have imagined normativity associated with such signals, with eventually a fully cemented practice of promising, and trusting in promises. When mutual assurances can be given and relied upon, we have the possibility of cooperation. It is integral to the account that the facts put in place at each stage of signalling and reliance can act as concerns. They motivate people, and they are supposed to do so.

In this story, someone else's legitimate expectation is a feature of the situation that has a positive affect of its own. Feeling this affect is not the same as altruism or benevolence. It is closest to Adam Smith's mechanism of having an internal voice whose sound we shy away from: the voice representing the potentially hostile and critical voices of others—those whom one would let down, by failing to fulfil their trust (Smith 1976: III.ii.3). We can find avoiding this voice to be one of our concerns even when, taken in itself, we do not care about the persons who are relying on us to act. Standard examples show the difference. Suppose others trusted me, and I let them down. Happily, events intervened so that it did them no harm, and they never learned of it. But I still feel badly about it. Or, they trusted me, and I did my bit. Unhappily, events intervened so that harm happened, and they never learned that I did my bit. But my self-respect lies easy.

Many features of actions have their own affect, that is, make their own contribution to the dynamic field of forces that sway decisions. It is not just that something is in my interests that sways me, but simple thoughts like: it's my job, it wouldn't be fair, it would disappoint Grandma, it would reduce the rainforests, it wouldn't be doing my bit, this would embarrass her, parents don't do that, it is not the action of a gentleman, how could I face her, and so on and so on. P. G. Wodehouse got his letters in the post in London in the thirties by the simple expedient of tossing them out of his hotel window, trusting that the average British pedestrian, seeing a stamped letter on the pavement, would pop it into the nearest postbox. He did not suppose that the strangers expected him to do them good in the future, nor that they had indirect expectations, for instance that if they acted well in this respect then . . . by some chain of causes . . . letters they tossed on the pavement would get posted. They just think: someone needs this letter posting, and then they do it. Similarly, if I trust someone to do something I do not necessarily suppose that they are motivated by any expectation of reciprocal favours. I trust the stranger from whom I ask the way to be telling the truth, but not because I impute any such expectation to him. I just suppose he has enough of the heterogeneous, self-effacing crowd of everyday concerns into which even the rational actors of game theory will have been inducted. And among our concerns we can number distaste for non-cooperative options. One of our concerns can be to cooperate, and good for us.

As we have already seen, the strategy for the rational actor theorist is either to condemn such facts as irrational, or to make them epiphenomenal, superfical skin over a forward-looking and self-interested core. But it is, in effect, provable that this cannot be right. As I already mentioned, we can appeal here to the literature that takes some bare competitive situations, most notably the prisoners' dilemma, and points out that for rational actors it is insoluble (that is, they end up in the socially worst corner). We can take the state of nature, characterized as in Hobbes, and ask whether rational actors, put in that situation, could ever decide upon the mechanisms that turn it into civil society. The difficulty is obvious: they cannot make promises when there is no reason to trust anyone to take them seriously; they cannot sensibly turn over power to a sovereign, when there is no reason to suppose that he will do anything except use those powers against them. So we are left with the melancholy thought that the rational actors are those that do badly: they stay in the state of war of all against all, or they continually fail to achieve the socially optimal outcome in prisoners' dilemmas. And they cannot give each other trustworthy signs and signals that they are willing to move to a cooperative stance, since no sign or signal could induce any other rational actor, who also knows of this rationality, to expect him to forgo his advantage when the time comes.

So if we present ourselves the puzzle of how rational actors ever come to do better, we seem faced with a kind of miracle, for we have managed to find ourselves in cooperative relations with each other. But one person's modus ponens is another's modus tollens, as philosophers like to say. It is perfectly proper to point out that since we have managed to achieve, sometimes, cooperative relations, in which we utilize others' willingness to act in some way because they are trusted to act in that way, and for no other reason, then any picture of human psychology that makes it impossible that we should do such a thing is false. The right response is not to deny the phenomena, but to save the phenomena and to deny the picture that made them seem impossible.

So we need to reject the conceptualization of our social situations that goes with the picture of the self-interested, forward-looking economic agent. We need a more organic model in which, rather than designing our way out of the war of all against all, we are seen as growing out of it, or rather, growing so that it never occurs. As Hume saw, we need not so much contract, as convention, and convention can just grow. A parent and child do not have to lever themselves miraculously into a relationship of trust by getting away from a 'natural' situation of war with each other. Neither do other kinfolk, these being people with whom you share rather than those with whom you compete. Our social relations are not all born from situations in which we fight competitively for limited resources, so that if one wins another loses.

We do not have to go all the way with Rousseau to realize that the Hobbesian miracle that transmutes war into cooperation never had to happen, for the actors that Hobbes imagined never existed. But of course there are social situations in which a version of the miracle is needed. These are cases where there is no history of trust, no loyalty to a shared pattern of action that has stood each agent in good stead. It is then indeed hard to find a strategy that would change, for instance, the Balkans into something more like the United States. And in our pessimistic moments we can all be aware of the fragility of cooperation: the tendency, as it were, of the United States to turn into something more like the Balkans. Parents can nurture trusting and trustworthy stances in their children, and politics can nurture similar stances in the relations citizens and states bear to each other, but only by fomenting a culture of trustworthiness, and relying on others to catch on. There is no shortcut. But the solution works.[3]

And here it may be worthwhile reflecting for a moment on the importance of the task. Some of our propensities may be hard-wired. In that case, theorizing about them will not disturb them. But our propensities to trust,

---

[3] See, for instance, empirical studies such as Braithwaite and Makkai 1993.

to act from various motivations, and to attribute them to others, are not so robust. Theory can disturb them. So rational actor theory is self-verifying in the sense that if we believe that others are untrustworthy, and ourselves feel we cannot afford to be better than they are, then we create a world in which there is no trust in people to act *because* they are trusted, or even because they have deliberately encouraged trust. And having created that world, we would be foolish to do anything except look out for ourselves. We will have reintroduced the war of all against all. The agents we would then have become would not be able to lever themselves out of the war. So we need to eschew any economists, game theorists, strategic experts, or evolutionary psychologists whose mantras tend to push us down into it.

6

Must We Weep for Sentimentalism?

1. A Misunderstanding

Hume said that the distinct boundaries and offices of reason and taste are easily ascertained, and he included under the heading of 'taste' the moral sentiments (Hume 1998: App. I, 163). Alas, he proved over-optimistic. I doubt if any question in moral theory has proved more vexatious. The area is confounded by difficulties over the identification of attitudes and beliefs, over the distinction between senses of the word 'reason' that sentimentalists can admit from those they must deny, over the relation between properties and concepts, over the metaphysics of the categorical imperative, and over much else besides. In this brief essay I cannot therefore attempt a full-scale defence of sentimentalism. I shall simply defend the theory against various recent assaults, one of which is mounted in Samuel Kerstein's defence of rationalism in this debate (Kerstein 2006). My impression is that Kerstein does not stand alone, but is a spokesman for a whole phalanx of people, perhaps calling themselves 'Kantians', who would sympathize with his assault, or at least fail to understand how a sentimentalist could withstand it.

It is fortunate, then, that the misunderstanding that permeates Kerstein's treatment of sentimentalism is highly visible, and I shall concentrate on one particularly exposed passage. After giving an account of my own neo-Humean description of the emotions and attitudes that underlie our propensity to go in for ethics and morals, he considers the issue of justice to strangers or outsiders. He writes that on my view:

It is a person's displeasing sentiments, ones such as unease or shame, that form the basis of her obligation to acquire the character trait of being just to strangers, or at least to act in a way that a person with this trait would act.   (Kerstein 2006: 135)

He continues:

This last point is crucial to the issue of whether sentimentalism coheres with the idea that there are categorical imperatives. On this account the basis for an agent's obligation to do something is a displeasing sentiment she has when, after taking the 'common point of view', she contemplates her not doing it or, perhaps, her not possessing the character of someone who would do it . . . If an agent does not have this sentiment, then she has no obligation. Of course, if an agent has no obligation to perform a certain action, then a principle commanding that action does not count as a categorical imperative. For it belongs to the concept of a categorical imperative that everyone within its scope is obligated to do what it enjoins. So in order for sentimentalism to ground a particular categorical imperative, each and every person, after taking the common point of view and so forth, must have a displeasing sentiment towards not doing what the imperative commands.   (Ibid.)

So, although Kerstein also chides me for failing to answer the question of how moral obligations 'stem from' the processes I have described, he supposes that such an account, were it provided, would inevitably suppose that someone without the sentiments is free of the obligation: the 'basis' of her obligation is a sentiment, so that 'if an agent does not have this sentiment, then she has no obligation'. In a similar vein he imagines someone with no sympathy for members of some minority within his society, and says that 'on Blackburn's sentimentalist account, you have at this point no obligation to refrain from abusing the minority'.

And then, unsurprisingly, he can go on to point out that there are legions of unhappily bad Samaritans, and what I called foreign-office knaves, when I was stressing and lamenting the same sad fact about humanity. These people do not have the appropriate sentiments. Hence, Kerstein concludes, for the sentimentalist, there are people who lie under no obligation to universal justice. Hence, there are no categorical imperatives, for the categorical imperative embraces everyone.

Whatever else is to be said about it, we should notice that this argument is remarkable for its scope. It can be directed not only against sentimentalism, but against any theory that seeks to explain our moral capacities in terms of contingent and potentially variable facets of human nature: language, culture, upbringing, acquired 'second nature', and so on. Even reason, insofar as it is empirically variable, or leaves its possessors liable to partial and self-serving policies, will not be enough. Only a universal birthright—and one strong enough to deliver commands to the will—could withstand it.

It is a pity, then, that Kerstein himself is not confident of a Kantian story of this kind, since it seems to be the only hope for a theory of the requisite standing. Otherwise there seems to be a straightforward empirical problem. If there is an inner mechanism of reason strong enough to dragoon us all into the ranks of the caring and just, it seems odd that so few of us get affected by it.

Why does Kerstein suppose that on a sentimentalist story, the knaves and villains are exempt from obligations? I should have thought no moral philosopher, except perhaps Gilbert Harman, and certainly not Hume nor myself, could have been thought to suggest such a thing. In fact, it seems to me such a shocking thing to say that I am at a loss to understand how Kerstein could have read Hume, or me, and perhaps others such as Allan Gibbard, as saying anything that implies it. For the record, I explicitly say the reverse, fairly often (e.g. Blackburn 1998: 210, 230, 265, and elsewhere. And why does Kerstein think I call the foreign-office knave a knave?).

The only explanation I can offer for the misreading is that it comes from conflating two different projects. One, the project of the anatomist, in Hume's terms, is to give an accurate and complete account of the states of mind that gain expression in moral thinking. The other, a moralistic project appropriate to Hume's painter, is to give an account of the 'sources' of our obligations. In my discussion of Christine Korsgaard's account of 'the normative question', I voice some doubts about how to conduct this second project. Like other pluralists, I think obligations arise for different reasons, and I am not myself wedded to the idea that any one, clear, univocal concept, such as 'utility' or 'self-legislation' might have been thought to be, plays the same explanatory role when we try to describe why we lie under one or another obligation. But it is the anatomist's project that occupies the bulk of my work, and that justifies calling me a 'sentimentalist'.

If you confuse these two projects, you might end up saying that moral obligations 'stem from' or 'are based in' psychological states, and thence infer that in the absence of the psychological states, the obligations disappear as well. The anatomical view is then supposed to lead to bad morals or bad painting. But it is not I who says that. I would say, for instance, that your obligations as a parent stem from the dependency of your children, their needs, and the absence of other social resources to provide a substitute if you fail to meet those needs. One of these needs is affection, so if you don't care about your child, you are in breach of the obligation that the child's need places on you.[1] The obligation does not come and go according to your affections, any more than your debt comes and goes depending on whether you care about it. And I think it shocking to suppose otherwise. The obligations you lie under, like the debts you owe, don't decrease or disappear when you stop caring about them.

I think, then, that parents of young children lie under a complex obligation, O. According to the sentimentalist, I say this by way of expressing a complex of attitudes and feelings towards the relationship between parents and their young children—what I shall call 'these sentiments'. Now let us say that someone who ignores or negligently or deliberately falls short in fulfilling an obligation, fails O. Finally, suppose we say that people who have no sentiments corresponding to feeling the weight of an obligation, laugh off O. Then all I ask is that we recognize the distinction between:

If I (we) had not had these sentiments, I (we) would not have been condemning parents who fail O or even those who laugh off O.

If I (we) had not had these sentiments, I (we) would have failed O or laughed off O.

If parents X do not have these sentiments, then they are likely to fail O or laugh off O.

If parents X do not have these sentiments, then they are under no obligation O.

The first three of these are true and harmless. The last is false and deadly. But it is the last that is foisted upon the sentimentalist in the passages I quoted.

I think the transition from the harmless to the deadly is lubricated by careless use of phrases like 'is based upon' or 'stems from'. If you ask me what moral thought itself stems from or is based upon, then, as an anatomist, I give the sentimentalist reply. If you ask me what a particular obligation or duty stems from or is based upon, then my painterly answer may vary, but will seldom cite the feelings of the agent. In this case it stems from the needs of the children, and the sociological structures that make the parent the person responsible for meeting those needs. In the case of justice to outsiders, again it may stem from the needs of the outsiders, or our overall

---

[1] If you (wrongly) think that we cannot lie under an obligation to feel various ways, perhaps because 'ought' implies 'can', read it as 'behaving as though you care for the child'.

needs for accommodation with them, or perhaps it stems from fundamental rights to equal treatment. I am not sure: the relationship between justice and mutual advantage, and reciprocity, and equality, is obscure enough for me and many others to feel insecure about exactly how best to paint it. What I am sure about is that you cannot get rid of the obligations by not feeling them, or laughing them off.

2. Peacocke's Hi-Tec Version

A trivial misunderstanding becomes worrying when you find it shared by enough people. As I have said, I fear that Kerstein is not alone. Christopher Peacocke (2004) has recently suggested that sufficient attention to two-dimensional modal logic conjures up a dependency claim which the quasi-realist must accept, but which offends against some conviction that we hold. So, contrary to what I have repeatedly claimed, there is a mind-dependency claim which causes trouble for any sentiment-oriented theory of value. The technology in Peacocke's discussion will doubtless shock and awe enough readers for it to be worth some trouble to show that it is in fact a smokescreen. The issues can be put simply enough, and when they are, the objection disappears.

In a nutshell, the issue goes like this. Peacocke recognizes the general strategy I have repeatedly used. It is an integral part of our ethical lives that we can evaluate scenarios that are described to us, whether past, present, or merely possible or fictional. So if you bring me a story about people and their doings, I can train my thoughts on it, and according to the attitudes it elicits, I will admire it, or condemn it, or hold a whole variety of more or less nuanced responses. If you tell me a story in which people fail to meet their children's needs, I react badly, and I express the conviction that what they are doing is cruel and wrong. I hope we all do. If asked why I condemn their behaviour, at least a prime part of my answer is about the needs that are not being met. Perhaps this simplifies a little, since the indifference of the perpetrators also matters, and that is a feature of the perpetrator rather than of the children. But for clarity, and as a harmless simplification, I shall say the verdict is child-dependent. If you told me a story about people causing pain to animals such as dogs, my verdict would be dog-dependent.

So far so good. Now suppose your story is more complicated. You tell me a story in which people not only ignore their children's needs, but *also* fail to condemn such behaviour, and maybe even admire it. They congratulate and esteem especially harsh or negligent parents. Their moral sensibilities are here the opposite from ours. What am I to say about this? It looks equally bad or somewhat worse to me. In the first story we could imagine some guilt attaching to the behaviour: perhaps it is mainly adolescents or criminals or failures who are bad with children, and their ordinary morality condemns it. But in the second story, there is no condemnation from the people who are described. They admire negligence or brutality. It is a horrible scenario, and I deplore it the more.

I have often stressed two further related points. The first is that someone *could* disagree with me about what I have just said. He could urge that the fact that they find it admirable makes all the difference, makes it admirable, in fact. We have a moral disagreement, for I deny that. I hold that it is the sad life of a child that is so shocking, and in this imagined society, the parents' self-congratulation at what they are doing takes none of that away, but actually adds to it, making it even more shocking. The second addition is that there might be examples—call them etiquette examples—where the structure looks similar, but my opponent would be right. For there are cases where the bad we do would not be bad at all were it not for the community's unfavourable take on it. I can imagine communities (perhaps there are some) where it is very bad form indeed to give a gift in return for a gift received. In such a community it would be insulting and wrong to do something which amongst us would be a normal expression of gratitude or reciprocated friendship, and it would be right to do something—omitting to reciprocate—which amongst us would be a breach of manners, and even insulting and wrong. In such a case it is true that had we had these different attitudes, different actions would have been right or wrong.[2] Their value is due to the conventions of etiquette that people follow, and these might have been harmlessly different. In the child case that is not so; as I said, it is due to the unmet needs of the child.

How does Peacocke hope to embarrass this analysis? He says some curious things about it. He says at the beginning of the discussion, 'it

---

[2] One could play with complexities introduced by the thought that in some sense 'not giving a gift back' in the described community is performing the same action as 'giving a gift back' in ours. They do not affect the point.

is very hard to see how it can be denied that, under [Blackburn's] approach, the conditions under which someone is correct in asserting a moral proposition have something to do with expressed mental states' (2004: 208). And the intention is to show that although, as he recognizes, I claim not to have a 'mind-dependent' treatment of morality, in fact I do. Unfortunately these wordings, like Kerstein's above, and others to which we shall come, are ambiguous. Obviously an expressivist treatment of ethics is 'mind-dependent' in one sense—it starts from reflections on the kind of mental state that gets expressed when values are made public and exchanged. Obviously, as well, 'the conditions under which someone is correct in asserting a moral proposition have something to do with expressed mental states', in one sense. Were the expressed mental states different, the proposition would be different and would be correct under different circumstances. For example, if the sentence 'kicking dogs is wrong' standardly expressed approval of kicking dogs, anyone voicing it would be correct only in quite different circumstances, such as ones in which dogs have no conscious states. But there is nothing worrying to the expressivist (or anyone else) in thoughts such as those. The conditions under which someone is correct in asserting *any* proposition have something to do with expressed mental states, in this sense. They have to do with which beliefs are being expressed. Of course, in another sense they have nothing to do with mental states: unless a proposition is explicitly about the mind, its truth condition will be world-dependent rather than mind-dependent. But similarly the truth (for I say it is a truth) that you have an obligation to your children is child-dependent, and the truth that you should not kick friendly dogs for fun is dog-dependent.

Peacocke pursues his attack via an indexing of propositions, correspond- ing to reference first to the 'world' from which an evaluation is made, and secondly to the 'world' that is being evaluated. To this end he introduces the double index $P(w_1, w_2)$, explained as:

Proposition P, when evaluated from the standpoint of psychological states in w_1, holds with respect to w_2. (Peacocke 2004: 210)

P here is some moral proposition, such as 'it is wrong to kick dogs for fun' or 'the infliction of avoidable pain is wrong'. The overall proposition $P(w_1, w_2)$ is, however, not entirely clear, because of the curious and treacherous word 'holds' (with its shades of 'based on' and 'stems from').

Suppose someone says that the proposition that the war in Iraq was justified holds from George Bush's point of view. I can hear that as a contorted way of saying that George Bush believes that the war in Iraq was justified, and it is probably true. What I should not do is hear it as some kind of insinuation that the war in Iraq was justified. It's a description of what George Bush thinks, not an endorsement of the way he thinks. Only a confused relativist of some sophomoric stamp would accept the transition from 'the war in Iraq is justified from George Bush's point of view' to 'the war in Iraq is justified'.

With that clear for the moment, we can turn to the 'w_2' variable. For that to do any work, there has to be some space between the proposition P and the variety of worlds to which it applies, or in which it is evaluated. And this may be granted. 'It is wrong to kick dogs for fun' can be tested against this world, or, if we are imaginative enough, against slightly different worlds, for instance in which there are still dogs and people, but only dogs that are unconscious, or in which there are only people who can survive by nutrition from the pain of other animals. And then it may turn out that the moral proposition is only true contingently on aspects of our world, and would get a different truth value were these other things different. Or of course, it may not. We may suppose that however worlds vary, it is always wrong to cause unnecessary pain, although even that may wobble if we bring in, for instance, apparently possible people who like pain.

With these explanations we can agree with Peacocke when he says that nobody can object to the employment of this doubly indexed proposition. Nobody can object to it, for $P(w_1, w_2)$ can be the form of good enough propositions, that can be regarded as true or as false in various cases, although they will often be indeterminate, when we have not given definite enough interpretations of the variables. Given what I have said, the evaluation of such propositions goes like this. We tell what we might call a *treble* story. First, we introduce a moral proposition P. Second, we introduce some possible people with attitudes. And third, we present a possible scenario, and we imagine the people we just introduced evaluating what goes on in the scenario, in accordance with the attitudes we gave them. If the people introduced evaluate the introduced scenario in the way that would properly gain expression by P, then $P(w_1, w_2)$ should be accorded T, otherwise not. It corresponds to 'the people we have introduced evaluate the scenario we imagined them to be contemplating, in a way that could be expressed by saying that P'. More concisely, we can say that the people we have introduced evaluate the scenario we imagine them to be contemplating, in the P-way.

Not surprisingly, we can vary the people or psychological states introduced, and we can vary the scenarios we conjure for them to be contemplating. So $P(w_i, w_j)$ can vary in two dimensions: there are two variables to be given interpretations before we turn it into a definite claim. And filling in one does not determine how we fill in the other. Or, of course we could quantify. $(\forall w_i)P(w_i, x)$ would mean that everyone from any possible story evaluates some given scenario x in the P-way, and $(\forall w_j)P(z, w_j)$ would mean that the introduced persons with the psychological states z, evaluate every possible scenario in the P-way. $(\forall w_i)$ $(\forall w_j)P(w_i, w_j)$ would mean that everyone, whatever their other differences, evaluates everything in the P-way.

This is the machinery, so what happens when it is set in motion? Alas, nothing at all. We get a variety of rather cumbersome descriptions of what different people think about different scenarios, and whether they would express themselves as agreeing with some moral or ethical proposition. We get things like 'we, as we are, think that in the world, as it is, kicking dogs is wrong' (true, I hope). Or, 'we, as we would be were we to become coarse and callous, would think that in the world as it is, kicking dogs is wrong' (false, no doubt). We can keep the people constant ('us'), giving what Peacocke calls the 'vertical' reading, or we can vary people and scenarios together, giving what he calls a 'diagonal' reading, such as the true 'we, as we would be were we to become coarse and callous, would think that in a possible world in which dogs feel pain slightly less than they do, kicking dogs is OK'.

Peacocke claims that since there is this diagonal reading, there is a 'mind-dependency' claim that the quasi-realist has not acknowledged. But that is just not true. Propositions such as this last one amount to *descriptions* of how people of some particular attitude (which we may or may not share) react to different scenarios. And there is nothing in general in these descriptions to offend the quasi-realist (or anyone else). It does not amount to giving our own verdict on those same scenarios, although if we make ourselves the topic, and describe ourselves rightly, there will be the coincidence that what we say about ourselves will be true just if we do assent to the verdict P.

The locutions that Peacocke uses reveal him to be in the same swamp as Kerstein:

on the quasi realist's theory the acceptability of basic moral principles depends on some psychological attitudes. However this dependence is formulated, it must be possible in thought to consider which propositions are correct when we vary the standpoint of evaluation; that is, when we vary the first parameter.   (Peacocke 2004: 214)

The first sentence is again ambiguous. On the quasi-realist's theory the question of which basic moral principles are accepted by people indeed depends upon (is the same thing as) their psychological attitudes. Whether they are right to accept those principles is a different thing altogether, and we will only settle it by ourselves finding a verdict on their approvals and disapprovals. If people in outer modal space, or for that matter people in benighted corners of the earth, accept the principle that it is OK to cause unnecessary pain to sentient creatures for fun, then they are cruel and callous and it would be good if they would change. The second of Peacocke's quoted sentences is therefore technically correct but highly misleading, for it implies that in general changing the first parameter, that is, considering different evaluative standpoints, changes the *correctness* of a verdict. But it doesn't. It only changes whether it is *supposed* to be correct, by whichever evaluators are introduced. Except in the cases that I called those of etiquette, it merely brings the evaluators into the embrace of our verdict, perhaps to their discredit, as in this case.

Peacocke continues:

Take a specific moral principle identified by its content, say 'Prima facie, the infliction of avoidable pain is wrong (w, w)'. It seems to me that the quasi-realist, like other mind-dependent theorists, must say this is false. It is false at those entries in the diagonal for worlds in which we have different attitudes to the infliction of avoidable pain.   (Peacocke 2004: 214)

This is hard to follow, because in accordance with his own explanation of the notation, propositions of the form $P(w_1, w_2)$, are not moral principles at all. First, they describe whether the evaluation from w_1, of the scenario of w_2, could gain expression by P: they are descriptions, not evaluations. And secondly, they are not propositions at all until the variables are bound or replaced by actual values, so neither the quasi-realist nor anyone else has any business saying that $P(w, w)$ is true, or false.

Perhaps Peacocke is thinking of the double universal quantification: 'Everyone, from whatever evaluative standpoint, and considering any scenario whatever, would agree that inflicting avoidable pain is wrong.' I do indeed doubt whether this is true, but that doubt has nothing to do with quasi-realism. It has more to do with pessimism about varieties of the wicked human heart, and if we are in outer modal space, the even more wicked Martian heart. And after all, Peacocke shares the doubt, for he allows worlds in which inhabitants have different attitudes to the infliction of pain. That's the point on the diagonal that he is inviting to the feast. Or perhaps it is not a double quantification but an anaphoric reference back to the world of the people with the evaluative standpoint: 'everyone, from whatever evaluative standpoint, and considering the world they inhabit, would agree that inflicting avoidable pain is wrong'. Alas, the same pessimism is appropriate.

Peacocke's ambition is clearly to get the quasi-realist *both* to treat some proposition of the form $P(w_1, w_2)$ as a genuine moral principle, *and* to evaluate it as false when we think of worlds in which the wicked hearts rule. But the machinery takes him not one inch nearer to that goal. Worlds in which the wicked hearts rule are still worlds in which, prima facie, the infliction of avoidable pain is wrong. The wicked hearts may not agree with this, but then that is just what's wrong with them.

I said that the word 'holds', as it occurs in the clarification of his notation, is treacherous, and at this point we are compelled to think that Peacocke has actually been betrayed by it. It seems he really does want to index the question of whether a moral principle is true to the various worlds whose inhabitants either agree or disagree with it. I think that is preposterous. It would be like saying that the proposition that the Iraq war was a good thing holds—really holds—in Republican circles in America, and really does not hold in most of the UK. And if that is what it means, the quasi-realist simply refuses to adopt the notation. It differs from the legitimate meaning we have so far allowed it, aiming at something more like this: 'The people we have introduced evaluate the scenario we imagined them to be contemplating, in a way that could be expressed by saying that P *and as a result P is true*.' But the quasi-realist has no use for this dog's breakfast of an assertion (it will be false except in etiquette cases). The Iraq war was a bad thing whatever other people think about it. This is not true in London but false in Texas. Nor is it a matter of etiquette, so that enough thinking it a good thing might make it one. That way lies sophomoric relativism, not sentimentalism. The criminality of the Iraq war is dead-innocent-Iraqi-dependent, not Republican-sentiment-dependent.

Far from taking him into the sunny uplands of rationalism, then, Peacocke's machinery grinds to a halt in the swamp of a relativism of his own devising. He finishes the discussion by considering the neighbouring case of colour, and the possibility that creatures with different perceptual systems might see physically different things and surfaces as red. He says that it is widely agreed that things would not stop being red if humans lost their colour vision and saw only in shades of grey. That may be so, although it ought also to be widely agreed that there is much more indeterminacy here than in the case of values. Jonathan Bennett's example of phenol-thio-urea, which tastes bitter to some people and bland to others, led many people to think that if the former group breeds into a huge majority, the world becomes one in which the stuff is bitter, while if the latter group does, the world becomes one in which it is bland. In other words, the 'response-dependency' of secondary properties is a much better candidate for providing a genuine truth condition for ascriptions of them, than any similar attempt to provide a 'truth condition' for ascriptions of value.

However, Peacocke is also correct that two-dimensionalism allows different formulations of the idea that colours are mind-dependent. Where Q is some underlying physical power, such as a disposition to reflect light of a certain wavelength more than other light, and we imagine varying perceptual systems, we could say that:

For any world, whatever perceptual systems its inhabitants have, Q objects are red, as they would be judged by us, as we actually are.

We would also want to say:

In some worlds, Q objects are not red, as judged by the inhabitants of those worlds.

And given Bennett's case, we might remain ambivalent about whether:

For any world, whatever perceptual systems its inhabitants have, Q objects are red

—since we would be ambivalent about, as it were, sticking with our own judgements, or entering into the world view of the people with the other perceptual system.

The reason this ambivalence is harmless is that once we bring other perceptual systems into view, then provided they are equally discriminatory, we lose any very robust attachment to the idea that ours is *right* and theirs is *wrong*. Similarly, we do not maintain sceptical fears that perhaps our sense of smell, or sense of colour, may in general be letting us down, so that perhaps things really smell different from the way we smell them, or have different hues from those we see them as having. People who taste phenol-thio-urea the other way are not wrong, just different. But there is no reason to suppose that this ambivalence extends similarly to the case of value. People who are coarse and brutal are not 'just' different. They are also depraved, and as a result they are rotten judges of value. If we are invited to 'see the world as they see it' we can, perhaps, manage it, but we ourselves can attach no weight to the verdicts we would imagine giving as we do so.

Before leaving this part of the discussion, it may be useful to reflect upon a difference between sentimentalism, as a theory of the origin of the moral sentiments, and a partly parallel exercise of quasi-realism, attempting to see our verdicts of modal necessity as the upshot of various features of the shape of our minds that determine what we can or cannot imagine. Here there is a legitimate pressure to see a contingent source of imaginative limitation as an undermining or debunking account of logical or metaphysical necessity (Blackburn 1987). If 'we cannot think otherwise' is sourced in contingent facts about us, an inference to 'things could not be otherwise' is compromised rather than explained.

Someone might be tempted to use the modal case as a Trojan horse, bringing the same worry into the theory of morals. But if so they would be wrong. The asymmetry lies in what we say about the states of mind in question and how it relates to the kinds of verdict we are making. In the modal case, if we find that the modes of thought, or the absence of alternatives, are only contingent, their source as an explanation of real necessity is compromised. But in the moral case, it would be not finding that they are *metaphysically* contingent that would give them a parallel debunking power. The parallel would be finding that they are *morally* indifferent. If it were morally all right to have the other sentiments—say, approving of cruelty to dogs or neglect of children—then it would be hard to believe that the ones we actually have could source a robust confidence in an obligation to refrain from cruelty and neglect. At least in general, if it is OK to think that some action is OK, then the action is OK.

But the sentimentalist is not saying that it is OK to have the contrary sentiments. As I have already said, the sentiments of those who would think otherwise fall within the scope of proper disapproval. We do not just disapprove of neglect of children, but perhaps even more so, and certainly just as much, we disapprove of those who approve of it or even tolerate it.

And rationalists had better not find the metaphysical contingency of modes of moral thought unsettling. If rationalist moral conviction is to falter whenever it comes upon people who do not share it or do not feel its force, then it is a fragile thing indeed. For knavery exists. Indeed, it often rules, and this is why a robust conviction of its baseness is so important.

3. Justice and Gentle Usage

Kerstein is not the first to worry about the scope of justice on Hume's theory. According to Manfred Kuehn's biography, Kant himself was led to reject Hutcheson's sentimentalism for a very similar reason (Kuehn 2001). Reading Rousseau apparently convinced Kant that while the sentimentalist allows that we have duties of charity to the dispossessed of the world, this is not enough. The poor or excluded have a right to more than charity. It is not charity they want or need, but justice. If sentimentalism cannot deliver that, then it delivers an inadequate account of the actual nature of our moral thought.

Hume makes himself a target for this kind of outraged reaction:

Were there a species of creatures intermingled with men, which, though rational, were possessed of such inferior strength, both of body and mind, that they were incapable of all resistance, and could never, upon the highest provocation, make us feel the effects of their resentment; the necessary consequence, I think, is that we should be bound by the laws of humanity to give gentle usage to these creatures, but should not, properly speaking, lie under any restraint of justice with regard to them, nor could they possess any right or property, exclusive of such arbitrary lords. Our intercourse with them could not be called society, which supposes a degree of equality; but absolute command on the one side, and servile obedience on the other. Whatever we covet, they must instantly resign: Our permission is the only tenure, by which they hold their possessions: Our compassion and kindness the only check, by which they curb our lawless will: And as no inconvenience ever results from the exercise of power, so firmly established in nature, the restraints of justice and property, being totally *useless*, would never have place in so unequal a confederacy.   (1998: 190–1)

There are many things to say about this passage, and quite how Hume thought it related to the human cases he goes on to discuss, which are firstly European relationships to indigenous American people, and secondly men's relationships with women. The clear implication is that the model applies in neither case, but only at best to our relationship with animals, or perhaps imagined animals.

Nevertheless we might want to modify the account to make justice clearly applicable, even in the circumstances of the thought experiment. I shall consider how that might be done in a moment. Meanwhile, the important point is that it is not Hume's sentimentalism that leads him here, but his strict delineation of the circumstances of justice and its source in mutual advantage. Hume does not deny that we have *obligations* to the creatures he presents. He says that we are 'bound by the laws of humanity' to give them gentle usage. The only issue is the way we are to understand this obligation. Remembering that for Hume the virtue of justice is both 'cautious and jealous' and above all artificial, it may not be so bad for these creatures if the source of that obligation lies elsewhere. But it is important to see that if we insist on the word 'justice', the sentimentalist can give it to us.

Hume mentions the resentment these creatures have, but which, because of their inferior strength and power, they can do nothing to visit upon us. This opens up a new sentimentalist vista, much more thoroughly explored by Adam Smith.[3] As D. D. Raphael explains, for Smith the sympathy that lies at the bottom of our capacity for morals has a slightly different shape than it does in Hume (Smith 1976: editor's introduction, 13). In Hume, we sympathize with the pleasure or pain that an action gives to a person. In Smith, we sympathize with different states of mind, including the motives of an agent, and more relevantly to the current case, with the gratitude or resentment of those affected by the action. Indeed, our sense of justice,

---

[3] In the paragraphs that follow, on Smith, I am much indebted to work by Michael Ridge.

for Smith, is dependent on reactions of resentment or gratitude to actions, which need not vary as the actual quantity of harm or benefit they bring about.

The 'sympathy' that is so prominent in each of Hume and Smith is translated, by the one into respect for the general point of view, and by the other into the voice of the impartial spectator, the 'man within the breast' who represents the reactions of those without. There is, of course, much to be said about the ways in which each writer identifies and handles the mechanism, and the relation between them (see, for instance, Cohon 1997; Korsgaard 1999; Radcliffe 1994; Sayre-McCord 1994). There is also much to be said about whether either mechanism implies some concession to rationalism, bringing in as they do some notion of 'corrected' sentiments. I cannot rehearse all that needs saying about that here, but shall have to take it as given that neither writer betrays sentimentalism by their construction of the more complex sensitivity. So suppose we bring in the lynchpin of Smith's sentimentalism, the 'real, revered, and impartial spectator' whose function is to bring home to us the resentment of those affected by our delinquencies. When the voice of this spectator is heard as it should be, we may recoil from our own contemplated or actual conduct. In Hume's terms, we can no longer bear our own survey. Recognizing this resentment of our conduct, and feeling no defence against it, we admit the injustice.

Suppose, then, that we have been minded to take from one of Hume's creatures something which they evidently cherish. They cannot visit their resentment upon us, but somehow we know that they feel it, and we know that we would feel it in their shoes. The man within the breast voices this resentment on their behalf, and we find we cannot dismiss it (we cannot resent their resentment, as we sometimes can). This unpleasant impact is the same as guilty awareness of the injustice of our conduct. What more could the sternest moralist ask from us?

Smith's modification of Hume may still leave us falling short of full-blown Kantian rationalism. But it is at least telling that the most fervent contemporary Kantians find it hard to do better. Christine Korsgaard, for instance, gives us the crucial moment in the genesis of obligation to others like this:

How does this obligation come about? Just the way that Nagel says that it does. I invite you to consider how you would like it if someone did that to you.

You realize that you would not merely dislike it, you would resent it. You would think that the other has a reason to stop—more, an obligation to stop. And that obligation would spring from your own objection to what he does to you.   (1996: 98)

Korsgaard goes on to employ a cognitive or rationalistic vocabulary, but it is hard not to feel that the central process is exactly the same as in Smith. The potential victim forces you to recognize his resentment, and to 'put yourself in his shoes'. His fundamental question is: 'How would you *like* it if someone did that to you?'—and once you find that you would not, then, other things being equal, his not liking or resenting it translates into your own discomfort at your own behaviour. Of course, as Smith sensibly recognizes, things are not always equal. We have an abundance of defence mechanisms against this incipient discomfort, including ignoring the impartial spectator, or more often convincing ourselves the he would be on our side or 'of our faction'. As Smith puts it: 'The propriety of our moral sentiments is never so apt to be corrupted, as when the indulgent and partial spectator is at hand, while the indifferent and impartial one is at a great distance' (1976: 154).

At this point the sentimentalist will certainly face another familiar challenge. The account finds the source of feelings of obligation and injustice in a certain emotional identification: in this case a contingent (of course) capacity to internalize the resentments of others. But might not this very notion of resentment itself import, and depend upon, an unacknowledged cognitivism? Resentment, as Korsgaard says, is more than mere dislike. Perhaps it is more like bitterness, but bitterness at the dispensation of some agent. Anyone suffering a third summer holiday in succession blighted by continuous rain might feel bitter, but only a theist can resent it. This quickly suggests that resentment is more like bitterness at the injustice of the behaviour, in which case a perception of injustice cannot be explained in terms of resentment and sympathy with it, but must be identified in some pre-existent cognition. Similar objections may be made to sentimentalist uses of notions like guilt, or even anger: if anger is the attitude or emotion of those who perceive themselves to have been wronged, and guilt is the attitude or emotion of those who recognize themselves to have done wrong, then we cannot understand the judgements by citing the emotions.

There is a simple lacuna in this popular line of thought. The equations in question are things like 'anger is perception of wrong' or 'resentment is recognition of injustice to oneself'. The objection implicitly supposes that these equations need to be read from right to left, so that the apparent cognition explains the emotion. The sentimentalist tradition, by contrast, reads them from left to right, so that the emotion or attitude explains the thought of wrong or injustice in terms of which it gets expressed. This is not the place to rehearse all the moves in this debate. You just have to try out the different directions of explanation, and you have to ask which is psychologically or metaphysically the more economical. But at least a preliminary remark is that as they stand, of course, the equations are absurdly simple. Anger is not perception of wrong, nor resentment recognition of injustice to oneself. Each is both more in one respect and less in another. More, because the pure cognition leaves out the upheaval and the motivational force, so that in fact perception of wrong may not lead to anger, and recognition of injustice to oneself may not lead to resentment. Less, because each has a primitive identity in which ethical thought is not yet present. After all, we should not forget that Darwin called his great work *The Expression of Emotion in Man and Animals*. The guard dog does a fair job of being angry at the intruder, and the pet which throws its food around the house on being left behind does a fair job of resenting being neglected.

A different strand in Smith is the idea that unlike obligations of benevolence, obligations of justice can be *exacted* from us. They bring in the potential force of the community or the civil power: 'the person himself who meditates an injustice is sensible of this, and feels that force may, with the utmost propriety, be made use of both by the person whom he is about to injure, and by others, either to obstruct the execution of his crime, or to punish him when he has executed it' (Smith 1976: 79–80). Applied to Hume's example, this suggests that the question of whether there is an obligation of justice may hinge on whether we think a spectator, contemplating a breach of 'gentle usage', should use pre-emptive or retaliatory force on the perpetrator. I am not sure whether we do think this in general. If we can take the case of animals as indicative, our actual animal welfare legislation suggests we think that if the breach is severe enough then the criminal law has a say, but at least in our jurisprudence, if not in our studies, we seem prepared to let a fair amount of not so gentle usage go on unprevented and unpunished.

However we solve this issue, if we stand back for a moment it should be obvious that this particular issue about justice is not a promising basis from which to attack sentimentalism. The structure of the case disqualifies it from that task. The idea is to arouse our sense of what is due to these creatures, and to encourage shock and outrage at the base behaviour to which Hume's agents might be led, or to excite us to lament the outrages which they might get away with, and to wring our hands over the sad plight of the poor defenceless creatures. All this is excellent. It shows us sympathizing with the downtrodden and their resentment, perhaps desiring or wishing for a civil order in which the powerful would be punished, feeling that things are out of joint unless they are brought to account for their crimes, and so on. In other words, it shows that our sense of outrage and injustice is mobilized, not merely our benevolence. But it cannot show more than that. It cannot show that what is mobilized lies outside the sentiments altogether. Hume's example may make us hot under the collar about the indignities the powerful may visit on the weak, but it does not afford any evidence that getting hot under the collar is anything else than feeling an attitude and emotion, directed upon a particular social structure and the abuses it looks set to allow.

4. Where this Leaves Us

I have not, in this essay, been exclusively defending expressivism. Other views which stress the place of sentiments, or imagination and culture, in the genesis of our ethical thought were equally possible targets of Kerstein's and Peacocke's attacks. Some of these others, perhaps less deft with the notion of 'mind-dependence', might even fall to such attacks, for instance by giving the moral judgement a truth condition that is not child-dependent or dog-dependent, but genuinely mind-dependent. Others may avoid them only by inappropriate reliance on 'actually' operators and other pieces of doubtful machinery. If so, I am glad to part company with them.

The popularity of rationalism, and the general feeling that there 'must be something to' the kinds of argument I have been discussing, are very deep-rooted. Partly, they represent a noble dream. They answer a wish that the knaves of the world can not only be confined and confounded, but refuted—refuted as well by standards that they have to acknowledge.

Ideally, they will be shown to be in a state akin to self-contradiction. Kerstein acknowledges that Kant and neo-Kantians have not achieved anything like this result. But it is still, tantalizingly, there as a goal or ideal, the Holy Grail of moral philosophy, and many suppose that all right-thinking people must join the pilgrimage to find it.

We sentimentalists do not like our good behaviour to be hostage to such a search. We don't altogether approve of Holy Grails. We do not see the need for them. We are not quite on all fours with those who do. And we do not quite see why, even if by some secret alchemy a philosopher managed to glimpse one, it should ameliorate his behaviour, let alone that of other people. We think instead that human beings are ruled by passions, and the best we can do is to educate them so that the best ones are the most forceful ones.

We say of rationalistic moral philosophy what Hume says of abstract reasonings in general, that when we leave our closet, and engage in the common affairs of life, its conclusions seem to vanish, like the phantoms of the night on the appearance of the morning (Hume 1978: III.i.1).

7

Through Thick and Thin

I

Like Allan Gibbard (Gibbard 1990), I am perplexed (both in the sense of puzzled, and as an expressivist, harassed) by the place people accord to thickness in ethical theory. But I think thickness is overrated. I do not think there are any thick concepts, as these have been understood. There may be words that are encrusted with the thickest of cultural deposits, but I shall urge that this is a different matter, and indeed one that subverts the normal notion of thickness.

Furthermore, although there are some thick words, they are of no great importance to the theory of ethics. And in fact, there are many fewer thick words than philosophers have been prone to suppose. I shall argue that attitude is much more typically, and flexibly, carried by other aspects of utterance than lexical ones. In the end I want to oppose the popular idea that a proper understanding of thickness tells us surprising things about ethical objectivity, and even perhaps undermines the fact-value distinction. However, I have attacked what I see as the argument before, so for the bulk of this paper I shall not be concerned with it (Blackburn 1981, 1984c). Instead I shall follow rather literally Austin's injunction to think about the dainty and the dumpy, before making some brief comments about Gibbard's own approach, and closing with some final comments about the thick.

When is a term a thick term? Hume says that discretion, caution, enterprise, industry, assiduity, frugality, economy, good-sense, prudence, discernment are endowments 'whose very names force an avowal of their merit' (Hume 1998: 126). This suggests that if you do not avow the merit, then you offend against meaning by using the term. The idea would be that if you are not prepared to avow the merit, you must search for some other term: taciturnity, cowardice, rashness, busyness might start us along the way. What Hume here says of his list of virtues is usually held true of a more Aristotelian list: it is supposed that unless it is present to the right degree you should not call it courage (but, for instance, rashness), nor temperance (but, for instance, anorexia). And the same might go for liberality, magnificence, proper pride, the giving of amusement, and so on.

Unfortunately, it is fairly plain that Hume is wrong if the 'forcing' of the avowal of merit is supposed to be done by conventions governing English usage. For we can easily hear any of these terms, except perhaps 'good sense', negatively. A previous master of my Oxford college was frequently praised as well-meaning, but condemned as frugal, a fatal flaw in someone whose main job is dispensing hospitality. If a person's industry is entirely misdirected and, like that of the prime minister Mrs Thatcher, a general cause of grief, we do not deny that it is industry. Her industry was misguided and objectionable, and people can be too prudent and even too discerning. But that does not *stop* them from being industrious, prudent, and discerning. Similarly we can talk of mad courage or Dutch courage without linguistic impropriety. The problem with the rash person is not that his excess of courage has transformed the courage into something different, but that his indubitable courage does not go with proper knowledge of danger.[1]

The dictionary puts no positive indicator of attitude by any of Hume's terms, in the way that it puts 'derog.' or 'usually contempt.' by certain epithets of abuse. In fact, dictionaries typically have no term signalling a convention of approval, in the way that these terms signal the standard attitude communicated by offensive epithets. I take this to suggest that language maintains few lexical conventions of this thickening kind. This may be because, as Kant pointed out, there is nothing unconditionally good about courage, temperance, and the rest. They may be put to bad uses, or they may be aspects of a situation that would have been much better had they not been present. Of course, we may *normally* expect someone who talks of a person's discretion, caution, etc. to be somehow implying or inviting a favourable attitude to them. But this is left to the passing

---

[1] Aristotle says this, but then says quickly that the man who 'exceeds in fearlessness' has no name, although the man who exceeds in confidence is rash. But of course the man who exceeds in fearlessness does have a name. He is really fearless. Or too fearless, or even absolutely fearless. *Nicomachean Ethics*, bk II, 1107b.

theory—the theory of what a particular speaker is doing on an occasion by making a particular utterance—rather than forged in steel by a prior theory or convention governing the terms. We might expect someone who talks of a house as containing south-facing windows to be implying or inviting a favourable attitude to that feature, yet 'contains south-facing windows' is not usually thought of as a thick term, and certainly there is no linguistic convention that a house with south-facing windows should be favourably regarded. Apart from anything else, there is no need for such a convention, given what people normally desire, and similarly, since exercises of courage and temperance are normally beneficial, we do not need additional semantic conventions governing the terms with which we refer to them.

I am not of course denying that there are terms where a positive, or more often negative, qualification is part of the dictionary meaning. A word can relate to another by qualifying it with 'offensively' or 'objectionably'. Niggardly may mean objectionably careful with money; buffoonery may be offensively high spirits. Something cloys if it is excessively sweet and satiating. But even here, I shall argue, we must be careful with talk of convention or meaning.

I should like to come at the reason by placing the discussion in a wider context. The communication of attitude in language (and gesture) is a subtle matter, and we may do well to widen our view in two different ways. First, consider the pervasive communication of information, force, and attitude by intonation. The study of this (prosody) distinguishes tone languages, such as Szechuanese, Ganda, and in fact the majority of the world's languages, in which tone is a lexical feature, from intonation languages. These include all European languages, although Norwegian and Swedish make limited use of tone to distinguish words (Cruttenden 1986). In an intonation language such as English the pitch, length, and loudness of parts of an utterance subserve difference of stress, accent, and rhythm, and these in turn are available to act as indicators of meaning. Familiar examples include the indication of force ('You're coming' can be said unambiguously as a question or a command by altering the intonation) and scope ('I am not going to perform anywhere,' where difference of stress distinguishes whether I am not going to perform at all, or whether I am, but not just anywhere). Equally certain is the effect of the flat low tone communicating indifference or boredom ('I have just seen Elton John!

Have you?') and a high tone followed by a low indicating excitement or interest ('Have you heard about Jane? She's (rising)preg (falling)nant'). Many complex effects are absolutely predictable: for example, a rise then fall on a positive word (brilliant, clever, splendid) easily turns the comment into a sarcasm. Furthermore, just as a tone can be unmistakably bored or excited, conciliatory or aggressive, so it can be condescending (try saying 'Let me help you do it' in different ways), menacing, hostile, jocular, ironic, and so on. Intonation can be thought of as a kind of tune to which a message is played, and there is no reason in principle why a semantics of a tune should not assign to it an abstract set of meanings. These, in conjunction with other pragmatic features, would yield local meanings. A complete description of these features would be the goal of theoretical prosody.

The second fact we should include in our view is the enormous variety of attitudes communicated by tone. Here is a sentence from a hypothetical novel: ' "John was using the computer again," she said, with . . . in her voice.' Depending on the rest of the novel, there are hundreds of possible fillings. From the realm of emotion and attitude we find excitement, horror, hope, anger, admiration, defeat, contempt, impatience, indifference, excitement, joy, grief, envy, pride, guilt, shame; epistemically we might have certainty, doubt, or confidence; and from the realm of pragmatics, telling us about the speaker's relation to the hearer, a whole new gallery would include menace, condescension, conspiracy, invitation, as well as command and question. The specifically moral dimensions of admiration and anger or contempt are but two among many. The sentence could have read: ' "John was using the computer," she said, . . .ly,' and adverbs can be constructed from nearly all the terms I listed with the same effect. The adverbial construction makes plain a separation of powers: here the words give us what was said and the pattern of intonation gives us the manner of saying it, but as we saw above, there are cases where the intonation is needed as well as the words to give us what was said, and whether it was an assertion or a question, for example.

The relation between the tune and the words is interesting in a way that Gibbard rightly highlights. Where the attitude or emotion is conveyed by a tune, there is a strong, almost indefeasible presupposition that it is on account of what else is said that the emotion or attitude, or pragmatic relationship exists. Even in: ' "She's just won the Nobel prize, I told him." '

' "She's strong, too," he said, admiringly,' the admiration has to be partly on account of her strength. The only exceptions I can think of may arise with moods: ' "The threat of global warming has been averted, I announced." ' ' "The toast's burned," she replied, with joy in her voice'—and even here the implication is extremely difficult to cancel.

Generally speaking, saying something with an attitude in your voice licenses the hearer to suppose that the attitude is expressed because of what is said. The parallel point applies to lexical elements. Calling someone a nerd is not so much saying that he is someone who is interested in mathematics etc. *and* contemptible, but that he is interested in mathematics, etc. and *on that account* contemptible. (If we dissent from the use of such a term, do we say that what was said was false, or inept in a different way? I regard this as indeterminate: the fact is we turn our backs. See Blackburn 1984c: 148–50.) As Gibbard also notes, this means that someone may hold in contempt those that others sneer at as nerds, but not despise them *as* nerds. Perhaps it is their typically pale complexions that bother her. But usage is actually quite flexible here, and we shall shortly come across cases where the distinction is ignored.

Obviously an intonation language can get us a long way in the communication of attitudes. Suppose the lexical items that are derog. and contempt. are excised from the language, as the politically correct would wish. The racist, sexist, fattist, or ageist can still convey all she needs by playing the information in neutral words, but to the contempt-conveying tune (curiously, as we shall see later, it is their opponents who lose most if the lexical way of doing it, with a special derog. vocabulary, is banned). Suppose, for instance, that the word 'gross' is correctly entered in the dictionary as applied to fat people and derog. The fattist can get by without it, by using the word 'fat' instead, with the right kind of sneery tone.

Thus the young sometimes call the old 'wrinklies' or 'crumblies', but before they did that they got by well enough by calling them 'old' in a kind of mock-horror, sepulchral, amazed tone. I shall transcribe 'fat' said with a sneer as 'fat↓' where the downward arrow signals the combination of emphasis on the first consonant and downward cadence that carries the sneer. 'Fat↓' will be heard most often in the mouths of those who are repelled by or despise fatness, or who sympathize with those who do. I shall talk of this group as sharing a sensibility (in the sense of Blackburn 1984c). They are fattists. Non-fattists will not be heard using the term, except in contexts of reportage (and even then, carefully, if they disapprove of the sensibility).

In some of these cases the descriptive side is fixed, and the sneer or other tone optional; whereas moral philosophers are mainly interested in the case where the description itself becomes contested, in the light of the norms governing attitude. But we can easily imagine just the same kinds of dispute over these terms, which combine description and tone. Amanda and Beryl may have been card-carrying fattists until Amanda met Clive. 'Clive is so fat↓,' challenges Beryl. 'No, not fat↓, stocky, well-built,' dreams Amanda. The dispute need not be one about vagueness, as we can see if we play it through with Pavarotti instead of Clive. Pavarotti was unquestionably fat, but probably many fattists would have refrained from calling him fat↓. They wanted to overlook the fact that he was fat to an extent that would normally repel them, since he was so transcendentally uncontemptible in other ways. 'Fat↓' shares with other derog. terms the property that where you do not want to express or endorse the attitude, you will refuse application of the term. Other dimensions of success or failure can enter to complicate the application or withholding, even in those inclined to share the general sensibility.

In other words, it is quite compatible with the attitude being carried by the tone that it then *plays a role* in determining the extension and in ruling out of the extension things which, for quite different reasons, escape the attitude. Where the word carries a tone, just as much as when it has a derogatory meaning, the tone may drive our propensity to apply or withhold.

So we have a model on which a term can optionally be pronounced according to a tune. When the tune expresses an attitude, the resulting disposition to apply or withhold the term + tune is subject to willingness to express or endorse the attitude. This gives rise to dispute in particular cases even among those inclined to share the disposition to feel the attitude on account of the original feature.

Allan Gibbard makes a slightly different proposal, so the question arises how mine relates to it. His model highlights a number of features that are not so far included in this story. The most notable is the judgement of warrant. On Gibbard's analysis we need three, or in the case of one of his examples, 'lewd', perhaps four, elements. In this example, we have a basic description of the kind of thing that may be judged lewd: a display of sexuality. We have an attitude expressed, which Gibbard calls 'L-censoriousness'. These parallel the two elements I have put in place for 'fat↓' . Thirdly, however, we have the acceptance of a presupposition, namely 'the general importance of limiting sexual displays'. These limits give a rationale for the fourth element, which is the judgement that the feeling of L-censoriousness is warranted. Since this judgement is in turn given an expressivist analysis in Gibbard's account, we see that *two* different states of mind are voiced: the L-censoriousness, and the acceptance of norms permitting L-censoriousness for acts of this type, as being, or in virtue of their being, acts of this type.

I have two reservations about this. The first is independent of my more general scepticism about the thick. I think it is possible to put into the background the last two elements of Gibbard's four. This is because we can distinguish between a particular feature of the meaning or use of a particular term, and general presuppositions of a wide sector of language use. I can illustrate the difference in a simple empirical case. Return to my saying that John is using the computer. What do I mean? That John is using the computer. But do I also express acceptance of a system of norms that permits my saying that in some circumstances, including the empirical circumstance I am now in? I do not think so. It may be a *general* presupposition of my saying something of this kind, that my situation warrants my saying it. If I were not involved in such a system of norms, I would not be a fully fledged ('licensed') user of the sentence to make an assertion. And if challenged I will typically draw upon such a system in defence, claiming that it is right to be confident of that here, or to describe that in this way, or to place trust in this or that informational channel. But there is no reason, I think, to make this a specific truth about the meaning of 'John is using the computer'.

It seems instead like this. I have an implicit or tacit or practical epistemology. When challenged I can try to articulate principles and norms from that epistemology, by way of justifying my assertion. I am probably bad at doing that, but it is the fact that my utterance is norm-governed, rather than our capacity to bring the norms to consciousness, that matters to our capacity to give my utterance its sense. I do not express my system of epistemological norms when I utter, because I may not know what they are, and communication is possible between people whose epistemologies differ, provided not too radically. In this way a norm-governed epistemology is in the *background* of meaning. Without it, there would be no empirical judgement. But it is not communicated in empirical judgement. The same seems to me to apply in the case of attitude. Gibbard rightly mentions the person who finds an act lewd unreflectively: 'he simply responds to the features of an act, feels L-censorious, and says "how lewd" ' (Gibbard 1990: 283). But, he argues, this does not display the concept of lewdness, specifically because I may countenance the possibility that I am wrong in my feelings: I recognize that my feeling may be unwarranted. The possibility is there sure enough, but it is a *general* truth about feeling and the voicing of feeling rather than a *specific* truth about the concept of lewdness. Suppose I communicate some information excitedly. 'Jane is pregnant,' I say, breathily. Then I must be prepared to countenance the possibility that my feeling is unwarranted. The audience burst into laughter at my excitement: 'So what,' one says, 'Jane is always pregnant.' Or, suppose I set about explaining something to someone condescendingly. Then I should be prepared to countenance the embarrassing possibility that my condescension is unwarranted. Perhaps the funny foreigner to whom I am explaining the function of a spark plug is Enrico Ferrari. But I think it would be Ptolemaic to say that as well as expressing excitement or condescension I also express acceptance of a system of norms that permit excitement and condescension. I will be judged by those norms, certainly, and have to defend myself by gesturing at such norms. But that is the common lot of any action, including expression of feeling. If I enter a house, I may be judged and defended by norms permitting the entering of that house, but it is unnecessary to suppose that in entering the house I express acceptance of any such system of norms.

It is certainly important that the feeling—the censoriousness, or the excitement, or the condescension—can be the target of attack. Indeed, I argue like Gibbard that it is this feature that above all justifies and explains our propensity to a propositional expression, moving us from a primitive tonal or 'boo–hooray' idiom to an idiom in which the primary vehicle of expression is a sentence that can be manipulated in indirect contexts. But I think this introduces no further need for expression of acceptance of norms as well as expression of feeling. If I yawn rudely at your dinner, I can be criticized both for feeling bored and for expressing my boredom, but I do not think the yawn expresses my acceptance of a system of norms for boredom. It is just once more that I shall have to scrabble for a system of such norms when I come under attack.

What the pervasive need to discuss and accept or reject feelings does introduce is a good reason to move to lexical expression rather than resting content with intonation. Although intonation is a reliable vehicle of meaning, it is evanescent, and hence deniable. 'Do let me help you,' I say, with condescension in my voice, and when you flare up I deny there is any reason: all I did was ask if I could help you. One of the best ways for an in-group to mock an outsider is to bandy words with tones of irony, sarcasm, and the rest that the outsider can recognize but cannot hold them to. But while we may not be able to pin the ugly tone onto the speaker, if she goes instead for a lexical device then the decks may be relatively clear for action. Having said that John is interested in nothing but mathematics and computer games, I can deny the scorn that was in my voice. But if I said that he was a nerd I can be held to it, and must defend my attitude. This is why it may be unwise to ban derogatory and abusive vocabulary: the result is not that the attitude disappears, or cannot be communicated, but that it is less likely to face the tribunal of criticism. Language responds to this need in the endless creation of new vocabulary with some attitude ostensibly built in: airhead, —babble, bimbo, bonk, brat pack, chattering classes, couch potato, would start a list of recent introductions, and toy-boy and yuppie could end it.

But the stabilizing function is only partly achieved. It is actually extremely difficult to say *which* attitude, if any, is fixed as part of the literal meaning of most of these terms. If Amanda and Clive set up house, something would lie behind my describing them as yuppies, but what exactly? I suggest that there is no stable connection between any single attitude and such a term. Rather, the social phenomena that give rise to it permit a wide variety of responses. Even if a term is introduced as a derogatory term, it can be washed cleaner: we refuse to be coerced by usage into accepting an attitude. Even a term of deliberate abuse stands ready to be orphaned. In Blackburn 1984c: 169, I gave the example of 'Kraut' as a term of abuse used by some English people for Germans. But it is very easy to think of contexts in which it is not that: faced with some marvel of engineering in my new BMW you might shake your head in wonder: 'Typical of the Krauts to think of that,' you say in awe, and all the term does is emphasize a sense of difference, that in turn reinforces the admiration. A few such cases, and the derogatoriness starts to slide into history, while the appreciation of the difference as a positive thing may come to be the default. So although lexical invention will sometimes and perhaps briefly stabilize expression compared with deniable intonation, it is itself not always easy to pin down. 'Buffoon' is, I suppose, generally a term of abuse, but Falstaff's buffoonery was his most attractive feature. What is clear is that a word's parentage is no certain guide to the best interpretation of any individual utterance, even if the knowing speaker may be aware of the deposits from the past.

In this, intonation is a firmer guide, and in Davidson's terms the 'passing theory' rules the 'prior theory'. Who knows what I am thinking if I describe Clive as Amanda's toy boy? The vocabulary might signal only that the phenomenon is interesting, and attitudes need voicing and comparing, rather than itself signalling any single response. As with metaphor, one kind of speech act performed by using the term may be to invite comparison (what are we to think of women who take younger lovers?). The choice of term is *significant*, but this is not to say that there is just one thing, still less a linguistically certified thing, that it signifies. And even if an attitude is convincingly attributable, it is unlikely to be specifically moralistic or ethical except in the largest sense. 'Thank God I can laugh at this' or 'Thank God I am different from them' seem to need expression at least as much as wooden approval and disapproval. Many slang terms exist in order simply to accentuate difference, like British terms of geographical origin: Taffy, Jock, Scouse, Geordie, Brummie. These are not in essence derogatory, but can be used on occasion in derogatory utterances.

Interestingly, when approval is needed, language typically finds not 'thick' words, but new words of straight commendation: ace, awesome, bad, crucial, and wicked might start a list of those that have acquired street credibility in the last decades.

The picture I want to paint, then, is of a multiplicity of attitudes and feelings, and a flexible and changing repertoire of linguistic expression, with feeling naturally signalled by signs such as intonation, and only unreliably read back from vocabulary except in very few cases.

And this brings me to my second reservation about Gibbard's treatment of 'lewd'. I would claim that while his picture is recognizable, it describes a particular culturally variable reaction to lewdness, and is in no way compulsory. I am not sure, for example, that censoriousness is part of the meaning of the term. 'Lewd' comes from the same neck of the woods as provocative, fruity, naughty, salacious, racy, bawdy, ribald, as well as the weightier obscene and gross. Attitudes to these things are complex, fluid, and mobile. One thinks of satyrs and Saturnalia, Carnival, Shakespeare's fools and porters, comedians and pantomime, Elvis Presley and Mick Jagger: necessary eruptions of the Dionysiac into the fragile Apollonian order. With lewdness we reaffirm control, defending ourselves by mockery and parody against the frightening tyranny of love and lust. In the same way, a wake defends us against the tyranny of grief. We rattle our chains and shake our fists at the gods. Language does not tell us how much we need the defence, but understanding this to be the actual function of lewdness, we might easily lament its suppression, or worry that this year's Carnival was not lewd enough. This is why instead of claiming that the concept is not thick, I could put my point by saying that it is too thick: it carries such a complex drapery of religious, cultural, and ritual history that thinking of it as tied to just one attitude is impossible. No single layer of its drapery is to be given the privilege of being essential.[2]

Nor is this picture confined to lewdness: it is not as though Gibbard accidentally chose a bad example. A person talking about industry, courage, and the rest can reflect in many directions, but will be part of the same conversation largely regardless of resulting idiosyncrasies of attitude or the surprising contours of the boundaries they suggest (so, in spite of his reticence I think Gibbard *is* a licensed user of the term 'lewd'). This is why the very same trait may start firmly entrenched as a virtue or vice but become subject to re-evaluation. Dispute between those who value differently humility or chastity or frugality is not settled by pointing to the dictionary.[3]

Certainly we can expect agreement in attitude, even to the lewd, because large numbers of people think the same way. In this case, they may be equally prudish. But their decorum is not guaranteed by semantics. My worry about Gibbard's treatment here is that by finding only an artificial construct ('L-censoriousness') he is playing into the hands of those who argue for ineliminable thick concepts. Whereas the reason we have no natural way of identifying *the* attitude expressed by 'lewd' is that there is no such thing as *the* attitude.

---

[2] In a paper not included in this volume, I express similar reservations about the idea that there is such a thing as *the* religious frame of mind. Indeed, it might be essential to religion that the adept oscillate between a succession of frames of mind.

[3] See also in this volume 'The Absolute Conception' and the discussion of Quentin Skinner's examples of linguistic change in history (essay 13, below).

II

Are there thick concepts? It might seem that by emphasizing the historical and psychological encrustations of lewdness I am reaffirming a Wittgensteinian complexity. Perhaps the term floats on a sea of associations that provide only a shifting, impermanent set of pressures on its application. Rather than a rule or even an overlapping number of distinct rules, as in the analogy with strands of a rope, perhaps we have something even more formless, a swirl of currents: thickness 'all the way down'. Even if this is right, the point remains that an individual element of the mix—moral disapprobation, for example—can be removed without semantic rupture. In this light, the usual notion of thickness, where attitude is cemented by convention, is the horrid offspring of marrying a Wittgensteinian picture of thought to a simple attachment to analyticities that the picture in fact undermines. Changing an attitude is not declining the conversation. But we should not overdramatize things. The term 'lewd', for instance, does have *some* semantic anchors: something to do with sexual display, something to do with mockery of normal proprieties, even if the rest of the swirl is so shapeless.

If I play a hitherto neutral description of something to a sneering tune, I do not deploy a new concept. No new concept is introduced when someone finds someone else 'fat↓'. To be repulsed at avoirdupois is not to deploy a new skill or new cognition. If language manages, however briefly, to standardize 'gross' as an alternative way of communicating just the same feeling, it does not thereby increase its expressive power. All that happens is that, having a fattist sensibility, a person can seize the linguistic tools provided by the term 'fat' and the intonation '↓', or the tool provided by the one term 'gross', at choice. If she does the former, the tone begins to determine the extension, but discussion, for instance, of whether Pavarotti is 'fat↓' is nothing new from discussion of whether to feel repelled or not at his weight.

The response to this detaching treatment by a defender of thick concepts must surely allow the pattern of analysis, but claim that it is not universal. More ambitiously, the claim should be that detachable examples are parasitic upon a prior, thick, conceptual repertoire. They could not form the basic elements of a moral sensibility. Once this is the issue, the debate parallels others, for example that over broad versus narrow content. That debate is endlessly conducted by imagining what is the same or different about a subject's thoughts if we vary the external circumstance she is in, without varying how the circumstance appears to her. It is just obvious—indeed, it is given in the thought experiment—that there will be many attributions of thought that are 'narrow', by staying constant throughout the change of environment. But what is not thereby established is either that there are any terms that are narrow in having no environmental responsibilities, or that if there were, their existence would be independent of the logically prior existence of other terms that do. Similarly here, while we can split description from feeling by understanding how tone can attach differently to terms, we do not thereby establish that all terms can be split into description + tone, nor that tones could be as significant as they are in the absence of a prior thick conceptual repertoire. Someone may argue that in this way, thick concepts are basic.

A thick concept might be thought of in chemical terms. It is not that the two elements of attitude and description cannot be understood as separate at some level (obviously, in searching for thick concepts or terms, we know that we are looking for items with implications of attitude on the one hand, and description on the other). But the idea must be that the two form a compound or an amalgam, rather than a mixture: the attitude and the description infuse each other, so that at the end, in the repertoire of the mature speaker, the two elements are no longer distinguishable. The speaker sees there as being just one rule, and can do nothing useful with the idea that she is guided by two. Since 'nothing is hidden', we ought to accept that there is just one rule, and not two. But to state it we must ourselves have been subject to the fusion, at least sufficiently to empathize with it. The chemical model ultimately breaks down, since it suggests that fundamentally there exist independent, self-standing elements out of which other compounds are formed. This defence of thickness will discard this element of the analogy, although the result will be a strain, as if we want to maintain the idea of a compound while discarding the idea of elements that are compounded together.

In any case, the model I offer for 'lewdness' and the arguments I have given that attitude is typically visible only to the passing theory, and not to the prior theory, undermine any such picture. For if there are basic, or at least important, thick concepts in ethics, it is surprising that they cannot more easily be found. Once we see Hume's list, or Aristotle's, correctly, the terms they contain prove not to work like this. We get nothing but detachable and flexible attitudes, coupled with delineations of traits of character or action. The attitudes, whichever they are, may partly drive debate about which traits fall into the extension, but that is no argument for new concepts and new rules of application. There is no more reason to find thick moral concepts in the background than there is to find thick concepts that amalgamate other feelings and their objects, as if someone exercises a new concept when she condescends to her friend's accent or place of origin. And if Hume and Aristotle cannot provide the fused, basic, thick concepts, where are they to be found?

It is, I think, just as well that we should not think of the matter differently. The defender of thick concepts must claim that a person loses the concept if a particular amalgam dissolves back into its elements. A form of life has gone, a way of seeing the world has vanished. But this is overdramatic again. It implies too ready a tendency to diagnose the discussions and re-evaluations that are the essence of ethical activity as exercises in talking past each other. For if you don't respond to lewdness as I do, then on this picture your amalgamated concept of lewdness is not mine, and we are left in incommunicable solitude. Whereas as Gibbard rightly emphasizes, the truth is that we have a well enough located object of agreement and disagreement, in the reactions we have, and wish to endorse or criticize, to a broadly located element of human experience.

POSTSCRIPT

Although this paper is one of the oldest in this collection, I confess to seeing little reason for retracting any of it. If anything, the intervening years have given me a more determined sense of the fluidities of language and the dangers of a slavish adherence to the Fregean template in which meaning is invariably approached through a set of categories including that of a 'concept', where this is thought of as a rule determining an extension.

It is not only the phenomena surrounding thickness that resist this degree of logicism. The related topic of vagueness does so as well, and I believe it is valuable to compare them. So consider a partition of people according to income or capital assets, going from poor, to comfortable, to rich. Vagueness strikes: there is no norm in heaven or earth saying that there is just one place to draw the lines. There are many permissible places, although there are also some that are too outlandish to be allowed. But then we have a sorites series, in which there is no one place at which the lines must be drawn, but on pain of absurdities on each occasion on which we pass along the series, the lines must be drawn somewhere.

The sorites, however, needs more careful expression than is usually given. The inductive premise—e.g. that if £n per annum leaves you poor, so does £n + 1—can appear in two quite different contexts. In setting up the paradox, we agree to it because we recognize that there is no rationally compulsory cut-off point, no 'tipping point' beyond which one pound propels you out of poverty into comfort or out of comfort into riches. But as we go through the series one pound at a time, somewhere we have to jump on pain of ending up with outlandish and indefensible applications of the terms in question. Wherever we jump, when we do we find ourselves saying that £n + 1 takes you into a new bracket, and we are then charged with the fact that we said that £n did not, and reminded of our original assent to the inductive premise. This is supposedly embarrassing, yet the natural (and correct) reaction is to laugh at the charge. You have to jump somewhere. I jumped here. I didn't say it was compulsory to jump where I did, any more than when I get out of bed I express adherence to a norm asserting that this was the compulsory time to get out of bed. I can get out of bed without thinking that there is any fact mandating just one time as the compulsory time to get out of bed. Similarly with deciding to say that with *this* income but none less, you enter the company of the rich.

If I jump at £n, saying that it leaves you poor but £n + 1 puts you at the bottom of the comfortable range, then of course I ought also to say that it is true that it does (by deflationism). So was the original inductive premise false? We must bring in an element of contextualism, and distinguish between a *theoretical* context and an *engaged* or *practical* context. In our theoretical moments there is an association between 'true' and 'rationally compulsory' or 'metaphysically grounded', and there is in this sense no rationally compulsory or metaphysically grounded jumping point in this series. But in our practical lives we have to let go of that idea when, as somewhere we have to do, we jump. So in the practical context we speak as if the words of the original inductive premise say something false, yet it was entirely justifiable that we assented to those very words in the theoretical context in which they first occurred. 'True' in the theoretical context maintains its associations with rationally compulsory, or metaphysically grounded. But it loses those associations in the practical world of descriptions of things and people, where we decide or legislate, rather than discover, where we wish to draw a boundary—and where, except in legalistic contexts, we need have no allegiance to where we drew the same boundary on other occasions.

Bringing in this difference between theoretical and practical contexts, coupled with as much of a laissez-faire attitude in the practical context as we find convenient, in fact enables us to explain the phenomena of vagueness without any non-classical logical apparatus, for we maintain only two truth values, and poor, comfortable, and rich remain contraries. But we also use them without imposing any implausible metaphysical picture on the phenomena themselves.

So now consider an argument between someone who says that (say) university professors are rich, and someone else who says that they are merely comfortable, but not really rich. The extensions these participants give to their terms is different. Yet each knows what he means: so must we say that although each apparently speaks English, in fact different rules determine these extensions, that is, they have different concepts, or even that it is unknowable which concepts they have? Surely not, for that implies that there is no identifiable proposition about which they disagree: they may as well be interpreted as talking past each other. And this is false, for one thing may be certain, which is that they are having an argument. So what are we to say?

A preliminary to answering that is to ask why we need vague terms in the first place. After all, on the transition from poor to rich, why don't we just make do with precise numerical measures of income and capital? On the transition from child to adult, why not make do with precise numerical ages? When we set out to count things, but find that we have identified the things in question in too vague a manner to allow ourselves to do so, we either give up or substitute a more precise definition of what we want (Robinson 2009). Why can't we just do the same kind of thing here? The answer, clearly, is that in each case we are attaching *significance* to particular numbers: the significance of a changing status or attitude. So what needs to be recognized is that two people may disagree because by choosing their terms each is encouraging a different practical cognitive attitude or direction of thought. One wants to suggest implicatures ('rich' meaning luxury, ease, freedom from care, a duty to give to charity, perhaps) that the other does not, preferring to substitute a different direction of thought or imagination ('comfortable' meaning freedom from serious want, certainly, but struggle, not too much to spare, a hard-won but vulnerable respectability, perhaps). It is only these implications, or implicatures, that give the dispute more than a verbal flavour. But they do so, just as effectively as more notorious choices of terms such as 'terrorist' versus 'freedom fighter' do. We need not be stupidly *engagé*, of course: we do not think that someone who has about as little as you can have while being called 'rich' deserves the same treatment as Bill Gates, or that a young adult is all that importantly different from a child on the last steps towards adulthood. But the terms point us in different directions, just as we are pointed in different practical directions if we call Gordon Brown resolute and if we call him pig-headed. This is why, even if we are legislating and deciding, we can find ourselves in dispute with people who conduct the legislation and decisions differently. It is also, incidentally, why societies signal when childhood is to be regarded as ended by the use of coming-of-age ceremonies. These also have an interesting self-verifying element, since being an adult is partly a matter of being treated as an adult.

The Fregean tradition in semantics, for all its virtues, maintains a hostility to psychologism; this hostility means that the delicate ways in which language encourages and discourages, invites and often profits from, movements of the mind that are nothing to do with logical implication, are too often invisible. I do not say that it is impossible to put all the necessary ingredients into a 'Fregean' recipe, in which what Frege, with his usual care, confined to the theory of an ideal scientific or mathematical language, is gaily applied to our own. But I do not find it particularly helpful to do so; and some of the more bizarre results of doing so, such as the idea that there is in truth a 'real' cut-off point, determined by concepts which are determined by linguistic use, but in such a way that neither man nor God can know what it is or how to approach it, should be a sufficient warning against investing too much in the attempt.

Returning finally to evaluations and thick terms, there is an enjoyable example of a surprising revaluation which nevertheless still stays within semantic boundaries in Thomas Mann's *The Magic Mountain*, which perfectly intelligibly describes the protagonist, Hans Castorp, as 'mediocre, although in a very honourable sense of that word' (Mann 1996: 31).

8

Perspectives, Fictions, Errors, Play

In a climate in which the idea of 'fictionalism' as a philosophy of this or that is flourishing, it is natural to salute Nietzsche as an honourable ancestor. For Nietzsche's work is shot through with references to the fictions which in his view make up at least a part of the machinery with which the mind copes with its world. The notion of fiction stands alongside the three other words in my title, in apparent amity—at least, it often seems to be a lottery whether Nietzsche will announce any particular one of them as the key to some diagnosis of our situation, or some recommendation for the men of the future. And fictionalists may feel comforted by another strand in Nietzsche, which is that calling something a fiction is not a put-down, or prelude to elimination. Or at least if it is, then whatever is so put down is in excellent company, since normal predication, logic, cause and effect, and indeed the very idea of the identity of things through time are equally passengers in the one boat.[1] Nor is this diagnosis an arbitrary caprice. Nietzsche was the first philosopher to try to take the measure of Darwinism, and to recognize that throughout nature adaptation trumps truth. If creatures such as us live by imitation, faking, deceiving, and self-deceiving, so be it. In summary, for Nietzsche (some) fictions *increase health*, and that is enough for us to cast off any sense of shame, and indeed to congratulate ourselves on our immersion in them. Perhaps our imaginations make up for the limitations of our cognitions or our reason. Of course, not all fictions will get this protection. Morality may depend upon fictions about human nature which are sufficiently fanciful, sufficiently at variance with the facts of life, to vitiate it. So the right response to finding fiction somewhere may vary from case to case. Indeed, there may be variation even within the case of morality,

---

[1] See, for instance, Nietzsche 1974: §111; Nietzsche 1969: III. §24.

where we have to balance the possibility of a healthy function of ethics in general, against the pallid and unhealthy tone it has taken in the Christian world. It is not a task that Nietzsche shows any signs of relishing, and the question of whether he himself ever got that balance right is surely moot.

In this essay I argue that the apparent amity between my four title words is camouflage. We have to make distinctions, and any idea that Nietzsche somehow enables us to overcome them or get beyond them is unsustainable. If so, we then need to ask whether Nietzsche at some point took a wrong turning, and whether a different, and perhaps more sober, diagnosis of our situation is possible. I shall argue that this is indeed so. The upshot is philosophical, rather than exegetical. My concern is not so much with what Nietzsche did say, but with how we ourselves should think about the things that exercised him. In doing this I shall have little to say about scientific truth, or cause and effect, or logic or identity through time. I shall concentrate on the central issue of values. It would have been nice to salute Nietzsche as an ancestor of my own position, an expressivism tolerant of many of the forms of thought that people wrongly take to be characteristic of realism. But I think that would stretch the evidence, and it is more likely that Nietzsche's own tools are different, but in unfortunate ways. This leaves it that although we may sympathize with his goals, there are better ways of achieving them.

To identify the kind of unsustainability I have in mind, we must investigate the relationship between perspectives, fictions, errors, and play. They consort together in a scattershot kind of way: adopting a perspective may result in our telling a story; if the story is fictional it may be an error to present it as fact, and one upshot may be to lighten up, substituting some more playful attitude for the sober concern with the truth. Or, we might argue that some of the things we say, taken as sober fact, are erroneous, but that the right rectification is not to stop saying them, but to preface them with an 'in the fiction' disclaimer, joyfully scattering myth about us as we go. This is one route to fictionalism.[2] But I shall argue that in the area of ethics, these scattershot associations soon dissipate, and with them the attractions of fictionalism. Other kinds of 'non-factualism' provide a

---

[2] It is that of David Lewis, in his exploration of the idea of moral fictionalism. See Lewis 2005a, and my reply, Blackburn 2005a.

much surer handle on the issues. The first relationship I shall consider is that between perspective and error.

I

As has often been noticed, in its origin, the metaphor of perspective does not consort with any notion of error. A view of St Paul's cathedral may be from front or back, near or far, pavement level or roof level, through a wide-angle lens or a telephoto. But no such view is erroneous per se, or erroneous just because of the possibility of shifting our point of view. We might, perhaps, concede that any single view is *partial*, although in context even that could be a tendentious thing to say. After all, we may read that from some belvedere you get a *complete* or full view of a city or a church, and if I subsequently try to beat the hotel tariff down on the grounds that the panorama gives me only a partial view of them, since from it I cannot see the back of the church or the back alleys of the city, I will gain little sympathy. If we do say it, and use it to belittle whatever is given to us by such a view, then the remedy is clear: walk on, change the perspective, conjoin and synthesize it with other views or other ways of looking at the object. Sometimes we will know of the particular defects of a particular view: some things are best seen from afar, others from quite close. A mere glimpse may indeed mislead us, or more often, fail to reveal something that more sustained or careful attention would bring to light, in which case, again, the remedy is to look harder, and from different points of view. If we worry that reading one chapter of a book does not give us a fair picture of the whole, we read on and put together what we read. We know perfectly well in general how to supplement glimpses, glimmers, peeks, whiffs, echoes, and snatches, by more sustained and extended attention.

To this it might be said that the metaphor of visual perspective is, indeed, only partially indicative of what Nietzsche wants. It is an analogy, and although it breaks down if pressed, it can nevertheless point us in the right direction. We can separate two different elements which may be disanalogies with the intended application of the metaphor. One is that which I have just mentioned, that we *can* shift visual perspective, and can typically do so easily and at will. And the other is that typically we *can* synthesize the different views we get as a result. There is no inconsistency between what we see from the front and the back, or near and far (when there is, we are of course nonplussed, and do search for a diagnosis of error). Perhaps neither possibility exists when we turn to intended applications. Suppose we said, for instance, that our colour vision gives us a particular perspective on the world. We cannot change our visual system, just like that. And we cannot well 'synthesize' what we get as things are, and anything we might imagine ourselves getting were we to see differently. In the case of valuations, we cannot well step outside our own skins, and shift our perspective so that we value what we presently do not. And if we think we can, perhaps by an exercise of imagination or empathy with a different culture, then we cannot conjoin the results to give us any synthesis parallel to that which we effortlessly achieve in the visual case. If from our actual perspective, women deserve equal political rights to men, and from an imagined perspective they do not, this gives us no possibility of a synthesis from which they both do and do not. Nor, if the conflict were less blatant so some sort of synthesis did exist, would that by itself give us any motive for moving towards it.

Do either of these disanalogies justify the transition from 'perspective', in this application, to error? They might do so, in some people's minds. What we have is a version of John Mackie's 'argument from relativism' (Mackie 1977: 36–8). It would be the idea that since there is 'nothing to' the world being coloured or people having rights beyond the fact that variously minded people will or might be appealed to in different ways and give various verdicts on such matters, then all such verdicts are erroneous, and all corresponding appearances falsify reality. But there is at least one missing premise in this line of thought—a premise that might be true in the case of colour, but which cannot be supposed true in the case of value. I certainly do not want to claim that supplying the missing premise makes the argument from relativism sound. But it does seem a necessary condition of its soundness, for without it the transition seems completely unmotivated.

The premise, of course, has to be that the verdicts or appearances that would make up the different views are all equally good, or equally 'no fault'. They are none of them better than another. But that only has to be stated to seem wrong in general. Perhaps in the case of colour we can imagine a defence: if we really think we can imagine a different kind of colour perception, and if we can also imagine that it stands its possessors in as good a position to discriminate surfaces and changes as we are, then indeed they might tie for first place with our own, and there would be no fault in implementing either (I abstract away from the question of why we would suppose them to be different in the first place). With colour, we do not have to quarrel with any imagined creatures who implement a different scheme. But with ethics we do. If I think that women deserve political equality with men, then I am not at all minded to admit that the perspective from which they do not ties with mine for first place, nor do I admit that there is no fault or flaw instanced by those who adopt it. It follows from my position that any such perspective is distorted or blind or deficient, and that there is at least one fault in people who adopt it, namely that they are wrong about the political equality deserved by women.

A reply to this might be that it does not get to the heart of the metaphysical issue, for in saying what I just did I am, inevitably, standing within my value system, and doling out verdicts of fault and deficiency to competing ones. Metaphysically, it might be said, there remains a symmetry between me doing this, and a competitor saying the same about me, from his standpoint of denying women's political rights. The vocabulary of fault and deficiency can be used by each of us of the other. Indeed, someone might continue, to get past the idea of 'no fault' disagreement by using this response begs the question. It seeks to shore up the status of one value judgement by pointing out that people making it also typically make another related judgement of the same kind. But since the original doubt applied equally to the status of all such judgements, the response has no traction, and is illegitimate in this context.

To which the counter is that the so-called 'metaphysical' symmetry is itself beside the point. The question was whether there is no fault in holding that women have different political rights, and the answer remains that there is. The question was not whether there was a *metaphysical* fault in holding it. Why should there be? The issue is a moral and political one, not a metaphysical one.[3] To suppose overall symmetry because of alleged metaphysical symmetry is like saying that since metaphysics is silent about whether

---

[3] Someone might come to the wrong conclusion about the issue because of further, weird, metaphysics, but that is an optional extra.

Switzerland has a coastline, the view that it does is neither better nor worse than the view that it does not, and neither implies a fault in their proponents.

Nobody, of course, is going to make that mistake. So why is the corresponding move so common and so tempting in ethics? The answer, surely, is because the notions of real truth, or fact, or objectivity get in the way. We would like our opinion to be not just true—a compliment we can always pay it without extra cost in the same breath as that in which we voice it—but objectively true, and that, we imagine vaguely, implies the metaphysical asymmetry—the backing from real fact—that we have not got. Perhaps, then, it is the loss of that backing that Nietzsche is lamenting, and which is to leave him talking of fiction, perspective, error, and play? That would be very disappointing. Such a thought has an ancestry sure enough, but hardly one that would recommend it to Nietzsche, for it is exactly that which leads Plato to buttress the ethical abilities of the elect with knowledge of the Form of the Good. Here metaphysics is called in to underpin ethics, and if it cannot do so, then the alternatives will seem to be either the wholesale loss of ethics which is nihilism, or a piece of necessary self-deception, whereby we slightly desperately maintain the fiction that it can. A Nietzsche who follows that line would be betraying almost everything for which he is usually supposed to stand. It would be more than a little disappointing to find Nietzsche, the great freethinker, the supposed patron saint of postmodernism, the iconoclast, and the hawk-eyed critic of metaphysics, blown about in the same vortex of 'piffle and hot air' as Plato.[4] It would mean that he is far from emancipated from the late-nineteenth-century view that 'if God is dead, everything is permitted'—culturally explicable perhaps, but philosophically naive and boring.

A clearer view of everything that objectivity can be in ethics should prevent us wanting to knock at the door of visionaries and spirit-seers, or feeling that if we cannot do this, then as a substitute we have to concoct the fiction that we have done so. The right response is to recognize that objectivity comes from within. Looking at St Paul's objectively just means being careful of slant or distortion, taking account of tricks of light or other influences, bringing to bear such knowledge of Baroque architecture

---

[4] Especially, of course, given the dismissive association of Plato with Christianity, in Nietzsche 1968: §4. For the idea that Platonic Forms introduce piffle and hot air, see Aristotle, *Metaphysics*, 991a 21–2. A passage showing that Nietzsche was emancipated from these imaginings about objectivity is Nietzsche 1969: III. §12.

or Wren's career as we can muster. It does not mean averting our gaze from St. Paul's, and looking at something else (except, perhaps, en route to making comparisons). Similarly looking at the political situation of women objectively requires thinking of it as it is, adopting a common point of view, avoiding prejudice and bias, subjecting our own cultural prejudices to the best light we can. It does not mean panting for a Platonic or Gnostic illumination, to be got by looking at something other than the political situation of women. By making a fuss about the loss of metaphysical underpinning Nietzsche would in fact be collaborating with Plato's misunderstanding of our situation, even if his eventual resolution would be different.[5] Each of them would be imagining a need where there is in fact no need.

All that is required to say this is a certain confidence in the way things appear or the verdicts we incline to give. But we have not yet been given an argument for abandoning such confidence, so all is well. The dialectic, incidentally, shows not only that John Mackie's argument from relativism ultimately depends on the argument from 'metaphysical queerness'—for that alone justifies the sense that it would be queer if there were anything other than metaphysical symmetry between the rival perspectives—but also depends on subtly displacing the nature of the judgements with which we are concerned, by making them beholden to some imagined metaphysics, piffle and hot air, rather than to the ethics and politics, where they actually belong.

II

Does Nietzsche do better if we turn to the other two notions on our list, fiction and play? To focus our thoughts, let us concentrate on one famous passage, paragraph 107 of *The Gay Science* (Nietzsche 1974):

If we had not welcomed the arts and invented this kind of cult of the untrue, then the realization of general untruth and mendaciousness that now comes to us through science—the realization that delusion and error are conditions of human

[5] Aristotle was the first to charge that Plato invents the need for the Forms, and that nothing of their kind could be of any use (see also *Nic. Eth.* 1097a 8–11). I am not here taking sides on whether Plato himself might have meant something more innocent by talk of the Forms. On this, see Annas 1999: ch. 5. The point is that the other-worldly interpretation was common, and is clearly that of Nietzsche himself.

knowledge and sensation—would be utterly unbearable. *Honesty* would lead to nausea and suicide . . .

[P]recisely because we are at bottom grave and serious human beings—really more weights than human beings—nothing does us as much good as a *fool's cap*: we need it in relation to ourselves—we need all exuberant, floating, dancing, mocking, childish, and blissful art lest we lose the *freedom above things* that our ideal demands of us. It would mean a *relapse* for us, with our irritable honesty, to get involved entirely in morality and, for the sake of the over-severe demands we make on ourselves in these matters, to become virtuous monsters and scarecrows. We should be *able* also to stand *above* morality—and not only to *stand* with the anxious stiffness of a man who is afraid of slipping and falling at any moment, but also to *float* above it and *play*. How then could we possibly dispense with art—and with the fool? —And as long as you are in any way *ashamed* before yourselves, you do not yet belong with us.[6]

In the first part of this passage it is we ourselves who have 'welcomed the arts and invented this kind of cult of the untrue'. The implication is that this diagnoses our actual situation. But in the second part of the passage the focus seems to switch. Now Nietzsche is talking of an ideal, and the 'exuberant, floating, dancing, mocking, childish, and blissful' attitude that it demands of us. The implication in this case is that it is just the men of the future, Zarathustra and his followers, who manage to float above morality and instead play. Art will enable them to do so unashamed of themselves.

I do not want to offer any view about which emphasis accords better with the bulk of Nietzsche's views, but only to warn that they are different. The former purports to describe our situation as we are, fenced against nausea and suicide only by the arts, and by our cult of the untrue. The latter talks of a special kind of person, a playful, joyous, healthy soul for whom it would be a 'relapse' to get involved entirely with morality, thereby becoming a 'virtuous monster' or a 'scarecrow'. There is no implication that we are like this joyous soul, nor even that we could improve to become like it without a massive transformation and rebirth.

We come to this view in a moment, but meanwhile it is the former view that puts Nietzsche in contact with contemporary appeals to the notion of a fiction. Fictionalism comes in different forms, but let us take

---

[6] The importance of this passage, and the possibility of divergent interpretations of it, was impressed upon me by Jonathan Ichikawa and Bronwyn Singleton, in a session at the University of Toronto graduate colloquium in 2005.

it first as a *practically conservative* doctrine. That is, we suppose that it is presented as a piece of theory that leaves everyday practice untouched. It only gives us a better picture of how to think about it. This better picture in turn can be presented either as an explanation of how we *do* actually think about the area, an interpretation of where we are, or perhaps more realistically as a revisionary claim about how we *should* think about the area, but one which nevertheless leaves our actual practice in the area just as it found it. In practice, these may not be as far apart as they sound, since the motivation for revision would presumably have to lie somewhere in things we actually think, and conversely the argument for saying that we do actually think about the area in this surprising way would almost certainly have to be that this is the right, reasonable, way to think about it.

For an example of a practically conservative fictionalism, consider one attitude to the institution of money. The attitude would be one of insisting that money is a social construction, a normative practice that we make up for ourselves. And it might express this insight in terms of fiction (although for reasons we shall explore, this ought actually to sound off-key). If it did, we need not anticipate the theorist campaigning for the abolition of money, or taking less seriously his or her debts and dues. The normative practice will sail on, whatever the theorist says, and the theorist may not mind that at all. He might think that the fiction is just what was needed—what Leibniz would have called a *phenomenon bene fundatum*. The theory is only conceived as placing the practice, not as undermining it.

For another example, we might consider idealizations in science: point masses, perfect conductors, or frictionless planes. Suppose a theory is couched in such terms, but also used to generate predictions and explanations. A novice might be alarmed. But he might then be reassured if, for instance, the effect of the idealization is well understood, and any discrepancy with empirical reality outweighed by the convenience of calculation or modelling. After the reassurance, it may be that he can go on using the theory just as he did before the fictional character of the idealizations dawned on him. Nietzsche sometimes talks of fictions when idealization is on his mind. For example, the 'fiction' of identity through time with its alleged implication of changelessness seems to be an idealization abstracting from the fact that things change slowly enough for us to cope with them.[7] Faced with slowly changing things, perhaps we idealize and imagine ourselves surrounded by things in stasis (notice that this would not be a metaphysical fantasy, but a physical one). Understanding the role of such fictions may also leave practice untouched.

The contrast is with fictionalism as a *practically revisionary* doctrine: one whose appreciation penetrates the everyday practice, altering it in one direction or another. Nietzsche clearly thought that some of the things he wanted to say about morality were practically revisionary, and the emphasis on fiction seems to have been part of this campaign, so if he is a fictionalist at least sometimes it seems better to interpret him as a practically revisionist member of the species. And he would not be alone, for the idea that morality involves fiction clearly often consorts with practical revision. If someone like Bentham asserts that rights are a fiction, we expect practical consequences. We expect Bentham to argue for particular practical policies in different terms, as indeed he did. If someone asserts that free will and responsibility are fictions, we expect her subsequent ethics to take on a certain hue, and we might expect her penal code to be rather different from that of someone who insists on the reality of the notion.

Closer to more lurid interpretations of Nietzsche than that is the tradition of Thrasymachus and Callicles. This gives us the kind of dismissive fictionalism espoused by Richard III:

> Conscience is but a word that cowards use,
> Devis'd at first to keep the strong in awe:
>
> (Shakespeare, *Richard III*, V.iii.336–7)

Some writers seem to thrill most to an imagined Nietzsche as the heroic amoralist, dismissing the timid voice of conscience with triumphant will and force. They forget, as it were, that Richard III is a treacherous murderer at bay, and I believe they forget Nietzsche's fundamental seriousness.

It may not always be clear whether fictionalism ought to be taken as practically conservative, as practically revisionary, or as out and out dismissive. For example, some people are fond of saying that personal identity is a fiction. Well and good, but is the idea supposed to change the way I think about my future or how I relate to the people I care about,

---

[7] For instance, Nietzsche 1968: §3, 5.

and if so, how?[8] Or does it leave my expectations and concerns untouched? Some theologians are cheerful about the continuation of religious practice in spite of the admission that God is a fiction. Others are not, but think the admission undermines the whole point and purpose of their religious activities. These theologians think of their states of mind as *beliefs* and these beliefs are straightforwardly inconsistent with the discovery that what we apparently believe in is actually a fiction. The former kind think only of other supposed benefits of immersion in ritual practice, and the fictional status of their God is no problem.

When fictions are revisionary or dismissive of practice, I think we can suppose it is simply because some things have been shown to be a fiction, while by contrast others remain true. A worried defendant may be relieved to find that it is a fiction that she owes a plaintiff money, but this is because things would have been very different if it had been discovered to be true. She is not likely to be relieved if some constructivist or ontologically parsimonious philosopher comes as a witness, declaring that all money is a fiction. This does not win her the suit. But fiction here works by contrast: it is equivalent to falsity. It is much harder to interpret the idea that 'everything' is a fiction, or that all our practical reasoning depends on fiction. Why should such a thought, if it makes sense at all, nudge us towards one reaction rather than another? If we were attached to the Platonic fantasy, perhaps the discovery that we are, as it were, treading water rather than set on solid ground might disturb us. But it doesn't by itself instruct us in which direction to move. It doesn't say either that now women's political equality does matter, or that now it does not. Insofar as Nietzsche was campaigning for us to ditch specifically Christian ethics we need such a steer—a way of satisfying ourselves that compassion is a corrupt motive compared to egoism, for example. After all, Richard III retains a code of how kings are to behave: decisively, nobly, and courageously. But if all we were given were a generalized interpretation of ethics as fiction, no such practical partiality could follow (nor do I believe that Nietzsche thought it would). We might just as well conclude that pagan self-assertion is corrupt and Christianity is by comparison the way to go. In other words, perhaps as a moralist Nietzsche can persuade us that Christian ethics is

---

[8] Derek Parfit notoriously argued (Parfit 1984) that it should loosen our attachment to ourselves, but observation of the world suggests that few if any have found it doing so.

indeed slavish, or that pagan ethics is preferable. But if so, it will not be by deploying any generalized notion of a fiction. It will be by persuading us to set ourselves against some specific attitudes and stances and postures of the mind: compassion, humility, general benevolence, and the like. And this is a move within ethics, not a move out of it altogether.

Bernard Williams sympathized with what he takes to be Nietzsche's move out of 'morality'—the bit of ethics that comes with concepts of obligation and duty and thoughts about what I ought to do (see e.g. Williams 1993). But we need to specify the target more closely, because these do not depend especially upon any illusion or any fiction. Consider Hume's artificial virtues, of respect for promises and property. I said above that we should not automatically pass from the language of construction to that of fiction, and these provide a central example. They remind us that constructions of our own matter, and they may matter centrally by way of rules and obligations. That is why we create them. Money, for instance, is well described in terms of social construction, but badly described in terms of a fiction, as badly as are other constructions such as Buckingham Palace or the game of cricket. If together we go through certain actions, it is then not a fiction that I have borrowed ten dollars from you, or that I owe you ten dollars. And this gives the notion of obligation a perfectly satisfactory foothold, just as it gives you the right to pursue me or my estate for the sum. The debt would be a fiction only if the contract were bogus or you fraudulently made up the story of the transaction, but not all contracts are bogus, and not all transactions are made up. My thought that I ought to pay you back is not a groundless thought; on the contrary, it is perfectly grounded in the monetary doings that have got us where we are.

More accurately specified, Williams's target was slightly different, and it was also a target of Nietzsche's. Both thought that the attitudes associated with specifically Christian practical reasoning, notably guilt, depend on fictions about ourselves, and in particular the false idea that we are responsible 'all the way down' for what we do and who we are. This is 'incompatibilism', or the view that 'real' free will is incompatible with things we know about ourselves, but is itself integrally involved with 'moral' practice, and this view is certainly found in Nietzsche.[9] Myself, I believe

---

[9] See Nietzsche 1968: 'The Four Great Errors'. I owe thanks to Brian Leiter for discussion on this passage.

that in detail it turns out to be less than convincing. The free will we can have, namely responsiveness to reasons, is the only free will we need. But in any event, incompatibilism certainly does not infect obligation, duty, debt, and associated attitudes of rejection and resentment across the board. Our institutions of money and promises do not hinge on some fanciful and demanding metaphysics of freedom, any more than the rules of cricket or chess do, yet as I have argued they give us a perfectly satisfactory grounding for these notions. One idea might be that these are merely conditional sources of obligation, or sources only of 'hypothetical' obligations: ones that we can escape, rather as we can escape any obligations that the rules of cricket place upon us by refusing to play. But in that case the difference is not in the metaphysics of freedom, but in the fact that others may for good reason demand that we involve ourselves with money and promising, whether or not we would like to do so. Except in fantasy or emergency, belonging to a social world is not something we can opt out of with impunity. I explore this further in the following section.

III

In this section I consider the notion of play, as it appears to be an object of admiration in the quotation from *The Gay Science* given above. However, I certainly do not want to imply that it is a serious or central part of Nietzsche's overall message, or that the apparent implications of that passage are ones that are intended in full generality, or as a general recipe for living. Nevertheless, like the Calliclean Nietzsche, they may excite some readers. So they need confronting.

It sounds rather gorgeous to be a man of the future, a free spirit, 'exuberant, floating, dancing, mocking, childish, and blissful'. But just like the notion of a fiction, the notion of *play* seldom seems perfectly in place when we consider our practical lives. Children can indeed play at buying and selling and borrowing money from one another, but only by imitating some part of what adults do when they actually *do* buy and sell and borrow money from each other, and the same applies to morality. I can play at admonishing you for some deficiency, but only by imitating some part of what I would do were I actually to admonish you. If I am a good enough actor I can simulate the emotion of white-hot indignation, but only because real white-hot indignation exists as a model for me to draw upon. So in the second part of the quotation, what exactly is Nietzsche recommending to the disciples of Zarathustra, and does it make sense?

If he is recommending a generalized ludic attitude to life, I suspect that it makes sense only at first glance, when we might see something enviable in the Stoics' capacity to treat all life as a game, or in the casual laugh of the Rortian ironist. We may be familiar with the sociological perspective that 'everything is a game', just as we are familiar with Wittgenstein's constant invocation of games, together with his suggestion that the notion of a game is itself indefinable. Each idea may help us believe that we understand Nietzsche's recommendation. I deny that we do—or rather, if we do we ought to recognize not a noble aristocrat or brave Zarathustra, a free spirit of the future, but a perfect pest, an annoying idiot along the lines of Charles Dickens's character Harold Skimpole in *Bleak House*. Here is the flavour, with the moral touchstone Esther Summerson speaking:

I was reluctant to enter minutely into that question; but as he begged I would, for he was really curious to know, I gave him to understand, in the gentlest words I could use, that his conduct seemed to involve a disregard of several moral obligations. He was much amused and interested when he heard this, and said, 'No, really?' with ingenuous simplicity.

'You know I don't intend to be responsible. I never could do it. Responsibility is a thing that has always been above me—or below me,' said Mr Skimpole. 'I don't even know which; but, as I understand the way in which my dear Miss Summerson (always remarkable for her practical good sense and clearness) puts this case, I should imagine it was chiefly a question of money, do you know?'

This by way of defence against Esther's contempt at him for betraying little Jo after being bribed by the police. Skimpole's character is real enough: it is an exasperated satire on the improvident and sponging Leigh Hunt. But his professions of childishness, his pose of being a mere spectator of life, his whimsical, mock-innocent stance towards the business of living, is far from an ideal, and Dickens has a great deal of fun with him, before finally dismissing him as a mere nothing. Insofar as Skimpole is blissful, and not just pretending to be, it has to be at the expense of any adult life, and in particular any normal humanity.[10] Red-blooded (or adolescent) admirers of Nietzsche may initially seize upon Skimpole as a fictional model of the manly, pagan, expulsion of compassion, but Dickens's own attitude is very different. In one episode among many, when Skimpole puts forward his gospel of merely pretending to pay the butcher, but expecting real meat in return, he is exposed as a thorough nuisance, not a hero. Nietzsche may not think much of English moralists in general, but here, at least, one of them is on solid ground.

Perhaps in taking Skimpole as a model, I am taking the notion of play too literally, whereas Nietzsche is more commonly associated with the tradition already mentioned, of Thrasymachus or Callicles or Richard III, for whom life is a nasty, bitter, dog-eat-dog business, not play at all. No doubt this is right, but it is still important to follow through what happens if we take the reference to play and bliss seriously. For they are not, I think, accidentally connected in many people's minds, and perhaps on and off in Nietzsche's, with the omnipresence of fiction and the recommended emancipation from conscience.

In a remarkable study, Bernard Suits ruminates on the life of the grasshopper, contrasted with that of the ant as a model of the life of play.[11] Notwithstanding Wittgenstein he gives highly illuminating analysis of the notion of a game. To play a game, Suits argues, is

to engage in activity directed towards bringing about a specific state of affairs, using only means permitted by rules, where the rules prohibit more efficient in favour of less efficient means, and where such rules are accepted just because they make possible such activity.[12]

The four elements involved are ends, means, rules, and the attitude of the players, the acceptance of the rules just because they make possible the activity (which then becomes a further end in itself). Suits defends his analysis against worries derived from many sources: games taken dead seriously, games whose ends are themselves defined in terms of rules, pure make-believe play, games played professionally or for the sake of

---

[10] His rather horrible indifference to the plight of others, including children, is portrayed throughout.
[11] Suits 1978. I would like to thank Tom Hurka for drawing this neglected tour-de-force to my attention.
[12] Ibid. 34.

psychological rewards, solitary games, and so on. A striking consequence of the account is that the 'lusory attitude' of the game-player is bound to be one of only conditional commitment: among human beings a game is an activity whose pursuit is set as an option within the background matrix of a life with needs and commitments that may at any time trump it.

In Suits's tale, the grasshopper has a dream in which he goes about persuading everyone that the activities of life are all really games. And in his dream, the moment people become persuaded of this, they vanish. His fable is an extended meditation on the meaning of this dream, which is that a life of pure play is not for human beings. This is not to suggest that a life of pure play is unimaginable. Indeed, Suits argues that game-playing is the only thing left to do in Utopia, where there are no unfulfilled needs, and where no instrumental activities remain. A Utopian might decide, for instance, to build himself a house, but the 'difference in quality' between his activity and ours is that his activity has no external instrumental value (in Utopia you can come to possess houses by snapping your fingers) and meets no unfulfilled need. Hence, it could exist only for the sake of the activity itself, and then becomes a pure option, like the solving of a puzzle, and is to be categorized as an instance of game-playing:

Thus all the things we now regard as trades, indeed all instances of organized endeavour whatever, would, if they continued to exist in Utopia, be sports. So that in addition to hockey, baseball, golf, tennis and so on, there would also be the sports of business administration, jurisprudence, philosophy, production management, motor mechanics *ad*, for all practical purposes, *infinitum*. (Suits 1978: 175)

But human beings are not grasshoppers, and in our actual lives these activities are not games. And in spite of the charm of utopias, it is doubtful if things would be better if we could jump free of our needs, so that they became only games. Setting ourselves games to play does not even stave off ennui for very long (let alone eternity).

This is not the place to explore all the ramifications of this account. Nor do I want to defend it to the last detail. However, it is plausible enough and offers enough insight into the notion of a game and of play for us to test the recommendation that we treat life as play against it. And as we might expect, the recommendation does not seem to stand up very well. Essentially, a life of play has to be a life without *needs* and without *unconditional commitments*. But this is unrecognizable as a human life, and only even works as an ideal so long as it is not thought through.

So we are forced to conclude that vocabulary of floating and mocking and putting on a fool's cap needs to be taken with a pinch of salt. You can mock needs and unconditional commitments only so long as you have neither, and while people can occupy such a state for a short period, and while as Stoics or ironists or even artists (of a certain kind) they may pretend to it for longer, it does not take much to puncture the balloon.

I do not actually believe that Nietzsche is recommending a generalized ludic attitude to life. It may be salutary to compare the passage from *The Gay Science* with *Beyond Good and Evil*, especially paragraphs 225 to 227. Here he is talking of a concern with what mankind could be, favourably contrasted with mere sympathy with rotten old humanity as it is:

Our sympathy is a loftier and further-sighted sympathy:—we see how *man* dwarfs himself, how *you* dwarf him! and there are moments when we view *your* sympathy with an indescribable anguish, when we resist it,—when we regard your seriousness as more dangerous than any kind of levity . . .

Honesty, granting that it is the virtue of which we cannot rid ourselves, we free spirits—well, we will labour at it with all our perversity and love, and not tire of 'perfecting' ourselves in *our* virtue, which alone remains: may its glance some day overspread like a gilded, blue, mocking twilight this aging civilization with its dull gloomy seriousness!   (Nietzsche 1997: 93–4)

Here the 'levity' and the mockery are those which come from unflinching awareness of life as it is, more like those of Swift or Pope than Harold Skimpole, and this is surely the tone and the moral complexion of Nietzsche himself. As he tells us, it is only 'fools and appearances' that say of such characters that these are men without duty.

IV

I have not had much good to say about errors, fictions, and play. They are notions needed only by philosophies that misunderstand what ethics is and why we have it, and who find it convenient to read that misunderstanding in Nietzsche. But we can extract the seeds of a much better philosophy of value from the notion of a point of view, or a perspective, provided this is used with care. So first a warning. It is not that we should take perceptual vocabulary very seriously, when we look for a philosophy of value. Indeed, when we hear philosophers talking of sensitivities, perceptual capacities, recognition of demands, and generally assimilating the state of the *phronimos* to that of a well-tuned observer, we need to ask how literally the visual analogies are intended. And we need to give the warning that they should not be intended literally at all. Moral facts, or interpretations, are not objects of sight, any more than they are objects of hearing or touch or taste. The senses are involved only in that it is the world we cope with and care about, and it is also the things of the world that we see, hear, or touch. Duties and obligations are not among them. It is right, of course, to talk sometimes of seeing or hearing facts as well as things. But while you can see or hear that something is near or far, hidden or in the open, you cannot literally see that ingratitude is a vice, any more than you can hear it or taste it. Rather, the judgement is the upshot of a stance, attitude, or posture of the mind: the dispositions of a practical engagement with the world, not a mere responsiveness to the way of the world. Indeed, if we were talking of mere responsiveness, the 'argument from relativism' would be more of a threat, encouraging the worry that since there are so many responses which therefore must be illusory, perhaps they all are. The argument from queerness would be more of a threat, encouraging the worry that we have no business to convince ourselves of the importance of 'things' that cannot be seen and touched. But no such worries attend the forthright understanding that what we voice are our own attitudes, and what we stand on as we do so is our own feet.

However, our practical dispositions give us something analogous to a point of view or a perspective. They give us a practical centre from which things dominate or subside, loom or fade in practical importance. The perspective of someone to whom something looms as important is indeed different from that of someone to whom it is trivial, and if something must be done, then they will be in disagreement as to what it is. As these practical concerns matter, we express our values and our ethics, our admirations and detestations, and the boundaries to behaviour that we insist upon and the spaces for it that we permit. There is no error in that, and as we have seen, we are not usually playing either. Requiring conduct of others, sanctioning them for failures, worrying about our own projects and plans, is typically about as far from play as can be imagined—as far as the consequences of going wrong, such as prison or war. Nor are we always imagining things, or making them up, or telling stories, any more than we are always imagining debts, or making up fictions about our needs, or telling fantasies about past gifts or slights. But my practical centre is in a slightly different place from yours, meaning that our different perspectives have to be engaged and negotiated as we look for a shared or general point of view. It is not easy to know how to think and feel, or what to do.

Nietzsche is of course right to be alert to signs of unhealth, and no doubt in the late nineteenth century he was right to smell it as even more pervasive than at present. There are indeed virtuous monsters and scarecrows, and the self-righteousness of the moralist can obviously cloak all kinds of human flaw. An over-inflated superego is not a lovable thing, while simple stupidity leads people to mount 'crusades against evil', and we need not look far to find cruelties and hatreds, self-loathing, boredom, disgust, and contempt, the desire for revenge or power, the hypocrisy and cunning of the slave. Perhaps the world would be better if we fenced ourselves round with fewer boundaries, and policed them with less enthusiasm. But if this is the problem, the solution is not an end to morality, but a better morality. Discount some of the rhetoric and the false starts, and we can perhaps find that this is what Nietzsche thought as well.[13]

---

[13] I owe thanks to the discussants at Richard Schacht and Michael Moore's outstanding Nietzsche colloquium at the University of Madison in 2003. I particularly recall contributions by Maudemarie Clark, Nadeem Hussein, John Richardson, and R. Lanier Anderson. Brian Leiter carefully steered me away from pitfalls in the interpretations of Nietzsche, and I am solely responsible for any tumbles I have nevertheless taken.

II

Language and Epistemology

9

The Steps from Doing to Saying

Rudolf Carnap wrote that

we must distinguish two kinds of questions of existence: first, questions of the existence of certain entities of the new kind *within the framework*; we call them *internal questions*; and second, questions concerning the existence or reality *of the system of entities as a whole*, called *external questions*. Internal questions and possible answers to them are formulated with the help of the new forms of expressions. The answers may be found either by purely logical methods or by empirical methods, depending upon whether the framework is a logical or a factual one. An external question is of a problematic character which is in need of closer examination. (Carnap 1958: 204)

The exact nature of this 'problematic character' is left undetermined by Carnap. He is clearly drawn partly to dismissing external questions as metaphysical, and therefore requiring no attention, but he is also drawn to seeing them as questions of attitude or policy: practical questions, for which the answer would be given in terms of the benefits of the framework in question. This has suggested to me a template for thinking about pragmatism in general, which I distil into the following suggestion. You will be a pragmatist about an area of discourse if you pose a Carnapian external question: How does it come about that we go in for this kind of discourse and thought? What function does it serve, and what therefore is the explanation of this bit of our language game? And then:

(1) you offer an explanation of what we are up to in going in for this discourse, and

(2) the explanation eschews any use of the referring expressions of the discourse; any appeal to anything that a Quinean would identify as the values of the bound variables if the discourse is regimented; or any semantic or ontological attempt to 'interpret' the discourse

in a domain, to find referents for its terms, or truth makers for its sentences. Instead:

(3) the explanation proceeds by talking in different terms of what is done by so talking, or by offering a revelatory psychology or genealogy or anthropology or even a just-so story about how this mode of talking and thinking and practising came about and the functions it serves.

I do not offer this as a prescriptive, defining description of pragmatism old or new. Some thinkers who like the label may reject the whole enterprise of answering a Carnapian external question, rather than giving an answer of a certain shape to it. Quine, who thought of himself as a pragmatist, disliked the whole external/internal distinction. But I find that it helps me to draw up a rough map of some of our more important philosophical alternatives. It also makes close contact with the way things are seen by prominent neo-pragmatists such as Michael Williams, Huw Price, and Bob Brandom. While Brandom calls his latest work *Between Doing and Saying*, the motto for my Wittgensteinian approach to things might be '*from* doing to saying': place the discourse in amongst life's activities, and you will gain a perspicuous representation of what is said when you use it.

To get a sense of the contrast, we might imagine the difference between a Wittgensteinian approach to the philosophy of mathematics, and a more standard set-theoretic approach. The Wittgensteinian tries to give a 'perspicuous representation' of our activities with mathematical discourse, perhaps in terms of familiar doings such as measuring out bricks or planning floor spaces or keeping track of money. He starts with applied mathematics, in other words, and hopes to see fully fledged systems of arithmetic as functioning as abstractions serving to book-keep for these homely activities. The contrast would be with an approach which takes 'reference to numbers' as a datum, and then puzzles over what numbers might be, how we might know about them, and why we should want to. Carnap's fears that such thought will prove too 'metaphysical' obviously hover around such an enterprise, and continue to hover even if we propose the reduction of all mathematical entitites to sets. Clearly we get the same shape of approach with expressivism in modal and normative or evaluative contexts, so called 'subjective' approaches to probability, expressive or even secondary quality approaches to causal thought, and many others.

Put this way, the natural opposite to a pragmatist approach might be described as referentialism or representationalism or in some equivalent terms, for instance, as providing a truth-conditional semantics or an 'account' of what makes true sayings in the area. But this way of putting the opposition needs careful handling, for deflationism in semantics introduces an awkward guest, and some would say a cuckoo in the nest.

Initially deflationism is a valuable ally of pragmatism. One of the salient features of any assertoric discourse is that we are free with the idioms of truth and of 'talking about' things, or in other words reference and representation. If I tell you that there is a chair in the kitchen, what I say is true under definite conditions, and we naturally say that I referred to the kitchen, represented it as containing a chair, and in a more general vein I was talking about how things stand. But the same is true when I talk about the distribution of prime numbers or the value of gratitude or the impossibility of perpetual motion. Abstract, modal, and normative vocabulary bedeck themselves just as naturally as any other with a propositional appearance and the associated semantic trimmings. But to the deflationist, this is no surprise and signifies no sinister flirtation with metaphysics. The vocabulary of truth is doing what it always does, and the vocabulary of representation the same.

Following Horwich (1990), I take deflationism in the theory of truth to be a combination of three theses:

(A) That there is complete cognitive equivalence between Tp and p;
(B) That conforming to that equivalence is all that is required to manifest complete understanding of the truth predicate;
(C) That the utility of the predicate is purely logical: it is a device of indirect reference and generalization.

The equivalence and the utility are the same whatever our subject matter. So if we are true to the folk, rather than seeking to debunk their sincere and intended sayings, or convict them of wholesale error in even deploying their favoured vocabularies, we will end up applying talk of truth and representation to whatever vehicles these sayings provide for the folk to travel in. For with truth comes a fully-fledged vocabulary of representation: when we speak truly we represent things as being thus-and-so, and the things we so represent are the things referred to or quantified over in our sayings.

In particular, notice that the word 'description' can go into the deflationist pot along with 'representation'. We describe how things stand with norms and values, possible worlds, or numbers and sets. We believe the results of our descriptions. Hence what Robert Kraut calls the 'bifurcation theses' between descriptive and non-descriptive uses of language itself goes into the deflationist mix, and is apparently dissolved as effectively as truth, reference, and represention (Kraut 1990). Other contrasts, such as that between belief and attitude, may go the same way. For there is nothing to prevent a theorist from allowing a promiscuous, catholic, universal notion of 'belief'—one that simply tags along with assertion, acceptance or commitment. But in that case, ask critics, what room is left in which to make pragmatism into something distinctive (Dreier 2002; Sinclair 2007)?

These points indeed show that it does not lie in where you end up. After deflationism, an expressivist, for instance, just as much as a Wittgensteinian in arithmetic or a Humean about causation, will be indistinguishable from anybody else in his everyday deployment of the relevant vocabulary. But we must not look only at the finishing line, after the race is run. Rather, whatever is distinctive comes in the route whereby you get to where you end up: the perspicuous representation that enables the pragmatist to put *sufficient* weight on the functions associated with the discourse to avoid putting *any* weight on the metaphysical imaginings that it might threaten to engender. It may be that any assertoric use of language associates itself with the same all-embracing semantic terms. Deflationism certifies as much. But the best functional story explaining how we ended up where we are may have a much finer grain. So, for instance, a perspicuous representation of how we have a descriptive-sounding evaluative language may itself eschew any truck with description, reference, facts or truth-makers but use as its only building blocks humdrum situations of choosing, preferring, recommending, or needing. Its promise is that with attention to these activities we come to see how our evaluative descriptions of things need no truck with the idea that we somehow respond to an autonomous realm of values: a metaphysical extra that we inexplicably care about on top of voicing and discussing our more humdrum concerns. It is here that a fine-grained distinction between, say, describing and desiring will have its place, and similarly for the plurality of functions associated with mathematics, modal assertions, normative assertions, and causal and dynamic assertions. All that the pluralisms of function would say is that we have to look below the surface, to see what belief *amounts to* in this area or that—Wittgenstein's 'I'll show you differences'. If you want to call the result 'belief', well and good—but it won't necessarily be much like belief in other areas. And, I would say, if the content of these beliefs is sufficiently removed from *explanation* in the Carnapian external context, then these beliefs can equally properly, and metaphysically much more illuminatingly, be thought of in other terms.

For the rest of this essay I want to compare the story I have developed with pragmatism as it is presented in more ambitious writings, which see it as a global recipe for a particular approach to meaning and use. The idea derives from Wilfrid Sellars, and in the hands of Brandom and Price says that an account of *use* can be given across the board, and that itself explains, in general, the meanings we manage to give to our sayings (Brandom 2008; Price 2010). However, within that broad camp there are differences: Price, for instance is a self-confessed functional pluralist, just like my pragmatists, whereas Brandom shows less interest in differences of function, apparently holding instead that a blanket account of assertoric function will do all the explanatory work that is necessary to give a full account of meaning adequate to any area whatsoever. This suggests not so much an alliance as a wholesale takeover of the territory occupied by functional pluralists, albeit by a global company with a cognate set of interests.

Even so, as with my Carnapian pragmatism, we have to start with some ingredients. The ingredients Brandom allows himself in order to characterize use in a way that fuels his project include activities of inference, and of criticism: a 'social deontic' world suggested, at least, by the idea of 'score keeping in a language game', where the game is one of making and rejecting inferences to and from individual sayings. The inferences in question are not purely logical inferences, but any of the wider class of material inferences, since these are a salient part of our linguistic behaviour and as much a target for endorsement or criticism as any of the much rarer class of logically valid inferences.

In spite of its auspicious pedigree, however, the notion of a language game is not really appropriate. Our inferential moves do not belong to a self-contained game, existing only for the pleasure that can be given by conforming to the constitutive rules that make up the activity, which I regard as the essential characteristic of a game. Nor is a harvest in which we only gather first the syntax of peoples' sayings, and then norms governing what they permit to be inferred from what else, sufficiently rich to bake the bread of semantics. The quick way of seeing that is to recognize that even if the social-deontic norms allow us to locate the logical constants and to conjecture their meanings, and allow us as well to distinguish out names and predicates, it is still bound to be true that if they are interpretable at all in some domain, then they can be interpreted in any of innumerable domains of the same cardinality. You simply cannot conjure semantics out of syntax. Hence inferentialists are driven to add some recognition of the landscape in which people's engagement with the world is more to the fore: fundamental use properties (Horwich 1998), or 'indication relations' (Field 1994).

In Brandom's richer treatment this means adding explicit recognition of a version of Wilfrid Sellars's entry and exit rules: starting with 'the practical involvement with objects exhibited by a sentient creature dealing skillfully with its world', progressing through a cycle of perception, performance, and assessment of results, and then further processes of 'feedback-governed performances', serving as the basis for the 'special case' of the practical intentionality exhibited by these transactions, which is semantic intentionality (Brandom 2008: 178–9). Such practices, he insists, are 'thick, in the sense of essentially involving objects, events, and worldly states of affairs. Bits of the world are *incorporated* in such practices, in the exercise of such abilities' (2008: 178). Such practices, we might add, are also far from games: they make up the serious business of life for any sentient creature.

Pragmatism is thus left only to fill in the space between any old sentient creature coping skilfully with its world, and specifically linguistic or semantic creatures, able to deploy the resources of language in order to aid that task. This may reasonably seem to be quite a diminution of its sphere of influence. For example, the creature coping skilfully with its world may be supposed to exhibit phenomena of attention, memory, and recognition, each of which seem to be at least as important an ingredient in a burgeoning notion of reference as any phenomenon, such as anaphora, that emerges from thinking solely about permissible or mandatory patterns of inference. The referents of its terms are ready to be picked out by its patterns of action, including the patterns of feedback that identify what counts as its success in action, or achievement of its purposes.

Bringing in the subject's worldly involvements in its world of desire and motivation, practice, and fulfilment is bringing in a great deal. Indeed, it makes pragmatism of this kind, with this much enrichment, quite difficult to distinguish from, say, a Davidsonian account of the business of the radical interpreter. To identify a practice, in Brandom's rich sense, is already to identify what counts as a perception or observation, as success in action, and as a modification of strategy in the light of success or failure. It is to endow the subject with a psychology, leaving only the task of mopping up the interpretation of any signals that seem to aid the social regulation and coordination of the psychologies of conspecifics with which it cooperates or competes. The Davidsonian radical interpreter triangulating holistically is using the same data in the same way. Yet Davidson is often offered as an example of someone advocating a theory based on truth conditions and therefore standing at some distance from modern pragmatism. It is desirable to understand that this opposition, at least, is much less substantial than it might have seemed.

It might seem that Brandom's emphasis on material inference, with no initial basis from which to distinguish strictly logical inference, makes his project different from anything in Davidson. But it is hard to believe that in the end this makes such a difference. Any emphasis on material inference must eventually be tempered by the requirement that people who have even quite extensively different beliefs about things can nevertheless be interpreted as sharing a language, or meaning the same by their words (this is why their beliefs can clash). As the initial debates between realists such as the then Putnam, and radical incommensurabilists in the philosophy of science showed a long time ago, shared reference is an interpretative move that can properly be imposed precisely to curb the idea that a small divergence in inferential pattern immediately suggests a large collapse of shared meaning. Pragmatists must, therefore, acknowledge something like a Quinean division between centre and periphery, and it takes little more than that, coupled with the isolation of logical vocabulary applied in any area and in connection with patterns of inference that may recur with any subject matter, to reinstate a much more realistic conception of sharing a language. But again, it will not be one that separates such an approach to meaning from that other descendant of Quine, Davidson.

Be these things as they may, the element I wish to highlight is rather different. Suppose we ask exactly *which* bits of the world are incorporated in the exercise of these abilities that make up practical intentionality? Some, we might surmise, will be much harder to do without than others.

Surrounding trees and rocks, prey and predators, will no doubt be parts of our practice, but what about the necessity of one event following another, or the duty to love our children, or the number 42? I have little idea how Brandom would answer such questions, but a natural line would bring him into closer alliance with Price, and with me. This natural line would recognize that a description of the sentient situation will necessarily employ some environmental landmarks, and for human beings in particular it will see us as surrounded by middle-sized dry goods, distinguished by features that are irresistibly borne in on us in the normal deployment of our senses (the objects for which, as evolutionary adaptations, the senses are fitted). These are things which, in Price's terminology, give rise to what he calls one of the 'attractors' of the undifferentiated idea of representation that he describes as environmental representation or e-representation. Cleaving to deflationism, Price does not think that e-representation exhausts the idea of representation: the other attractor for the notion is the inferentialist notion, or in more general terms the promiscuous deflationist notion we have already saluted.

We now see room for a rapprochement between the Carnapian pragmatist and the post-Sellarsian camp. The route to metaphysics opens up precisely when the notion of the 'environment' is expanded sufficiently to include any old thing: properties, classes, numbers, propositions, values, norms, abstracta, necessities. But there is no reason, if we want to understand our cognitive functioning in terms that are remotely naturalistic, for doing that. It is confusing items which it may be reasonable to call 'parts of our world'—for after all we talk in terms of them—with items which are 'just there anyway': parts of *the* world in which we must inescapably see ourselves placed if we are to give any remotely realistic yet naturalistically economical account of human cognitive functioning, or the human situation.

I do not see this development as in any sense hostage to what are vaguely referred to as the 'rule-following considerations'. By stressing the contingencies underlying all our classifications, Wittgenstein's discussion certainly has the potential to alter the way we look at ourselves (even if, as some commentators suppose, only by warding off philosophical mistakes responsible for erroneous ways in which we might look at ourselves). But adding the equivalent of 'that's how we look at it' or 'that's what we say' after all our sayings is a wearisome game, and as Wittgenstein himself insisted, does nothing to obliterate working distinctions between what we find ourselves having to say, and what we can more or less easily imagine ourselves not saying, or not having said at some historical juncture, or not being about to say in the future (Wittgenstein 1969). And as I have argued at length elsewhere, the rule-following considerations most certainly did not, for Wittgenstein, operate as a 'metaphysical wet blanket' smothering distinctions within language, and muting all its rainbow hues into a uniform muddy brown of response dependency (see also Essay 11).

However, closely allied to the rule-following considerations is the thought that different parts of discourse blend into each other, or that there is no 'disentangling' leaving us an area of clean fact, and a distinct area of clean value, or in the empirical case a world of clean 'is' and a world of clean 'must be', or natural or causal law. This latter entanglement is saluted by Brandom as a major discovery of Kant, reinforced by Sellars: 'the ability to use ordinary empirical descriptive terms such as "green", "rigid", and "mass" already presupposes grasp of the kinds of properties and relations made explicit by modal vocabulary' (Brandom 2008: 96–7). According to Brandom, Sellars saw that this licensed the idea that modal vocabulary makes explicit what is already implicit in the inferential powers associated with more ordinary items of vocabulary. To say that a cat necessarily has weight, for instance, makes explicit an inferential licence already possessed by anyone understanding the concept of a cat and of weight. Such an idea clearly has the potential to undermine any kind of simple empiricism, and any kind of simple foundationalism. On the other hand, it does not have the potential to undermine the distinctness of the contribution the modal element is making to the concept in question: this is why the Kantian thesis is worth stating (and the only reason that it can be stated). Similar remarks apply to the factual and the evaluative. Even if it could be established that, as it is put metaphorically by Hilary Putnam, values everywhere cast at least a little shade of pink over the grey of fact, this would not stop it being true that by so doing they do something distinctive and something that it is important to distinguish if we are to make explicit the architecture of cognition.

Environmental representation is essentially a matter of causal co-variation. It can be thought of by comparing ourselves with the instruments we build to co-vary with environmental states: petrol gauges, voltmeters, windsocks, and so forth. What the rule-following considerations can remind us is that this is not a matter of wholesale opposition between the space of causes and the space of reasons. One of the functions of our cognitive machinery is to monitor our own capacities as input/output devices, and this is where

Brandom's notion of iterated episodes of feedback and adjustment is useful. I may be aware, for instance, that a verdict on the state of the world has not just popped into my head, but was the result of my having placed myself intelligently into a situation in which that verdict would not have resulted had the world not been thus-and-so. Or, I may entertain doubts whether I did indeed do this, and adjust my confidence accordingly, or go and look another time, or go over my notes again, or whatever is required. In this way I can monitor my own functioning: applied to myself, the question, 'Did I dream it up or am I remembering seeing it?' is much the same as the question asked of a voltmeter, 'Is it stuck at this reading, or is it co-varying its output with the input in the way in which it is supposed to do?' And in each case the empirical investigation of the question proceeds in much the same way. We look for evidence of causal receptivity, and if it is lacking we may take steps to improve the instrumentation operating on the subject matter. Kant was right that without such a grounding in our own reception of causal impacts from the immediate environment, the whole world of thought would be empty. The spaces of causation and reason cannot therefore be separated: by seeing ourselves as reasoning beings we do not stop ourselves from being at the same time natural animals.

Let us return to the pragmatic approach to particular metaphysical danger areas. We now decide to treat some part of what we say not in terms of environment—but how, then? What is the contrast, and how, having started with the contrast, do we regain entry into the world of 'inferential representation' or in other words aptness for assessment as true and false, and the resulting right to wear any semantic vocabulary that we care to deploy? Approaching this question takes us into the domain of what I christened 'quasi-realism', although I no longer like the connotation of 'as if', which does endless amounts of trouble, nor the implication that 'realism' is a well-developed 'ism' which can and should be imitated. Nevertheless, the task is properly identified. It is that of getting from some kind of *doing*, now thought of as the function of the sayings in question, to being comfortable with their assertoric status or propositional clothing—their fit into the domains of truth and falsity. And this territory must be crossed without supposing that the doing in question is one of responding to an environment of an enriched kind: a modal or moral environment, for example. For that is precisely the kind of explanation that would explode the pretension to pragmatism and open the door to metaphysics once more.

It seems to me, as it has always done, that the right approach must be to see what happens if we do without the propositional surface. Suppose we did not have this piece of vocabulary; in what way would our practices be hampered? Provided the cost is identifiable and we therefore can be seen to have had a motivation to avoid it, then the way should be open to see ourselves, precisely, as having done just enough in order to avoid it. We can see ourselves as having enriched our inferential practices or our dealings with the world, without having licensed the philosopher to enrich our conception of the world with which we are dealing.

I think it is not often recognized (or perhaps it is a question of myself having been slow to recognize) that far from threatening this project, deflationism itself offers an example of the very same strategy in action. We have already placed deflationism as giving a logical, i.e. inferential, role to the truth predicate. And this supersedes any idea that the predicate serves to introduce some arcane property or relation to which we are equally mysteriously sensitive. But this is exactly an example of the strategy about which I am talking (see also essay 2 in this volume).

Now consider the 'good' predicate. What would be the cost of doing without it? The second clause in deflationism about truth gives the cognitive equivalence that establishes the conditions for understanding the truth predicate. The natural equivalent clause for the 'good' predicate would be that in a straightforward application to an identified subject, such as someone's action or character, you assent to the assertion using it if and only if you are disposed to endorse, choose, recommend, or otherwise practically orientate yourself in favour of the action or the character. And then the story of function proceeds in parallel with the alethic case: we can now generalize and refer indirectly, talking of John's good deed (without telling you what it was he did), saying that everything John did was good or that John's character is spotlessly good, and so forth. In other words, we now bring the practical orientation into the sphere of the propositional, ready to take its place either as the conclusion or as a premise in inference. If used as a premise, then its eventual output may be other approvals, or a modification of beliefs, or whatever else the addition of the proposition may do to affect inferences downstream of it. If we are 'on line', or in other words asserting the proposition, then the output is itself primed to be on line. If we are 'off line' or merely playing with the approval in our imagination, then the proposition is put into inferences as a supposition, which may or may not be discharged, exactly like any other.

Giving this kind of pragmatic story about the role of certain propositions—for we can now use the term in good faith—does not diminish the care they deserve nor our responsibility for verdicts cast in their terms, or in other words, our responsibility for doing our best to get them right. If I say that a proposition is necessary when it is not or that an act is obligatory when a better verdict would say that it is not, then my intellectual or practical life is set to go wrong. I would be insisting too much, since the verdict of necessity plays the role of ruling out alternatives, and this may be a very bad thing indeed to do. So self-scrutiny is just as urgent in any such case as it is anywhere else.

There are things which little companies do better before they are taken over by large conglomerates. I hope I have done something to defend the idea that the piecemeal investigation of different uses of language, of the kind suggested so forcibly by Wittgenstein, may be more fruitful than acceptance of the prairie landscape insisted on by those global behemoths, realism and pragmatism.

10

Success Semantics

How come we are so successful, unless we are hooked up right to the world? A good question, and one that suggests a way of thinking of our hook-up to the world. Success semantics is the result of that suggestion. It is the view that a theory of *success in action* is a possible basis for a theory of *representation*, or a theory of *content* or *intentionality* (throughout this essay I shall use these interchangeably). At its most simple we can think of representation in terms of disquotation, as in the famous 'Fido'–Fido relationship. Then the idea is that the disquotation of representation is explained or illuminated or even analysed by the disquotation of explanation, where whatever is represented explains something about the person representing it. And what it explains is primarily the success of the actions that the person bases upon the representing.

The view is an heir to the pragmatist tradition. At the most general level, the idea is that we get our way, or flourish, or fulfil our desires or our needs because we get things right about the world. The contents of our sentences are then whatever it is that we get right.

The ancestor of success semantics, as of so much else, is Frank Ramsey, who wrote that it is right to talk of a chicken's belief that a certain sort of caterpillar is poisonous if the chicken's actions were such as to be useful if, and only if, the caterpillars were actually poisonous. 'Thus any set of actions for whose utility p is a necessary and sufficient condition might be called a belief that p, and so would be true if p, i.e. if they are useful' (Ramsey 1990: 144). Ramsey did not develop the idea, and it may even be doubted whether his chicken was thought of in representative terms at all. Perhaps it was a primitive precursor of a representing agent. But the idea is too tempting to let lie. It was later picked up and paraphrased, by Jamie Whyte, in terms of the truth condition of a belief being that condition that guarantees the success of desires based on that belief (Whyte 1990: 147).

But the idea that the truth condition of a belief would be whatever *guarantees* success in action based on the belief meets trouble, because nothing at all guarantees such success. X's belief may have the truth condition that Cambridge is NNE of London, and X may act on that belief, yoking it to his other belief that the way to travel NNE out of London is to take the first departure from Paddington. X lands up in Bristol, failing in his desire to get to Cambridge.[1] This suggests that no fact guarantees success in action, because even when an agent apprehends a fact correctly, there may be an indefinite amount of other rubbish in her head, waiting to misdirect action based upon it. This is the familiar holism of the mental. And there may also be an indefinite number of things not wrong with the agent, as in this example, but wrong with the environment: unknown and unthought-of obstacles waiting to trip her up.

Recently, Jérôme Dokic and Pascal Engel have attempted to protect the Ramsey–Whyte view against these difficulties (Dokic and Engel 2002: 46). Their idea is to bring into view the whole range of actual and possible desires that might join with a given belief, and to suggest that 'true beliefs are those that lead to successful action whatever the underlying motivating desires'. They quote approvingly Ruth Millikan, who says of percepts of the world:

> The same percept of the world may be used to guide any of very many and diverse activities, practical or theoretical. What stays the same is that the percept must correspond to environmental configurations in accordance with the same correspondence rules for each of these activities. For example, if the position of the chair in the room does not correspond, so, to my visual representation of its position, that will hinder me equally in my attempts to avoid the chair when passing through the room, to move the chair, to sit in it, to remove the cat from it, to make judgements about it, and so on.   (Quoted in Dokic and Engel 2002: 46)

However, although Millikan is right that a false belief (here, a percept that does not represent a position correctly) stands ready to *wreck* an indefinite number of projects, it does not follow that a true percept similarly stands ready to *guarantee* the success of an indefinite number of projects, whatever the underlying desires. 'Guarantee' remains too strong. Taken strictly, the Paddington case alone falsifies the view that my saying about Cambridge, 'It's NNE of London,' represents the fact that it does. For with this desire it

---

[1] For non-English readers: trains from Paddington go westward.

failed to guarantee success, yet the formula requires that a truth condition guarantee success whatever the underlying desires.

One kind of defence is that the theory works only for ideal agents, meaning ones who never believe anything false, and are (vividly) aware of any obstacle that may wait to trip them up. For such agents, perhaps a fact does guarantee the success of action based on a representation of it. But these are agents that have to be described in the first place in terms of representational successes—indeed massive, unqualified representational successes—so there will be a lurking circularity in approaching the issue by restricting the relevant agents in this way.

I believe we have to recognize that a true belief will certainly *aid* an indefinite number of possible projects, but it can do this while guaranteeing none, and realistically, we must still expect a failure rate, depending, as already indicated, on what else is in the agent's head, and how cooperative the environment proves to be.

In this essay I try to show that we can do better, without in any way departing from the spirit of Ramsey's position.

Success semantics might be wedded to a theory of biological function, as in some versions of teleo-semantics. But I regard that as an option, and one that we should not take. Suppose we want to say that a particular brain state in a frog represents the proximity of a fly (and not of any old small black thing). We could work in terms of some version of this:

(A) The brain state represents the proximity of a fly = it is an adaptation, and evolution selected it because it is triggered by flies.

Or we could work with some version of this:

(B) The brain state represents the proximity of a fly = the state is involved in the genesis of action (behaviour) by the frog, and that behaviour is typically successful because of the proximity of flies.

I shall argue in favour of approaches taking the second option. The second approach is equally a success-based approach, but it confines itself to the present, or at least the extended present in which we can talk of what typically causes what. It is by getting flies now that the frog flourishes. Evolution can stay in the background. It provides, no doubt, the correct explanation of the emergence of the system at all. But it leaves the content of any element in the system, such as the brain state, to hinge upon the kinds of behaviour in which it is implicated, and the kinds of function this behaviour has. This is an advantage. David Papineau, for instance, once defended the other choice, talking of a desire's 'real satisfaction condition as that effect which it is the desire's biological purpose to produce' (Papineau 1987: 64). But this cannot generally be right, since many beliefs and desires have contents that are too late for any evolutionary process to have selected for them, and hence for any notion of biological purpose to apply. If Amanda wants a mobile phone, we cannot talk of this being an adaptation, nor of the 'evolutionary purpose' of her desire. Evolution has had no chance to act selectively on people who do or do not desire mobile phones. Of course, Amanda may be instancing some evolutionary successful and much older strategy, such as acting like the rest of her group, or acting so as to attract a mate. But those are poor bricks out of which to build a theory of content, since desires, or beliefs, with almost any content can be seen in the same light. If Amanda can be said to instance such a strategy here, she presumably equally instances it when she wants a tattoo or a Britney Spears record. But these are different desires.

There are many choices for a theory of content. It can take language as primary, or something else. It can take the individual as primary, or the language-sharing group or community. It can help itself to notions such as action, or it can regard them as too heavily involved with intentionality to be part of any explanatory project. It can be heavily marinaded in normativity, or it can try to make do without. It can be wedded to some kind of project called naturalism, or it can turn its back on any such motivation. It can take sentences, or sub-sentential parts, or larger units such as theories as primary. It can be presented as a kind of realism about the mental, or it can come in the spirit of an intentional stance or interpretative manual. It can put up with, or celebrate, indeterminacies and underdeterminations, or it can insist upon facts of the matter. My approach remains neutral on these issues for as long as possible. How long that is, remains to be seen.

What is the problem of content, or of intentionality, or representation? It is usually expressed in terms of the mind's relationship with external things and states of affairs: things and states of affairs that may or may not exist, or may be relatively near to the subject, or that may be far, in space and time. It is the fact that we can think of distant things, past and future things, or even just imagined things. Sometimes the problem is put as the problem that these thoughts, identified as they are in terms of things different from ourselves, cannot supervene upon brain states of our own. That by itself need not strike us as much of a difficulty. Many facts about ourselves would not be facts but for the relations we have with other things. But we like to be able to say what those relations are, and therein lies the problem.

1. The Theory

Any theory of mind that takes our representational or intentional capacities as something to be explained seems likely to work in terms of some kind of distinction between vehicle and content, and that is what I shall do. The vehicle of representation, or what Ramsey called 'the subjective factor', is usually thought of in terms of the sentence, identified by features *other* than those intrinsically connected with meaning. So it is contingent whether a sentence has the content that it does. This standard approach need not preclude a wider theory, according to which there might be or actually are other kinds of representational vehicles. For example, there may be non-linguistic vehicles, or we might want to work towards a theory in which the whole person represents things, without there being anything as it were smaller to count as a specific vehicle at all. We come to say something about such extensions in due course, but for the moment it will do no harm to think in terms of sentences as paradigm representational vehicles.

So consider a subject S. S gets about the world, and we suppose that some of her actions are successful. She achieves what she desires. And suppose some of her actions are based upon a vehicle V. It is not going to be easy to say exactly what that means, but at a first pass it may mean that it is because of an event, whereby V becomes *salient* in her overall psychological state. Some writers like to think in terms of a sentence, such as V may be, entering S's 'belief box'. Without being so literal, or geometric, we can use that as a model, again if only for the purpose of approaching a wider theory. A slightly more realistic version for humans might be that S gets into a state in which, were she to be asked why she is doing what she is, the answer would contain V as an ineliminable ingredient. As for what distinguishes one's belief box from one's entertainment box, containing vehicles of content which we entertain without believing, we should look to functionalism. We should concentrate upon *force*, meaning that a belief differs from a mere entertainment of a thought precisely in that beliefs are, as it were, in gear. They are playing a role in the machinery of agency. So for the moment we are to think of an event, which I shall call the tokening of a vehicle, precipitating a vehicle into that machinery.

In order to come at the idea of V bearing a content (being a representation, having intentionality) we think in terms of explanation. What explains S's success as she acts upon the belief expressed by 'the University Library is over there'? In the typical or paradigm case, she is successful because the university library is over there. She is not, on the other hand, typically successful because of the whereabouts of Heffers or Trinity College or Grantchester. Why were S and R successful in meeting this afternoon? Because they exchanged tokens, 'Let's meet at the university library,' and the university library was where they then went. Once more, it is their going to the university library, not their going past Heffers or through Trinity that explains their successful tryst. Why was S successful in her shopping? Because she said, 'Can I have some haddock?' and haddock was what she got. The properties of neighbouring halibut and cod are not typically relevant to the success the actions based upon that tokening.

We could at this point go directly for an attempt to describe the representative content of the whole vehicle, the sentence. We might try something like this:

A vehicle V has the content *p* if and only if behaviour based on V is typically successful, when it is, because *p*.

However, difficulties lie down that direct road. I have in mind difficulties connected with the utility of false belief, which can accrue in various ways. Consider, for instance the vehicle, 'I am popular.' Psychologists say that this is a useful thing to get into your belief box. It promotes your ability to get on well, even if it is false (maybe, especially if it is false). So it will not be true that behaviour based on tokening this sentence is typically successful, when it is, because the subject is popular. Yet this is the content of the sentence.

It would be possible to try to handle this kind of example as Engel and Dokic do, by bringing into view the variety of possible desires that might accompany the tokening. Then, while a false content explains occasional success, only true content could explain a general pattern of success across all these possible applications. I think this may work, although it takes us some distance from our actual evidence. We have no general access to the requisite patterns. We have to invent scenarios in which the tokening of 'I am popular' conspires with other desires to generate a whole pattern of actions, most of which are unsuccessful if, but only if, it is false.

A different range of problems comes into view if we think of approximations. Behaviour based on tokening the standard expression of the Boyle–Charles gas law (pressure times volume = constant times temperature) is typically successful, when it is, because of the truth of van der Waal's equation.[2] But the sentence does not express the same thing as that equation. Here, expanding our gaze to take in possible but non-actual desires does not seem likely to help, since it will always be true that it is the more complex relationship between the magnitudes involved that explains success in relying upon the simpler relationship.

In addition, there will be sentences that are too seldom tokened for there to be a typical way in which behaviour based on them is successful, let alone an explanation of any such pattern of success in terms of their truth. All in all, then, a direct approach looks unlikely to give us what we want.

If we want to stay more closely to the evidence, the remedy must be to go compositional. We do not want to ignore the structure of the representing sentence. So let us look at reference first, and try what I shall call the fundamental schema:

(FS) Suppose the presence of 'a' is a feature of a vehicle 'a . . .'. Then 'a' refers to a if and only if actual and possible actions based upon the vehicle 'a . . .' are typically successful, when they are, at least partly because of something about a.

Here we imagine a sentence containing a name. Actions are sometimes based upon it. When they are successful, this is typically at least partly because of something about some object. And that is the object that is referred to in the sentence.

At this point we may wonder why 'success' is allowed to muscle its way to the front. After all, 'a' may represent something, and then actions based upon a tokening that includes it would typically *fail*, when they do, at least

[2] This is the more complex equation that corrects for the finite volume of gas molecules, and the attraction between them, which are ignored in the Boyle–Charles law.

partly because of something about whatever it represents. The university library being far from a mile away would explain why I failed to get there, acting on the tokening, 'The university library is about a mile away.' Perhaps 'action semantics' would be a better title than 'success semantics'. I think this point is right, as far as it goes. But I also think that sucesss in action is the fundamental notion: like Davidson and Wittgenstein, I incline to think that failure only exists against a background of success. It is only because of our successes that the representational powers we have are adaptive, and exist in the first place. So I shall retain the title, while remembering that it is the place of representation in the overall life of an agent that is the focus.

For any actual term, there will of course be a huge variety of possible sentences in which it may occur. So the pattern of success illustrated here for any one particular sentence can be enormously bolstered by thinking of other sentences alike in containing the term 'a'—enough so that the credentials of the object a as the focus, the uniquely invariant explanans of a huge variety of doings, will be abundantly established.

Some might worry that the 'something about a' introduces something suspicious and unscientific, such as surreptitious mention of facts.[3] But that is just an artefact of the generality of the proposal. The fundamental schema collects together a pattern of explanation, and as is often the case, to generalize in this way we need mention of truth or fact. But in any particular case, the explaining is done without anything suspicious of the kind. Why was John's action based on tokening 'The university library is about a mile away' successful? Because the university library is about a mile away. In other words, the introduction of a vocabulary of fact or truth is necessary for theorists generalizing about the phenomenon. But it does not indicate any mysterious residue in the phenomena themselves.

Before expanding this, and confronting objections, we should notice a few points. Some are obvious enough, but others deserve separate mention.

(1) There is a disquotation, in that the name, or other feature of the vehicle mentioned, is used in the sentence following 'because'. It is in this sense that the schema reproduces the idea of representation as a vehicle–world relationship.

---

[3] This objection was urged upon me by Gary Kemp.

(2) There is a 'typically' qualification, corresponding to the fact that we want to tiptoe past deviant causal chains and the like. We gain our point of entry by thinking of the typical or normal case, just as we gain our point of entry to a causal theory of, say, vision by thinking of the typical or normal case. There may follow a choice about how seriously we should look on deviant cases.

(3) There is an attempt to accommodate the thought that sometimes we refer to things which never enter into our action plans by expanding the explanatory range to actual and possible actions. I do not plan much on the basis of a tokening of 'Henry VIII', but were I to do so, or to have done so, and generated a class of successful actions, that would be because Henry VIII was one way or another.

(4) The actions specified may or may not be those of the agent. A baby may say 'biccy', and the fact that the word signifies biscuits is certified by the fact that other people's actual or possible actions based upon his saying are typically successful if, but only if, they involve biscuits. Things go well just when biscuits are provided by someone else, in response. If the baby is at a stage where this is not so—for instance, the success rate is the same if cereal is provided—then reference is not so specific. Of course, 'biccy' in the baby's mouth may express desire rather than belief. But that is an advantage of the account: representation is different from force.

(5) There is no necessary restriction to linguistic vehicles. The schema would apply, for instance, to maps. If a feature of my map of Cambridge is the presence of a big picture of a tower, here, then that can refer to *the position of the university library* if actions based upon that feature of the map are typically successful, when they are, because of *the position of the university library*. Similarly, if we are moderately realistic about mental imagery, there is no principled objection to features of the imagery carrying intentional content. If we reify perceptions (I do not claim that we should, or even that it is permissible to do so), then elements of perceptions can carry content, referring to libraries, features, distances, and so on.

(6) The schema speaks directly to *compositionality*. That is, its point of entry is a feature of a sentence, correlating with a feature of the world. Thinking intuitively, if we imagine an atomic sentence 'Fa', if one clause certifies the contribution made by the presence of 'a',

another clause would certify the contribution made by the presence of 'F', in the obvious way (the presence of 'F' would refer to a property F if and only if actual and possible actions based upon the vehicle '. . . F' are typically successful, when they are, at least partly because of something about the property F). This compositionality is put into the shop window, as it were, because it is *kinds* of vehicles that correlate with *kinds* of explanations of success, and the 'sub-sentential components', or as I prefer to call them, features of vehicles, identify the kinds. Of course, our standard model would be the presence of words in a sentence, but other features of vehicles could easily have content on this methodology. I believe this aspect is actually true to Ramsey, who introduced the chicken example only as a preface to considering other sorts of belief, that is, ones expressed in composite linguistic vehicles.

(7) Although the point of entry is sub-sentential, there is no conflict with Frege's insistence on the priority of the overall vehicle or sentence. That priority can be maintained provided the idea of action being *based on* a vehicle requires a whole or unified vehicle: something like a sentence. But in this sense, a picture could *serve as* a sentence.

(8) Similarly, there is no necessary conflict with a holistic view of language, for two reasons. Firstly, a feature may only be able to gain content, given this explanation, if it occurs in many different sentences, differently successful in different ways, provided there is a unifying thread in the explanation of those successes. This will be the various properties some thing has (if it refers to a thing) or the varying instantiations or lacks of them that some property has (if it refers to a property). And secondly, it remains possible, for all that the schema implies, that an action can never be regarded as being based upon a single vehicle, but only on any given vehicle in conjunction with others.

(9) The notion of 'the' explanation may worry some. In the simple, point-of-entry case, we imagine something like this. A person tokens a succession of vehicles, 'The university library is over there,' 'The university library is a mile away,' 'The university library contains books,' and so forth. He performs acts based upon these tokenings and is successful in some typical ways. Then the

idea is that there is no 'total explanation' of the success of the first that fails to include the position of the university library relative to the subject, or of the second that neglects its distance from the subject, or of the third that neglects the fact that it contains books. Although in particular cases we might choose to emphasize something else, these facts will merely have been suppressed. They would need to be cited in a full story. Equally, we might wish to stress the differential or contrastive nature of explanation, in order to avoid the outcome that we are always referring to the presence of oxygen or the continuation of the gravitational field—things that are background general conditions of success.

(10) The explanations in question need not be causal. Reference need not be confined to items that are causally anterior to the tokening of the vehicle. Actions successfully based on tokens such as 'Tomorrow will be wet,' 'Tomorrow will bring the examination,' and so on, may typically be successful because the day after their tokening is wet, or does bring the examination. In that case the day after the tokening is in good standing as the content or reference introduced by 'tomorrow' as an element of the vehicle. Abstract objects can be referents, insofar as (say) nineteen being one thing or another is the explanation of the success of action based on the vehicle 'nineteen . . .'. Reference to complexes such as aggregates or species and kinds clearly follows on seamlessly. Actions based on the vehicle 'Crowds are dangerous' are typically successful, when they are, because crowds are dangerous, and similarly for sheep being tasty or water being wet. Indeed it is the very promiscuity of explanation, and its Protean capacity for covering all kinds of topics, that largely explains the failure of causal theories and other attempted naturalistic reductions of semantic notions (there is a comparison here with similar frustrations in defining knowledge in other terms).

(11) On the other hand, we could draw back at some putative cases of reference. Can one refer to non-actual possible worlds, for example? That will depend on how we can explain the success of actions based on putative mention of them. If such explanations can cite the way possible worlds are, as the explanans of this success, then reference is saved. But if this is not so, then the referential

credentials of the terms is put into question. I myself have grave doubts whether useful explanations of our propensity to modality can take this shape. If those doubts are well founded, then by the fundamental schema there is no such thing as reference to possible worlds. The schema does not solve our problems here, but it helps to pinpoint them.

(12) The fundamental schema fleshes out the thought that our doings are successful because we are hooked up rightly to the world. This kind of formula may ring alarm bells, implying to some people an 'Archimedean point' or God's eye view whereby we Stand Above and Behind our own theories and applaud them for their real contact with Elements of the World. But this fear, whatever it amounts to, is in any event groundless. The explanation of our success that we give, when we cite the university library being one way or another, is not the offspring of some transcendental, Archimedean viewpoint. It is an explanation from within. It is no more mysterious than the way the university library blocks the view or costs money. These are things the library does, and there are others, and these are amongst them. The way it is in various dimensions sometimes explains the success of human doings, based on tokenings. (I should say myself that this 'deflationist' stance also explains what force there is to the 'no miracles' argument for realism about scientific theories. It is not that there is a metatheory, called realism, required to explain this success. It is that just as science explains pressures and temperatures, so it explains the successes of actions based on reference to those pressures and temperatures, and so on for the other theoretical elements of science.)

(13) Many people hold that representation is somehow essentially normative, and that this normative dimension is, fatally, missing from naturalized accounts such as that of the fundamental schema (FS). This is difficult terrain, but at least *standards* for normative assessment are closely implicated by FS. For the notion of success is at the heart of the analysis. Where there is success there is also the chance of failure, either in a subject's state, or in the way his signals are taken by others. It will not require any other source to give us all that is needed from a notion of correctness or incorrectness in representation.

(14) The disquotation in (FS) is one that *we* give. It is one we give
when describing our own representations. So there is a sense in
which, if it is the last word, we cannot stand outside our own
skins—perhaps there is even a sense in which the early Carnap and
others were right, that semantics is a very limited enterprise. But this
does not mean that the proposal achieves nothing, or nothing more
than a strictly modest or quietistic disquotational semantics does. It
does not leave us with starkly irreducible notions like reference or
predication, backed up, for all it tells us, by noetic rays. On the
contrary, it naturalizes these notions by seeing them as applying
to relational features of things we say to ourselves, or pictures or
anything else we give ourselves, responsible for our success as agents
acting in a surrounding world.

And so to difficulties. Some are easy to cope with, but others are less so.
The hardest, I believe, is voiced by Papineau. Papineau talks of Ramsey's
different suggestion, criticized above. But the present proposal is just as
vulnerable to the objection. Papineau complains:

It explains truth for beliefs, only by assuming the notion of satisfaction, for desires.
Yet satisfaction is as much a representational notion as truth, and so ought itself to
be explained by an adequate philosophical theory of representation.   (Papineau
1993: 70–1)

So, for instance, consider our agent who wants a particular book, believes
that the book is in the university library, and that the university library
is in some direction from where he stands. Suppose all goes well. We
can say that his success is explained by the book being in the university
library, and the university library being where he expected. But his success
is identified in terms of getting what he wanted, and that requires content
or intentionality: he wanted a particular book, which he therefore had to
represent to himself. If we cannot say that much about him, we have no
reason, it seems, to talk of success at all. But to say that much requires
some pre-existing representation, and that vitiates the proposal as a general
account.

Should this objection silence us? It does not falsify the fundamental
schema, but only suggests a limit to its utility. Yet how severe is this limit?
If we were trying to give a reduction of *all* intentionality at a blow, it
would be serious. But perhaps we do not have to claim any such ambition.

It remains true that for any *particular* representative feature of a vehicle, we can use (FS) to give a truth condition or account of its representative power. That account only works, it is true, by imagining the feature embedded in the psychology of an active, desiring agent. And it is true that when we turn to the fact of desire, other representative powers will be implicated. But these in turn can be explained by a reapplication of the schema. Suppose the book our agent desired was *Emma*, and suppose his desire was activated by the tokening of a representative vehicle: 'I must read *Emma*.' Then the fact that the term '*Emma*' represents *Emma* is given, according to (FS), by the fact that actual and possible actions based upon the vehicle '*Emma* . . .' are typically successful, when they are, because of something about *Emma*. Notice that among these examples of success we can number the very occasion under discussion: the agent's success on this occasion arose because *Emma* was in the university library. Faced with this, it is not very clear how damaging Papineau's problem is. But in addition, we can approach it from a different angle.

Papineau's problem will probably seem most intractable if we think synchronically. We might imagine the simultaneous tokening of two vehicles, V_B carrying the content of the belief, and V_D carrying the content of a desire. And we perplex ourselves because 'success' underdetermines the identity of these two things together. 'Success' could consist in the belief having one content, and the desire a related content, or the belief having a different content with an accommodating difference in desire, and so on indefinitely. Underdetermination stares us in the face.

But suppose we think a little more diachronically. We find out what baby wants by finding what brings peace. We could be wrong: baby may have wanted a biscuit, but be pacified by a rattle. But as the days go by, typical patterns emerge. If 'biccy' reliably correlates with pacification by a biscuit, we get one entry into our lexicon. If when baby seems to want a biscuit we direct his attention successfully by saying where it is, and the words we use become part of baby's repertoire, then we take them to be representing wherever it is. And so it goes, entry by entry. But at the end of the process there is only one thing to think, sometimes, about what the emergent child believes and wants. And by then representative features of vehicles are available either to enter the function of pushing and pulling, the 'desire box', or the function of guiding the actions appropriate to the pushings and pullings, the 'belief box'.

This solves the epistemological problem. We play off macrobehaviour and microstructure of vocabulary, and just as with a crossword puzzle, one clue at a time, fallibly, but eventually uniquely, a solution emerges. But does it solve the metaphysical or ontological problem? Does it tell us what representation *is*, or how intentionality is *possible*? Does it, for instance, make room for misrepresentation?

I believe so. Consider misunderstanding first. Suppose subjects S and R want to meet, and S says, 'Let's meet in New York,' and R hears, 'Let's meet in Newark.' They will fail to meet. S intended R to token something with one kind of power, and he tokened something with a different kind. Instead of directing him to New York, the event set him off towards Newark. It is an event which reliably does that, because there is a feature of the vehicle (which might be 'Newark is the place to go'), and actual and possible actions based upon the vehicle are typically successful, when they are, because Newark is the place to go. On this occasion, it is not, and action will fail.

With falsity we imagine an agent whose tokenings of 'a' and of 'F' generally slot into the fundamental schema so as to compel interpretations as referring to a, and to the property F, respectively. We suppose that the (syntactic) structure (or some other feature) of the vehicle ensures its indicative form. So the subject bases action on 'Fa', interpreted as a being F.[4] In other words, he acts on the belief that a is F. Unfortunately a is not F. So either the subject will be unsuccessful, or his success will not be explicable in the typical, disquotational fashion. He is not successful because a is F, but in spite of a not being F. There is no principled difficulty about isolating such cases, and saying the right thing about them.

If the theory allows misrepresentation to fall nicely into place, it is difficult to see what remains of the idea that it is at best epistemologically adequate, but failing on some metaphysical or ontological ground. However, another general problem looms.

So far, we have run representation and reference together, imagining that a theory of the latter, in terms of explanations of success, will automatically give us a theory of the former. But there are difficulties here, since obviously a subject can represent without referring. This is the problem of empty

---

[4] Clearly, I am assuming that 'concatenation' in a simple atomic sentence as vehicle has the consequence that the vehicle represents whatever is referred to by the name term as having whichever property is represented by the predicate.

names (or predicates that fail to pick out properties, although historically that seems not to have been so worrisome). Johnny represents Santa Claus to himself (and success may attend his actions based on this representation). But his tokenings do not refer to Santa Claus, or to anything, since the explanation of his success does not consist in Santa Claus being one way or another. Johnny himself may suppose the explanation of his success to be the doings of Santa Claus, but he is wrong about that.

Maybe the typical explanation of the success of Johnny's actions, such as hanging up a stocking, are the doings of Johnny's father. So can we avoid the result that his tokenings in fact refer to his father? We may not want to avoid it: it is no accident that when Johnny grows up, one way for his father to reveal the truth is to say, 'I was Santa Claus all along,' or, 'It was me to whom you wrote all those letters.' If we want to avoid the interpretation, we can invoke several other features of the situation. Johnny's friends all suppose one person to be the common reference of the name, but no one person explains their successes equally. Johnny's conception of what Santa Claus is like is quite at variance with what Johnny's father is like, and although that does not preclude reference, it at least counts against it. But there still remains the question: how are we to analyse the distinction between representation and reference that the case opens up?

What we need to cope with this is the idea of Johnny's mindset being appropriate to a Santa Claus world, although we do not inhabit such a world. We can do this if we use the notion of a dossier that Johnny associates with the tokening of 'Santa Claus': giving presents, visiting once a year, climbing down chimneys, and so forth. This dossier corresponds to beliefs Johnny has about what Santa Claus is like and what he does. The existential quantifications associated with those descriptions should not be problematic, for we have already suggested an approach to the general problem of misrepresentation. That he ties these quantifications together under the heading of Santa Claus gives us our understanding of Johnny's mindset. It is inappropriate to the actual world, and its token 'Santa Claus' has no reference. But it does not show us a Johnny who is irrational or uninterpretable, and certainly not one whose tokenings fail of content, so that he fails to think at all. Johnny thinks, hopes, desires, is grateful, just as if Santa Claus were a real person.

There is more to be said about fiction, and fantasy (I have imagined Johnny in the grip of a real mistake, not fantasizing about non-existents in full awareness that this is what he is doing). But I do not see that the phenomena will force any significant move away from (FS).

Less global difficulties may remain. One intriguing worry might be that the theory falls into a mirror image of one problem that afflicts a causal theory. Causal theories of reference do not easily allow reference to the future. Is it possible that success-based theories do not easily allow reference to the past? For after all what causes success is a matter of what will be the case when the time to reap rewards comes, which will be the future. So, for instance, how can I refer to the present position of my car, when it is the future position of my car that will explain my success or failure as I walk in the direction in which I am prompted by some tokening?

There are two kinds of answer to this. One would point out that explanations cast a wide net, and we do not confine explanations to immediate or proximate explanations. True, it is whether the car will be in a place to which I walk that proximately determines my future success. But it is where it is now that explains where it will be (in the normal case, in which the car is stationary). The other kind of answer reminds us of the wide class of actual and possible actions. My actual actions, based on a tokening of the present position of the car, reap their rewards in the future. But *possible* actions based on the same tokening could have reaped their rewards now or in the past. Hence, there is a wider class of possible actions whose success would typically be, or have been, explained in accordance with the fundamental schema by facts about past or present objects.

I have talked throughout of tokenings as events, in which a vehicle is somehow summoned into an active area of the brain or mind: a belief box or desire box, implicated in the machinery of action. We may wish to point out that as well as episodic events like this, there are 'standing beliefs', or for that matter standing desires, which may seem to be implicated in action but with no event of this kind taking place. To accommodate this idea, I take it we can expand our conception of what it is for action to be based on vehicles. We might think of some vehicles exerting a standing pull. The words, 'It is a bad idea to walk into a wall,' do indeed not have to go through my mind for me to act daily on the belief that it is a bad idea to walk into a wall. But the fact that it is *that* belief upon which I am acting has to lie somewhere. Presumably it lies in my being in a state both in which I am strongly disposed to avoid walls, and in which I am disposed to cite something like the belief mentioned as the rationale for my first disposition. In the habituated agent, a tokening does not have to precede an action based on the belief that the tokening expresses. Similarly, we can say that the batsman played the stroke as he did because he foresaw the flight of the ball. But we don't have to think of an antecedent mental picture with elements representing that flight. It is enough that afterwards he could produce such a picture, either mentally or on paper or in any other way.

I have talked in very simple terms of actions being based on tokenings, and some may be poised to object that this makes a mockery of the delicate space of reasons. Representational tokenings should not be thought of as pushing action in some hydraulic or mechanical way. Rather, they inject contents into the space of reasons, and whatever action emerges is only the resultant of operations within that space.

But it is a mistake to think that the simplicity of the conception is inconsistent with the complexity of our reasonings. The simplicity of the conception is supposed to take some of the mystery out of representation or intentionality. It does require a notion of basing an action upon a tokening (or background disposition to token). Such 'basing' may become more complex than any simple two-factor, desire–belief model suggests. Actions may turn out almost never to be based upon one tokening at a time. Standing beliefs and desires complicate things indefinitely. But at the end of the day there is such a thing as basing action on belief, and expressing belief in vehicles, just as there is such a thing as basing the direction of movement on a map. And this is all that is required to launch success semantics as a going concern.

POSTSCRIPT

It might be profitable to compare the position advocated in this essay with the views in 'The Steps from Doing to Saying' (essay 9). That essay highlights both the input and output features of sayings: the experiential side and the exit into action. There might seem to be a tension with this paper, which is concerned only to highlight the ouput in action, and the explanation of that output by attributing representational or semantic properties to the terms we use en route to action. I do not intend any conflict (which is not to say that none might emerge with further thought).

The problem addressed here is that causal impacts, themselves giving rise to experience, have not generally given us helpful material from which to understand semantic notions, so it seemed to be worth trying whether the output end could do better. But of course in concentrating upon output into action, one is not forgetting that the agent acting is doing so in an environment to which he is causally sensitive. It may be true that a better theory would be more even-handed in stressing both elements. My concern in this paper was at least to give the fact of agency its proper importance, getting away from the idea that the thinking agent can be thought of purely as a spectator of the passing show.

11

Wittgenstein's Irrealism

One keeps forgetting to go right down to the foundations. One doesn't put the question marks deep enough down.

Wiggenstein 1980a: 62

Introduction

Was Wittgenstein a realist? Was he an anti-realist? Or did he offer materials to 'deconstruct' the debate, being sceptical whether either side had a coherent position, or fought over a coherent issue? The answer, I shall show, is not at all simple. And it bears heavily on the correct interpretation of the famous rule-following passages.

Here is a view of the later work, given forthright expression by Sabina Lovibond:

What Wittgenstein offers us, in the *Philosophical Investigations* and elsewhere in his later work, is a homogeneous or 'seamless' conception of language. It is a conception free from invidious comparisons between different regions of discourse . . . On this view, the only legitimate role for the idea of 'reality' is that in which it is coordinated with (or, as Wittgenstein might have said—cf. *Philosophical Investigations* * 136—'belongs with') the metaphysically neutral idea of 'talking about something' . . . It follows that 'reference to an objective reality' cannot intelligibly be set up as a target which some propositions—or rather, some utterances couched in the indicative mood—may hit, while others fall short. If something has the grammatical form of a proposition, then it is a proposition.   (Lovibond 1983: 25–6)

This view of the later Wittgenstein is not unique to Lovibond. It is a view that many writers have put into the service of a fairly blanket 'unpretentious realism' about all areas of discourse. Richard Rorty, who is probably the best-known advocate of the view, talks of the Wittgenstein—Sellars—Quine—Davidson attack on distinctions between classes of sentences, an outcome of the impossibility of any 'attempt to say "how language relates to the world" by saying what *makes* certain sentences true' (Rorty 1982: xviii). He presents Wittgenstein as sharing a broadly Davidsonian attitude to any attempt to develop either a substantive realism, or a substantive anti-realism, about such topics as the moral, the modal, or the psychological. These attempts founder through being attempts to 'step outside our own skins', contemplating from some superior standpoint how well we are managing to depict reality. But there is no such standpoint. Let us call this attitude to Wittgenstein 'the received view'. On a polemical version of the received view, it is not only that Wittgenstein himself was hostile to theorizing in either a realistic or an anti-realistic direction about one area or another, but that he was right to be hostile: we have learned from him that no such issues arise.

It is one thing to deconstruct a debate, but another to announce that one side has won. However, one can see why someone might want to describe this Wittgenstein as an unpretentious realist. For holding, as he did, a redundancy theory of truth, he can pass without cost from any assertion p, to 'p is true', and to 'p is really true/corresponds to the facts/says how things are or really are . . .'. Nothing is *added* by these locutions; hence we can hear Wittgenstein saying things that supposedly define realism—there really are values, numbers, possible worlds, rules, intentions. It is just that an old-style realist thought these things implied a theory, or that they were difficult to say, or took some earning. The new style thinks that they need no theory; they go without saying, once one is committed to the discourse. And since they go without saying, any attempt to rebut them—to say that an assertion does not correspond to the facts, etc.—is merely a way of denying it. It is not a *second order* remark of any kind.

I return to Wittgenstein's use of the redundancy theory in due course, after seeking to show that virtually everything in the received view is false to his later philosophy.

There is just one element of Lovibond's quotation with which I am not concerned. I believe she is right that Wittgenstein was not interested in 'invidious' comparisons. He had no interest in the role of philosophy as critic of any aspect of our form of life, and these are the aspects that issue in one linguistic form, one language game or another. Wittgenstein had little sympathy with scepticism about areas, or 'error theories', although he did, as I shall show, have sympathy with close cousins: the view that in some areas the surface form of discourse misleads us into bad philosophical theory. What I do deny is that he was not interested in any comparison at all, of a kind that could properly lead us to think that one kind of theory ('realism') sustains the attributions of truth and falsity in one domain, and another kind ('anti-realism') in another.

So do we have, in the later Wittgenstein, a writer bent on showing that reference to an objective reality is something that is aimed at by all indicative sentences, all of which express propositions, in the same way? Even before looking at detail, it ought to seem uncomfortable. At the most cursory glance, Wittgenstein's later work is shot through with warnings against taking surface uniformity as a safe guide to deep similarity of linguistic functioning. He wrote that 'we remain unconscious of the prodigious diversity of all the everyday language-games because the clothing of our language makes everything alike' (Wittgenstein 1953: Pt II, xi, p. 224). Or 'the basic evil of Russell's logic, as also of mine in the *Tractatus*, is that what a proposition is is illustrated by a few commonplace examples, and then pre-supposed as understood in full generality' (Wittgenstein 1980b: I, *48). He even told Drury that he had thought of using a quotation from *King Lear*, 'I'll teach you differences,' as a motto for the *Philosophical Investigations*.[1] So how could a doctrine that simply ploughs through potential differences of function, usefully be attributed to him?

The defence has to be that the doctrine in question is, as it were, too *little* to be intended to plough through anything. Its import is that terms like 'corresponds with (describes, refers to) reality (the facts)' are to be given the same deflationary interpretation as 'is true' on the redundancy view. And this, it will be urged, is not a doctrine that irons out differ-ences—it leaves all the room there can be for charting the differences of activity, or differences of 'language game', lying behind the emer-gence of different kinds of content. It is not, for example, that ethics is science, or that mathematics is psychology, but that if each of them issues in propositions, then those propositions equally purport to describe

---

[1] Drury 1981: 157. The quotation from *Lear* occurs in Act I, sc. iv, in which Kent upbraids Oswald. Interestingly, it is an invidious distinction, or at any rate one of rank, that Kent is emphasizing; perhaps the received view will say that this is why Wittgenstein discarded the motto.

their respective aspects of reality—the scientific, ethical, mathematical, or psychological.

Let us suppose we allow this. Its main effect, one might think, is to shift attention away from *proposition*—a term that is now firmly cemented to the notions of reality and fact—and onto the prior question of whether all indicative sentences express propositions—that is, whether they all share the role of purporting to describe reality or the facts. Lovibond canters straight past this one. She leaves no doubt that Wittgenstein offers us a picture in which it is automatic: 'if something has the grammatical form of a proposition, then it is a proposition.' In other words, her Wittgenstein holds not only (a) that propositions are all equally subject to assessment as true or false, in terms of correlative notions of fact or reality, but also (b) anything with the grammatical form of an indicative sentence expresses a proposition.

Considered by itself, (a) is not obviously objectionable, for it may merely ask us to rope together the family of terms: proposition, true, false, description, fact, reality. However, even here we must be careful. As already explained, it is tempting to see (a) as justifying a universal 'metaphysically unpretentious' realism. But more accurate theorists (including, we shall see, Wittgenstein) see it as justifying no 'ism' at all. It is a name without a doctrine, simply not in the space in which illuminating descriptions of discourse can exist. But this does not mean that there is no such space. Nor did Wittgenstein think that it did mean this. Nor does it follow that descriptions from that space cannot properly be thought of as realistic or anti-realistic. I shall try to justify each of these claims in time, but meanwhile note how very much more ambitious is the conjunction of (a) with (b). For with (b) we have an uncontentious, syntactic, road to propositions, and thence, via (a), to the constitution of reality as represented in our thought.

We might indeed notice that thesis (b) may be ambiguous, depending on whether we use 'grammar' in a normal sense, or in a more specialist, Wittgensteinian sense, in which virtually anything philosophical contributes to grammar. I take it that the former reading is intended, firstly because the class of sentences at issue is defined grammatically in that sense (indicatives), but secondly because the latter reading trivializes the thesis (grammatical indicative coming to equal propositions by definition), leaving us to find yet another term for indicatives-by-normal-standards, whose proposition-expressing function needs thought.

I now look in detail at four different areas in which the later philosophy is quite explicitly concerned with the very differences that, according to the received view, it denies. These are the philosophy of ethics, of necessity and arithmetic, of psychology, and of knowledge. They are, in fact, the four areas in which Wittgenstein worked in sufficient detail for us to know how he thought of the family of indicative sentences.[2] In each of them he explicitly and centrally contradicts the conjunction of (a) and (b), and sometimes each separately.

1. Ethics

In the 'Lecture on Ethics' Wittgenstein considers what he calls judgements of absolute value, by contrast with the 'trivial or relative' sense in which we talk of good chairs, good tennis players (Wittgenstein 1965: 5–6). He makes many claims about such judgements, the central one of which is that no statement of fact can ever be, or imply, a judgement of absolute value. He considers the 'book of the world' as it might be written by an omniscient person, containing 'all relative judgments of value and all true scientific propositions and in fact all true propositions that can be made' (1965: 6; note especially the last clause). Even if we make sure that our book describes all human feelings, 'there will simply be facts, facts, and facts but no Ethics'. 'Ethics, if it is anything, is supernatural and our words will only express fact; as a teacup will only hold a teacup full of water and if I were to pour out a gallon over it.' Considering statements of absolute value he urges that 'no state of affairs has the coercive power of an absolute judge', and goes on to consider various states of mind lying in the region of the ethical (wonder, fear, or a feeling of safety, or of the miracle of existence) en route to the idea that a certain characteristic misuse of our language runs through *all* ethical and religious expressions. It is as if they are similes, but 'as soon as we try to drop the simile and simply to state the facts which stand behind it, we find that there are no such facts'. He can see 'not only that no description that I can think of would do to describe what I mean by absolute value, but that I would reject every significant description that anybody could possibly suggest, *ab initio*, on the ground of its significance'.

---

[2] Perhaps the philosophy of religion is a fifth, and here too the material illustrates the argument.

Finally, what it (ethics) says 'does not add to our knowledge in any sense. But it is a document of a tendency in the human mind which I personally cannot help respecting deeply and I would not for my life ridicule it.'[3]

I have heard the 'Lecture on Ethics' discounted as a 'positivist' work, written as it was in 1929–30.[4] But there is no evidence that he ever changed his view. It is not as if later he said, as the received Wittgenstein ought to say, 'Of course my lecture was hopeless: ethics describes facts—ethical facts.' Nor is he *merely* contrasting ethical facts with scientific ones. For he explicitly adds that the book of the world contains not only all scientific truths, but all truths, but still no ethics. And the *thrust* of the lecture must surely be that it is from a different standpoint than that of description that ethics is found. It is found when it is *felt*, or perhaps even when we think not of description but of *feelings* and the will, and this explains the elusiveness, even the threat of vanishing, of the ethical proposition.

What does happen later is actually highly relevant. In a conversation of 1942, Rush Rhees reports, Wittgenstein considers an ethical dilemma: 'Someone might ask whether the treatment of such a question in Christian ethics is *right* or not. I want to say that this question does not make sense' (Rhees 1965: 23). If we imagine deciding which solution is right and which is wrong, he complains:

But we do not know what this decision would be like—how it would be determined, what sort of criteria would be used and so on. Compare saying that is must be possible to decide which of two standards of accuracy is the right one. We do not even know what a person who asks this question is after.   (Rhees 1965: 23)

And finally, in 1945, a passage that needs full quotation:

Someone may say, 'There is still the difference between truth and falsity. Any ethical judgment in whatever system may be true or false.' Remember that 'p is true' means simply 'p'. If I say 'Although I believe that so and so is good, I may be wrong': this says no more than that what I assert may be denied. Or suppose someone says, 'One of the ethical systems must be the right one—or nearer the right one.' Well, suppose I say Christian ethics is the right one. Then I am making a judgment of value. It amounts to adopting Christian ethics. It is not like saying

---

[3] Wittgenstein 1965: 12. My previous quotations are from the preceding five pages.

[4] Compare also the entry in *Culture and Value* (Wittgenstein 1980a) for 1929: 'The good is outside the space of facts.'

that one of these physical theories must be the right one. The way in which some reality corresponds—or conflicts—with a physical theory has no counterpart here. (Rhees 1965: 24)

This passage contradicts the received view not only on thesis (b), but also on thesis (a). For in it Wittgenstein not only turns his back on the appeal to a moral reality, serving to make one opinion 'the right one'. He explicitly contrasts the case with that of physics where, he says, there is a different way in which reality does correspond or conflict with theory—the very antithesis of the received view.

What is apparent in this passage, and in others I shall come to in time, is a dismissive attitude, an impatience, with the introduction of truth, reality, or fact as somehow containing the key to the use of the language game. His constant, characteristic, stance is against using facts and the rest as a separate element in our description of the language game, something that we can use to 'place' or understand the activity of judgement, or that we can use as a constraint in any such attempt.

2. Necessity and Arithmetic

A great deal of the interest of the *Remarks on the Foundations of Mathematics* hinges on a theme to which Wittgenstein constantly returns: the use of the mathematical sentence not as a description, but as a norm, as something that lays down a rule for description, or serves as a framework within which description can occur. Here are four illustrative quotations:

Let us remember that in mathematics we are convinced of *grammatical* propositions; so the expression, the result, of our being convinced is that *we accept a rule*.

Nothing is more likely than that the verbal expression of the result of a mathematical proof is calculated to delude us with a myth.   (Wittgenstein 1978: Pt II, 26, p. 77)

Why do you want always to consider mathematics under the aspect of discovering and not of doing? If must influence us a great deal that in calculating we use the words 'correct' and 'true' and 'false' and the form of statements. (Shaking and nodding one's head) . . . There is no doubt at all that in certain language games mathematical propositions play the part of rules of description, as opposed to descriptive propositions.

But that is not to say that this contrast does not shade off in all directions. And that in turn is not to say that the contrast is not of the greatest importance. (Wittgenstein 1978: Pt V, 6, p. 173)

To be practical mathematics must tell us facts.—But do these facts have to be the mathematical facts? But why should not mathematics instead of 'teaching us facts' create the forms of what we call facts?   (Wittgenstein 1978: Pt V, 15, p. 173)

We say: 'If you really follow the rule in multiplying, it must come out the same.' Now when this is merely the slightly hysterical style of university talk, we have no need to be particularly interested. It is however the expression of an attitude towards the technique of multiplying, which comes out everywhere in our lives. The emphasis of the 'must' corresponds only to the inexorability of this attitude, not merely towards the technique of calculating, but also towards innumerable related practices.   (Wittgenstein 1967: *299)

So: the verbal form of mathematical statements can delude us with a myth; in certain language games mathematical propositions play the part of rules of description, as opposed to descriptive propositions; perhaps mathematics teaches us no mathematical facts, but creates the form of what we call facts; a statement of necessity corresponds only to the inexorability of an attitude, not to anything that the slightly hysterical style of university talk might make of it.

None of these theses make any sense on the received interpretation. For on that view, the indicative form of a mathematical statement makes it a proposition, which makes it automatically descriptive of mathematical reality; equally with a statement of necessity and a modal reality. Yet this is exactly what Wittgenstein is interested in denying. It is not as if he turns around and says, 'but they have indicative form—so mathematical realism triumphs!' Notice especially the first and second quotations, which openly embrace the possibility of a surprising or puzzling verbal form masking the real function of the mathematical remark, its place in the game. One might almost use as a motto for the *Remarks on the Foundations of Mathematics*, Part IV, section 28: 'the words don't determine the language game in which the proposition functions.' And the game is described in many ways better than saying that it is the one in which we attempt to describe the mathematical or modal facts. The 'myth' against which he warns us, and that the verbal expression of mathematical statements deludes us into, is precisely the realist's myth of the selfstanding world of mathematical fact, explored as the external world is explored.

Notice again the context in which Wittgenstein invokes the redundancy theory of truth in Part I, section 5. When the alter ego invokes truth ('isn't it true that this follows from that?'), Wittgenstein replies that this just means that it does so—but immediately goes on to explore what this comes to, what goes wrong if the game changes, or the background against which it is played shifts. The effect is the same as with ethics: invocation of truth and fact is *useless*, playing no part in an illuminating description of the activity, the form of life, from which the judgement emerges (one could compare this too with the last paragraph of the *Philosophical Investigations*, p. 226).

3. Psychology

Are there explicit counterexamples to the received interpretation in this domain as well? Consider what is sometimes called the 'doctrine of avowals'. Here it is hardly necessary to cite examples—the whole discussion in *Philosophical Investigations*, Part II, sections ix and x, shows Wittgenstein again taking seriously the idea that an apparently descriptive sentence—the first-person indicative form of 'I believe . . .', 'I intend . . .', and so on serves not as a description of anything, but as an avowal of a certain kind. ' "I intend" is never a description, although in certain circumstances a description can be derived from it.' And he emphasizes the problem this puts in front of him:

Don't look at it as a matter of course, but as a most remarkable thing, that the verbs 'believe', 'wish', 'will' display all the inflexions possessed by 'cut', 'chew', 'run'.   (Wittgenstein 1953: 190)[5]

This is not yet to take on the issue of an irrealist or anti-realist construal of the famous rule-following discussion, and the heart of propositional attitude psychology. My immediate point is much more limited. It is just that once more we have a use of indicative sentences that is *not* correctly thought of in terms of describing a truth or a fact, or of corresponding with a state of affairs. To understand the language game in which they occur, we need to see their use in other terms. And this he suggests is the key to

[5] The point is that it is in its inflexions that the sentence's propositional function seems undeniable—giving rise to the famous Frege–Geach problem with non-propositional theories.

the problem of how the intention and its fulfilment seem mysteriously to fit together, although the diagnosis here is certainly obscure.[6]

4. Knowledge

By now the citation of texts may be becoming tedious, and in any event the discussion of the use of 'I know . . .' and its status of avowal, rather than a description, in *On Certainty* is spread throughout the work. More interesting is the role accorded to those propositions that have the status of hinges, or the riverbed, or framework within which ordinary debate about correctness and mistakes takes place. These include, of course, many (uses of) sentences that have normal indicative expression: cars do not grow out of the ground, the earth has existed for many years, objects don't just appear and disappear, and so on. On acquiring this status a proposition turns from an empirical proposition into a norm of description (Wittgenstein 1969: *167). Of such a matter-of-course foundation, something that goes unnoticed, 'there is something misleading' about using the expression 'true or false': 'Really, "the proposition is either true or false" only means that it must be possible to decide for or against it. But this does not say what the ground for such a decision is like' (1969: *200). In the case of framework propositions, the ground is nothing less than a change of form of life, a change of game: something that changes everything. As in the discussion of mathematics, we are told that there is a boundary between a rule on the one hand, and an empirical proposition on the other, although the boundary is not a sharp one: 'here one must, I believe, remember that the concept "proposition" itself is not a sharp one' (1969: *320).[7]

The impression—for I admit that Wittgenstein never makes the consequence explicit—is very much that in some uses, sentences expressing commitments that belong to the methodological framework—the ones of which you could not say 'that's false' without being regarded as mad, as changing the game—do not express propositions (one can almost hear Wittgenstein saying that if they cannot be false, they cannot be true either). Changing them is changing the game. And on this, since it gives another important example of a non-descriptive thesis, see *Zettel*:

[6] Wittgenstein 1967: *53. The paragraphs through to *57 are also relevant.
[7] The remarks are a culmination of the discussion arising from *309.

What does it mean to say: 'But that's no longer the same game!' How do I use this sentence? As information? Well, perhaps to introduce some information in which differences are enumerated and their consequences explained. But also to express that just for that reason I don't join in here, or at any rate take up a different attitude to the game.   (1967: *330)

In sum, Wittgenstein is constantly battling with the difficulty of seeing the norm as at the same time a proposition, but he will not surrender the view that a proper view of the language game demands that we respect the difference of function.

5. The Redundancy Theory of Truth

The 1945 remark on ethics that I quoted above shows Wittgenstein's dismissive attitude to any invocation of reality and its cognates in these investigations. He does almost exactly the same in *On Certainty*:

Well, if everything speaks for an hypothesis and nothing against it—is it then certainly true? One may designate it as such.—But does it certainly agree with reality, with the facts?—With this question you are already going round in a circle. (1969: *191)

He returns to the circle in *203:

If everything speaks *for* an hypothesis and nothing against it, is it objectively *certain*? One can *call* it that. But does it *necessarily* agree with the world of facts? At the very best it shows us what 'agreement' means. We find it difficult to imagine it to be false, but also difficult to make use of it.

And this is almost immediately followed by the pregnant warning that it is not a kind of *seeing* on our part, but our *acting* which lies at the bottom of the language game. Seeing, of course, implies a relationship to something else, and this is exactly what cannot be usefully invoked in the discussion of knowledge, certainty, and truth.

   With this in mind, we can now see the proper place for *136 of the *Philosophical Investigations*. What we in fact have, in the context of *134–*137, is exactly the same attitude. Proposition, truth, reality, 'this is how things are', indeed come in a tight family, but for that very reason none of them is of any help in elucidating the other. To *understand* a language game—to attain the complete clarity we are after, constantly 'giving prominence to distinctions which our ordinary forms of language easily make us overlook'—we must turn elsewhere, to the more intricate and detailed kind of description Wittgenstein then offers. The constant theme, unmistakable in each of these works, is that a blanket invocation of a descriptive function, of a concept of a mathematical or ethical or modal 'reality' represented in our thought, is absolutely useless. It not only irons out differences, but *precisely because of the redundancy theory* it merely pretends to presenting a theory at all. It fails to go beyond whatever proposition you start with, fails to get out of the circle.

6. Realism and its Alternatives

It may be tempting to think that at least in areas in which we do have propositions, realism must win. If 'p' and 'p corresponds with reality' mean the same, and we accept p, then we accept what many would suppose to be a commitment to realism. But the important point is that no 'ism' at all is involved—all that has so far happened is that you have accepted p. The redundancy theory gives you nothing. It does not give you even an unpretentious 'ism', only for free. But in that case is there nothing that can be opposed, either?

Not in these terms. Accepting the redundancy theory means accepting that truth is not a substantive predicate about which different conceptions might be held (see also essay 2 in this volume). But I have shown that Wittgenstein is intensely interested in what I shall call 'non-descriptive functionalism'—the attempt to understand the function or use of commitments in other terms than those of description. Charting their actual role in our activities and our lives shows some to be used as norms, others as rules, as expressions, as endorsements, and as attitudes, and so on. As I have shown, this is the toolkit to which he naturally turns when he wants to inscribe detail.

Now there are two ways that detail can develop. One is to allow the emergence of a proposition—something capable of truth or falsity—as an expression, even given the non-descriptive function of the expression.

This is the route I call 'quasi-realism'.[8] Another is to insist on a sharp separation of spheres: if a non-descriptive functional story best fits a given sentence then it does not express a proposition and is not capable of truth. Wittgenstein tends to write as if this second option is the better.[9] But he nowhere, I believe, squares up to the looming problem that it threatens to be a revisionary view (yet philosophy 'leaves everything as it is'). Because it is obviously a feature of our language game with 'true' and 'false' that we pretty promiscuously *call* even bedrock sentences, those functioning as norms, first-person statements of intention, and the rest, true or false. There may be even better things to say, but one good thing to say is that it is false (not true) that motorcars grow on trees, that I intend to take up tightrope walking, and so on. And these are not just false in certain contexts (which Wittgenstein would allow), but in any normal situation in which the embedded sentence might occur. Nor does Wittgenstein give us any inkling of how much of the propositional appearance of such commitments ought to be abandoned, if we faced up to their non-descriptive function in our lives. One has a strong sense that he would prefer the answer: 'None of it.' And that is to embrace the first, quasi-realist alternative. To do philosophy, to understand the language game, we start with the non-descriptive function of these commitments in our activities; the result is an appreciation of just *how* a content emerges, giving us a proposition—something properly called true or false, properly subject to argument and doubt and properly embedded in various contexts. In telling this story about *how* a content emerges, no explanatory work can be done by mathematical, ethical, etc. 'reality'. But it does not follow that mention of such a reality cannot be tossed in at the end—for, given the redundancy theory, that is to toss in nothing extra.

A trifling reason for doubting this picture of (part of) Wittgenstein might be that it presents him as too much of a *theorist*, seeking *explanations* rather than descriptions, whereas he frequently rails against any conception of the philosopher as theorist. But this is not a real danger. Even if, when he reflected on it, he mistrusted calling his own activity one of explaining or theorizing, it is certainly one of seeking illuminating descriptions of our

[8] For an introduction, see Blackburn 1984c, ch. 6.
[9] I am grateful to Donna Summerfield for emphasizing this.

sayings and doings, avoiding philosophical traps and puzzles. There is no reason at all why a quasi-realist story, seeking to place the emergence of content in mathematics or ethics or modality, but starting from a firm grasp of a non-descriptive function for commitments in these areas, should not conform to this pattern. It may even be a story of a fairly unsystematic kind, compared with the supposedly more streamlined vehicles of truth-conditional semantics. And of course it is anti-realist in the sense in which Hume presents an anti-realist theory of causation, or Ayer an anti-realist theory of ethics. This completes my proof that Wittgenstein cannot rightly be seen as hostile to finding, if not theory, then at least illumination, in exactly this space. In it no explanatory weight is pulled by thinking in terms of a described reality: the discourse is understood in other terms.

7. Anti-Realism and Rules

It will be apparent that if Kripke's Wittgenstein were presented in this guise, he would avoid many of the brickbats hurled at him, and lose nothing fundamental. The root idea is that rule following is to be understood not by searching for the 'fact' that it consists in, but by considering the practice of embracing, or dignifying, various activities in terms of correctness and incorrectness, and this idea survives quite intact. The end point would not be expressed by saying that there is no fact or truth that people follow rules. It would be expressed by saying that there is, but since saying that is saying only that people follow rules, that does not amount to an advance. The advance comes by seeing the judgement emerging as the expression of a stance we do take, and no doubt need to take, to the activities of ourselves and others.[10]

I do not think it is plain sailing to make quasi-realism work here. The fundamental difficulty is whether we need to understand the activity of dignifying oneself or others as rule followers *in advance* of having any other source of understanding of what it might be to follow a rule. It is not clear that we do have this understanding. For me to deem you to be following

---

[10] 'Ourselves and others' in order not to prejudge the question of whether a public is necessary, or whether the stance might be taken towards his own activities by an individual considered in isolation.

the rule for what it is to be a tree or a sum of two numbers seems to require my own ability to determinately think in terms of one thing or another. If my own thought is subject to endless indeterminacy, then what I deem you to be doing is so as well, and the introduction of interpersonal attitudes will not help to defeat the Kripkean sceptic.[11] He will be within his rights to disallow the resources that even a 'sceptical solution', or 'assertibility condition' theory, needs to provide an answer. Put starkly, the problem is that if the 'truth-conditional' approach fails, finding nothing for the fact that I mean 'plus' and not 'quus' to consist in, then assertibility condition approaches seem set to fail too, there being no difference between possible worlds in which I dignify or embrace you as a fellow 'plus' follower, and those in which I dignify you as a fellow 'quus' follower.[12] However, a quasi-realism as a philosophy of rule following has recently come under attack for other reasons, and I shall conclude by fending these off, partly in order to introduce one more relevant facet of Wittgenstein's thought.

The attack I have in mind is developed by Paul Boghossian in his survey article on rule following (Boghossian 1989). I follow his numbering in isolating the relevant premises.

Let us suppose that we pursue a quasi-realist or projective approach to rule following and meaning by claiming:

(3) For any S, p: 'S means that p' is not truth-conditional.

Boghossian says that Kripke extends this globally to:

(4) For any S: S is not truth-conditional.

This is apparently a much more general doctrine. Whereas the problem of the fugitive fact of rule following might lead us to cast in the direction of (3), surely (4) is a different kettle of fish, and one of doubtful value. What can it mean to say that all sentences have a projective or quasi-realist metatheory? So the question arises, why extend (3) to (4)? Because the global character is *forced*: according to Boghossian, (3) entails:

---

[11] A dangerous word, but I take it that by now it is well understood that the 'scepticism' is not an epistemological doctrine, but an exploration of the lack of any fact for rule following to consist in.

[12] This is why I think a quasi-realist approach needs to solve Kripke's other problem, that of the infinitary character of meaning, in order to provide standards for the correct deemings and dignifying. See Blackburn 1984a.

(5) for all S, p: 'S has truth conditions p' is not truth-conditional.

But then, 'via the disquotational properties of the truth predicate',

'S has truth condition p' is true if and only if S has truth condition p,

and 'since (5) has it that "S has truth conditions p" is never simply true', it follows that (4).

Boghossian calls this a 'fascinating consequence' and it is one he goes on to rebut, basically on the grounds that we need the idea of at least some sentences being truth-conditional, if only to draw the contrast whereby others might be seen as something else. But is it a consequence at all? To see the difficulty, I shall reconstruct the argument in terms nearer those that I advocate. We shall then see that it fails to avoid the trap of use/mention confusion.

Suppose we call commitments—moral, modal, or rule-attributing—for which our metatheory is quasi-realist, QR commitments. As explained, the route to understanding them lies in first considering them in the light of a non-descriptive function they have. Suppose we want to contrast these with more ordinary commitments for which no such theory works: OD, or ordinary descriptive commitments. Derivatively we can call sentences expressing these different kinds of commitments QR on the one hand, and OD on the other. The charge is that if a QR status is given to attributions of rule following, all commitments become QR. But is this so?

In these terms Boghossian's (3), (4), and (5) would translate as:

(3!) For any S, p: 'S means that p' is QR
(4!) For any S, S is QR
(5!) For any S, p: 'S has truth condition p' is QR

—the claim being that (3!) entails (5!) and thence, 'via the disquotational properties of the truth predicate', entails (4), thus ruling out the existence of OD sentences. But this is not so. For (5!) only gives us that the attribution of a truth condition p to a sentence S is QR. It does not follow that the commitment expressed by S (and thence S itself) is QR.

To see the difference here, compare how it goes if instead of QR we substitute a harmless remark about attributions of meaning—say, that they are dependent on the use of language in some population. With this reading, (3!) is true, and entails (5!). But it does not follow at all that every sentence (e.g. 'Glaciers flow downhill') says something whose truth is dependent on the use of language in some population. *That* the sentence says what it does is so dependent; *what* it says is not. Boghossian thinks otherwise, because he relies on the 'disquotational properties of the truth predicate'. But those properties are often poor bridges for entailments, since it is familiar that the sentences that express them are themselves contingent. Consider:

(6!) 'Glaciers flow downhill' is true in English iff glaciers flow downhill.

This is true enough, but it is not a necessary truth, which it would need to be to preserve entailment. What makes the left-hand side true varies with the uses the English give their words; what makes the right-hand side true does not. And equally it might be so that the best theory of the left-hand side, since it ascribes a semantic property to a particular sentence, sees it as QR; the best theory of the right-hand side may remain OD.

Interestingly enough, Wittgenstein himself returned quite often to just this point. In the *Remarks* he is very careful to distinguish the presuppositions of the game, or things that make measuring and counting possible and that enable our sentences to have the sense they do, from the propositions they express:

Does this mean that I have to say that the proposition '12 inches = 1 foot' asserts all those things which give measuring its present point?

No, the proposition *is grounded* in a technique. And, if you like, also in the physical and psychological facts that make the technique *possible*. But it doesn't follow that its sense is to express these conditions. The opposite of that proposition 'twelve inches = 1 foot' does not say that rulers are not rigid enough or that we don't all count and calculate in the same way.   (Wittgenstein 1978: V, 1, p. 159)

Or, as he puts it in *Zettel*:

Our language game only works, of course, when a certain agreement prevails, but the concept of agreement does not enter into the language-game.   (1967: *403)

Compare finally the famous:

'But mathematical truth is independent of whether human beings know it or not!'—Certainly, the propositions 'Human beings believe that twice two is four' and 'Twice two is four' do not mean the same. The latter is a mathematical proposition; the other, if it makes sense at all, may perhaps mean: human beings have *arrived* at the mathematical proposition. The two propositions have entirely different uses.   (1953: Pt II, xi, p. 226)

Paraphrasing, we could say that a proposition might be grounded in a technique of mutually holding each other to be subjects of normative appraisal, since without that there would be no such thing as holding a sentence to express it. But none of that would be apparent in its sense. It is simply no part of the way we use sentences to let the human condition underlying their meaning into their sense, any more than natural history is part of mathematics.

Perhaps Boghossian did not intend his (4) to pass over the mention/use division as I am claiming. It is, after all, still talking of whether sentences, not propositions, are truth-conditional. But that is to protect the argument by an ambiguity:

(4a) For any S, p: it is QR whether S means that p.
(4b) For any S, S is QR in the sense that the proposition expressed by S is QR, not OD.

The difficulty is that while (4a) indeed follows from (3), and indeed merely paraphrases it, (4b) does not, yet it is only (4b) that gives Boghossian his subsequent argument that, on an irrealist reaction to the rule-following considerations, ordinary descriptive truth disappears.

However, although there is no easy argument against the quasi-realist approach at this point, unease may remain. As usual, appeal to the language-independent Fregean thought or Moorean proposition is only using terms that presuppose a solution, not telling us how to get there. The mutual dignities and attitudes that are the background to verdicts of rule following may seem to be unpromising sources of any such thing. How out of this crooked timber can anything straight be made? How can the OD status of a *proposition* emerge, how can it be *operational*, when all that we have in linguistic behaviour is the disposition to assert or withdraw sentences?

8. Hard Mistakes for Irrealists

Suppose, for example, dissent breaks out—someone insists that glaciers do not flow downhill, that they do not flow at all. How can this be uncontaminatedly an OD dispute, if the question of correct application of the terms is QR? Perhaps the dissident refuses the term 'flow'—refuses to be impressed by the analogies between the movement of ice and that of liquids. We can mobilize social dissent, take up an admonitory attitude, but given the quasi-realist view of rule following, talk of his making a *mistake* seems only the upshot of these attitudes—a classic QR commitment. Our sense that the dissident is *wrong* loses its hardness, and as it were blurs into mere irritation with him.

Now suppose by contrast that the dissident insists that glacier ice does not move at all. Here we are more in the domain of hard, descriptive mistake—something disproved by ordinary tests for movement. We show him the tests, and he admits he was wrong. He had made a mistake—a hard, OD mistake. Why? Because no question of reinterpretation arises: the *procedures* are agreed and so is their result. If someone suggests that by 'move' the dissident might have meant shmove, where something shmoves if . . . (e.g. if it is not ice, and moves, or is ice, and stays still), we might reply that nothing in the subsequent conversation confirms this or causes us to take any notice of it. We deem the mistake hard when our eyes are shut to any such doubt.

Notice that in neither of these cases is the dissident completely out of court—one can find one's feet with someone who is shocked by the idea of solids flowing, and the second character made a simple mistake. The third case might be someone who denies that glacier ice moves, but does not budge even when given all the evidence. Apparently the methodology of movement has changed; the riverbed has shifted, the door has become unhinged.[13] We are at a loss—all we can do is deem him to be out of the game (see *Zettel* *330, quoted above).

The question is whether these three classifications, together with the blurred borderlines to which they give rise, are just as available to the QR treatment of rule following as to any other theory. The second is the hard one. Here is an approach. When our eyes are shut to possibilities of reinterpretation, we deem dissidence to be the making of a mistake, and subsequent events often prove us right, as the dissident himself comes to share our attitude to the original saying. It may seem surprising that we so often shut our eyes to the possibility of reinterpretation, or so seldom avail

---

[13] Both these analogies are used in *On Certainty* (Wittgenstein 1969).

ourselves of it as an excuse when we make mistakes. It is only seen when scientific or historical change forces us to think of meanings as flexible. Schoolteachers never think of 'quus'-type hypotheses in connection with the mistakes of their pupils. But on a QR treatment, this attitude is entirely defensible. (I doubt whether it is so on a realist view unless some sort of reductionism about meaning is contemplated. For on a non-reductive view, who is to say how many transient facts of meaning may have flitted in and out of control of a subject?) The defence is that we only dignify a dissident as in command of a different concept when we can admit his sayings to be part of a technique—a way of classifying things that has a use. And experience suggests that the mistakes of schoolchildren do not have this property. Since they remain irregular, forgotten, part of no practices, questions of reinterpretation do not arise, and we take ourselves to be in the realm of mistakes. Similarly, we know that we cannot make good any such claim on behalf of our own errors, and seldom pretend to be able to do so.

It may be compared to the way in which we properly treat the moral 'ought' as categorical. It is binding upon people who may have no desires on which it can catch: we say this to disallow such a defect from serving as an excuse. The comparable hardness of the rule-following 'ought'—you ought not to call that an apple; this is the wrong answer—arises because we are sure, as we often are, that no new technique prompted it. Of course, in saying this I am aware that many people find the hardness of the moral ought endangered by a quasi-realist treatment of morals. But their fears are groundless, and equally so in the case of the proposition.

The upshot is that a community can perfectly well distinguish in its attitudes between the embedding of one classificatory scheme or another —something that may in principle be a 'soft' question of decision, and that in any case will depend upon human nature and human interests and the use or misuse of a classification that is embedded—something that may well be hard and enable us to conceive of truths and falsehoods which are themselves independent of any such foundation. Perhaps, before Wittgenstein, we might have wanted more—not just rails to infinity, which we can have, but rails laid by no human practices which we cannot.

12

Circles, Finks, Smells, and Biconditionals

1. Setting the Scene

An interest in 'response-dependent' concepts has generated a large, impressive, and increasingly complex literature, although contributors to that literature differ widely in how important they take such concepts to be.[1] Optimists include Philip Pettit, who believes in a global form of response-dependence (Pettit 1991: 588), and others such as Crispin Wright, who give it modified but important work to do (Wright 1989). They also include Michael Smith, David Lewis, and Mark Johnston, who in their 1989 symposium all present such accounts of evaluative concepts (Smith 1989; Lewis 1989; Johnston 1989). Pessimists include Huw Price (Price 1993) and, under a different hat, Mark Johnston (Johnston 1993), who thinks that our actual concepts are seldom response dependent, although he is also sympathetic to an error theory of our actual concepts, and a programme of replacing them with hygienic cousins that are so.[2] At least two optimists, Johnston and Wright, have directly expressed the belief that response-dependent analyses, for instance of evaluative terms, supersede and sideline expressivist accounts, and others like Lewis clearly sympathize. They thus turn the whirligig of time one more round, since historically expressivist accounts of concepts came in partly because of the failure of the subjectivist analyses to which response dependence is a successor. My aim in this essay is to show that the whirligig should have stayed where it was.

What are the issues? The central idea has been to refurbish a form of analysis of concepts that seem somehow anthropocentric, used and

[1] Volumes substantially devoted to the subject include Menzies 1993 and, given the scale of the papers by Mark Johnston and Crispin Wright, Haldane and Wright 1993.

[2] My exploration of this issue owes a great deal to Price's paper.

understood only because we have particular sensory or affective systems. The standard examples include concepts of colour and other secondary qualities, concepts like being fashionable or chic that centrally reflect the tastes of some identifiable group, or those like being boring or comical, where the application clearly depends somehow on the reactions of people (or some particular people). The idea rapidly generalizes, and values, intentional concepts, and even causation have been advertised as response-dependent concepts.

The idea of a subjective analysis of some concept is not of course new: those of us brought up on G. E. Moore cut our teeth on refutations of such analyses. But the recent interest has quickened because we have become more sophisticated, or more relaxed, about what a response-dependent 'account' of a concept might involve, and the kinds of argument to which it might succumb. In fact, it is no longer plain to many philosophers that a notion of analysis needs to be put into play at all. Our standards for an 'account' may not involve providing a straight equation, expressing the same concept in other terms. One of my main aims is to pour some cold water on this modern sophistication. But to begin with, what is agreed on all sides is that we can usefully start by thinking in terms of a biconditional whose form we can write as follows:

X is ϕ ≡ [persons] are disposed to [reaction] under [circumstances]

A variation on this equation would be:

X is ϕ ≡ X tends to elicit [reaction] from [persons] under [circumstances]

and for the purposes of this paper the two forms may be taken as equivalent (in case 'tends' worries the reader, it gets modified later). Instances of the basic equation would be:

X is red ≡ normal people would be disposed to judge X red in normal light
X is good ≡ ordinary people would be disposed to choose X when faced with it
X is boring ≡ most people would go to sleep on coming across X

and so on. A common view of such equations is that they work well for some concepts but not others, and that where they work well it is because they have an interesting a priori form. Another view is that they work well where they do because they can be read 'right to left'. This means in effect that we can see them as claiming that X is red/good/boring *in virtue of* the dispositions mentioned on the right-hand side, and this is suggested by the notion of dependence. These refinements occupy us later.

Complexity obviously arises because the form of the biconditional gives us three different places for fillings, and different choices can be made for each. Amongst the possibilities we have:

> [persons]: myself, all of us, those who are normal, the experts, us as we actually are, us as we would be after improving, us as we would be after some specified empirical process . . .
>
> [reaction]: a non-cognitive reaction, a cognitive reaction, a judgement that something is ϕ, a judgement couched in other terms, an experience, a piece of behaviour . . .
>
> [circumstances]: common conditions of acquaintance, standard conditions, conditions appropriate especially to X, conditions of paying appropriate attention to X or having X as an intentional object, ideal conditions, whatever-conditions-it-takes . . .

I shall abbreviate these three place-holders as [P], [R], and [C]. When nothing hinges on separating them, I shall lump [P] and [C] together as [P,C]. The many degrees of freedom they introduce are increased when we turn to another choice point. For any equation of this kind might be advanced for different philosophical purposes, and we should keep in mind at least these. There is the purpose of old-fashioned analysis. This is to display on the right-hand side the very concept from the left, with its structure made visible on the model of 'to be a vixen is to be a female fox'. The biconditionals could therefore be rewritten as straight analyses:

> The concept of ϕ is that of tending to elicit [R] from [P,C]

but the sophistication I have mentioned allows that we do not have to be saying this. The purpose of identifying something about the 'logic' of the concept or 'explicating' it or giving the conditions governing its application may not demand a strict identity. Why will something less than an analysis do? Notably, it has been suggested, a condition on an old-fashioned analysis will be non-circularity, whereas for other elucidatory purposes this need not be so. We might presumably learn something about the application conditions of 'boring' by being told that the conditions governing its application are that X is boring ≡ we tend to be bored by X under normal conditions. That this is a substantive claim is proved by its actually being false (normal conditions might be the noisy, crowded, theatrical milieu hostile to realizing that X is not at all boring, but imaginative and demanding).[3] Adopting a useful term from Richard Holton, we can say that we have an 'echo' proposal when ϕ reappears on the right-hand side (Holton 1993). Echoing biconditionals can clearly be true (X is ϕ ≡ X is ϕ), and the claim now is that the echo does not disqualify them from doing at least some philosophical work.[4] How much remains to be seen.

A different purpose might be that of giving a substantive truth condition. This can be supposed to be something different from the above, modelled on the 'substantive' identity of water and H_2O or heat of a gas and the kinetic energy of its molecules. But few of those investigating these biconditionals see them as playing this role. Accepting Kripke's account, these scientific identities are necessarily true, but not a priori. But the kind of biconditional envisaged for, say, boring or red is usually thought of as a priori: part of the interest of the matter is that if true they enable us to know a priori that what [P] [react to] under [C] is indeed boring or red.[5]

At this point it is important to keep in mind a distinction. I have laid out the landscape so far as if our interest is in a kind of *concept*, or equivalently a kind of *judgement*, which the right-hand side is supposed to illuminate in some way. We need to keep in mind that another focus of interest might be the *property* referred to by the predicate 'ϕ'. For some of us there is not much of a difference here: I myself see properties as the semantic shadows of predicates, not as self-standing objects of investigation. But others see the matter differently: they think of there being a substantive science of identifying the property ϕ which is not the same thing as identifying the concept ϕ, or the role ϕ judgements play in our thought. Thus a popular kind of moral realism ('Cornell realism') searches for natural properties with which to identify the property of being good. Property identity becomes a topic of its own. I shall call this the substantive way of thinking of properties. With it we get a sense/reference distinction for predicates. Two

---

[3] See also Johnston 1989: 147–8.

[4] Echoing explications are endorsed by, among many others, McGinn 1983 and McDowell 1985. The idea of opening them up is often credited to David Wiggins.

[5] The value of a prioricity here is stressed by Wright 1988. The difficulty of filling the placeholders so that the biconditionals are not trivial but remain a priori is well brought out by Holton 1993 and Edwards 1992.

predicates might denote the same property, but in different ways. The judgement that X is good is not the judgement that X creates happiness, even if, on such a philosophy, there is but the one property, creation of happiness, which is also to be seen as goodness, although seeing it this way is doing something extra. We can put this by saying that there is something special about seeing the creation of happiness *under the heading of* being good, and we would not understand ethical *judgement* until we have a sense of what is special about that heading. I return to this point below, but for the moment the topic is its impact on the basic biconditionals.

To make this plain, let us focus on a simple example:

(P) X is poisonous ≡ X tends to elicit illness or death from most of us on being ingested.

This, I hope, sounds about right, and any rough edges are not presently to the point.[6] In fact, it looks like a good old-fashioned analysis of the *concept*, but in any event it affords some elucidation or explication of it. What does it tell us about the property? The substantive way of thinking means that it allows a further hunt for finding what the property of being poisonous actually is. For instance, suppose that all and only things with cyanide molecules are poisonous. Then having cyanide molecules might be the property of being poisonous. This one property can be seen under the one heading—chemically—or the other—medically—and no doubt many others—economically or sociologically.

As I say, I am not myself an advocate of this way of thinking about the semantics of predicates. But at present I am not objecting to it, but pointing out its consequences for the present issues. What it means is that it is quite consistent to hold that (P) tells us everything we need about the *concept* of being poisonous, although it is also true that the *property* of being poisonous is that of containing cyanide molecules. (P) identifies the property under one heading, and this identifies it under another, and each is perfectly acceptable. To take a more interesting example, suppose we have

(C) X is red ≡ X tends to make normal people see-redly under suitable conditions of observation

---

[6] It is right for foodstuffs, but not for many snakes, which are poisonous although benign when ingested. This shows that [C] may vary with X.

then this is quite compatible with the kind of physicalist hunt for the property of redness, that hopes to locate some disjunction of physical properties holding of all and only red things.[7] On the substantive picture, this hunt is not a rival to an analysis like (C), any more than in the poisonous case, but a supplement to it.

If (P) is necessary, then things with cyanide molecules would not be poisonous unless they tended to elicit illness or death from most of us on being ingested. The right-hand side of the biconditional gives us the identifying condition, or that in virtue of which the property of having cyanide molecules is that of being poisonous. It explains why having cyanide molecules can be seen under that heading. Similarly, the right-hand side of (C) tells us why reflecting light of 700 nanometers (or . . . , or . . .) can be seen under the heading of being red.

Here we should notice one cost of the substantive way of thinking. So far all is well: we have it that containing cyanide molecules is the same property as being poisonous, and we have the biconditional telling us what it is about the property that makes it deserve that appellation. But we might reflect that even if true, it seems highly contingent if things of just one or another molecular structure elicit illness and death. So we seem to be peddling a contingently true property identity: the property of containing cyanide molecules is the property of being poisonous, but it might not have been. This is quite compatible with the substantive way of thinking, but it offends against one strong semantic intuition, which is that when we turn the predicate 'ϕ' into the noun phrase 'the property of being ϕ' we end up with a rigid designator of a property. If the property of being ϕ is the property of being ψ, there ought not to be possible worlds in which they ('they') are not identical. If we want to heed this intuition we should abandon (thankfully in my view) the substantive way of thinking of properties, and go back to saying that if the biconditionals give us the property, then further investigation is simply one of telling us what explains why things are poisonous or what explains why things are red. We need not then worry whether these are the only things that *could* have been poisonous or red, as we have to if rigid reference is in play. But for this essay I am not going to take this argument as decisive, and shall allow the

<hr>

[7] Of course, it is known that this disjunction will be hopelessly unwieldy. To repeat, I am not advocating that we think of any such thing as 'being the property of redness', because I do not advocate thinking in these terms at all.

substantive way of thinking as an alternative. It is not wholly foreign to everyday ways of thought, although I shall argue later that it has caused considerable confusion in the area.

2. Dispositions and Finks

Before assessing the work these biconditionals may do, a further point remains to be made about them. I have deliberately couched them in terms of dispositions and tendencies. A more ambitious project would remove that terminology, and substitute conditionals:

X is ϕ ≡ if [P] encounter X in [C] there arises [R]

A subjunctive form might be used instead. Elaborating on the notion of a 'finkish' situation, Mark Johnston has been active in generating counterexamples to analyses of this form.[8] In a finkish situation, a thing is disposed in some way, but if circumstances apt for manifesting the disposition come about, it will not manifest it. Or conversely, a thing may not be disposed in some way, but if circumstances apt for manifesting the disposition come about, it will do so. This may be because it changes when the antecedent of the conditional is fulfilled. Or it may be because the disposition is what Johnston calls 'masked', or that although the disposition is absent it is mimicked. Examples of finkish situations are: a thing may be brittle, but an angel has decided that if it is dropped she will make it hard; so although it is brittle, if it is dropped it will not break. A thing may be hard, but the same angel has decided that she will render it brittle if it is dropped, and so if it is dropped it will break.

Johnston suggests that these cases and others like them show that we make a distinction between what is 'underwritten by the thing's intrinsic nature and the laws' and what would happen if . . . In finkish situations, a thing's intrinsic nature and the laws make it *such as to* break when dropped, although actually it will not, or vice versa. There are costs in appealing to intrinsic natures, for we may well wonder whether we have any notion at all of a thing's nature and of the laws of nature, that is not itself couched in

---

[8] Johnston 1994: App. 2. I owe the term 'finkish' to David Lewis; Johnston avoids calling his situations finkish, but the term is useful.

dispositional terms.[9] But we need not follow Johnston to intrinsic natures as far as these cases go. For we should also notice that insofar as the cases involve supernatural agency this response can hardly be needed: we can just invoke nature, *tout court*: a thing is brittle if its breaking when dropped is in accordance with nature and its laws.

It is not so easy to construct finkish cases where we try to put the angel on board, as it were, or in other words imagine a thing being brittle but naturally such that when it is dropped its nature transforms into that of something hard. If it continually fails to break, it seems not to be brittle, whatever the underlying evolutions of physical state. This is certainly so for other dispositions. Suppose that I have the 'intrinsic nature' of a capable rock climber: I am strong, agile, trained, and eager. Except that I have one more quirk: the proximity of rock causes me to change (my hands become sweaty), and this temporarily stops me having the same nature as a capable rock climber and I become apt to fall off. The natural description is not that I am a capable rock climber most of the time, but finked when I get on the rock, but that I am a bad rock climber. This is usually what it feels like being a bad rock climber or bad pianist: it feels as if the circumstances of performance conspire to make your real merit shrink. But this is false consciousness. My rock climber is not a capable rock climber who generates a 'standing illusion' of being worse than he is. The disposition is assessed by the conditional, and *natural* changes in a thing arising on the circumstance of manifestation of the conditional do not affect the description.

We can signal this difference between external or supernatural finkish situations, and natural evolutions, by writing the biconditionals:

$$X \text{ is } \phi \equiv X \text{ is naturally such as to elicit [R] from [P] in [C]}$$

where the 'naturally such as to' warns that something might be ϕ although adventitious angels stop it performing as such. But this formula does not allow something to be ϕ if its own mechanisms trip in to prevent manifestation.

Johnston's further case for invoking intrinsic natures is also supposed to unseat response-dependent analyses of secondary properties such as colour. This is the case of the 'shy but intuitive' chameleon. This sits in the dark having one colour, green, but ready to change to a different colour, red,

[9] See Blackburn 1990.

if the light is put on. It is actually green, but by the equation (C) it is red. But although Johnston sees such cases as support for his invocation of an intrinsic nature, the matter is not so simple. After all, in such a story it *is* the intrinsic nature of this chameleon to go into its red mode, so we should expect the parallel result to the rock climber case, namely that it is always red. Perhaps it is important to distinguish between the thing and its surface, and Johnston's claim will be that the intrinsic nature of the surface is that of a green surface in the dark, so the right thing to say is that the chameleon's surface, and hence the chameleon, is green in the dark. So suppose instead a light-sensitive surface that instantly reacts to bombardment by photons by changing its structure slightly, like photographic paper, only more so. Perhaps my red ruby is like that. It is never ever seen as green, and indeed could not be, although in the dark its surface is physically isomorphic with that of things which, when like that in good light, look green. Is it green in the dark? Johnston's formula gives us no clear guideline. The 'intrinsic nature' of this surface and the laws ensure that when the light goes on it reflects red light. So taken one way we should think of it as red in the dark; on the other hand, its physical structure is such that were it to stay as it is when put in the light it would reflect green light.

The case seems to be a 'don't care', hinging on the elasticity of being such as to do something: in some respects, the surface of the ruby is such as to appear red, and in other respects, it is such as to appear green, because if it stayed with the reflective properties it has in the dark that is how it would appear. We make a verdict on these cases by *imagining* seeing the surface *as it now is*, and retailing the visual experience we imagine ourselves to have. What the case gives us is two ways of looking at how the surface now is, and concentrating on one way we think of ourselves as seeing green, and the other way we think of ourselves as seeing red (for this surface stays *as it now is* by clicking into red mode when there is any light).

Here are some other examples of this Berkeleyan genre.

Case 1: the finkish skunk. Suppose skunks with the magic property of sucking all the molecules they emit back in when olfactory systems come near enough to detect any. Do they emit bad smells? We might think not: you can safely have one of these as a pet, but you don't want smelly pets. Now suppose that when an olfactory system is present they retract all the bad molecules and release Chanel No 5. Are they fragrant—even when they are alone in the forest? If the purely retractive skunks have no smell, then these have a wonderful smell. Or, we may, like Hylas, be tempted to say that the skunks emit good or bad smells depending on the molecules and regardless of the lawlike impossibility of any smell being perceived. Again, I suggest we have a 'don't care': looked at one way, the space round the skunks is not a space you would want to be in (keep the molecules constant, and imagine sniffing). Looked at another, it is fine (keep the nature of the skunks constant, and imagine sniffing). We can exercise the imagination either way.

Case 2: the finkish pig. The flesh of these pigs would taste frightful as it is actually constituted. It contains molecules that have well-known bad effects on taste-buds. But death or dismemberment destroys the molecules, and makes them taste delicious. Are these pigs delicious as they gambol round the yard, or should our mouths not water as we look at them? Here there is less temptation to be even temporarily puzzled, and there is even something off-colour and irritating about the question.[10] But we are surely inclined to give the same answer as for the rock climber. These pigs are delicious, *tout court*. (Maybe pigs and pheasants are actually like this.) 'Delicious' may be analysed by slightly rephrasing our biconditional:

$$X \text{ is delicious at } t \equiv X \text{ is naturally such that if } [C] \text{ then } [P] \text{ give } [R]$$

making it plain that it is what happens in [C] that counts. For pigs, whatever else it includes, [C] includes being dead. It does not follow that being delicious cannot be predicated of live pigs, because the left-hand side does not include the qualification 'in [C]'. It could read 'X is delicious always $\equiv \ldots$'. Equally we could modify both sides with 'at t'. Quite possibly ordinary thought simply does not care what temporal modifier goes there, and this would explain our irritation with the question whether the live pig is delicious.[11]

---

[10] We feel quite free with other janus-faced dispositions where it is not change that is involved. Many snakes inject several different kinds of venom. Suppose a snake adapted not to poison mammals but only birds, and suppose that only one of its venoms is poisonous in mammals while its second chemical acts so as to neutralize the poison. Is it a poisonous snake? It injects a poison, but you can step on it with impunity. We don't much care: in some respects it is such as to poison, and in others not. Do guardian angels guard from danger, or mean that there is no danger?

[11] Crispin Wright reacts to the shy but intuitive chameleon by a slightly different modification. He revokes the simple biconditional, and substitutes a 'provisional' equation, of the form 'if [C], then a thing is ϕ iff [R]'. No verdict is given on the chameleon or the lone skunk or the live pig, because the circumstances of good observation do not hold. This certainly chimes with the irritation we feel with questions like 'is he a good rock climber, when there is no rock about?' My reason for avoiding it is that I believe that the right equation should show us how a dispositional property can be instanced even when not manifested.

So far, we have it that we solve the rock climber and the finkish pig fairly definitely one way. With the skunk we are more apt to be ambivalent, and I have suggested that this is a consequence of not having settled what has to stay the same as we put ourselves in the situation of smelling the skunk. Johnston's problem with colour, I take it, is that he thinks there is a definite verdict going the other way. The chameleon is supposed to be green, not red, in the dark. People want to say that colours are categorically present in the dark, and one way of tightening up that intuition would be to say that we have no freedom to insert temporal modifications as we wish on the left-hand side.

I cannot see this telling us anything deep about colour, nor putting an obstacle in front of a dispositional analysis. For even if we share Johnston's intuition, the dispositional analysis can accommodate us. Suppose we are adamant that the chameleon is green. Then, just as if we are adamant that the lone skunk smells awful, all we need to do is to weight our selection of the feature dominating the 'is naturally such that' clause. Perhaps simple-minded faith in colours correlating straightforwardly with physical properties of surfaces encourages this selection, so that we imagine the chameleon's colour or the skunk's smell by imagining good circumstance of seeing and smelling but fixing the corrugations of the surface or the distribution of molecules. We then soft-pedal the fact that in good circumstances of seeing and smelling this will not be the set-up any more. Also, if we were attracted to the substantial view of properties, we may have identified the colour green with the property of having such-and-such a corrugated surface, and this will tip our judgement violently that way, and even do the same for the skunk and pig. Otherwise it is hard to see the argument, and I suspect that those who place great importance on objects being coloured one way or another in the dark forget that we imagine the colours of reflective surfaces in the dark by imagining the light on.

The upshot is that we can avoid finkish problems by staying with the dispositional suggestions with which I started, and we can sidestep chameleons, skunks, pigs, and their ilk by looking out for elasticities in how we think of things as being, or what we think it would be for things to stay the same. We mark this by rephrasing the biconditionals:

X is ϕ ≡ X (is naturally such as to) tend to elicit [R] from [P] under [C] where the bracketed phrase reminds us that something may be such as to do this in some respects and not in others, and that these will give rise to wrongly disputed cases.

3. Explanatory Priorities and Analysis

The points already in play enable us to deflect one across-the-board reservation about the success of response-dependent accounts of concepts. Mark Johnston puts it by finding a tension between the a priori status the biconditionals have, and the way in which the left-hand side functions as an empirical explanation of the right (Johnston 1993). The 'missing explanation argument' is that frequently it is explanatory to say that it is because X is ϕ that it has or we have the dispositions identified on the right-hand side; this being so we cannot see the biconditionals as a priori true. Johnston suggests that this argument works at least except for concepts that wear their response dependence on their face (pleasing, shy-making, nauseating). In particular, it works for values and it works for secondary properties. He suggests that the argument shows that ordinary concepts are *not* response dependent, although he concedes that this leaves open a programme of reform, suggesting that their response independence is the upshot of something like a projective error.

The argument is a daring one, in the light of all the well-known pragmatic and contextual factors that lead us to allow that one thing is an explanation of another. We can undoubtedly hear ourselves saying that things are disposed to look green to us in favourable circumstances because they are green; seem boring to us because they are boring, and so on. But the superficial linguistic data will not carry the load of this argument, because it is quite compatible with an a priori equivalence between explanans and explanandum. As Wright points out, we can equally hear ourselves saying that the figure is a circle because it is the locus of a line equidistant from a point, or that such and such a connective is material implication because it has the truth table TFTT. An a priori status is jeopardized only if the explanation is a contingent one. Johnston recognizes this, and in a response to Wright emphasizes that the explanations in question are contingent, empirical, and causal, although he also makes it plain that their causal status is less important than the other two (Johnston 1993).

As well as showing that the use of the left-hand side to explain the right is use of a contingent or empirical or causal connection, the argument needs extreme care over the explanandum and explanans. The biconditionals may be a priori and indeed analytic, but still we would be able to explain why we found something boring on an occasion, or why I find X boring, by saying that X is boring, and such explanations may be contingently true or false. For it may be contingent whether on this occasion I or we were bored because of X being such as to excite boredom from [P,C]. It may be contingent whether the occasion counted as [C], or I or we as [P]. It may be that we were bored because of something quite different: we were out of sorts, or there were roadworks outside the theatre. The explanation rules out these possibilities: it works by saying that we were *true to form* by being bored. (This point parallels one commonly made about opium and its dormitive virtue.)

To put this aside, suppose we take the whole population, as we should be doing:

X elicits [R] from [P] in [C] *because* it is ϕ.

Can we get a reading which is contingent or empirical or causal, for the appropriate cases, and thereby rules out the a priori equivalence of the two sides? It seems strange that there should be an empirical or causal science of whether it is boring things that bore us, or red things that we see as red. I suspect there are ways of reading such sentences as contingent, and even empirical and causal. But on no way of so reading them does the conclusion follow. These ways are quite compatible with the a priori status of the biconditional. Here are four such possibilities.

(1) [C] or [P] or [R] could be chosen so badly that there is indeed a contingent, causal, and empirical gap between the two sides with the inept substitutions in place. But this is clearly irrelevant to the a priori status of the conditional with better-judged substitutions. The different question of whether any substitutions fit the bill entirely occupies us in the next section.

(2) Even when [C] and [P] and [R] are chosen with care, there may be an empirical investigation in the offing. Suppose we identify some favourable circumstances. The question may still arise why these *are* the favourable circumstances, and contingent and causal factors may enter the answer. But this does not impugn the a prioricity. For example, a kite is well designed $\equiv$

it flies well in favourable wind conditions. Which are those? Let us say
between force two and six. Why are those the favourable conditions?
Because they prevail quite frequently, because we are comfortable in them,
because air has the density it does. All of these are contingent, and they
underlie the choice of these conditions. But that does not impugn the
definitional status of the original biconditional. It simply introduces a new
topic of interest.

(3) Perhaps 'because' contexts introduce reference to properties, so the
explanation reads in effect that X elicits [R], etc., because of having the
property ϕ. Given a substantive theory of properties (see above) this may
be contingent, but we saw in section 1 that this contingency is compatible
with an analytic status for the biconditional.

Johnston misses this possibility. He cites against Wright the 'Cornell
realists' in ethics, who emphasize the propriety of putting ethical predicates
into explanatory contexts, and allow, for instance, that it is contingent that
we generally approve of things because they are good. But he does not see
that the Cornell realists are bad allies at this point. They have a substantive
theory of properties, and the properties referred to in the explanation
are those natural properties that contingently excite our approval. The
contingency of the explanation is perfectly compatible with the a prioricity
of the related biconditional (a thing is good $\equiv$ it is such as to excite
[R] in [P,C]); this is the point I made above in connection with the
notion of a thing being poisonous. The point is that a prioricity concerns
information, or its constituent concepts. Explanation here concerns the
relationship between properties. Since properties are here treated as capable
of being apprehended in different ways, an a priori proposition can mask
a contingent relationship between them. The point was made familiar
by Davidson in connection with events: if something caused ϕ, then the
proposition that the event ϕ was caused by the cause of ϕ is a priori, but
the events stand in a contingent causal relationship.

(4) Through time a thing may have evolved to be as it is because of the
effect that induces: it may be the colour that has made the flower successful.
This gives us one way of reading the explanatory claim the other way
round. But it also gives us a way of reading it as Johnston does. This is
easier to see if we use the longer form:

X is naturally such as to elicit [R] from [P] in [C] because it is ϕ

and here the 'such as to' formula points us to thinking of the same properties as before—the base or underlying properties—now said to be there because of the redness or whatever that they underlie. Compare: this circuit diminishes the voltage because it has a resistor in it; this circuit has a resistor in it because it diminishes the voltage. Each can be true, and contingent, and each is compatible with there being an analytic equivalence between a component being for diminishing the voltage and it being a resistor.

In these last two cases the substantive view of properties confuses the issue of contingency and makes Johnston's claim look superficially plausible. But as the sense/reference distinction reminds us, it then has no consequences for the a priori status of the biconditionals.

On the other hand, if we eschew the substantive theory of properties, what reading can we give to the explanation? Russell once said it was favouritism to suppose that the things that seem to us blue are the things that are blue, and I suppose the proposal that there might be an empirical and causal investigation of whether this is so in general reflects the same idea. But it does not grip us for long. If it is contingent whether our colour vision is adapted for the real colour of things, then it is very likely contingently false, but what kind of investigation could anybody holding that be envisaging? Might ammonia really have no odor? Has a finkish nature resulted in us being poisoned by things that are not really poisonous? Anybody interested in the dispositional account of secondary properties will reply with justice that part of the point of the analysis is to get away from a general gap between the judgements we are disposed to make and the truth.

The case of values introduces further issues. Once more, however, it is incredible that a scientific, empirical, causal investigation is capable of raising a general gap between the right- and left-hand sides—unless the right-hand side is chosen so badly that one of the four options above is in play. What is true is that we can always distinguish in our thought between something being good and it eliciting any reaction in a given population, and we can prosecute that possibility not by a causal empirical investigation, but by an ethical one, as we mull over the defects of the population (or their reaction, or the circumstances). But this irreducible normativity waits for the next sections. Meanwhile, the upshot is that the 'missing explanation' argument puts no obstacle in front of an a priori status for the biconditionals.

4. Analyses and Circularity

With such excavations behind us, these biconditionals may seem to be well set to do the work claimed for them, and provide a suitable explication of various concepts. So it is time to concentrate on what seems to me to be a real problem, which is that of circularity. As I have said, it is often claimed that a feature of echo in these biconditionals—the reappearance of ϕ on the right-hand side—need not matter, since our goal is explication of a concept rather than analysis. But this is at best a half truth: in fact, more like a one-tenth truth, and often wholly false. The principle to keep hold of is that if you want some things, your biconditional will need to observe some constraints, when if you want others, it might not. Suppose, for instance, that your concern is with what it is to judge that something is ϕ. Then you will be disappointed with an echoing biconditional of this kind:

X is $\phi \equiv$ X (is such as to) dispose [P] in [C] to judge it to be ϕ

because it is what these persons are *doing* in judging something to be ϕ that you wanted explained. For example, if you want to know what it is to judge that something is good, your quest has not been advanced by:

X is good $\equiv$ X (is such as to) dispose [P] in [C] to judge it to be good,

for even if this is true, you gain no understanding of what the persons are doing (what it has to do with their rationality, or emotions, or standards, or social situations, or whatever troubles you).

Obviously a regress arises if we try to make the proposal help with this question by substituting the right-hand side into the content of the judgement:

X is good $\equiv$ X (is such as to) dispose [P] in [C] to judge that X (is such as to) dispose [P] in [C] to judge . . .

And this regress is vicious, because either it is never closed, or it leaves the very activity you wanted explained unanalysed on the clause on which it is closed.

Our goal is frequently to understand judgement that something is ϕ. Indeed, since we are supposedly investigating the concept of ϕ, and since concepts and judgements are the same topic, it may be hard to see how we can be doing anything else, in which case insouciance about the echo is completely inappropriate. It is, however, true that if, surprisingly, understanding judgement had not been your concern, the very same proposal might have had some point. You might feel you understand well enough what people are up to who judge that things are good, but lack any understanding of what could make their judgements *true*, and in the context of that predicament the suggestion could be helpful: what makes it true is that (it is such that) [P] in [C] so judge it. Thus I might feel no philosophical problems about what it is to judge that something is boring (perhaps I have a simple functional story: 'tending to make people fall asleep on contemplating it') and be helped by being told that a thing actually is boring ≡ [P] in [C] judge it boring. So it all depends what we want explaining.

In this context the regress does not arise, because there is no reason to substitute in the content of the judgement. The judging is understood in another way, and the regress sidestepped. But it is essential too to notice that this benefit incurs a cost. For there is a certain lack of harmony between the reaction as specified—tending to fall asleep—and the content that, on this account, that judgement actually has. Naturally I might tend to fall asleep without judging that [P] in [C] so tend, and I might judge this, as it were, in an anthropological spirit, without myself tending to fall asleep. My own disposition to the reaction will be one thing, but the judgement that X has ϕ (i.e. is such as to elicit [R] from [P,C]) is here quite another. This remains true even if as pure subjectivists we replace [P] with me, since I may tend to fall asleep without judging that I do, and without judging that the conditions are [C]. The lack of harmony is that a prominent semantic anchor for 'X is boring' is that I am absolutely and straightforwardly entitled to voice it on having been bored by X (see also essay 2 in this volume). Whereas I am by no means entitled to voice the left-hand side on having been bored by X, unless I can take myself to be representative of [P] and my circumstances to have been in the set [C]. The problems this causes return in the final two sections.

Suppose we stay with the goal of understanding the judgement that X is ϕ. The next problem we meet is not one of regress, but one of navigating between two disasters, that I shall call Scylla and Charybdis. Scylla is that we falsify the kind of judgement 'X is ϕ' actually makes. Charybdis is that we get this right—but at the cost of making (not mentioning, as in the regress problem) the same kind of judgement at some place within the right-hand side. It may be no objection that we make the same kind of judgement with the overall right-hand side, and indeed it can with justice be urged that this will be the point of the biconditional taken as an analysis. But it can well be objectionable when this is achieved by including the very same kind of judgement within the right-hand side.

This structure is familiar in the case of value. Scylla is that we go naturalistic or empirical; Charybdis that we make an ethical judgement on the right-hand side. Contrast:

X is good $\equiv$ X is such as to elicit desires from us as we actually are, when we come across it.

X is good $\equiv$ X is such as to elicit desires from good people when they come across it.

The first, considered as an attempt to understand ethical judgement, must be deemed to fail, because it only gives us an equation with a natural judgement about X, certifiable by empirical means. Notice that if our interest had been in a substantive theory of ethical properties, this might have been acceptable. We would say, in the spirit of Cornell realism, that this is a candidate for being the property of goodness. This leaves to one side the question of what it is to see this property under the heading of the good, as opposed to seeing it as just another natural property, possibly instanced by very regrettable things. But since we are supposing that our interest is in understanding ethical judgement, seeing it under the special heading is the very topic we are pursuing, and this suggestion has mistaken it. Thus Scylla.

The second proposal fails in the complementary way, since what it has done is equate one ethical judgement with another: it takes not observation but ethical judgement to determine whether something is such as to elicit desires from good people, since you have to judge who are the good people. Of course, in principle an advance *within* ethics could come about this way, since it might be somehow easier to judge who are the good people than it appears to be to judge X's. But this will not be an advance in our understanding of ethical judgement per se. It would be a strictly local advance in first order moral theory.

How wide does Charybdis gape? For a particularly spectacular dive into it, consider:

X is good ≡ X is such as to elicit desires from people under the ideal circumstances, i.e. those under which people desire good things.

Everybody accepts that this is trivial. The running-on-the-spot here is indeed emphasized by the irrelevance of the way the each of [R] and [P] is identified. That is, you might just as well have:

X is good ≡ X is such as to elicit astonishment from polar bears under the ideal circumstances

if you identify ideal circumstances as those under which polar bears are astonished at good things. Obviously similar equations can be constructed for any judgement at all. But how much ethical can be left in the right-hand side? Again, it will depend how much context you bring to it. But so long as the right-hand side makes the same *kind* of judgement as the left, it will not serve to elucidate the kind. In the following schema the presence of just one of the curly bracketed terms will disqualify the equation from the task of understanding ethical judgement and colour judgement respectively:

X is good ≡ X {deserves} the judgement that it is {good} from {good/improved/virtuous} . . . persons under {ideal} conditions.

X is red ≡ X is naturally such as to elicit the judgement that it is {red} from non-{colourblind} persons under conditions favourable for {colour} discrimination.

The question will be whether the brackets can be removed without stripping the equations of any a priori status they ought to have, and falling into the clutches of Scylla. Putting fig leaves over the bracketed terms only postpones the problem.[12]

Scylla and Charybdis will flank any attempt to understand judgement of a particular *sui generis* kind by means of these biconditionals. But it may be hard to believe that there is no room to navigate between them. Remembering that the goal is to understand some kind of judgement, we should recall that an increase in understanding may be contextual. For instance,

X is boring ≡ X is such as to elicit sleep dispositions from normal people under circumstances that are good for appreciating X

---

[12] Potential fig leaves: merits, standard, normal, suitable, sees-redly, sees red', has a visual experience as of seeing English pillar boxes . . .

might look as if it drowns in Charybdis. It will if the best we can say about circumstances good for appreciating X are: circumstances such that if X is funny, we laugh; if X is tragic, we heave, if X is boring, we get bored . . . (equally, we drown if the best that can be said about normal people is that they are the ones who laugh at what is funny . . . and get bored by what is boring). But if we can do better than that, the equation might be an advance. It will be if we already understand other kinds of appreciation, and can understand a general notion of evaluating circumstances of appreciation, and have a general notion of normal people. We then learn to place the judgement that something is boring within this family, and that could be the understanding we needed. Once more, this will be a strictly local advance, placing one of a family of concepts at the table, but not helping to place the general appreciative table. Again, then, the issue hinges on the explanatory context.

All the attempts that I know of to understand value judgements in general by giving dispositional accounts meet Scylla or drown in Charybdis.

5. Looking at Ourselves?

Ordinary thought seems to have been rather casual about the identity of [P], [C], and even [R], if we are to judge by the limited success philosophers have had in recommending privileged instances. This confirms the evident truth that to enable a learner to use and communicate regarding smells or colours, we do not have to load them with something like:

> X smells foxy ≡ X is naturally such that it elicits from most normal people who do not have colds or other relevant disabilities, in circumstances of still air with no other smells (!) present, the judgement that X smells like a fox.

On the face of it, using and understanding the concepts here displayed betokens a much greater conceptual sophistication than knowing how to report that there is a foxy smell in the garden, which will have been taught by ostension, and by induction into a fairly flexible practice of subjecting such claims to a certain amount of critical scrutiny (for which, see more below). Of course, the response-dependence theorist may reply that he is not trying for an analysis, but as we saw above this has costs: she is after all trying for some elucidation of the judgement, and the point is that we have no reason for confidence that the biconditional shows us how the judgement *works* (Wittgenstein 1966: 1–3 is good on this).

Connected with this is the point that often these judgements are more like *verdicts* than hypotheses about the suspected reactions of some other group under some putative circumstances. If I am asked whether the picture was beautiful or the play interesting, I dissemble if I say that it was *because* I hypothesize that most people find it so, although I personally couldn't stand it. What is expected is that I give my own verdict. 'Yes, it was fascinating' expresses how I found it. My verdict can be challenged, of course, but the challenge is not itself a hypothesis about [P] and [C], but an attempt to show that my feeling was unwarranted—that I ought not to have found it beautiful or fascinating. Notice, too, that if I then retreat to say (huffily, as it might be), 'Well, *I* thought it was fascinating,' I am not retreating to saying that *my* hypothesis was that it was such as to elicit [R] form [P,C]. I am repeating my own verdict or expressing my own reaction.

We here have what I earlier called the lack of harmony between the reaction and the things that make true the biconditional elaborated upon it. The logical space I enter when I make my verdict is not that of an empirical hypothesis about the reactions of some identifiable group of people. As Kant put it for the case of beauty, the judgement of taste does not 'postulate' the agreement of everyone, but 'imputes' it, or 'exacts it from everyone else as necessary' (Kant 1952: 52–9). 'The assertion is not that everyone *will* fall in with our judgement, but that everyone *ought* to agree with it' (Kant 1952: 84).

Kant's insight is confirmed by another phenomenon that is prominent in these cases. I may know empirically that X is such as to elicit [R] from [P,C], but because I have no experience of X, I cannot without misrepresentation answer the question, 'Is X beautiful/boring/fascinating . . .?' I can only answer that other people think so, or that I am longing to see it. I cannot say *tout court* that it was one or the other without giving an overwhelming impression that I have myself been in a position to make a judgement, and have made it. This is highly mysterious on the hypothesis that the judgement functions as a straight description of the reactions of an identified group in identified circumstances.

Of course, a normative element can be overtly included on the right-hand side:

X is $\phi \equiv$ X is such that [P] in [C] ought to give [R].

And typically this is right enough as far as it goes. A thing is boring $\equiv$ people ought to be bored by it. As Kant saw, the whole question then turns on our right to invoke norms at this point, or in his terms, on why our judgements do not retain a purely 'subjective validity'.[13] This is the same as the question of how the judgement of taste is even possible—how can there be *space* for a genuine judgement here? The quasi-realist project of earning our right to a judgemental form is by no means bypassed but is actually highlighted and centre stage if this is the kind of biconditional on offer. And this is inevitable, given that where value terms are in play the echo is not at all benign, but points us straight at Charybdis. For the right-hand side is another example of the kind of judgement we might have been hoping to understand.

6. Secondary Properties Again

Let us return to secondary properties. Even if the biconditionals have lost ground as a device for showing us how evaluation works, might they retain a place here? We have deflected the argument from the missing explanation and from the finkish complexities, so the way might seem relatively clear to relying on them. On the other hand, reluctance to take the echoing impredicativity lightly will be difficult to accommodate. For enough work has stressed the impropriety of avoiding the echo by going private and imagining a different property of experience whose presence amounts to the reaction in question. If that route is closed, as I think it is, then the only way of identifying the reaction is as that of someone who judges that something is red, or smells like ammonia, or sounds like concert A. So the form of the offering is now:

X is $\phi \equiv$ X is such as to elicit the judgement that it is ϕ from [P,C].

Does this kind of offering (or the claim that it is a priori) help us to understand the way judgement of colour or smell or sound works, in

---

[13] For aesthetics, many people now probably think in effect that they do.

spite of the echo? The flexibility in [P] and [C] complicates the issue. But for any substantive fillings, something is wrong, akin to the misdirection these equations introduce in the case of values. There we do not, as I put it, turn our gaze through ninety degrees and concern ourselves with our reactions. And here, too, we do not turn our gaze on our population or circumstances. Certainly we do have a sense of our judgements being corrigible, if enough people do not confirm them, or the light turns out to have been deceptive.[14] But we do not wrap this practice of corrigibility, necessary as it is for the purpose of communicating what to expect, into the content for the actual judgement of colour. If we did, those of us unfortunate enough not to have a grip on some favoured fillings for [P] and [C] would be unable to judge colour.

The point here can be easy to miss. In the context of defending a dispositional account, John McDowell once asked rhetorically: 'What would one expect it to be like to experience something's being such as to look red, if not to experience the thing in question (in the right circumstances) as looking, precisely, red?' (McDowell 1985: 112). The answer is straightforward. Imagine anyone able to determine whether something is such as to elicit the judgement that it is red from [P,C] by any means we like: touch, sound when struck, monochromatic contrast with other objects. Just as a chemist might determine that a thing is poisonous by giving himself visual experience of its molecular construction, so any of these methods may certify the disposition of a thing. It will be purely contingent whether there exist such methods for any particular secondary quality. The point is, of course, that anybody arriving at a hypothesis about a secondary quality in such a way is not judging its *colour*. She is in the same position as someone who, not having seen the painting, says in the anthropological spirit that it is beautiful because she knows the reactions of those who have. It is the reaction of those who are judging the colour or the beauty that we need to understand; the fact that an outsider could plug into the existence of their reaction, and make the dispositional judgement

---

[14] Although the way we actually work this latter is interesting. We do not only say, 'It wasn't green: the light was misleading,' but also, 'Funny: it is green in that light.' Our attachment to single colours for objects is quite casual. Metamerism is not usually described as things of the same colour, which appear different from each other in different lights, but things of the same colour in one light, and different colour in different lights.

on her own account, shows that the dispositional judgement is not what was wanted.

McDowell insists that the crucial reaction 'presents itself as perceptual awareness of properties genuinely possessed by the objects that confront one', and in this he may be right. But the perceptual awareness does not typically include in its scope [C] (most people cannot just see, for instance, whether it is a clear northern light, or one of a different colour temperature). Still less does it include [P] and how they would be disposed to react.

Similarly, by tasting a substance and being poisoned, I may be in a position to guess that others would be so too, but I am certainly not in a position to know that, and still less do I have the content of that judgement presented perceptually. *That* would be something quite different, like a movie of people collapsing.

The crucial residual problem for secondary quality perception is now apparent. Colours are seen, sounds heard, smells smelled. The problem is not that McDowell's remark is true, but that it is hard to understand how it can be true. Our reactions *do* present themselves as perceptual awareness, yet we have no stable conception of their *right* to so present themselves. The true situation is probably much more easily understood with smell and taste than with colour: we are more easily led by Berkeley to think that the nose or palate tells us nothing about the world, than that chromatic vision tells us nothing either. The problem of their right to do so is exactly analogous to Kant's problem with the judgement of beauty, but the solution that we want a normative practice of demanding a similar response from others is not nearly so plausible. Dispositional accounts solve the problem of right, but make colours and the rest essentially imperceptible. Rebounding from that, we confront the problem of how the bare subjectivity of response transforms itself into a genuine awareness of a property.[15] Once more, then, far from superseding approaches which wrestle with the problem of how to understand the emergence of judgement from human response,

---

[15] In an excellent paper (Smith 1990), A. D. Smith highlights Descartes saying that 'even bodies are not properly speaking known by the senses or by the faculty of imagination'. It is one thing to think that Descartes was wrong, but quite another to understand how.

concentration on the dispositional biconditionals threatens to conceal even the need for just such an understanding.

POSTSCRIPT

This essay goes through a number of scholastic hoops in order to make a point about an essentially scholastic literature. It takes seriously more of a 'post-Kripkean' approach to metaphysics and analysis than I now believe to be valuable. But perhaps its own intricacies are the best guide I can offer to why I doubt much of the value that has been attributed to modern 'analytic metaphysics', and for that reason I have included it here. It also bears upon some of the discussion in essay 13, in which I consider the debate between Bernard Williams and Hilary Putnam on closely related matters.

13

The Absolute Conception:
Putnam vs. Williams

Science deals exclusively with things as they are in themselves; and art exclusively with things as they affect the human sense and human soul. Her work is to portray the appearances of things, and to deepen the natural impressions which they produce upon living creatures. The work of science is to substitute facts for appearances, and demonstrations for impressions. Both, observe, are equally concerned with truth; the one with truth of aspect, the other with truth of essence. Art does not represent things falsely, but truly as they appear to mankind. Science studies the relations of things to each other: but art studies only their relations to man.

John Ruskin, *Stones of Venice*, 11.47–8

Williams wrote that his 'notion of an absolute conception' can serve to make effective a distinction between 'the world as it is independent of our experience' and 'the world as it seems to us'. It does this by understanding 'the world as it seems to us' as 'the world as it seems peculiarly to us'; the absolute conception will, correspondingly, be 'a conception of the world that might be arrived at by any investigators, even if they were very different from us' (Williams 1985: 139). It contrasts with parochial or 'perspectival' or what Williams calls peculiar conceptions, ones available only to a more or less restricted set of subjects, who share a contingent sensory apparatus, or culture, or history. The question that I want to discuss is, first, whether this gives us a reliable distinction.

Williams also says that 'the substance of the absolute conception . . . lies in the idea that it could nonvacuously explain how it itself, and the various perspectival views of the world, are possible' (Williams 1978: 246). This is a different, and apparently a more ambitious claim. One might think, for instance, that any sufficiently advanced investigators of a world like ours, even if they are very different from us, might converge on, say, something like Newton's laws of motion, or even on subsequent physics and mathematics. But there is no evident reason why that should equip them to explain how our perspectival view of the world is possible, if only because they may not be equipped to understand our view of the world or to know what it is. Indeed, Williams's well-known and highly developed sense of history suggests that his view ought to be that often they will *not* be equipped to understand some of our social, political, and ethical concepts, precisely because these are the contingent growths of our peculiar history, and need to be understood in historical terms. Williams himself says as much (1978: 301–2). There is a tension here in his thought, or even an outright inconsistency, and Hilary Putnam and others are right to notice it.[1]

Williams's distinction is a cousin, at least, of the primary/secondary quality distinction. It is sometimes suggested that this in turn was the child of a particular historical time, the result of one phase of science, but with no claim on those before, or by implication those of us now past, that time. This is not true, for some version of the distinction long precedes seventeenth-century science. It was widely found in the classical world, being a side-product of ancient atomism, and implicit in the standard tropes of scepticism.[2] It remains true, of course, that the distinction was very much highlighted in the seventeenth century, not only because of the resurgence of materialism and atomism, but also with the Copernican recognition of the role of the observer. It is also highly debatable how that distinction was to be drawn, and both Locke's arguments for the distinction, and the distinction itself, were rapidly contested (Smith 1990). Berkeley, perhaps following Pierre Bayle, who in turn credited Simon Foucher, denied that the distinction had any substance at all.[3] Notably, he did this by using a precursor of Putnam's 'entanglement' arguments (Berkeley puts it in terms of hostility to 'abstraction') to urge that we could have no idea of a world conceived in purely primary quality terms. Berkeley argues that if we take away the features that relate to our specific senses in the way, whatever it

---

[1] Putnam pounces on the inconsistency in his 1992: 99. See also Rosen 1994.

[2] See e.g. Hankinson 1995: 155–92.

[3] Berkeley 1988: *Principles* §§9–10; Bayle 1965: entry for 'Pyrrho'.

may be, that colour is specific to sight, we are left with no conception of an object at all, and hence no conception of the bearer of some reduced set of primary qualities.

In Berkeley a conception, or what he calls an idea, is of course an empirically tinged notion, identified with a presentation in the imagination, so it may be that a Lockean can evade the argument by admitting that even if we have no conception by these standards of a purely primary qualitied object, we can nevertheless perfectly well understand the notion. For what follows, it is important as well to notice that while Locke's distinction is in essence *metaphysical*, or at least physical, Berkeley's objection is in terms of what we can *conceive* of, or what we have an idea of, or can represent to ourselves. We should also notice that Locke defended his distinction by calling on the relative *stability* of primary quality perception compared to the potential *variability* of secondary quality perception, and this asymmetry, whatever it may come to, does not require that anyone can conceive of the world in purely primary terms. The asymmetry is denied by Berkeley, but it is hard not to feel that there is something to it (Berkeley 1988: *Principles* §§14–15). So something like Williams's contrast has an initial appeal. It is not implausible to suppose that rational Martians would, if intelligent and scientific enough, come to share with us the scientific framework we employ, deploying thoughts about spatial configuration, temporal passage, velocity, mass, energy, electric charge, and no doubt others, while there would be less presumption that they would taste as we do, smell the same smells, feel heat or cold as we do, or respond to colours in our way. There is just as little presumption that they would have anything like our moral sensibilities or our political or normative sensibilities, any more than we should expect them to share our senses of humour. Everyone knows that in these areas variations of sensibility are to be expected.

Williams updates Locke in terms of descriptions of the world that have some claim to represent what is 'just there anyway' as opposed to descriptions that are 'peculiar', that is, that are available to us only as creatures with particular constitutions and modes of perception, which we could not suppose to be shared by all rational enquirers. But this introduces a crucially different issue, since we ought to wonder whether at least some concepts that are in his sense peculiar might enable us to represent what is just there anyway, attributing to things *properties* which are just there anyway, but which we pick out or respond to in our own parochial, peculiar way. We can get a vivid sense of this possibility if we think of Nagel's problem with imagining what it is like to be a bat. The bat's *take* on the world, if Nagel is right, remains always opaque to us, for we are not equipped to share it. But what the bat does is certainly to detect things that are just there anyway—solid three-dimensional things, since that's what echolocation is for. Nagel may not be right about the inevitable opacity to us of the bat's take on things. But even his prima facie case for this shows that there is a crucial distinction between the property represented, and the conceptions enabling this representation to occur, and it is one that also opens Williams to Putnam's attack, to which I now turn.[4]

I

In *Renewing Philosophy*, Putnam opens his opposition to Williams by considering two cases where our modes of receptivity seem to be to the fore, namely heat and colour. In each case he rejects the idea that our responses in any sense determine the properties we perceive. In the case of heat, he directs us to the scientifically central concept of temperature. In the case of colour, he draws on the approach of Jonathan Westphal (Westphal 1991). A surface is green just in case it *refuses* to reflect a significant percentage of red light relative to light of other colours, including green. This enables Putnam to write: 'The view that green is a perfectly good property of things, one which is relational in the sense of involving the relations of the surface to light, but not relational in the sense of involving the relations of the surface to *people*, is alive and well' (Putnam 1992: 96). He urges, and we should agree, that whatever dispositionality appears in these accounts is no bar to the idea of these properties appearing in the best scientific conception of the world—our best approximation to Williams's absolute conception.

But this is a question of a *property* appearing in the scientific understanding of the world. Williams's concern initially seemed aimed at a contrast between social and ethical *thinking* and scientific *thinking*. We might put it by saying that while Putnam can follow Westphal in putting *reference*, colour

---

[4] Also noticed by Rosen 1994: 307.

properties themselves, and properties of heat and temperature, firmly into the scientific sphere, that leaves open the question of *sense*, or what above I called different subjects' *take* on things. Someone feeling heat does not usually feel it *as* motion, and somebody thinking of colour, unless he is especially well educated, is unlikely to think of it in terms of refusal of light. Rather, his tactile or visual system substitutes for any need to theorize, delivering a phenomenology instead, a view of the world that indeed selects the properties Westphal and Putnam talk about, but in a way that, for all we can yet see, may be peculiar to us, or peculiar to those of us who have unimpaired tactile and visual systems.

There is of course no single story about the relationship between concept and property. For instance, Putnam here diverges from John McDowell, whose writings on these matters he has otherwise tended to endorse. McDowell says outright that the concept of a sensory quality 'cannot be understood in abstraction from the sensory character of experience. What it is for something to be red, say, is not intelligible unless packaged with an understanding of what it is for something to look red' (McDowell 1996: 29). It is important that McDowell here writes not only of our phenomenological conception of red colour, but of the property or quality itself. But Putnam's approach to redness purely in terms of the relation between a surface and incident light appears to leave out altogether the fact that redness is a *perceptible* property, for us, or any implications for the *concept* that arise from that fact.

Perhaps Williams could leave McDowell and Putnam to wrestle over what is to be said about the *property* of being red. For *some* of his purposes, he could even side with Putnam, so far as that is concerned. For, to repeat, it is enough for some of Williams's purposes if the *concept*, linked at least to the mode of presentation or mode of experience associated with heat or colour, is peculiar to us. And that might be so whatever our best theory of the propety of being coloured or hot turned out to be.

Putnam writes as though if we are talking of our conception of heat or colour, given by experience, the subject has in effect become the *sensation* of heat and colour, and he points out that Williams offers no arguments for denying that sensations are brain processes (Putnam 1992: 94). But it is not clear at all whether this interpretation of a sense/reference distinction is justified, nor how the point about the possibly material nature of sensations relates to Williams's concerns. To take the second point first, put in terms of sensations, when he is talking of a peculiar *conception* of the world, Williams's concern is not to defend any particular ontology of sensations or qualia, but to defend the idea of a special or peculiar kind of judgement, that is enabled by the experience, or by the sensation if we talk that way. It does not matter in the least whether the sensation is a brain process. This special kind of judgement is what has subsequently become familiar as a perceptual demonstrative thought, the kind of thought that would be voiced when we say '*that* red is too sombre' or 'that smell is still lingering'. What matters is that the perceptual demonstrative thought is *peculiarly* ours, and perhaps can only be ours at some evolutionary or historical or cultural juncture. The question is whether having this element of subjectivity enables us to to make a specific kind of judgement, and one that could not be made by creatures with a different subjectivity. If having the subjectivity is itself a matter of being in a particular brain state, the distinction and the defence still remains. After all, our brains themselves are peculiarly ours, and peculiarly configured by evolution, history, and culture.

Perhaps thinking further about the different sensory modality of smell will make the matter clearer. Scientists interested in olfactory perception study the influence of emotion and mood on such perception, and how alongside things like associative learning, gender, and even according to some researchers sexual orientation, they influence the hedonic tone and the sensory threshold for different odours. The experience of smelling is substantially different depending on these factors. The odorant itself, i.e. the pheromone or other chemical, remains identical, and just like the reflectance properties of a surface, can be scientifically isolated and described, in this case chemically. So can the specialized proteins in the olfactory receptors that bind odorant molecules, just as the differential wavelength sensitivities of different cones in the eye can be found. But the experience of smelling requires more. It requires that the brain generate an organized response to the arrival of those molecules, just as it must respond to levels and differences in energy at the short, medium, and long end of the light spectrum in ways that can only be approximated by a quite complex algorithm (which is one reason for caution about a casual notion of 'red light'). Currently the science of smell tells us that different odorants set up different patterns of spatial activity in the glomerular layer of the olfactory bulb, suggesting a combinatorial mechanism for olfactory coding. With different subjects, different patterns of activity arise, and then the 'take' or the phenomenology of odour perception is altered. Nobody doubts that this take or phenomenology is in some sense brain located, and certainly brain dependent. But the point is that it gives different subjects different takes on the one chemical (the thing that is just there, anyway), up to the point where one subject has no olfactory experience at all, smells nothing, in circumstances in which the other does. Goodman's description of the situation in terms of different worlds seems especially apt: it is natural to think that the dog's olfactory world is entirely distinct from mine, and in many respects mine may be distinct from yours. We have, on this account, no reason to think in terms of one world of smells, from which different creatures make different selections. There is one chemical world, perhaps many different combinations of philia and receptors, and different spatial and combinatorial algorithms, set by other factors, before we smell anything in our own distinctive, or as Williams would put it, peculiar, ways. No doubt similar things are true of taste, and the different ways things taste to different people, or the same person at different times, is a matter of everyday remark.

I do not think that everything about smells generalizes to colour or heat: for a start, the scientific underpinnings of different smellings are chemicals themselves, not properties of other things, such as a disposition not to reflect red light. But the example illustrates the overwhelming importance of keeping conception apart from property. With this in hand, let us ask: why did Putnam think it necessary to confine the property of being coloured to having a relationship to light, rather than, for instance, having a three-way relationship to light and us, such as having the power to reflect or to refuse to reflect a kind of light apt to strike us in one way or another? Obviously enough, once the possibility of mind–brain identity is on the board, it clearly makes no difference to the *scientific* status of colour or smell whether they are best analysed without invoking any relation to us, or whether such a relation is central to them. Since we are part of the same scientific world, a relation to us is as good a scientific property as, say, being poisonous to us.

This three-way relation can do justice to the thought developed by Jonathan Bennett, that you can change a thing's secondary qualities, but not its primary qualities, by changing us rather than it (Bennett 1965). At present phenol-thio-urea (and, apparently, Brussels sprouts) taste bitter to some proportion of people, and insipid to others. Genetic drift or evolutionary advantage means that we *could* change so that phenol-thio-urea (or Brussels sprouts) become insipid or tasteless, or so that they become bitter or astringent. There is no reason why the same kind of structure should not exist with colour or sound, tactile feelings, or odours. And where a change in us produces a change in a property, we will naturally want either to analyse it in relational terms, or at least to give an account of how it supervenes on some scientific truth which may concern reflectance and light, but also concerns us. The only alternative would be to try the heroic ploy of holding that after such a change, Brussels sprouts remain *really* bitter, although everyone finds them bland. But that way, I take it, lies a general scepticism about our knowledge of secondary qualities that few would want to hold.[5]

We can say more about how firmly we get into the picture if we look in a little more detail at the teleology of the senses: what they are for. So, for example, with smell we get a very different story than with colour constancy. Smells are provoked by events. The electrical energy passed from the receptors in the cilia is greatest just *when* the original binding takes place. Hence, we habituate to them quite quickly: witness the smoker who does not realize the fug he carries around with him. This is presumably how people could bear to live in medieval cities and castles. Colours, by contrast, are perceived as the same for as long as we care to look, and through large variations of incident light, and therefore through large variations of patterns of energy falling on us.[6] It is therefore tempting, and I think correct, to speculate that smells essentially alert us to things, and especially things likely to affect us. This is their function, and once they have done this job, they die away. The teleology of colour perception is different. It is not the registration of locations in the spectrum of reflected light, for if it were we would be much more sensitive to features such as intensity of light, and colour temperature, as both film and digital cameras are. Instead, we ourselves are concerned with the discrimination and tracking of objects by their surfaces. It matters to us when surfaces change: at sunset we don't want to be misled into thinking that the berries are ripening just because the ambient light temperature has got warmer, for example. Tracking things is what colour vision is *for*. By contrast,

---

[5] Although I have heard this über-realism defended on occasion, and it presumably lies behind Bertrand Russell's view in *Problems of Philosophy* that it would be 'favouritism' to suppose that what we see as blue is actually blue (Russell 1980: ch. 1). Putnam's emphasis on there being a *correct* way to perceive colour, raises the question of how he himself would respond to Bennett's case.

[6] The classic account is Hardin 1988.

the teleology of smell is essentially one of warning us, in this case of the presence of the kinds of substances that carry effects on our well-being, for good or ill. Again, there is no prospect of an account that makes sense of any of that without bringing us ourselves firmly into the relationship. But as I have insisted, that does nothing to impugn the scientific or objective status of the relations that science discovers.

II

Perhaps Putnam's most serious objection to Williams is that he needs an 'absolute notion of "absoluteness" ', yet cannot, on his own grounds, sustain it. This is because '*his* denial that semantic relations could figure in any purely scientific conception—not *mine*—leaves Williams with only a *perspectival* notion of absoluteness, not an absolute one' (Putnam 2001: 608). And there is no doubt that Williams does say things that deny him an 'absolute notion of "absoluteness" ', for Putnam's reasons. These can be summarized as follows. The question of whether some conception features in an absolute account of the world is the question whether we can expect convergence upon it from sensorily diverse, but rational, investigators. But the question whether we have such convergence will inevitably be a question of interpretation, and such questions are only settled by the best, most *reasonable* interpretations that can be given of the different communities of investigators. In Quinean terms, that leaves them open to indeterminacies of translation: within the perspective afforded by one way of taking some investigators (one translation manual) there may be convergence, but within another there may be none. Hence, the question of absoluteness is itself perspectival, and there is no 'absolute notion of "absoluteness" '.

The argument is sufficiently strong in its own right, but is particularly difficult for Williams, since as Putnam makes plain, Williams is himself committed to its premises. Williams accepts a Quinean or Davidsonian view of interpretation, and the corollary of semantic indeterminacy. He may have been wrong to do so: several philosophers have argued that the various doctrines of semantic indeterminacy are much more difficult to make sense of than is usually acknowledged, and I incline to agree with them. In my view it is a non-negotiable truth that 'cats' in my mouth, and in yours too, refers to cats, and furthermore this is one determinate truth, so that we do not just have one sentence that can with equal propriety be interpreted as expressing any of an indefinite and vast number of different truths. But without adjudicating that, what of the other part? What is the argument that Williams does need a concept of 'absoluteness' that would itself feature in a scientific view of the world, or even a view of the world 'couched in the language of mathematical physics'?

This is much less certain. As we have already remarked, when Williams talks of the powers of the absolute conception, it is in terms of its ability to explain all manner of things, including how it is itself possible, and also how the various perspectival conceptions we have are also possible. This is where its substance is said to lie (Williams 1985: 139). And he happily concedes that such explanations will be 'to some extent perspectival': this is the part where he concedes that they would *not* themselves be available to any investigator, since others may lack a capacity to grasp the conception which we ourselves, through possessing it, can grasp. These other investigators would therefore lack an adequate conception of the explanandum. (For instance, having no sense of smell, they would be unable to explain scientifically how our sense of smell works—Williams is less explicit about what kind of explanation of this, doing full justice to the explandandum, we would ourselves ever be able to mount, however much science we learn.) So it seems that wearing one hat at least, he is himself happily committed to a perspectival conception of absoluteness, and the question is whether this indeed vitiates his position, as Putnam claims.

Putnam's only argument that it does so, in the paper replying to Williams, is that even Rorty could agree to a perspectival conception of absoluteness, yet Rorty has no time for the spectrum that Williams is offering. Perhaps Putnam is right that Rorty could have agreed, but one of Williams's complaints about him is that in fact he did not. Here is the passage in which he expresses what he calls the second fault in Rorty's account, the first being that he fails entirely to explain why the picture of the world being 'already there' and helping to control our descriptions of it is so compelling. Williams writes:

[This] leads directly to the second fault in Rorty's account: it is self defeating. If the story he tells were true, then there would be no perspective from which he could express it in this way. If it is overwhelmingly convenient to say that science describes what is already there, and if there are no deep metaphysical or epistemological issues here but only a question of what is convenient (it is 'simply because' of this that we speak as we do), then what everyone should be saying, including Rorty, is that science describes a world already there. But Rorty urges us not to say that, and in doing so, in insisting, as *opposed* to that, on our talking of what it is convenient to say, he is trying to reoccupy the transcendental standpoint outside human speech and activity, which is precisely what he wants us to renounce.   (Williams 1985: 137–8)

Anyone going this way becomes a 'perspectival absolutist': someone who goes around saying that science describes what is just there, anyway, but who regards themselves as a pragmatist, reserving a place for further comment about our own involvement in attaining the scientific perspective. Williams's objection is not that this position is untenable, but that it is in fact not the one Rorty is advocating, while the one he is advocating instead is unavailable to him by his own lights. Earlier pragmatists had in fact noticed the problem, and embraced the position that Williams thinks Rorty ought to hold. The Oxford pragmatist F. C. Schiller wrote that

Realism manifestly is a theory of very great pragmatic value. In ordinary life we all assume that we live in an 'external' world, which is 'independent' of us, and peopled by other persons as real and as good, or better, than ourselves. And it would be a great calamity if any philosophy should feel it its duty to upset this assumption. For it works splendidly, and the philosophy which attacked it would only hurt itself.   (Schiller 1907: 459)

This is Williams's position as well. It is therefore not at all clear that Putnam can frighten Williams by dangling the spectre of Rorty in front of him, when on Williams's own account there is clear water between himself and Rorty, which enables him to escape the problems he poses for the latter.

    There is indeed a remaining question whether perspectival absolutism is a coherent position, and without invoking the spectre of Rorty, Putnam might certainly claim that it is not, although the rhetorical tone of his discussion suggests that he thinks it is coherent but trivial. It may be difficult to prove incoherence, if we remember how perspective got into the picture in the first place. It was not by insisting on a peculiarly human or parochial element in our perception and thought about shape or mass, motion or temperature, for instance. It was only by insisting on the indeterminacy of interpretation, meaning that whether *other* people or other creatures are thought to be similarly responsive to shape, mass, or the rest is assessed only perspectivally. And that difference of focus surely leaves a coherent position that contrasts the lack of 'peculiarity' of judgements of shape or mass, while allowing the 'peculiarity' of interpretation. Or, the position might move in David Lewis's direction, towards supposing that the absolute status of shape or mass, their position as privileged properties, itself serves to diminish, perhaps to vanishing point, any indeterminacy of interpretation that a more catholic or egalitarian attitude to properties allows (Lewis 1983). On that view, Williams was conceding too much to Quine and Davidson when he talked of interpretation, but was entirely on the right track when he talked about science.

A subsidiary reason for supposing that this might be the best line for Williams to follow is also mentioned by Putnam. This is that in doffing his cap to Davidson, in particular, Williams should remember that Davidson believes he has a transcendental argument that there are some concepts that all rational creatures must have in their repertoire: concepts such as belief and truth and falsity. For rational creatures must manage to communicate, which implies interpreting each other, which implies the deployment of just these concepts. Yet Williams does not want to say that truth or belief belong to the absolute conception of the world, marking out the equivalent of Lockean primary qualities. This is awkward, certainly, but Williams could reply with a distinction. In the cases of scientific primary qualities, he may say, what we can properly expect is convergence not only in possession of those concepts, but in their application. We would not expect Martian scientists to work in terms of mass, but systematically diverge from us about whether one body has greater mass than another. But if Quine and Davidson are right, while we may expect the Martians to have concepts of truth and belief, there is no expectation at all that they will apply them just as we do. Their different perspective on sayings may be quite intractable, unless Lewis is right and we can expect their judgements of interpretation to be, like ours, governed by the privileged universals that are instanced in the world around us and whose instancings have a monopoly in explaining things.

III

The upshot is that Williams has room to defend his distinction as one among our concepts. He can continue to hold that the modes of thought that our sensibilities give us are more peculiarly tied to the contingent nature of those sensibilities in some cases than others. And he might do well to tiptoe past the issue of whether the reference of these modes of thought, the properties of things that they represent, are always things, properties, powers, or dispositions of things that are also visible to fundamental science, and in that sense 'just there anyway'. But it is quite clear that for both him and Putnam the central issue is not with heat, colour, or odour, but with concepts that help to structure our social and moral worlds. It is the concepts of the human sciences rather than bare empirical concepts that excite both authors.

Why is Putnam opposed? He has often claimed solidarity with those Oxford philosophers, from Philippa Foot and Elizabeth Anscombe onwards, who have sought safety from wicked prescriptivists and emotivists by highlighting the place of so-called 'thick' concepts in our sayings about people and things. Thick concepts knead together 'facts' and 'values' in one package, and many writers, including Putnam and Williams alike, think that they resist attempts to disentangle them into two separable components, the facts and the values. Putnam frequently uses this amalgamation, and the impossibility of disentangling *any* description of the world from some tinge of valuation, to generate his own response to Williams's spectrum. Yet this is a surprising ploy, for thick concepts are just the ones whose perspectival and often peculiar or parochial identities are most apparent. Their contingent, historical, and cultural peculiarity is written on their face, as it were. I shall illustrate the problem by drawing upon a piece of history.

The noted historian Quentin Skinner details some of the rhetorical strategies employed at the beginning of the seventeenth century by the newly emergent commercial class, in order to legitimize their activities and deflect the opprobrium that was then easily expressed against wicked usurers, 'city cormorants', and the practitioners of ungodly worldly activities in general (Skinner 2002: ch. 8). His analysis works entirely against a background of shifting forces contending for the possession of 'thick terms'—terms which in Skinner's analysis 'perform an evaluative as well as a descriptive function in our language' (Skinner 2002: 146). The strategies available to the new 'innovative ideologists' included extending or refiguring the descriptive background to an acknowledged positive term in such a light that it could be seen to extend to the questionable activity that the ideological innovators were seeking to legitimize. Thus the innovators would co-opt religious terms with an established positive ring, for instance by representing commercial ability as 'provident', or 'prudent', and representing commercial activity in terms of a 'dedicated' life, a worldly 'asceticism', or 'devotion to a calling'. Sometimes their course included taking hitherto neutral terms and adding a positive gloss: 'discerning' and 'penetrating'—neither of which name aristocratic virtues—begin at this time to emerge as terms of approbation, for example. And sometimes hitherto negative words were taken and revalued: 'ambitious' is a good example. Conversely, hitherto positive terms such as 'profligate', 'obsequious', or 'condescending'—each of them actually used as *commendations* in the courtly, hierarchical, and aristocratic society that was gradually being replaced—began to gain their current load of disapproval and even resentment.

In other words, the new social forces bent and adapted both the evaluative and descriptive bases for socially important terms, bringing the questionable activities within their orbit, and exploiting, or when necessary changing, their evalutive load in order to align the favourable ring with the intended application.

Now proponents of entangling and of thick concepts are quite coy about telling us when one thick concept gives way to another, as I complain in essay 7. Are we to say that at the beginning of the seventeenth century one set of concepts disappeared, and quite different ones, unfortunately expressed in homophonic terms, replaced it? The real question for anyone such as Putnam, pleased to call himself a pragmatist or sympathizer with pragmatism, is how can an equivalently interesting, insightful, description of how the new ideology generated the innovation be given, without first recognizing the lynchpin of Skinner's account, the interpenetration of description, which is one thing, and evaluation, which is another, however often they happen together? It is no accident that the 'new' concepts arrived, nor that the particular appropriations took the form that they did. If historical analysis had to stop short with the vacuous commentary that what happened at the beginning of the seventeenth century was the replacement of one set of concepts by another, historical understanding would be stopped in its tracks.

It is, in one respect, worse than this. Historical understanding would not be so much stopped as smothered, prevented from getting underway at all. For in general, diversity of concept does not imply disagreement. There are many different compatible descriptions of any one subject matter, as of course Goodman and Putnam have often reminded us. So if the change at the beginning of the seventeenth century was simply to be described as the gradual displacement of one set of thick concepts by another, there would be no reason to see the change as involving conflict: it would in principle be open to someone to conjoin both descriptions without there being any necessary reason to see a tension between them. But if *that* is where we remain, we lose sight of the essential historical fact, which is that the change was indeed one of ideological conflict. The displacement was not unmotivated; it was not one of random conceptual drift, but the deliberate deployment of persuasive speech to foment a revaluation of different activities and qualities that they demanded. You simply cannot say that, without noticing that we are in the domains of both description and evaluation, the same things differently valued and differently compared to other paradigms of virtue or vice.

A final remark about this example may also help. If we say we are in the conceptual domain, and leave it there, then via the rule-following considerations the practices of those applying the terms pre-seventeenth century followed a rule: where there is a concept, there is a rule of application. And the ideological innovators broke rules. But I do not think that is true, at least in any interesting sense. They introduced new practices, like someone who bakes a cake a new way, or takes a new route for a journey, but such people do not break rules. They are more like someone who in some context stretches a vague term a little further or less far than some statistical majority. You can call a suitcase heavy, if you are tired, even if to the majority who are not it would be regarded as reasonably light.

The peculiarity, in Williams's sense, in perception of odour is not a philosopher's construct, but a matter of everyday experience as we notice habituation and change in ourselves. As my example shows, the similar peculiarity of *thick* thinking is similarly visible not only to philosophers, but to historians. They can not only recognize change, but chart the different rhetorical strategies employed by people deliberately driving change. In the period Skinner is considering, it was words like 'godly', 'pious', 'ambitious', 'prudent' that were pulled into the service of legitimizing the new commercial order. At another time we might chart the rise and fall of terms like 'cad' or 'gentleman', of virtues like politeness and courtesy, and of the various extensions and importances according to being saved, pure, provident, or godly. These vary historically, just as olfactory perception varies with personal factors.

This example suggests that thick terms are richly peculiar. It also suggests that Williams's spectrum should be deeply congenial to pragmatism. As Huw Price and David Macarthur have recently written, pragmatism is essentially in the business of substituting anthropology and genealogy for metaphysics (Price and Macarthur 2007). In many areas it avoids 'representation' because it sees it as empty. We do not get a theory, or add to theory, but only set off down a blind alley if we hope for a story whereby we can pat ourselves on the backs, complacently content that the term 'cad' refers to caddishness, and so on for all our thick terms. Rather, pragmatism looks to the relation between the term and practice. The genealogy lies in the practices of a society in which, for example, being a gentleman was a passport to status, and being a cad was the dishonourable failure to live up to the gentlemanly code. It is the *opponents* of pragmatism, the metaphysical realists, who find it important to talk of receptivity and representation, of qualities in the world that merit the application of the term, or who think of more or less static rules governing its application, in place of the fluid and contested realities which historians chart (see also essay 9).

Out-and-out pragmatists such as Rorty or Price think that what is true of these historically mutable terms is true of everything. Representation is always the enemy and our practice in making judgements is always the right focus to substitute for it. Williams, evidently, held that in the case of common sense and in at least what we might call the inshore waters of science, this was otherwise. One reason for thinking he was right is that genealogy and anthropology, like Skinner's piece of history, can only go on against the background of a shared world. We need to suppose things about the environment within which adaptation took place and practice was moulded in order to give a historical narrative, or even the sketchiest just-so stories about the evolution of a way of thought. So we would again find ourselves respecting something bearing some resemblance to Williams's spectrum: not necessarily put in terms of 'an absolute conception', but rather in terms of explanatory depth and explanatory importance. If these concepts themselves import 'perspective', or are themselves peculiar to a point of view, as Putnam's semantic argument suggests, then that neither renders them unfit for purpose nor redundant for pragmatists.

There is a general view amongst many philosophers that, somehow, the rule-following considerations put an obstacle in front of this way of distinguishing a bare, primary-qualited reality from anything more richly described. But this is also not an easy case to make. Suppose we agree that there is a moral to be drawn from those considerations, along the lines that representation is not to be thought of as a two-way traffic between single subject and a (part of) the world, but as a normative transaction governed by some kind of rule or convention tying us to a language, to the interpretive strategies of other people, or to a *practice*. This way we might arrive somewhere in the vicinity of Rorty and think of truth being supplanted by solidarity, or we might find ourselves nearing those authors who put a constitutive role for the *consentium gentium* in determining the rightness of application of any term, and who believe that this much presence of the human serpent flattens out any interesting distinction along Williams's lines.

We might, but if so we will certainly have left Wittgenstein somewhere behind. Wittgenstein does not emphasize conformity with others, still less any kind of Rortian solidarity or self-absorption, but a *technique*. It was engineering, not social solidarity, that the misanthropic Wittgenstein had in his blood. And in the first instance techniques give us abilities and successes explained by the intractable physical properties of things: their size, shape, elasticity, friction, charge, mass, velocity, and acceleration. Again, the moral is going to be that there is no getting started on more indirect or interesting teleologies for particular parts of our judgemental repertoires without standing firm on the fact that we are situated as we are. And Williams remains right that the terms in which that situation can be the most barely presented must occupy a special role in any of our explanatory endeavours (see also essay 9).

14

Julius Caesar and George Berkeley Play Leapfrog

Some twenty years ago I voiced reservations about John McDowell's embrace of a spatial metaphor, whereby we should expand our idea of the 'space' occupied by the mind, locating its boundaries far outside the skin, way into the world (Blackburn1984b). I thought at the time that the spatial metaphor was a flourish McDowell had been betrayed into, particularly by some of the terminology of his dispute with Dummett over 'manifestation'. But over the years it began to be clear that it was more than that, being one of several metaphors that figure centrally in his extensive and influential meditations on the relationship between ourselves and our world. Indeed, the best thumbnail description of his aim would be to show that the world is not 'blankly external' to the mind, and this description uses the metaphor. So the reservation went unheeded, and years later the metaphor and its cousins occupied large parts of *Mind and World* (McDowell 1996), which is the principal text which I shall consider, although they liberally sprinkle other writings as well. I shall use this opportunity to try to sensitize others to my reasons for discomfort.

My discomfort equally concerns the metaphor of the two spaces, the space of reasons and the space of causes, or as McDowell prefers to put it, the contrast between the space of reasons and the 'realm of law'.

Why should one worry about these two metaphors? I think we should acknowledge immediately that they do some sterling work in McDowell's criticism of others. Quine, for instance, makes the same mistake that, according to T. H. Green, Locke and Hume made, of conflating data in the sense of brute causal impingements from without, and data in the sense of basic reasons for beliefs (Green 1874). This can be put by saying that he confuses denizens in the space of reason with those in the space of causes.

Davidson makes the mistake of avoiding pure coherentism only by a global assurance that (from without) you will be seen as possessing mostly true beliefs, although God knows what their content will be. This is no substitute for wanting beliefs known true by local attention to the way of the world. Rorty jettisons too much of what makes the space of reasons what it is, giving us only a substitute that, because of its avoidance of representation and truth, is essentially mindless. These criticisms are compelling, and what is right about them can be indicated in part by use of the metaphor.

Yet there is danger at hand, because a metaphor can pave the way for inferences, inviting us to frame problems one way rather than another. A metaphor can blind us to possibilities, including the possibilities that give us philosophical control of an area. For that matter, a metaphor can also make it easy to demonize those who do not see the subject in quite the same way. And I believe the spatial metaphors put us in peril of framing issues in a misleading and ultimately unsustainable way, a way that disappears with a more complete emancipation from a false view of the mind. So, as I read it, while much of *Mind and World* is written in terms of these metaphors, including its positive theses, they fit badly with what is best in the book. They show that McDowell is not as free of the presuppositions of an old and discredited philosophy of mind as his own animadversions on that philosophy would lead the innocent to believe.

I believe that this accounts for the sense some readers must surely have, that somehow in the course of the work, rather large rabbits are pulled out of a rather small hat. For then, not wanting to devalue the hat, seduced by the metaphors and perhaps by the almost sacerdotal progress of McDowell's persuasive prose, the unwary reader sees no option but to confess that it must indeed hold these rabbits.

The best parts I am referring to, as well as the criticisms of other major players already mentioned, are the Austinian or Strawsonian parts, seeking to substitute a better theory of perception and its objects for anything modelled on old-fashioned sense-datum theory. The rabbits include the metaphysical inflation, railing against the bald and shallow metaphysics of the scientific world view. They include the dismissal of the standpoint of the 'cosmic exile', or 'sideways views' from which we attempt to understand ourselves as parts of a natural world. They include the doctrine that when we evaluate things we simply display a sensitivity to the values things have. And above all, perhaps, they include the doctrine of 'disjunctivitis', or the denial of a highest common psychological factor between cases where we perceive things rightly and cases where we do not.

So what we have, I shall argue, is an admirable adherence to modern views about perception, made to deliver ambitious results, but only via allegiance to a way of framing the issues that are undermined in part by those views themselves, properly understood.

I

Early in *Mind and World* we are introduced to the Sellarsian concept of the space of reasons, and made to face up to the idea that only conceptual items, things within that space, are capable of justifying or being justified. The idea of the Given is the enemy, and

[t]he idea of the Given is the idea that the space of reasons, the space of justifications or warrants, extends more widely than the conceptual sphere. The extra extent of the space of reasons is supposed to allow it to incorporate non-conceptual impacts from outside the realm of thought. But we cannot really understand the relations in virtue of which a judgment is warranted except as relations within the space of concepts: relations such as implication or probabilification, which hold between potential exercises of conceptual capacities. The attempt to extend the scope of justificatory relations outside the conceptual sphere cannot do what it is supposed to do.   (1996: 7)

McDowell goes on to elaborate:

What we wanted was a reassurance that when we use our concepts in judgment, our freedom—our spontaneity in the exercise of our understanding—is constrained from outside thought, and constrained in a way that we can appeal to in displaying the judgments as justified. But when we make out that the space of reasons is more extensive than the conceptual sphere, so that it can incorporate extra conceptual impingements from the world, the result is a picture in which constraint from outside is exerted at the outer boundary of the expanded space of reasons, in what we are committed to depicting as a brute impact from the exterior.   (1996: 8)

McDowell goes on to talk of an 'alien force', the causal impact of the world, operating outside the control of our spontaneity, or reason, or judgement. In a well-known footnote, he compares the result of such an impact to that of being deposited somewhere by a tornado, giving us an event that might exculpate us (if, for instance, the question arose of whether we are somewhere we have any right to be), but that cannot be said to justify us, or give us reason for being where we are (McDowell 1996: 8 n. 7).

This enables McDowell to both set up a problem and give his solution to it. The problem is to stop the exercise of judgement from being entirely self-contained, disengaged from a reality outside the mind. In this picture it would be the play of what, in Kantian terms, would be concepts without intuitions, or concepts without responsiveness to anything other than themselves, in a self-contained dance of inferences. McDowell fears that Davidson has fallen into the trap of presenting a picture in which our thinking is thus self-contained, or only rescued by the inadequate global subterfuge indicated above, and it is frequently raised as a charge against his colleague Robert Brandom. It is as if a thought only maintains friendly relations with other thoughts, and never with things outside the realm of thought. This would be a version of idealism, and while it may be mischievous to say that it might remind us of Berkeley, it is sufficiently similar to his doctrine that an idea can only resemble (have representational relations with) another idea to explain one part of my title.[1] Of course, this is consistent with McDowell's point that the real problem is not one of epistemology, but is 'transcendental', in that what in Berkeley purport to be ideas, or in Davidson purport to be thoughts, in this scenario would fail to be ideas or thoughts at all.

McDowell wants to rescue us from the oscillation between this threat of idealism, on the one hand, in which, as he nicely puts it, thought (or, better, fake thought, something that is only the façade of thought) spins frictionlessly in the void, and the lame solution represented by the Myth of the Given on the other hand, whereby impingements from outside the space of reason nevertheless anchor that balloon nicely to the world. His own proposal is what he calls the 'unboundedness of the conceptual'. An independent reality does exercise control over our thinking, and this

---

[1] More pedantically, the parallel is that Berkeley makes it impossible that an idea should have rational relationships with anything except another idea, just as Davidson makes it impossible that a belief or concept should have rational relations with anything except another belief or concept. The moral of quite popular transcendental arguments, such as that of Putnam's brain-in-a-vat thought experiment, would be that this means that in the absence of a commonsense world, we could not be the subjects of genuine ideas or concepts at all. With these arguments in place, the idea is not so much one of thought spinning frictionlessly in the void, as of what purports to be thought not really being thought at all. I am indebted to Mark de Silva for conversation on this point.

control is rational control. But it can only do this because it is itself in some sense 'conceptual'. The bad picture is one of an

outer boundary around the sphere of the conceptual, with a reality outside the boundary impinging inward on the system. Any impingements across such an outer boundary could only be causal, and not rational.   (1996: 34)

Since experience, or what McDowell likes to call receptivity, certainly gives us rational control over what we believe, it is itself to be regarded as a kind of judgement, a judgement that typically discloses how things stand.

   Thus begin McDowell's battles with writers such as Evans and Peacocke, who have found it necessary to notice a 'non-conceptual' element within experience. According to McDowell, Evans, for example, falls for the Myth of the Given, by first acknowledging a non-conceptual element in experience (the kind of modification of consciousness that we might share with animals, for instance), and then trying to see the non-conceptual part as standing in some rational relationship to whatever judgement expresses what we experience.[2]

   This is a very interesting issue, and has probably prompted most of the reactions to *Mind and World*. But whatever its intrinsic interest, it is not actually central to the theory of mind and world, and by McDowell's own lights we ought to be able to put it to one side. We can see this by thinking for a moment of the Davidsonian coherentist slogan that nothing can count as a reason for holding a belief except another belief. What strikes us as uncomfortable about that slogan is not the presence or absence of various non-conceptual elements in experience. As McDowell initially and rightly emphasizes, we are made uncomfortable by the absence of rational links to the world. If experience is introduced to allay this discomfort, it had better not figure as just another *belief*. And neither can it figure as just more belief, only tricked out with something else: modifications of experience such as

---

[2] There is a scholarly question about whether it is fair to criticize Evans for falling for the Myth of the Given. Sellars's own attack on the myth takes as a premise a distinction between the materials of sense and the inputs to the processes of reason. It presupposes, therefore, that the sensory experiences and the conceptualizations are not the same thing, as indeed he says repeatedly, for instance between sections 25 and 32 of *Empiricism and the Philosophy of Mind* (Sellars 1997). We should also remember that Sellars thought there were two mind–body problems. One was understanding how sensory qualities can be in brains, and the other is understanding how thoughts can be in brains. Sellars is not a monist about the contents of consciousness. In his own attack on the myth, Sellars was primarily concerned to deny that sensations can play the role of empiricist foundations for belief, so the question is whether Evans thinks that they do.

sensations or qualia or the rest. So far as establishing contact with the world goes, these would simply function as decorations, having at best a causal role in making us believe things. Davidson's slogan would still rule. The question of sensation, a component of experience that we may well share with brute animals, is not fundamental. It simply would not matter whether consciousness included such stuff. If it could only function causally, it would be as if we were victims of an incessant succession of belief-inducing injections, we would still be left with idealism or coherentism. It wouldn't matter in the least if the injections also felt one way or another. To sum up, what is missing is not the idea of experience as belief plus an add-on of sensation or feeling or anything non-conceptual, for no add-on would do the work of showing that in experience beliefs are formed in ways, whatever they may be, that make them more likely to be true. It is clear that no phenomenal extra, intrinsic to the experience itself, could do that.

If non-conceptual content is not thought of in this way, because the idea of genuine content is played up beyond anything recognizable as mere sensation, then it has a very narrow path to find, being neither phenomenologically self-standing as sensations and qualia might be, nor articulable by the agent as the reason for a belief (since that would make it conceptual again). It is indeed hard to see what it could be, and for the purpose of this paper I am happy to let McDowell's rejection of it stand (I am not here bothered by the problem of animal thought). It is, of course, an entirely different matter whether an episode of perceiving something, say for a definite duration, is to be assimilated to a different event, such as believing something for the same duration. Sidelining the word 'content' does not mean sidelining perceptual events, nor dismissing everything that is distinctive about perception, distinguishing it from the simple arrivals and departures of beliefs.[3]

II

Should we then avoid extending 'the scope of justificatory relations outside the conceptual sphere'? I think it is too unclear what this means for us to

---

[3] To take just one instance: the arrivals and departures of experience command attention in the way that arrivals and departures of beliefs need not. The enjoyment of experiences is episodic, whereas the having of a belief is not.

judge. Let us consider an everyday observation. Mary has come to believe that there is butter in the fridge. How? Suppose that she saw it. She went and looked, and there was the butter. What justifies her belief? Most obviously, *that* she saw it. Here we can agree with Strawson, Evans, and nearly all contemporary philosophers, that her doing so is necessarily but a tiny exercise of a vast set of dispositions. Mary has learned to interpret what she sees. She has learned how far she can see. She has some practised confidence (she gets butter right) and surrounding modesties (she cannot tell contraband butter from legitimate butter, or Jersey from Guernsey, just at sight). She knows in the same way how to find out if there is butter in the fridge, a car in the garage, or a cat in the garden, and she knows that if there was butter in the fridge a few minutes ago and nobody in the room, then it is probably there now, that if it can be seen from one angle it can be seen from others, that it has a life of its own when she departs, and she can tell if other things are in the fridge and if the butter is in other places, and so on and so on.

So when we say that Mary is justified because the butter was there and she saw it, are we taking justificatory relations 'outside the conceptual sphere'? We are taking them as far as the butter and the fridge. Mary is certainly justified, and by that plenipotent way of earning the title, namely that she got the right result, and did so by exercising an activity exactly adapted to getting the right result, and that she knew to be so adapted. She would not be displaying confidence about the butter had she not gone and looked; she does not find herself in the grip of strange and inexplicable beliefs on such matters, and she gets things right markedly more often when she does go and look. We might say that Mary is abundantly justified, leaving it open how much of this abundance she could jettison while still being justified.

McDowell does not of course deny any of the commonsense thoughts about observation. Indeed, it is part of his project to establish them. But he thinks he can only do so by firmly placing the facts about butter, cars, and cats 'within' the conceptual sphere. More precisely, it is the very things that Mary knows—that the butter is in the fridge and so on—that are to be enfolded in the sphere or space of concepts. So in turn, the question now becomes where we know what is referred to by such clauses, and hence what it means to think of their referents as being in some space or another.

One might hazard that it is a fact that is referred to, and McDowell often describes himself as insisting that the mind reaches as far as facts. And we can say that it is the fact that butter is in the fridge, together with the other things

I have mentioned, that justifies Mary. But facts are queer referents, queer enough not even to be regarded as referents by many philosophers (including Strawson). They are not spatial entities. If they were, as Wittgenstein remarked, they could move around, but they cannot. Some of their queerness as referents comes out if we consider again the central sentence of the first quotation from McDowell that I gave: 'But we cannot really understand the relations in virtue of which a judgement is warranted except as relations within the space of concepts: relations such as implication or probabilification, which hold between potential exercises of conceptual capacities.' That the butter is in the fridge is a potential exercise of conceptual capacities? Surely not. That the butter is in the fridge might be, for instance, a reasonable matter for gratitude or a source of amazement, but it is not a potential exercise of a conceptual capacity for which one is then grateful or at which one is amazed. That the butter is in the fridge may put us at risk of getting fatter. But it is not the exercise of a conceptual capacity that puts us at such risk.

So do we recoil to the allegedly sole alternative, so that 'that the butter is in the fridge' becomes tornado-like, brute, alien, merely a provider of 'impacts from the exterior'? Not if we refuse to work in terms of the spatial metaphor. There are of course a number of things that make this language inappropriate to Mary. One is that her activities as an observer—her goings and lookings—are intelligently directed. She knows what she is doing, and what she is doing is exactly what is needed to discover what she wants to know. Mary is in control, precisely unlike someone deposited here and there by tornadoes. Like Julius Caesar, she comes, she sees, and she conquers. What she conquers is her ignorance of where the butter is, or of what is in the fridge.

A related thing to say is that when we describe Mary, we are not confined to listing the onset of her beliefs, as we might be if we were making the diary of the mental life of a delusive paranoid. This is one thing that is jarring about Davidson's slogan. It makes it sound as though a sufficient list of her beliefs, made independently of any concern with how they were formed, would tell us everything we need to know about Mary's status as a reasonable person. But this is quite wrong. We applaud Mary as reasonable only because we know, as she does, not only that beliefs were formed, but why they were formed.

The butter is firmly within the realm of law, and that the butter is in the fridge might be so as well (if we were worried about both butter and fridges being human artefacts we could change the example). Things like butter have a chemical constitution, shape, size, weight, and mass and behave in predictable ways. That is why we can see them. The butter impinges on Mary, and if she is a typical fridge-gazer, it will generate an impact from the exterior, from outside her boundaries, in fact from about three or four feet away from her. But then many things 'within' the realm of law seem to be understood by us, and so in some sense at any rate fall 'within' the sphere of our concepts. Otherwise we could not talk about them.

Minimalists about truth and facts will deny that 'that the butter is in the fridge' has a referent at all. Others think it does. Some will hold that it refers to a proposition, others that sometimes it splits into a demonstrative, and the production of a saying which is then demonstrated (Davidson 1968). Others again, including Davidson, celebrate the notorious slingshot argument, as showing that all facts collapse into one. I can afford to remain agnostic about that. All I am denying is that any referent we may devise for it is an appropriate candidate for spatial imagery. Indeed, if we were to adopt McDowell's spatial imagery, we might say that Mary's receptivity is within the sphere of her spontaneity, meaning that the way she makes observations is something over which she exercises rational control. But then we might equally find ourselves saying that her spontaneity is within the sphere of her receptivity, meaning that the way she thinks about things is responsive to what she observes. Perhaps we want to be able to say both these things, but the metaphor of spaces and spheres then gets in the way. It leaves us with the uncomfortable image of my title. One moment Julius Caesar—our information-gathering techniques and activities exercised in the realm of law—is on top; the next moment George Berkeley—the fact that all this is understood by us, and can be made to appear to be just one more element in our system of beliefs—gains the ascendance; and so it goes on.[4]

The problem here is that McDowell does not succeed in cementing the idea of an observation firmly into the idea of *activities* within the world, *techniques* of discovery and manipulation which are possible to us only as situated within the same spatial and causal world as the things which concern us, the realm of law.

---

[4] There is an echo here of the 'just more theory' debate between David Lewis (here representing the Julius Caesar tendency) and Hilary Putnam. See Putnam 1983; Lewis 1984; Taylor 1991.

Nothing we have said about Mary takes what she saw outside the realm of law. But neither does it take Mary. Mary's belief that butter is in the fridge is certainly one on which she can exercise reason. At the limit, if she has excellent reason for doubting that such a thing could be, she will doubt the evidence of her senses. But without the dualistic metaphors (realm of spontaneity versus realm of law; space of reasons versus space of causes) this should not worry us. Philosophers enamoured of the scientific world view never denied that Mary would be complex, able to juggle observations against memory or testimony or other ancillary evidences. The baldest of scientific metaphysics will accommodate Mary, or, if it will not, it will be because of some other way in which intentionality escapes the realm of law, and that other way is not yet on the table.

III

The butter caused Mary's belief. Had it not been there, reflecting light or doing other buttery things, Mary would not have formed her confidence that it was there. We know of this causal relationship, which is why we can use it to effect changes in Mary's belief. If we know she will be worried about having butter over Christmas, we can reassure her best by putting the butter where she will lay eyes on it.

I do not want to charge McDowell with ignoring such platitudes, although I believe that some have taken the oneness of mind and world to exclude any conceptual linkage between causation and observation (Snowdon 1990). But it is fair to worry whether causation is entirely central to McDowell's thinking. Could the notion of spontaneity take its leading role if it were? There is nothing spontaneous in any ordinary sense about Mary's coming into awareness of the butter, however many conceptual abilities are in play as she does so. But for ancillary evidence that causation may need to make its voice heard more loudly, I should like to turn briefly to a different work.

In his paper 'Non-Cognitivism and Rule Following', McDowell introduces his interpretation of the rule-following considerations.[5] In particular

---

[5] John McDowell, 'Non-Cognitivism and Rule-Following', in S. Holtzman and C. Leich, eds., *Wittgenstein: To Follow a Rule*, London: Routledge, 1981.

he discusses their significance for the issue of objectivity in moral philosophy, by quoting what he ringingly endorses as a marvellous passage from Stanley Cavell:

We learn and teach words in certain contexts, and then we are expected, and expect others, to be able to project them into further contexts. Nothing insures that this projection will take place (in particular, not the grasping of universals nor the grasping of books of rules), just as nothing insures that we will make, and understand, the same projections. That on the whole we do is a matter of our sharing routes of interest and feeling, senses of humour and of significance and of fulfillment, of what is outrageous, of what is similar to what else, what a rebuke, what forgiveness, of when an utterance is an assertion, when an appeal, when an explanation—all the whirl of organism Wittgenstein calls 'forms of life'. Human speech and activity, sanity and community, rest upon nothing more, but nothing less, than this. It is a vision as simple as it is difficult, and as difficult as it is (and because it is) terrifying.   (Cavell 1969: 52)

It is I think a little surprising to find this passage as an icon for a philosophy so hostile to attempts to gain 'sideways-on' views of ourselves. In this passage Cavell manages to tell us rather a lot from what might seem to be an external or sideways-on standpoint on our language and thought. He tells us both what language does 'rest upon', and what it does not. Perhaps this is not in the relevant sense to be thought of as taking up a sideways-on viewpoint. But that merely raises the question of what, then, is to be tarred with that particular brush.

But before we return to that, while we are worrying about causation there is a different problem. Consider the things upon which language is here said to rest: routes of interest and feeling, senses of humour, and so on. All of the things Cavell cites are reasonably called aspects of human nature. Cavell simply ignores any aspects of the world apart from human nature. He might have mentioned the properties and powers of things, or the existence of causal laws or substances or space or time. For one would have thought at the very least that our language rests upon the surroundings in which we find ourselves and live our lives, just as firmly as it rests upon us ourselves. But natural kinds are absent, and with them causal powers and the influence of those powers. The 'realm of law' is just not invited.

This omission is not just an accident or an oversight. For the vision that Cavell talks of at the climax of his account is 'terrifying' *only* because of the absence of the world. Suppose instead Cavell had said that we teach and learn words in connection with kinds of things; people catch on to which kinds of things these are; nothing logically guarantees that we will, but our shared natures make it very likely that we will, and human speech and activity rest on nothing more nor less than that, together of course with our senses of humour and the rest. There is no vertiginous vision, and nothing terrifying there. The vertigo we are invited to suffer (and the thrill of suffering it) depend entirely on the absence of anything to anchor us, and the resulting image of ourselves as either spinning in a void, or at best in a world entirely of our own making. And although it is incidental to this essay, I myself doubt if this purely anthropocentric emphasis is faithful to Wittgenstein. On p. 230 of the *Investigations*, Wittgenstein says: 'Our interest certainly includes the correspondence between concepts and very general facts of nature.' I do not hear Wittgenstein intending anything vertiginous.

But Cavell's neglect is explicable. He will not seem to have neglected anything important when Berkeley is on top. The things Julius Caesar stands for—placing ourselves, manipulating things, exploiting what we know of the ways things work—are not denied. They are just assimilated to other conceptual exercises, such as the making of inferences, or the popping of new ideas into the mind. Hence, they do not deserve separate mention.

This becomes important when we remember that Strawson, McDowell, and practically all philosophers for the last half-century have emphasized both the non-inferential nature of observation and the range of things we can properly be said to observe. Things do not come to us as raw stimuli tagged in some empiricist language—what Quine himself called the fancifully fanciless medium of unvarnished news. Instead, an observation is more like the first thought that comes into our head. It is this that enables McDowell to bring into the *Geisteswissenschaften* the equivalent of the collapse of the observation/theory distinction in the *Naturwissenschaften*. The well-trained natural scientist, at home with his instruments, sees the nebula, the mitochondria, or the electrical field. The human being, with a second nature properly developed, sees or hears the meaning of another's words, the intention of their action, or the villainy or innocence of their demeanour. In neither case is there any conscious inference, so in each case we can talk unblushingly of observation.

If we put together the Berkeleian turn represented by Cavell, and Strawson's generosity, the way is open to our deeming ourselves to observe more or less what we like: the past, the future, norms, forces, counterfactual truths, the meaning of the Constitution or Picasso's intentions, and if we are so minded, the grace of God or impending doom.

IV

I said that Mary knew why she came to believe that there was butter in the fridge, and so do we. Possibly, neither Mary nor we made any conscious inference, although of course it is also possible that we did. But why would that be an interesting question? Observation is a source of authority, but it makes little difference to Mary's authority whether she had to make an inference, or whether a training and a habituation meant that the first thought that came into her head already gave her its conclusion. Her inference, had she needed to make one, might have been unwarranted. But then her training and habituation might have warped her mind as well. Indeed, we might think that Cavell himself, as well as boycotting reality, goes out of his way to invite a certain pessimism about the credentials of observation. At any rate, virtually all the features of human nature that he cites are very clearly empirically variable. On the face of it they would be of more service to a Kuhn or a Foucault than to the project of recovering an Aristotelian innocence. If we are denied a sideways look at ourselves, the result, in cases of ideology and ethics, would be not so much confidence that our particular *Bildung* has resulted in an unbounded openness of world to mind, as fear that it has trapped us so firmly within our paradigms or our *episteme* that we no longer recognize our prison as a confinement. If we are deaf to the threat of scepticism or relativism at this point, it will not so much seem like an exercise of Aristotelian innocence or magnificence, as an exercise of, well, deafness.[6]

If we put agency and causation back in the centre of the picture, we can say some more things than this. We can in principle discover which of Mary's subconscious or subdoxastic systems was involved with the observation she made, and we can talk of the links between the ways such systems work, and the truth or falsity that Mary enunciates. Suppose, for

---

[6] This is where we can feel the attractions of Rorty's attempt simply to abandon any notion of representation at all. I do the same in the case of ethics, but not across the board.

instance, Mary hears the sarcasm in someone's voice. We can ask what caused her so to hear him. We might get the plonking reply that it was the sarcasm (in one terminology, this is called a modest reply, but it is at least as natural to hear it as incipiently self-congratulatory). But we might also get a more informative reply: the contours of his intonation, or the fact that he avoided this word, or stressed that one. And in turn these factors can be expanded or detailed further, and we could build up a picture of Mary's reliability as a detector of sarcasm. We might find, for instance, that in some contexts she is very good, but in others fails to notice sarcasm, or invents it where it does not exist. She might be good amongst her peers, but get thrown completely by the accents of a different class or place.

If she possesses more than a rudimentary self-consciousness, Mary will herself be able to conduct this thinking, and test her own diagnosis of sarcasm. Children manage to learn that not everybody who sounds slightly different is mocking them. Of course, as we measure ourselves, we also use our own judgements, but that is quite in order, provided that there is enough independent confirmation or disconfirmation of what we spontaneously judged to give us a handle on the nature of our spontaneous judgement and its reliability.

This independence, of course, can only be granted up to a certain point. Mary, or people observing her, can come upon the question of whether such-and-such an intonation is a reliable sign of sarcasm, but they cannot answer it independently of *any* use of *some* indication of sarcasm. There are currently suggestions that microscopic muscular changes around the eyes betoken dishonesty, and that while only gifted human observers are sensitive to these cues, machines could be developed that register them much more reliably. Well and good, but we need (and of course, have) less subtle manifestations of dishonesty against which to calibrate the gifted observers, or the machines.

Quine and Rorty have said things like this:

An observation sentence is one on which all speakers of the language give the same verdict when given the same concurrent stimulation. To put the point negatively, an observation sentence is one that is not sensitive to differences in past experience within the speech community.   (Quine 1969: 86)

An observation is, in effect, what enough other people will accept as an authoritative first thought to pop into your head in one circumstance or another. McDowell is right to guard against the democratic air of this. There is such a thing as the development of sensitivity, or the trained observer or *phronimos* who may indeed observe things that other people cannot. But once we bring causation back into the picture, we see that the authority of the trained observer is not, as it were, self-standing. His or her credentials are established, and in difficult cases, either in science or in human life, there are procedures for querying them, and procedures for self-checking that an intelligent agent can use. These procedures take us back to less theoretical or less ambitious conceptions of what made the agent give the verdict they did, and the links between the situation described in those terms, and the situation as interpreted in the original terms.

It is possible, then, to distinguish two different cases. Sometimes, but not always, the procedures can start from asking what was actually seen or heard in stripped-down terms, less ambitious terms than the subject first used. We have the lawyer's injunction to 'just stick to the facts'. Some cases always fit such a request. The first thought in the subject's head may have been 'impending rain', but we can request an answer to what was observed that sticks to the present. 'That it is going to rain' can be seen or felt, but only because something else is seen or felt. This in no way implies that the thought that it is about to rain is the conclusion of an inference: our natural belief formation can be more automatic, and just as rational as anything deserving the name of inference. Ethical observation also conforms to this model. In Harman's famous example (Harman 1977: 4), in one sense the first thought in the spectators' minds may have been, 'What a dreadful thing to do,' but there is a stripped-down report that they are also able to give: 'First they caught the cat, then they got the gasoline . . .' Furthermore, spectators who were genuinely unable to give that second report would be highly suspect as moralists. It is not a signal of good moralists that they find the thought that something was a dreadful thing to do popping into their heads without their having anything to say about why (there are fascinating contrasts here with aesthetics, arising from the strong justificatory demands that good moralizing has to meet). In fact, a sufficient inability to retreat will disqualify the subject from being properly regarded as a moralist at all. In McDowell's own phrase, he will just begin to seem to be somebody who on occasion sounds off.

In other cases, however, the subject may have nowhere to which to retreat, while the interlocutor does. The subject just heard the melody or the sarcasm or saw the benevolence or the beauty, and when asked by the lawyer to stick to exactly what was seen or heard, is at a loss. It does not follow that the interlocutor has nowhere to which to retreat. He or she can discover what else it was about the situation that prompted the subject's verdict, just as the artist may know what shapes and shadings to create to prompt the seeing of the drawing as a picture of a sneer or a smile, or the investigator might discover what the conjuror did in order that the audience saw him produce an egg from his ear.

Finally, there are cases of what we might call bare receptivity. Here, neither the subject nor any investigator can retreat to a stripped-down story. Suppose, for instance, the subject saw a straight black line on a white page. Faced with the demand to tell exactly what he saw, there is unlikely to be anything further he can say. And in an ordinary case there is unlikely to be anything else an investigator can say either: there is no story of the kind 'This is how it was done' except that it was done by a straight black line on a white page. Of course, there will be further things to know about the retina and the optic nerve and the visual cortex. But these form no part of normal self-reflective practice. They are not used in everyday procedures. It does not follow that they should be banished from philosophy, of course, and the theory of secondary qualities hinges very importantly on knowing just how they get in. But for the present purpose what is telling, and what surely motivated traditional philosophy of science and traditional moral and mental epistemology alike at this point, is that even if we are receptive to quarks, duties, and other minds, we are surely not *barely* receptive to them.

The point of these thoughts about observation and judgement is not to reintroduce some version of the idea that anything to which we are not barely receptive is the result of inference, or even to reintroduce an observation/theory distinction. The point is just that in cases where we are not barely receptive to one or another feature of things, there is available an ordinary sideways-on perspective on what we do. It is this sideways-on perspective, a refinement of common sense, that motivates worries about the enchanted world which McDowell takes to be 'disclosed' to us. Of course, the worries will not be felt by anyone secure enough in her own sense of her own receptivity not to raise any questions. The believer feels within herself the working of divine grace, and her confrères think she does too. They never have to raise the question of whether this is the operation of bare receptivity, and neither do we, unless of course we want to understand things better.

Properly read, even Cavell does not have us stop before these thoughts, since he leaves it quite possible that the confidence that we have observed the working of divine grace in our own souls is the function of some other element of our whirl of life: our self-importance or our resentment or our imperial will to power, for instance, after which it will be impossible to think of it as a simple openness of mind to world.

V

The spatial metaphor more or less forces the allied doctrine of 'disjunctivitis' upon us, and it is a tribute to McDowell's strength of mind that he has been able to accept it. In its industrial-strength version, disjunctivitis is the view that there is nothing fundamental in common, no 'highest common factor' between someone whose mind embraces a fact, and someone whose mind does not. One mind has a bit in it (the referent of the 'that' clause, construed as telling of the fact that is 'within' the mind) and the other does not. Their minds are unlike, as unlike as a nest with an egg in it and a nest without one. And there is nothing else to say about how they are similar, except in the most general terms: that each satisfies the disjunction of being either genuinely faced with a fact, or not (each either has an egg in it, or is empty). The quietist potential of this doctrine is apparent: either you embrace the facts or you do not, and if you do you owe no explanation—indeed there simply is no explanation—of your doing that starts, as it were, from anywhere psychologically or metaphysically further back.

Disjunctivists might be thought to hold that there is no such thing as false belief. For if there is nothing in common, no highest common factor, between minds perceiving (containing, reaching as far as, disclosed to by) a fact, and failed minds appeared to in such a way that they take the same thing to be a fact when it is not, then how can there be anything in common between minds believing something to be a fact when it is, and those other failures believing it to be a fact when it is not? For some reason, however, and in spite of the general trend to assimilate perception to belief, the doctrine is usually confined to perceptual experience.

If we avoid the spatial metaphor for the mind, will anything motivate disjunctivitis? Indeed, can we so much as believe that we *understand* the doctrine, without a fatal distortion of the whole philosophy of mind?

Mary and Twin Mary can equally be told by their experience that there is butter in front of them, when one is faced with butter, and the other only with fool's butter (margarine, perhaps). Third Twin Mary, further out in modal space, who is faced with nothing, but is having her optic nerve stimulated by the mad scientist, is equally being told by her experience that there is butter in front of her. But according to this version of disjunctivitis, there is no more in common between these sisters than between Mary and anyone else who is not faced with butter: a twin facing an elephant, or another sky-diving, for instance.

What could motivate this view? Some things certainly will not. The position that experience is intrinsically or fundamentally 'presentational' will not. This is the doctrine that an experience could not be what it is, did it not present things to us as being one way or another. But each of these sisters is being told, by her experience, how things stand, and each can absorb what they are told and factor it into their other beliefs and desires.[7] In other words, each can behave rationally as a result. This is what made it so unappealing to deny that one using a term empty of reference, as one of these three would be doing if she said, 'Lo, that butter is rancid,' is thereby denied the status of thinking anything, while the other two qualify. In fact this last claim is a pure example of the spatial way of thinking in action: here an empty demonstrative is diagnosed as leaving a hole in a complex called 'content'—a hole in the head, as it were.

A second fear that we can discount is that if we admit a commonality between our Marys, we will be ignoring Austin's or Sellars's claim for the priority of 'is' over 'appears'. Not at all, for we can give the veridical case priority in all kinds of ways. Alexander Bain said that a belief was a preparation for action (Bain 1859), so we might try the idea that it appearing to one as if there is butter there is a state disposing one to readiness for actions that, given one's desires, would be successful if and only if there is butter in the environment. This kind of suggestion, crude though it may be, accords

---

[7] If we are fastidious about the dangers of metaphor, we will worry about the locution of their 'being told' something by their experience. All that I want is that this is the understanding of what they are faced with that is all-but-irresistibly borne in upon them by what they see, and we can add for basic cases that they have no retreat to a less demanding conception of what they are faced with.

with Sellars's priority, for it approaches 'appears' only in terms of 'is'. And it is only a suggestion, for there would be many other similar approaches.

Another fear that should be put aside is that unless we embrace disjunctivitis, the old grim problems of Cartesian epistemology will once more overwhelm us.[8] The idea will be that to defeat these problems Mary will need to strip what she is allowed to know down to some subjective core that she shares with her siblings, and enter on the forlorn attempt to regain the whole sphere of empirical knowledge from just such a string of subjective cores. But this is in no way implied by agreeing to what we have said about Mary and her siblings. The world is presented as being a certain way, the same way, to each of them. Two are mistaken. But this does not mean that they are never justified in taking their experience at face value. Nor does it mean that they ever gain anything except confusion by attempting to subject all their experience, en bloc, to a process of Cartesian doubt. We can admit a shared psychological state between a Mary who remembers childhood abuse, and another who is the victim of induced false memory syndrome, without falling into a pit in which memory is regarded as intrinsically untrustworthy, or only otherwise by the grace of God. We can admit shared beliefs between those who believe truly and those who believe falsely without making a single step to thinking that our beliefs together form a set of presences from which we vainly try to infer facts about the world.

Such an idea may well sound absurd in the case of beliefs, but it is no more absurd than the fear that the 'highest common factor' must be thought of in terms of the presence of a proxy: mental butter, perhaps something like an extremely thin slice of butter or an 'extremely thin coloured picture' of ordinary butter.[9] To think that is just to reapply the bad old spatial metaphor. The sisters, we have said, are each in the same state of experiencing the world as having butter before them. This is the highest common factor. There is simply no reason to think of this 'state' as reified, a Tractarian configuration in which mind contains some sinister thing which in one of the cases is a fact, but in two of the cases fails to be, and so is nothing of this world but only something 'in the head'.

In the grip of the spatial metaphor, one might uncritically find oneself heaping scorn on those who reject disjunctivitis. They will be leaving

---

[8] This especially grips McDowell at 1996: 111–13.
[9] This phrase parodying sense-datum theory comes from Wisdom 1936–7: 75.

facts blankly external to minds. They will be denying transparency of mind to world. They will be condemned to failure of understanding altogether, to darkness within. But shake off the grip, and all is well. People finding an interesting commonality between Mary and her twins are as commonsensical as those finding an interesting commonality between believing that it is Mary in the room when it is Mary, and believing that it is Mary when it is her indistinguishable Twin Mary.

It is interesting that in a discussion of McDowell on this matter, Hilary Putnam in effect interprets this as being McDowell's own point (Putnam 2000: 152). According to Putnam, McDowell would of course admit to the highest common factor I talked of (let us call it the highest common *feature*): the fact that each of them is being told by their experience that there is butter in front of them. According to Putnam, McDowell's point is simply to exorcise the tendency to think of this shared feature in terms of the presence of a proxy, a mental object or intermediate thing. He thus sees McDowell as simply following the Jamesian, or Austinian, path of distinguishing sharply between a quality being 'in' an experience intentionally (it is how the experience presents things as being) and it being something else, a proxy, described adjectivally. This is not an industrial-strength disjunctivitis, but a pussy-cat disjunctivitis, telling us to avoid thinking of the highest common feature spatially.

Often, McDowell's own language is indeed interpretable either way. For example, he identifies the highest common factor conception as:

The idea that even when things go well, cognitively speaking, our subjective position can only be something common between such cases and cases in which things do not go well.   (McDowell 1996: 113)

But that description of an idea straddles the harmless, indeed essential, things we have said about Mary and her twins, and the harmful spatialization of it that suggests the idea of a proxy. It is indeterminate from this whether McDowell intended a denial of the apparently harmless and essential things, which certainly makes the doctrine of disjunctivitis radical, but also quite unacceptable, or only a denial of something like old-fashioned sense data, which leaves it quite innocuous. My claim is that McDowell does not bring the difference into focus and does not speak unambiguously precisely because of the power of the spatial metaphor in his thought. It means that whenever subjectivity becomes the topic, the fear of the mind as retreating 'within' takes over, and then the harmless and essential things to say about delusive perception and false belief get caught up in the panic.

I said above that even taking oneself to understand the doctrine of disjunctivitis already implies a contaminated philosophy of mind, and it may still not be apparent why this is so. Well, what could be meant by saying that those who have experience as of butter being present when it is not, and those who have experience as of butter being present when it is (I almost wrote, 'those who have the same experience when it is'), share no single state of mind? Quite apart from the phantom fears that motivate the doctrine, what can we make of the doctrine itself? It is admitted that Mary and Twin Mary and Third Twin Mary are in indistinguishable states (if the butter flickered into margarine and back, or was miraculously substituted by proximate or distal stimuli of just the right kind, Mary or her twins could not tell). So there are *lots* of descriptions that apply equally to them, such as the one about action derived from Alexander Bain. Their functioning, and their dispositions such as their preparations for agency, are identical, insofar as these are functions of how things appear. So what is not identical?

The only answer is their 'mental states' conceived as these would be by a spatially contaminated philosophy of mind (it does not matter how obese this mind has become, for the image is still fatal). These 'mental states' are reified states like structures, occupying a region that either contains something or does not. And then it is indeed possible to think that Mary has a real egg in her nest, Twin Mary only a cuckoo's egg, and Third Twin Mary has nothing there at all. Their inner spaces differ, just because its boundaries now extend so far.

McDowell on Putnam's interpretation ought, therefore, to be counselling us firmly *against* the blandishments of disjunctivitis. There is nothing to be said for it once the spatial metaphor is abandoned. And McDowell's embrace of the doctrine undermines any claim to be free of the ghosts of the past. But even if Putnam were right, our interpretations would agree about this: that one of the results of *Mind and World*—and it is not a negligible result—should be an even more profound mistrust of the spatial metaphors which alarm me by presenting themselves so much as crucial parts of its argument, and of its solution to the problem of relating world and mind.

15

The Majesty of Reason

I. Introduction

In this essay I contemplate two phenomena that have impressed theorists concerned with the domain of reasons and of what is now called 'normativity'.[1] One is the much-discussed 'externality' of reasons. According to this, reasons are just there, anyway. They exist whether or not agents take any notice of them. They do not only exist in the light of contingent desires or mere inclinations. They are 'external', not 'internal'. They bear on us, even when through ignorance or wickedness we take no notice of them. They thus very conspicuously shine the lights of objectivity, and independence, and even necessity. By basking in this light, ethics is rescued from the slough of sentiment and preference, and regains the dignity denied to it by theorists such as Hobbes or Hume, Williams, Gibbard, or myself. Hence, many contemporary philosophers compete to stress and to extol the external nature of reasons, their shining objectivity (Broome 2004; Dancy 2000; Nagel 1970; Parfit 1997; Raz 1975, 1978, 2003; Shafer-Landau 2003; Wallace 1999).

The other phenomenon is that of the inescapable 'normativity' of means–ends reasoning. Here the irrationality of intending an end but failing to intend the means is a different shining beacon. It is that of pure practical reason in operation: an indisputable norm, again showing a sublime indifference to whatever weaknesses people actually have, and ideally fitted to provide a Trojan horse for inserting rationality into practical life. If the means–end principle is both unmistakably practical and yet the darling child of rationality itself, then other principles of consistency or of humanity, or of universalizing the maxims of our action, can perhaps

---

[1] I should say that I have misgivings about the term, and usually find myself writing it *sous rasure*. I believe Fodor has said that 'cows go "moo", but philosophers go "norm" ', and I agree.

follow through the breach in the Humean citadel that it has spearheaded. And so we get the dazzling prospect that if people who choose badly are choosing against reason, then this can be seen to be a special and grave defect. It would locate the kind of fault they are indulging. It would give us, the people of reason, a special lever with which to dislodge their vices. Being able to corral knaves and villains in a compound reserved for those who trespass against reason and rationality therefore represents definite progress.

It is sad to have to spoil the party, but I fear that these apotheoses of reason contain much less than meets the eye. Ethics is given no new light, nor is its armoury in the least strengthened, nor is its status beyond anything dreamed of by Hume remotely established, by these contemporary ethusiasms. In fact, the massive amount of work that has gone into the coronation of reason has been almost entirely misdirected.

II. Moving the Mind

Clearly we should not start by being deluded by the noun, thinking of Reason as a kind of magical faculty or structure. We should start with the relation. Reasons are reasons *for* something: the primary datum is relational. The field of the relation is less clear, or rather, more diffuse. Propositions are reasons for propositions, facts are reasons for intentions and desires, some intentions are reasons for others. Actions have reasons, and one action may be another person's reason for a different action. But corresponding to each of these and other relations there is a potential movement of the mind, a movement *guided* by the first mental state, and *issuing* in the second, when the reason is accepted or operative. So when we talk in the abstract of one proposition being a reason for another, or a fact being a reason for a norm or decision, the field is one of abstract representations corresponding to potential movements of a mind so guided. The movement in question might be one from one cognitive state or true belief state to another: this is when we talk of theoretical reason. Or it might be one from the apprehension of a fact about a situation to an action or a desire or the formation of a motive or intention: this is when we talk of practical reason. We can also include movements that have action itself as its terminus, if we wish. A movement might also be that from a plan or an intention, or the supposition that a policy is settled, coupled with belief about the means that are open, to the postulation or adoption of a strategy for realizing the intention. A particular movement of the mind might therefore consist in Sally noticing that there is a dead mouse under the chair and inferring that the cat is somewhere around, or noticing that her scratching the blackboard is distressing Molly and then, guided by this thought, supposing she should continue.

The notion of guidance is intended to suggest the difference between taking one thing as a reason for another, and being subject to some kind of free association in which one thing leads to another, but not by a process of reasoning. It is the difference between thinking that a restaurant is expensive, and for that reason going elsewhere, and finding (either consciously or unconsciously) that the restaurant reminds you of an evening long ago with your mother-in-law, and finding yourself going elsewhere. Since the relationship between reasoning and causes of behaviour is puzzling, it may be hard to say in what the difference consists, and there will certainly be cases that are neither clearly one nor the other. Psychologists in Newcastle found that in a communal coffee room, in weeks when a picture of eyes looking at subjects was added as a kind of banner headline to a poster indicating suggested prices for coffee, the amount stumped up in the honesty box went up by nearly three times compared with weeks when a neutral image of flowers was substituted (Bateson, Nettle, and Roberts 2006). Is this a case of free association between a cue suggestive of being watched, leading to an unconscious fear of exposure, or is it a case of unconscious reasoning, triggered by that same cue, from the possibility of being watched to feeling you should not be a free rider? For the purposes of this paper we can choose either way. I shall mostly be concerned with conscious sensitivity to the starting point and to its tendency to steer the movement of mind in question, rather than with subliminal or subdoxastic forces which may or may not be counted as giving reasons.

By an abstract representation I mean simply that we can leave out mention of actual agents and their actual states of mind, and contemplate the guidance purely in the abstract, considered as a relation between truths, or one between truths and possible intentions or desires. We can say, for instance, that the fact that an action is distressing people is a reason for desisting, or the fact that there is a dead mouse under the chair is a reason for inferring that there is a cat around. It is often difficult to frame such abstract relations without a *ceteris paribus* clause, since the particular circumstances of particular cases may nullify the reason. If you keep a pet mink, a dead mouse may not be a reason for inferring the presence of a cat, and if someone has no business being distressed because what you are doing is harmless, there may perhaps be no reason to desist. Nevertheless, the abstract generalization may be a useful general guide, even when it is liable to exceptions.

Some philosophers insist that the actual and potential movements of the mind must start from genuine cognitions, or even facts. I shall mostly defer to this usage, in which a false belief or a misapprehension does not provide a reason for anything. We might say that it does not provide a *real* reason for anything, although unfortunately some people take it to do so. I do not entirely like the stipulation, since it forces us to say that people who through little or no fault of their own misapprehended the facts and inferred or acted accordingly, had no good reason, or no real reason, for what they did. And that sounds harsh, for they may not have been at all irrational, after all. They certainly had *their* reasons for what they did, and they may have acted well in the light of them. The general who is misinformed by a normally reliable source about the disposition of enemy troops, but who then plans well accordingly, is only unfairly accused of having had no reason for what he did, unlike the one who has proper information and then thoroughly botches his plans. The second might be court-martialled for acting irrationally or for no reason, but surely not the first. Similarly the victim of hallucination, taking himself to perceive a rat in the drawer, acts reasonably enough in then shutting it, although his movement of mind does not start with apprehension of a fact. However, nothing important hinges on this stipulation in what follows, and we could in these cases follow the course of saying that there were after all 'factive' reasons in play: not the fact of the enemy troops being thus-and-so, nor the fact of the rat's proximity, for these were not facts, but the fact that the informant reported as he did, or the fact that it looked as if there were a rat there. Similarly in the Newcastle case we cannot say that the subjects reasoned from the fact of being watched, but we might choose to say that they reasoned from the fact that there was a possibility of being watched.

Of course aims and intentions as well as apprehensions provide reasons, and introduce another need for care in our scorekeeping. Sally's reason for scratching on the blackboard may be to annoy Molly. If we say, as no doubt we should, that this was a bad reason, what we say is unfortunately ambiguous between negatively evaluating Sally's intention, and negatively evaluating the means she adopted to realize it, for instance, if we approve of Sally's mischief, but Molly was unfortunately out of earshot. It is important to distinguish these, since they impute quite different faults to Sally. It would matter, for instance, if we are wondering whether to employ Sally to annoy Molly in the future.

When we say that the field of reason is that of movements of the mind, we must be include *failures* to move as the kind of thing which excite verdicts of reasonable or the reverse. Gordon may be unreasonable in ignoring Jack's interventions, or failing to pick up Molly's signs of distress. This is just an instance of the way in which more generally we criticize failures to act as well as positive actions.

So what are we saying about the actual or potential movement of the mind? We say that p is a reason for q or that the fact of x is a reason for doing y when we think it is good to infer q from p, or to be moved towards doing y upon apprehending x. By invoking the relation we *commend* or *endorse* the kind of guidance of the mind that it indicates. Molly's distress is therefore a reason for Sally to stop scratching the blackboard. Movement from apprehension of that distress to her stopping would be a good movement of Sally's mind. It would be good even if in fact Sally does not know about Molly's distress, or does not care a jot about it, or is actively enjoying it. It would be good even if Sally could not implement it, perhaps because of some kind of ingrained insensitivity or some equally ingrained and immovable determination to ignore or humiliate Molly. The reason for Sally to stop is just there anyway—it is Molly's distress—and Sally, or a slightly improved version of Sally, can apprehend it by normal perception. But this does not imply that she needs nothing more to apprehend it *as* a reason for stopping. She may or may not be guided by it. If she is, we say she is being reasonable, by way of commending her.

III. A Blind Alley

An agent's blindness or malformation may prevent a good reason for a movement from being *his* reason for doing anything. When we describe *his* reason, we are simply producing a fact about him and the explanation of his states—the way his mind was guided. It has nothing to do with how it would have been good for him to be guided. When agents not only are not moved but cannot be moved in the right direction, they are still liable to criticism, and this is the sense in which reasons are external. This in turn means that there is absolutely no need to follow Bernard Williams's regrettable move of making the contingent profiles of *actual* concern of an agent determine what is to be said in the context of evaluation. This is so even if, like Williams, we expand the domain of an agent's actual concerns to include an idealized set of concerns, the ones to which they could deliberate in ways they themselves approve. Thus when Williams considers an agent who is a confirmed wife-beater and who has not got sufficient internal resources to deliberate to a better way of being, he finds it difficult to judge that there is good reason for him to stop (Williams 1995: 191). I say instead that there is no difficulty here. There is indeed good reason—excellent reason—for him to stop. *He* sees no reason to stop, and perhaps his mind is too corrupt or impoverished ever to be guided in that way, or even for him to comprehend improvement in this respect. Nevertheless, it would be better if he did. Some may be optimistic enough to suppose that all human beings have enough resources within them to come to adopt, as their reason for acting, anything which actually is a reason for acting. It is a nice, pious, hope, but our language and our thoughts are far from presupposing that at the outset. There need be no optimistic assumption that any agent can be moved by any reason.

With this understood, this whole debate between 'internalists' and 'externalist' in the theory of reason collapses. Externalists were right that reasons are just there anyway, for the starting points of guidances of the mind are there anyway—i.e. regardless of whether particular people notice them, or could bring themselves to move in good directions because of them. But this is an entirely hollow victory, for internalists remain right that it is only in the light of the contingent ways we are that we can instance movements, and just as obviously it is only in the light of the contingent ways we are that we commend and endorse them. So the phenomenon is of no interest to the debate between Humeans in the theory of motivation and value, and others.

IV. Kinds of Guidance

We should notice that it is the *kind* of guidance that we are commending, not its end point nor its consequences. It may be a pity that Sally came to believe that the cat was around, because her project was to decapitate it, although her reason for believing it was the perfectly good one that there was a dead mouse under the chair. It may be good that Cedric brought Sally flowers on her birthday, even if his reason for doing so was the bad one that it would exacerbate her allergies. You can move in a bad way but get to truths, and to doing the right thing or the fortunate thing. And conversely, you can move well, but be moving to falsehoods, and to doing the wrong thing or the unfortunate thing, although we should accept that there are some destinations so bad that nothing could count as a good journey ending up with them: an intention to commit genocide, for instance.

A distinction that we need not dwell upon holds between movements that are in some sense deliberate, those with which the agent himself is comfortable or which he endorses, and movements that the agent either does not consciously know about or might wish away. This is close to Gibbard's distinction between accepting a norm and being in the grip of one (Gibbard 1990). Thus someone in the grip of a fetish or a compulsion might be said not to have a reason for doing what he does, but only find himself caused to do it, as if by some outside force. But he could equally be said to have had a reason for acting as he did. Plato's Leontius, who had a shameful thing about recently executed corpses, found himself sufficiently gripped by the consideration that there were corpses to be seen to go and see them (*Republic* IV, 439e). He may have felt as if he were doing so 'almost' against his own will. But we can properly say that he had his reason for going. What we will not say is that the fact that there are recently executed corpses somewhere is *actually* a reason for going and looking, unless we wish to commend the process, for instance to medical students.

In the case of theoretical reason, our sense of how truths relate to each other gives us our standards for good or bad movements. Of course, it is not entirely easy to describe the relations behind these standards. But we know the general pattern. The premise p makes q more probable, or q provides the best explanation of p, or the simplest or only plausible explanation of p. The gold standard, of course, is that p could not be true without q being true, but few movements of the mind are guided by relations that meet the gold standard, except in logic lecture rooms and mathematics classes. In most cases we have to settle for less, or, if we use the modal term it may be because we are operating under a tacit contextual assumption that some possibilities are too outlandish or irrelevant to take into consideration (Lewis 1996). When we settle for less, we may only want to say that in the circumstances, p was a good enough reason for assuming q, and here the circumstances may determine not only the probability of q being false, but the gravity of getting it wrong and the cost of investigating further. It may only correspond to a good movement of the mind if nothing much hangs on it. This touches upon the relation between alethic standards and pragmatic ones, an area in which there is a clear difference between the 'right' kind of reason for believing something, and the 'wrong' kind of reason, such as the advantage in doing so. A similar distinction arises in practical reasoning, where it hinges on the difference between a reason for admiring something, which is on account of the way it merits or deserves admiration, and an extraneous or 'wrong' kind of reason, such as strategic or political reasons for doing the same. The difference lies in the kind of movement of the mind in question. If we are egging someone on to admire something because it will be politic to do so, we are not commending the kind of movement that takes in only the relevant properties the thing possesses—those we take to be indicators of merit—and is guided to admiration on their account. It is if, but only if, we were prepared to commend this kind of movement we would say that the thing merits or deserves admiration. But if we see advantage in admiring it, for instance in becoming one of the club or sneaking a financial return, we are only hoping for a particular end point, and the only movement of the mind that is commended is one that takes account of the advantage and sets about gaining it. In the alethic case there are deep issues here, going to the heart of pragmatism, about the connections between success in action on the one hand and a general cognitive ability to represent the world on the other (see also essay 10). However, they do not concern us in this paper.

In the case of practical reason, the widest standards are those for evaluation in general. In saying that Molly's being in distress is a reason for Sally to desist, I commend or endorse or express approval of the movement of mind in which Sally takes in Molly's distress and as a result desists. This is entering an ethical judgement. I will have my own reasons for it: I hold that things go better if people are guided like this. If I go further and say that it is a decisive reason or a compulsory reason for Sally to desist, then I do not merely commend the movement, but insist upon it or regard it as compulsory, and stand ready to censure Sally if she fails to move in the appropriate way.

In standard cases of succumbing to temptation, we can be described, albeit unhelpfully, as being unreasonable. Seeing the situation as it is, and judging which action is best to perform given how things stand, and then doing the other thing, will generally (although not always) be an instance of a bad or inferior movement of the mind, that is, a case of being unreasonable.[2]

If life were simple, the virtue of reason would simply be a matter of moving well, one dyadic relation at a time. But of course it is not. Many considerations clamour for attention; many movements which would otherwise be good are nullified or outweighed by others. The *phronimos* or person of judgement and practical reason needs not only sensitivity to reasons one at a time, but a capacity to amalgamate them, weigh them, and prioritize them. The better he does this, the more reasonable we allow him to be.

Since movements of the mind, in the generous sense we have given ourselves, occupy so much of the territory of ethics, it should be little surprise that Scanlon's project of 'buck passing', or seeing talk of good and bad, right and wrong, obligation and trespass, as verdicts entered in terms of 'reasons', might be feasible (Scanlon 1998). Nor is it surprising that Michael Smith can urge the sovereignty of the ideally rational self, since this will just be the self whose mind moves exactly as it should (Smith 1994).[3] But of course, the takeover is merely nominal. For all we are given are moves within the ethical. We are not provided any independent methodology, or independent underwriting of the ethical as a domain. The

---

[2] The exceptions I have in mind are Huckleberry Finn style cases. See Bennett 1974.

[3] I do not in this paper highlight any differences between 'rational' and 'reasonable'. Pruned of theoretical accretions, I think they come to little more than, as Edward Craig once put it to me, being reasonable just means being reasonably rational.

suggestion we have been following out tells us nothing about the authority of these verdicts on good or bad practical movements of the mind. It merely uses the judgements themselves. If, for instance, we were troubled by objectivity before, we will be troubled by it after. For in spite of any contrary appearance, this talk of reasons imports no new standards and no new buttress for whatever standards we deploy.

V. Unkindness to Animals

Derek Parfit writes: 'Other animals can be motivated by desires and beliefs. Only we can understand and respond to reasons' (Parfit 1997: 127). But we now see that this is not so. That there is a snake in the path is an excellent reason for me to step aside. But it is also an excellent reason for my dog to step aside, and the dog will probably do so every bit as quickly as me. The dog responds to the reason with an alacrity more than matching my own. Parfit had earlier said, correctly, that 'reasons for acting are facts that count in favour of some act' (1997: 121), and on this occasion the dog understood and responded smartly to one of those, the fact that counted in favour of jumping aside, just as I did.

Parfit probably did not intend to deny, as he actually did, that the dog responds to reasons. The tenor of his discussion, as of many others, is that we ourselves are not just responding to the presence of the snake, but to some 'normative feature' of the snake, or in other words, a further evaluative or deontic fact about the situation of its being in the path, a halo or nimbus of normativity beatifying the union between the presence of the snake and a subsequent sidestep, a radiance in which Parfit, but not the dog, can bask. Needless to say, this is pure fantasy. The position of the snake can be quite sufficient to set one's legs racing. We do not need to respond to anything more or anything different; indeed, since speed is probably of the essence, we need not to do so. There is no time for extra processing. And since stepping aside is highly appropriate, this is a good movement of the mind, and equally so for the dog. We could, if we wish, give *some* meaning to saying that we, but not the dog, see the snake *as* a reason to jump aside. If this is to mean more than that we are disposed so to act, a property we share with the dog, it must be along the lines of our satisfaction with the movement, or willingness to endorse it and recommend it for similar occasions, or in other words, our own positive valuation of our own conduct. This is all that separates us from the dog. If we put them in the negative and say rather that we do not regret the movement, or feel ashamed of it, or feel inclined to apologize for it, then once again the dog and we are on all fours, since it too feels no regret or tendency to apologize. Perhaps a young mongoose would feel some proto-version of these emotions, were its sidestep derided for cowardice by its mongoose mentors. But not the dog, and we share everything essential to walking with equal safety through the forest. Hence, there is nothing about our thoughts conducted in terms of reasons that affords any evidence at all for Parfit's speciesist intuitionism.

Do we gain anything by subscribing to the thesis that if an agent has a reason to do something and is properly aware that the reason obtains, then he must be motivated to do it 'on pain of irrationality' (Wallace 1999: 218, citing many others)? First, notice that it is not very apparent how severe this pain is: Sally and her mischievous ilk can evidently put up with it quite contentedly. If we want to improve Sally by threatening pain, it had better be of a different sort. And most people find it sufficient to call children like Sally naughty, insensitive, mischievous, careless, callous, or even wicked, while after all it was the pain the snake might cause rather than any other imagined pain that explained our sidestep. We thought, 'Oh heavens, it might bite me,' rather than, 'Oh heavens, how horrid to feel irrational.' The invocation of irrationality is not an improvement, but an abstraction that washes out the interesting textures or particular contours of individual cases of vice and virtue. We would of course like Sally's mind to move in better ways. We would like her to take Molly's distress to guide her more reliably, and in the reverse way than it evidently does at present. We have familiar devices of persuasion and argument. 'How would you like it if Molly did the same to you?' we might ask. Perhaps Sally does not mind the sound of fingernails on the blackboard, but Molly can reciprocate by playing her bagpipes, which annoys Sally just as much. Sally wouldn't like it at all. We hope that thinking about that will motivate her to stop. But it may not. She can gamble on the kind and forgiving Molly not playing her bagpipes, or gamble on her parents stopping her if she does. Or, she can expect Molly to play her bagpipes, and be getting her own strike in first. Or, she can usually beat Molly in a fight. Or, she knows she may have to pay for her fun later, but still finds it irresistible to be naughty now. So we might try rubbing Sally's nose in Molly's distress, hoping to activate empathy or pity, and thence remorse and a better frame of mind. But perhaps we fail. It was, after all, the prospect of Molly's distress that excited Sally's mischief in the first place. Suggesting that it is Sally's 'rationality' that is at fault now looks simply like a *déformation professionelle* that afflicts moral philosophers, rather than an open road to new proofs of Sally's wrongness, or new therapies for bringing her back to the straight and narrow. It is in this vein that Bernard Williams scoffed at that *ignis fatuus* of moral philosophy, 'the argument that will stop them in their tracks when they come to take you away'.

VI. The Authority of Reason

A problem area which my proposal clears up nicely is that of the 'authority' of reason, a problem some writers have found in 'Humean' proposals about motivation and desire. In an influential paper on this theme, Warren Quinn urged that there is a basic issue between rationalists such as himself, and 'subjectivists' or 'noncognitivists' (Quinn 1995). Although I disown the labels, he clearly has in mind expressivist and in general naturalistic approaches to ethics of the kind that I favour. He writes that:

The basic issue here is more fundamental: whether pro- and con-attitudes conceived as functional states that dispose us to act have any power to rationalize those acts.

He points out that bizarre, pointless, functional states (such as a disposition to switch on any radio that I find not to be on), do not 'give me even a *prima facie* reason to turn on radios'. The disposition may explain how I am, but by itself it cannot make any resulting act of turning on a random radio sensible. And after rejecting any attempt to invoke higher-order states, such as pro- or con-attitudes to the having of this first order disposition, to help with this problem, he concludes that in themselves dispositions such as tendencies to try to obtain things or to feel pained by things do not 'rationalize' choices. Even choices of means to given ends are not rationalized unless the ends themselves are, and only a genuine cognition of the objects of choice as 'good' could do that. Parfit enthusiastically takes the same line (Parfit 1997: 128).

It seems strange to say that a movement towards, say, eating a proffered piece of pie is not 'rationalized' by my occurrent hunger, so we need to take a closer look at this line of thought. First of all, which movement of the mind is in question? One proposal would be that it is movement from an awareness of a desire to a tendency to satisfy the desire. But that is not the typical case. When acting on a desire we are not typically self-reflective, taking a fact about ourselves as our starting point. Rather, we take in a fact about our situation, and our desires are functional states manifested in the relationship between the fact we apprehend, and the tendency towards action which results.[4] As the desire for food, hunger is manifested in the way in which a tendency to take the pie issues from and is guided by an awareness that it is being proferred. Does the desire, then, 'rationalize' the tendency? It explains it, in whichever way dispositions may be said to explain their manifestations. But Quinn is indeed right that it does not by itself show that the movement of mind is either good or bad, admirable or despicable, and so does not fund evaluative talk in terms of reason or rationality. That is not its job. However, all that shows is that Quinn's demand that desire *should* validate or rationalize choice was entirely misplaced. To enter on the enterprise of arguing that a movement of the mind was a good one is a different business. To do this one has to step back, and see if one can fit the movement into whichever practices in the area one endorses, or at least shares or understands or accepts as immune to criticism. The compulsive, oddball desire, such as the addiction to turning silent radios on, is pointless, and potentially costly and irritating. So of course we are not inclined to endorse the movement of the mind from awareness of a silent radio to the motivation to turn it on, that manifests the compulsion.

Quinn and Parfit may have thought that if particular desires cannot rationalize themselves, then nothing in our conative dispositions, taken as a whole, could do so either: the picture is that the Humean world is one with 'normativity' bleached out of it. This would be a dangerous form of argument, whose weakness is more familiar from discussions of coherentism and foundationalism as they apply to cognitive states. While many writers accept that a belief cannot validate itself, they tend to suppose that its

---

[4] In my 1998: 254 I call this the 'leading, characteristic mistake of a whole generation of theorists wanting to go beyond Hume', and more than a decade later I can add around a third of a new generation.

membership of a sufficiently coherent set may do so. Or, if other things than beliefs are allowed into the justificatory pool, they may include things like processes and actions, such as the engagement of perceptual processes in causal interaction with the world, or the experiences resulting from such engagement. If this begins to paint a satisfactory picture of cognitive justification, which it had better do because it is really the only game in town, then a parallel story can do a parallel job for practical dispositions, first invoking a whole matrix of surrounding dispositions, and then potentially invoking experience of the way those dispositions stand the test of time, as they are tried out in human practice. These together provide the only tribunal that a single desire could ever face. In other words, although we can stand apart from any particular desire or disposition, and consider the good of it in the light of other desires and dispositions, taken as a whole, there is no process of standing back from all of them at once, any more than there is in the case of belief. Someone with Quinn's orientation might try urging that so long as this is 'just us', it can only tells us what we actually value, but not what *is* of value. But little is gained by denigrating the only methods we use, or could use. Insisting upon a wholesale cleavage between 'fact' and 'value' at this point would not so much be protecting the autonomy of the normative world, as making it on the one hand immune to awareness, and on the other hand of no conceivable interest. It is in fact only philosophers' illusions, not valuations and norms, that are bleached out of the Humean world.

VII. Open Questions

Nevertheless, the contemporary enthusiasm for reasons suggests that in many minds, the substitution of the sovereignty of the good by the sovereignty of reasons is to be not just a change of idiom, but a change of regime. It is to open the way to a new dawn of philosophy, a new dispensation, and new philosophical territory to occupy and explore. It is important therefore to consider the view that by moving onto the territory of reason we are, actually, moving. I suggest that the only remaining temptation to think this arises because of the possibility of an 'open question' akin to Moore's famous open question about goodness. However, in this application this question opens not between goodness and some natural property, but between reason and goodness. Thus if everything I have said is true, a critic may complain, how can there be the open and difficult question of whether it is always reasonable to be good? How can there be an issue, for instance, of whether reason might sometimes demand a sacrifice of goodness in favour of such competing candidates as self-interest? How could we so much as worry whether reason stands on the side of prudence and self-interest, or on the side of justice or benevolence or the common good?

The question is very real, and fertilizes the idea of reason as a particular kind of authority, a self-standing normative structure magnificent enough to be used to measure and assay even the claims of virtue themselves. But I want to explain this open question differently.

For since 'reasonable' and its clan are general terms of commendation, like other such terms they can take on a particular cast. They can be confined to commendation within a subset of possible dimensions. This happens whenever we talk of 'good for (the economy, the crops)' or 'good from (the point of view of the banks, the farmers)', and in the same way we talk of reasons of state, economic reasons, reasons of health, personal reasons, or strategic reasons. In chapter XVIII of *The Prince* Machiavelli notoriously claims that the prince sometimes has overwhelming reason to behave cruelly and inhumanely, treacherously and in bad faith. In short, he must behave badly. The dimension within which the commendation is given is simply that of his own survival, and Machiavelli notoriously thinks that when that competes with conventional goodness, not only does it win in men's actual conduct, but that it is necessary that it should. Here what the prince has most reason to do is not what is best: the movement of mind that is commended may be crafty, deceitful, treacherous, and inhumane. He has to be these things (while appearing not to be) in order to survive.

All this is in accord with our proposal. The point is that the crafty and strategic movement of mind is indeed *commended*. It may not be being commended in conventional terms—that is why Machiavelli prompted such shock and gained his dark reputation—but it is commendation within what he regarded as the most important dimensions of statecraft, namely survival and success. The example generalizes. Whenever anyone describes a potential conflict between reason and virtue, what we find is that reasons are restricted to within a dimension, and the question is whether wider, more humane, virtues of justice or benevolence need curtailing because of the insistent demands of that dimension.

So we can open the question whether it is always reasonable to be good, not because reason is an autonomous lawgiver at some unspecified distance from the good, whose injunctions have their own authority yet may conflict with the injunctions of virtue or obligation. We open it, for instance, when we explicitly or implicitly worry about the old and uneasy conflict between self-interest and the other-regarding virtues. In an ideal world, perhaps, we could commend each without ever ranking them, for they march in step. But in the real world, and in spite of the optimism of some classical philosophers, any coincidence between them is a fragile business; servants of the world are not necessarily good trustees of their own interests, and indeed it is a political achievement to bring them into anything resembling an alignment. Machiavelli thought that in the Italy of his time, no such alignment obtained; hence, reasons of state had to trump better-known virtues, and the ideal prince had better be aware of that ugly fact.[5]

To solve this we cannot appeal to the autonomous court of reason. We can only walk around our own moral and ethical thought, and then campaign for whatever resolution appeals to us.

VIII. Means and Ends

We now turn to the much-discussed issue of means–ends reasoning, which is so frequently paraded as a prize specimen of 'practical rationality', a normative constraint of almost divine authority, and even a Trojan horse to insert into the citadel of naturalism. If Humean naturalism cannot even account for the majesty of this norm, then it is indeed in trouble.

It may be worth remarking that Kant did not think of it like that. Kant thought it is *analytic* that if we will the end, we will what is known to be the only means to it:

---

[5] We can also open the question the other way around. Low-church sects have often declaimed against reason in the name of inner light, faith, revelation, and the rest. Here 'reason' is associated with particular kinds of procedure to which these are supposed to be superior, rather as Nietzschians associate 'goodness' with a particular kind of soggy Christian benevolence, which they then despise. See Holton 1996.

In the volition of an object as my effect, my causality as acting cause, that is, the use of means, is already thought, and the imperative extracts the concept of actions necessary to this end merely from the concept of a volition of this end . . . when I know that only by such an action can the proposed effect take place it is an analytic proposition that if I fully will the effect I also will the action requisite to it; for it is one and the same thing to represent something as an effect possible by me in a certain way and to represent myself as acting in this way with respect to it.   (Kant 1997: 4.417, p. 70)

One can see why he might have thought this if we consider the problem of interpretation offered by the agent who might at first sight seem to intend (which I shall use as synonymous with 'will') an end, yet shows little or no inclination to adopt what he knows to be necessary means. It is at least plausible that we cannot be sure *where he stands* on the issue.[6] Does he really intend to meet me for golf, if he said he would, but has not bothered to collect his clubs or put gas in his car? Perhaps he said so, but if he is comfortably resting in front of the television as the necessary time ticks away, interpretation falters. Kant only says that if we *fully* will the end we intend the means, and that seems about right. Our friend's intention may be half-hearted, or his knowledge of the necessary means may be insufficiently robust, as when he knows that the time at which he might have got himself to the course has gone, but 'hopes that something might turn up'. What is clear is that we cannot rely on him; we do not know where he stands on the project of playing golf, and perhaps he does not either, and probably there is no determinate reality about where he does stand. Socially he is a thundering nuisance, since on the basis of his apparently sincere say-so, we turn up, only to find he is not going to be there.

A norm of action is something to which we can conform, or fail to conform. But if Kant is right then there is a difficulty about failing to conform to the 'norm' of means–ends rationality. It cannot be done. There is however a cluster of very closely related norms, and indeed our errant golf partner exhibits what it is to fail to conform to them. He is a nuisance, as already noticed. He is incapable of following through on apparent commitments, for communicating an intention on which the audience is likely to rely is normally undertaking a commitment. He is weak-willed,

---

[6] I gratefully adopt this useful expression from Michael Bratman.

in the sense properly made prominent by Richard Holton, and that builds on Michael Bratman's pathbreaking discussions of the virtue of diachronic consistency in aims (Bratman 1987; Holton 1999). All that is sufficiently serious, and after all, it has been known to be important for a long time: 'No man, having put his hand to the plough, and turning back, is fit for the Kingdom of God.' But what remains unclear is whether there is a more specific 'norm' of means–ends rationality against which he has trespassed, or against which anyone can trespass. It is here that Kant's doctrine stands in the way.

If there is such a more specific norm, then it requires careful formulation. Let us consider only situations in which it is known, sufficiently vividly or wholeheartedly, that means M is the only means to end E. Suppose we try:

If a person intends the end E, then they ought to intend means M.

We then meet problems of 'factual detachment', made prominent in deontic logic by the paradox of gentle murder (Forrester's paradox), and recently resurrected by John Broome and Joseph Raz. The original paradox, we may recall, goes:

If you murder someone, then you ought to murder them gently
You murder someone
Hence: you ought to murder them gently
Hence: you ought to murder them.

And the problem is how to interpret the first premise so that the conclusion does not follow, firstly by a simple application of modus ponens, and secondly by the principle that if a complex ought to occur then its consituents ought to occur.

Before continuing, it will be as well to remember some points drummed into us in elementary formal logic. An argument takes us from premises to conclusions, not from beliefs to beliefs. If we talk of conclusions of arguments being 'detached', this does not imply that they are accepted or that it is a good idea to believe them. That is only so if it is a good idea to accept the premises, and the very fact that they imply the conclusion may count against that. Secondly, within an argument, a conclusion may be detached, but remain under an assumption. Detachment is not the same as discharging all the assumptions still in play. There is no limit, for instance, to the assumptions in play under which premises of a modus ponens may be assumed, and its conclusion appropriately detached—but still remain under assumption. The importance of remembering these distinctions will shortly appear.

A second point to remember is that the auxiliary in the consequent, the 'ought' of deliberation, is not on its face an 'ought' of ethics. It is not, in 'If we want to get to London, we ought to go by train.' In fact, everyday English idiom is quite happy to substitute other modal auxiliaries with more flavour of necessity and less of obligation: 'To get to London, you must/have to/should/had better take the train,' and we can quite equally substitute a conditional prescription: 'To get to London, take the train.' Things are clearer if we generally reserve 'ought' for cases where there is genuinely a moral or evaluative element. The point to keep hold of is that generally we are advising a course of action in the context of the assumption of an end to be achieved.

A final preliminary warning is that we should notice something treacherous about our habit of introducing apparent reference to states of mind, such as desires or intentions, into the antecedent of such conditionals. In the context of deliberation, the most the conditional can easily be heard to mean is that if we are to *achieve* the end, we have to intend the means; that is, in a normal world in which the end is to be achieved, such-and-such is the plan to adopt. In the context of deliberation, 'If we *want* him to come, we have to write a letter,' 'If we *would like* a good time, we had better not go to Torremolinos,' or 'If we *wish* to get home tonight, we had better leave now' would normally be taken to have as antecedents *not* states of mind, but their satisfaction: we could equally or better have put it by saying, 'If he is to come, . . .,' 'If we are to have a good time, . . .,' or 'If we are to get home, . . .' The reference to wants, intentions, or wishes is, in my view, an incidental way of indicating *why* we are interested in planning for those outcomes, rather than an integral way of specifying the condition in question itself. There is no inference, no movement of the mind, from the recognition of a state of mind itself to a demand or plan, but only an inference from the presumption that an end is to be achieved, to proposing a plan for achieving it. Such auxiliary mention of intentions, wants, or wishes may also get into the consequents of conditionals. I might say, 'If you are to do the washing up, you will want to wear an apron,' when I suppose that (a) you are to do the washing up, (b) you do not want to do it, and (c) you do not and will not want to wear an apron either. The conditional does not induce contradiction, because the mention of a want is incidental to its real content, which is to recommend that if you are to do the washing up, wear an apron.

A popular suggestion is that in the paradox of gentle murder the detachment is invalid because the first premise should be interpreted in terms of a wide scope 'ought'. We only have:

> It ought to be that (either you do not murder anybody, or you murder them gently).

And that together with 'You murder someone' yields no inference to murder having been what you ought to have done.

But the wide scope reading seems unlikely on the face of it. Advice for what to do if a contingency arises is clearly *not* advice to make a disjunction true. Imagine a three-horse race. I advise my bookmaker friend, 'If Galloper does not run, sell bets at evens on Trotter.' This is not: 'Sell bets at evens on (either Galloper running or Trotter winning).' The evens bet that I advised might be a good one to sell, since Trotter is not really as good a horse as the third contender, Canter, so by selling the bet I suggested the bookmaker may expect to make money. But selling the bet on the disjunction may be a very bad idea, for instance if there is a much better than evens chance that Galloper will run. Nor is the advice to bring it about that either Galloper runs or you sell the evens bet, since you could follow this advice, but not the original, by arranging that Galloper runs. If you so clearly cannot export the advice in this case, it is very unlikely to be different if I arbitrarily choose to give it by using an auxiliary verb: 'If Galloper does not run, you should/better/might want to/ought to sell bets at evens on Trotter.'

The proposed reformulation is inadequate in other important ways. Consider this conversation, in which Donald, Dick, Condi, and George are four co-conspirators:

Donald:	We are agreed, then, on a policy of imprisoning random Iraquis (IRI).
Dick:	If we imprison them, we ought to humiliate them inhumanely (H).

Condi:	No, if we imprison them, we ought to treat them with decency and compassion (not-H). What do you think, George?
George:	I agree with both Dick and Condi.
Condi/Dick/Donald:	What?!

Surely Condi, Dick, and Donald are right to gape. In the context of deliberation about what to do *supposing* that we are to imprison random Iraquis, George's remark is completely at sea.[7] It is simply not open to George to agree with both treating them humanely and treating them inhumanely.

This is obvious if we look again at the way we naturally formulate the conditionals. We might say: 'If you *are to* murder someone, you ought to do it gently.' The activity is one of *supposing* that the end is given, and then recommending means, and this is a quite different activity from that of assessing the pair of <ends/means> together, which is all the proposed wide scope recommendation of the disjunction shows us doing. *In the deliberative context*, IRI is being taken as given, just as the advice to sell the evens bet only becomes live if Galloper scratches. I think the best way of putting this is to say that the conditional has us consider the nearest normal world in which the end is to be achieved, and proposes a plan: a plan of what has to be done or is best to be done either in that world, or to bring about that world.[8] The question of whether it was a good idea to achieve this end simply does not enter in, any more than when we say 'If the giant slime is coming, flee for your lives!' we express any attitude either to the probability or the desirability of the giant slime coming, or of any complex that has this as a component. The English variant closest to the Latin is perhaps more perspicuous here: *when* you murder someone, you ought to murder them gently.

---

[7] The separation of contexts of deliberation from contexts of judgement was recommended in Thomason 1981: 180.

[8] I talk of the closest normal world, following Bonevac 1998. The view is that conditionals take us to the closest normal world in which their antecedent is satisfied. This is not necessarily the closest world, since the actual world may be abnormal. A consequence is that conditional logic is not monotonic. Conditionals in ordinary discourse do not accept strengthening: 'If you turn the ignition, the car will start' may be true, while 'If you turn the ignition after taking out the battery, the car will start' is not.

With these points understood, it is clear that George's contribution is in effect a contradiction, an endorsement of both of two incompatible plans, and this would not be true, of course, if the conditional were simply a wide scope 'ought' governing a disjunction. Were that so, George's remark would be perfectly intelligible as a way of saying or implying that we ought not to imprison random Iraquis. But I hope that most of us do not, simply because of that, agree with Dick in the above conversation. Whereas if the wide scope disjunctive account were correct, we might well do so. Similarly consider:

Donald: The Iraquis ought not to resent us being there.
Dick: If they do, we ought to beat them to death.
Condi: I agree with Donald, but not with Dick.

If Dick's remark were parsed as, 'It ought to be the case that either they do not resent us or they get beaten to death,' then it follows from what Donald said, and there would be no room for Condi's position. But of course, there is.

In the context of deliberation, the conditional 'If we murder someone, then we ought to do it gently' is a perfectly acceptable recommendation of a plan for the nearest normal world in which we are in fact to murder someone. Much better do it gently! The 'ought' of planning detaches. The plan is conditional upon an antecedent being satisfied: it is only when or if we are to murder someone that we should follow the plan to do it gently. This is most obvious when the murder is unavoidable or irrevocable: the assassins we employed are on their way and beyond recall, but we can somehow get a painkiller to the victim before they arrive, so that is what we ought to do (Setiya 2007). But mere supposition or postulation of the end *takes us to the same deliberative context* as actual irrevocability. The consequent is detachable even if the murder is not irrevocable or inevitable; it may be still under consideration, and the consequent only detached, as I reminded us of at the outset, in the way that any consequent is detached in a formal argument, potentially en route to a reductio or a modus tollens:

Dick: Are we to murder prisoners?
Colin: If we do so, we ought to do it gently.
Donald: There is a major difficulty about that, since none of
                our soldiers know how.

Condi: Still, Colin is right, so perhaps after all we had better
                                not murder prisoners.

Here the consequent is provisionally detached, an implication worked out
(the plan requires resources we do not have), and turned into an objection
to the proposal of murdering prisoners. The consequent is detached just
as any proposition may be detached in the course of any inference,
not necessarily as something to be accepted in its own right, but under an
assumption, provisionally en route to further inference, and then potentially
to a backtracking on the original antecedent assumption. It is here that we
must remember the remarks I made about detachment not being the same
as acceptance.

All this is the context of deliberation. To repeat, in that context, the
conditional 'If we intend E, we ought to do M' signals the endorsement
of a plan of action (M) in the normal world in which we are to perform
or bring about E. Nothing is said about whether it was a good idea, or
morally acceptable, or inevitable, or anything else, to have the intention
itself. A consequence of deliberations in which the conditional works just
as conditionals normally do (sustaining modus ponens, opening the way to
modus tollens) may be to make it clearer than before that we had better
abandon the intention itself. And in that context, 'If we intend the end,
then we ought to intend the means' is clearly a good principle. 'Taken to
the closest normal world in which the end is to be achieved, plan on using
the means.' Of course you should, and if Kant was right, you must, on pain
of forfeiting your claim genuinely to intend the end.

But this does not mean that if we switch to the different context, that of
external judgement, we need to see anything good either about having the
intention, or about using whichever means the intention requires if it is to
be fulfilled.

IX. Evaluation

Although the language of reasons can be used carefully, so that the necessary
distinctions are maintained, it makes it very easy to get all this wrong. Thus
consider the question whether Iago's villainous intention to destroy Othello
'provides a reason' or 'provides a normative reason' for him to manufacture

lies about Desdemona. We naturally recoil from saying that it does: we do not want to hear ourselves recommending anything about Iago's end, nor the means he adopts. On the other hand, Iago does his planning impeccably; having turned his hand to the plough, he does not turn back, even if he is ploughing the wrong field. How are we to combine our out-and-out rejection of Iago's intention and its handmaidens, with acknowledgement of his abilities as a planner?

Fortunately, we have ample ways of saying what needs to be said. There are two terrible things to say about Iago: he had villainous ends in view, and he chose villainous means to execute them. There is one, perhaps grudging, good thing to say about him: he is an able planner. When he contemplated and intended the closest normal world in which he is to effect Othello's destruction, he planned efficiently and as it turns out successfully to bring it about. If we imagine instead an Iago who (at least apparently, if we remember Kant), intends Othello's destruction, but does little or nothing effective to execute it, then things are reversed. There is one bad thing to say about him—he is not an effective or efficient planner—and two slightly better things can be said than are to be said in the Shakespearean scenario: first that he does not set up Desdemona, and second that his intention to destroy Othello seems relatively insecure or half-hearted. It is a mistake to try to shoehorn all these, and perhaps more, distinctions into the one verdict on whether Iago did or did not have a 'normative reason' for his behaviour or any part of it. The language simply will not bear the complexity of the distinction between the perspective of deliberation and that of external assessment, and it also encourages inattention to the crucial difference between description of Iago (given in terms of his reasons for doing one thing or another) and endorsement of one or another facet of the movements of his mind.

A conflation that assists in confusing this issue is that the conditional, 'If we intend the end, we ought to intend the means,' can sound as if the antecedent locates a state of mind, and then it looks as if the issue is to be whether our having that state of mind provides some sort of reason for supposing that we 'ought', perhaps in some strong ethical sense, to intend the means. And that sounds in general outrageous: how can we bootstrap ourselves into having reasons, or even obligations, so easily? But as I have already argued, in the context of deliberation the apparent reference to a state of mind is incidental. There is no inference from a state of mind to a plan, but only a supposition that something is to be done, to the conditional selection of a plan for doing it. And with this, the appearance that means–ends rationality or means–ends normativity provides a problem for Humeans, a shining jewel that they cannot pick up, and hence that gives theorists an incentive to mine for others, disappears.

X. The Plasticity of Reason

If we throw away attention to the particular nature of people's flaws, preferring a blanket diagnosis of 'unreasonable' or 'irrational' whenever their minds move in ways we think inferior, we not only lose important textures and distinctions, but we also lose most chances of engagement and improvement. For 'unreasonable' and still more 'irrational' not only function as general terms for denigrating the movement of people's minds. They usually have further, sinister connotations that the defect is irredeemable, that it is not sensitive to discursive pressure, that it licenses us to treat the subject as a patient or in other ways as beyond the human pale, or out of the game. Let us return to errant Sally. We can say, of course, that Sally is irrational or unreasonable—her mind is guided in bad ways. What we cannot do is invest the term with more interest than it gains from gesturing at the more specific and insightful descriptions of the particular flaws that infect Sally's character. But if we are to improve Sally, it is her particular flaws that need particular attention. We might want to cherish Sally a little more, be careful how we praise Molly when Sally is present, be more watchful against providing opportunities for envy and jealousy, and so forth. In harsher climates, we might have wanted to frighten or bribe her. Whatever rationalists, intuitionists, realists, Kantians, or Platonists may say, these are the only tools anyone has. We may win in the end. Sally may not be irredeemable after all. For one implication of all this is that reason is every bit as pliable as sentiment.

16

Fiction and Conviction

It is bad to be a fantasist, although sometimes it may not be that bad. We are, after all, sympathetic with Walter Mitty, whose fantasies remained largely where they should be, in his head. Fantasies only become problematic when they trespass across the reality barrier. It is some difficult cases about the nature of that trespass that are going to concern us.

Bernard Williams confronts a version of the problem I want to face (Williams 2002). In that book Williams gives us a state-of-nature story in which, by a natural evolution, truth and its attendant qualities of sincerity and accuracy come to be regarded as virtues. But having done that, he starts off in what he calls a different direction. He has not assumed that the people in his state of nature have what he calls an 'objective' conception of the past. According to that conception, which is our own, there is a temporal ordering in which every event has a fixed place. Every event either precedes, or follows, or is simultaneous with every other event. No event is outside the ordering, which is therefore complete. Niceties like the relativity of simultaneity to the motion of an observer do not concern us here. Furthermore, every event is determinately placed in the order: it is determinate how distant any event is from us, either in the past or the future. We may not know that distance, but in principle it has a magnitude.

Williams does not think that this objective conception is part of a heritage that goes back as far as recognizable human life, or that would have been there already in the state of nature. Indeed, he thinks that this objective conception arrived at a distinct point in history. In the West it arrived in the fifth century BC. It was absent, according to Williams, in Herodotus, but present in Thucydides. At one point Williams follows Hume in billing it as the arrival of and interest in fact instead of fable, or truth instead of myth (2002: 152). But describing it like that, in Williams's view, leaves out the interesting textures, which become visible only if we go on to ask whether Herodotus or his audience are supposed to have *believed* their stories about the gods. Although he does not put it quite like that, Williams gives us reason for doubting that they did. He says that in the context of doing whatever Herodotus was doing, the question, 'Is this a story we should tell?' would have had the force of 'Is this a story to be told now, to this audience?' meaning, 'Would it—as we may put it—suit them?' He goes on:

There is nothing in those people's practice to make us say that if they asked about such a story, 'Is it true?' there was some *further* consideration that might be brought in: that question, if it was asked was not an independent question. It is a question that indeed arises, everywhere, in relation to what is familiar and recent; relatedly everywhere it is one possible reason for not telling some stories to some people that one knows them not to be true. But those considerations did not press on those stories about the old days, with their strange content and their indeterminate temporal remoteness.   (Williams 2002: 160)

The idea is that there are 'familiar and recent' events, and that in anything recognizable as human life, there is a question of truth that arises about them. We want to know where the tiger went, or who ate the nuts, or whether as many people are now on the hunting party as when we set out. As soon as talk arrives, we want to sift true from false reports on such matters. Indeed, it is plausible that the relevant talk could not arrive in the first place, without a notion of truth arriving simultaneously. For the word 'tiger' to represent tigers, or be capable of functioning in a report that the tiger went into the cave, there has to be an operating notion of correctness and incorrectness, of the possibility of the reporter having got something right, or having got it wrong. For the word 'five' to deliver a contribution to the semantics of 'five of us started, but there are only three now', there has to be a technique of counting, and with the idea of technique goes that of something that can be done properly or improperly, correctly or wrongly.

II

Along with Williams, we can already sketch part of an answer to one question why being a fantasist is a vice, and calling someone a fantasist is an insult. The fantasist in whom the reality barrier has broken down is unreliable, believing things when he should not, and telling things as true when they are not. His inaccuracy, or insincerity (for they may blend together), is a nuisance, and one of an extremely important kind, both to himself and to others who rely upon him.

We can describe the connection between representation and action in a little more detail. Pieces of information can indeed be acted upon, and we can isolate the sub-sentential components and their specific contribution to typical explanations of actions and their outcomes. We might say, for instance, that

> 'tigers' represents tigers if and only if tigers typically play some role in explaining the successes and failures of action based upon sentences involving tokenings of the term.

This is the beginning of a programme of 'success semantics' (see essay 10). Obviously it requires expansion. We need some notion of an action as based on a tokening. And we need some confidence in the notion of a 'typical' explanation of the upshot of action. But the prospects seem bright enough for each aspect of the approach. When I token to myself, 'The tiger went in there,' and then behave warily and cautiously, the explanation of my survival will typically need to cite something about the tiger—that it went in there, or even if it didn't, that the chance of it being in there given my evidence was sufficiently high that caution in such a circumstance was highly desirable. The explanation does not typically cite corresponding facts about polar bears or beetles, and according to the suggestion, this is why 'tigers' refers to tigers rather than them. If we set out to hunt gazelle believing them to be in this patch of grass, the explanation of our failure may be that the gazelle were somewhere else. The explanation of this failure will not cite the whereabouts of buffalo or barnacles, although the explanation of other successes and failures may do so. Similarly, if I give you the message, 'Meet at Marble Arch,' and you act on it, then typically the explanation of our successful meeting is that we both go to Marble Arch. There will be other, atypical cases, but across the huge spectrum of communication the mundane explanations of our various successes cite the various things we represent, and the properties we represent them as having.

The idea, then, is that the disquotation of representation is illuminated by the disquotation of explanation. Now, these typical patterns of explanation emerge most clearly when we are engaged with the here-and-now, and the recent past or immediate future. There are naturally unfolding ways of acting on remarks about the immediate environment. This is why the simple fantasist is a nuisance.

We could suggest that the cases that interested Williams are ones where no such typical pattern of explanation is forthcoming. When we deal with the dim and mythical past, the very notion of success and its typical explanation blur. So, for instance, imagine a Herodotus writing the sentence: 'In those days, Athena helped the Greeks to overcome Troy.' This is not a sentence whose tokening readily prompts action in any very repeatable pattern. It has no typical engagement with current needs and desires. It is not clear how it belongs to any kind of technique for living. And if it is (for instance, through being part of a ritual which in turn has some kind of social or other function), we, who put no credence in Athena, are in no position to say that the typical explanation of success is that Athena has some property or other. Not ourselves in the grip of the Athena story, we disbelieve in her explanatory potential. We would suppose instead that the typical explanation of whatever successes or failures ensue on a tokening of the sentence should bypass Athena altogether, and simply cite the role an Athena character plays in the peoples' imaginings or narratives. All that is required is, in Williams's words, that the Athena story suits the people. Its representational properties play no role in explaining why that is so. It needs no connection with any particular stretch of space and time for life to unfold as it does.

In saying this we have jumped over a range of cases that do not concern the here-and-now, but where we certainly want to maintain genuine representation. I take it that, however it was with Herodotus, for us 'Henry VIII' represents a particular historical figure who had his own niche in objective historical time. We hold beliefs about him, and we suppose those beliefs to be true, although we may be aware that, beholden as they are to historical fact, some of them may be false. Now, there may seem not to be a typical pattern of success in action associated with speaking in such terms. A child may be successful in writing, 'Henry VIII lived from 1491 to 1547,' but the explanation of his success need not concentrate so much on Henry VIII and his actual lifespan, but only on what the child's teacher or examiner takes to have been the lifespan. Here Rorty's 'solidarity' serves the child just as well as truth does.

But this is not the end of the story. We who are realists about historical truth suppose that there is a 'typical' explanation of the centuries of acceptance of sentences translatable as 'Henry VIII lived from 1491 to 1547', and the explanation has it that that Henry VIII did live for that period, or at least was taken to have done so by his contemporaries and the records of the time. Our explanation does not stop with an explanation of why this story suits the people. It goes on to say why it suits the people, and it is there that it comes upon Henry VIII and his particular time and place. We might say that the *proximate* explanation of the child's success is that he gives the answer his teacher also gives. But the *full* explanation includes a long trail that, we take it, leads from Henry VIII, through the records, to teacher and child alike. The status of 'Henry VIII' as fully representational is restored once we bring in our full explanatory picture.

Returning to our theme, one way of tackling Williams's question whether Herodotus and his circle *believed* the mythological content of their writings, would be to ask what explanation they themselves would give of successes derived from thinking that Athena helped the Greeks. If they say, in effect, that the full explanation of why this story suits the people is that Athena did help the Greeks, then they sound like true believers. If, on the other hand, they rest content with something more sociological, then they do not. They may give grounds for a more nuanced explanation which mentions stories, but will not mention Athena. But of course in practice any such test will be highly imperfect. For there is no particular reason to expect people in general to be in control of the status of their own sayings, or to have a very reliable tacit understanding of it. We return to this point below.

III

Herodotus, as interpreted by Williams, is quite a long way from us—that is what makes Williams's suggestion so exciting. But is he, in fact, so far away? Is Williams right that the way Herodotus interleaves his history with myth suggests that he had not our objective conception of historical time and historical truth? Are we to believe that Herodotus literally cannot hear the question 'Is it true?' as a further question beyond 'Does it suit?'? I am not sure we are to believe this. And even if Herodotus is thus (by our lights) disabled, it is by no means clear that this in turn suggests he lacks a conception of objective historical time.

There are a number of reasons for scepticism about Williams's interpretation. First, in passages at the beginning of his history that Williams himself cites, Herodotus presents himself as pretty firmly in control of some basic historical method, such as the difficulty of reconciling what Persian historians and Greek historians say. He announces a preference for what he himself knows, and indeed throughout the narrative prefaces his innumerable delightful stories with cautious disclaimers. Secondly, following Williams's method, we risk having to say that if the objective concept of time arrived with Thucydides, it was fairly soon lost. For many Christian chronicles are at least as enthusiastic as Herodotus in the interleaving of history and myth. Indeed, it is something of a refrain in historians up to and including Leopold von Ranke to bemoan their predecessor's lamentable inability to distinguish the mythical from the actual. Williams would be faced with saying that the objective conception itself waxes and wanes with time. But a different hermeneutic method would suggest the less radical, and more charitable, interpretation that the point of writing at all changes with time, and for some purposes myth is just as good as what we would call history.

For example, it is just as good or better at revealing universal features of the human condition. We do not want to say that Wagner lacked a conception of objective time because he found it supremely valuable to rework ancient myths in order to do precisely this.

Consider another example of the same phenomenon. We, I take it, have a conception of objective space (or space-time). Yet some people are religious, and many of those who are go round talking of heaven as a 'better place' to which people go after they are dead, and where they live roughly the same kinds of life as people in ordinary space live, only free from woe. I do not want at this stage to call these people believers, for one of our issues is the nature of belief. Neutrally, I shall say that they are in the grip of a story. This story, like those of Herodotus, involves strange events and a 'place' of indeterminate remoteness, albeit spatial rather than temporal (although I suppose that heavenly events may be indeterminate in time as well). Those who talk like this may typically shrug off questions such as, 'How far away is heaven?' or, 'In which direction did the Virgin Mary fly off?' But I suggest that it is uncharitable to suppose that this undermines their credentials as having the same conception of objective space as the rest of us. They shrug off the question of what supports God's throne, but that by itself does not suggest that they lack other people's conception of mass or gravity.

In Wittgensteinian terms, we might say that it is no part of the religious language game that one has an answer to the question, 'How far away is heaven?' Indeed, it may be quite integral to the game that such a question not get asked. In the eyes of those in the grip of the story, it is a *crass* question. It shows misunderstanding, like the question Wittgenstein mocks, of asking whether if God sees everything, he must also have eyebrows (Wittgenstein 1966: 71). It mixes the religious too much with the profane, as would an expedition to discover the remains of Valhalla.

In Williams's view, our religious people suppose that ordinary space or time 'smear out', become indeterminate, and involve distances that cannot be measured. There are events that happen in time, but at no particular time from us, and there are events that happen in places, but at no specific distance from us. There are thrones that support people, but with no mass.

If we want to avoid this imputation, we face the question of how the religious language game is to be thought of. If people who talk of heaven and events in heaven are not describing an exotic part of space, with a distance and a direction from earth, what are they doing? There are many suggestions, some compatible with others, of which these are just a few:

> They are describing what they took to be events in a separate space or time, distinct from ours, in which people can nevertheless find themselves.
>
> They are telling stories: satisfying fictions.
>
> They are finding metaphors through which to gain some understanding of the human condition.
>
> They are insisting upon, expressing, or enacting certain emotional reactions to the human condition: hope, desire, rebellion, acceptance.
>
> They are performing, analogously to performing dances and songs, or reciting poetry.
>
> They are promoting the old human favourites: self-interest, self-importance, the will to power, the illusion of control over events.
>
> They are affirming identities, or separating themselves from others.

The first of these indeed offends against the completeness of the objective spatial order. But it involves a particular kind of claim, and one that is not readily applicable back to Herodotus. It must represent an over-interpretation of him. For a historian gripped by the idea of two times could behave in a number of ways. Plausibly, he might at the outset announce that he is only concerned with one of them, such as our objective time, and then he might be just like one of us. Similarly, a Christian physicist might be expected to do his physics just like anyone else: he does not have to confuse what he says about the space of our cosmos with what he says about the space which heaven occupies. Interleaving the two is more the subject of jokes, such as spoof calculations of how big angels' muscles need to be to support their wings.

Williams does not interpret Herodotus like this. The claim is that he lacked something we have, not that he had something we have, but an additional complication on top of it. I do not think the breakdown of completeness of the ordering, brought in by the 'two times' interpretation, shows any such lack. By analogy, imagine a mathematics concerned only with cardinal numbers and their ordering. It is not a disability, from the standpoint of this mathematics, if someone comes along and claims that as well as cardinal numbers there are complex numbers that do not fit naturally into the ordering of the cardinals. This discovery represents an advance rather than a disability.

None of the interpretations following the first impute a cognitive disability to the storytellers either. We may be inclined to grumble that if they are doing these later things, it is a pity that they chose a story told so like a recital of plain historical truth, in an apparently descriptive, factual language, in order to do them. But it is crucial to our exploration of the boundary between fact and fiction that this grumble may be misplaced. It seems entirely possible that there should be no better kind of language to use to do whatever it is that the religious storyteller is doing. This is suggested by Wittgenstein at one point: 'It says what it says. Why should you be able to substitute anything else?' (1966: 71). We might even mount a Darwinian argument: if there were better ways of doing it, it is surprising that they should not have emerged during the centuries of writing and wrestling that religious people have put into the task. So, for example, suppose the religious person finds 'I know that I shall see my Redeemer' a profoundly satisfactory and important thing to say. It seems presumptuous to suppose both that we know just what the satisfaction and importance are, and that we also know of a better way of achieving it. On the face of it, neither claim is easily sustained.

At this point reason totters, and we may be apt to feel a strong sense of outrage. Wittgensteinian theology sounds shifty, and priests who try to explain themselves in such terms are often thought of as atheists in all but name. Furthermore, an abyss of 'anything goes' relativism might seem to open up. We seem in danger of offering the sayings of religious storytellers a general-purpose immunity to any kind of alethic evaluation. And then the all-important barrier between fantasy and fact is being dismantled on their behalf.

This is indeed a threat. But at least the Wittgensteinian interpretation does not exempt the religious language from *ethical* criticism. We might know enough of what the satisfaction is to wish that religious people would not go in for it. We might gesture at some of the things that go into the mix, and if we find them distasteful we may campaign against the persistence of the sayings and doings. The storytelling might leave people who go in for it worse than they would otherwise have been.

Or it may be that we can connect their sayings with nothing at all. Wittgenstein says he comes close to this, when he considers the sayings of spiritualists. God is indeed dead, and those who go on being gripped by the stories become incomprehensible.

Bertrand Russell liked to compare religious belief with straightforwardly factual kinds of belief that were as improbable, scientifically, as anything could be: the belief that there is a china teapot in its own orbit around the sun, for example. It is fair to say that this identifies religion with mere superstition, foolishness. But now imagine that this teapot undergoes a sea change. Suppose it becomes an authority (out of its spout come forth important commands and promises). Suppose it becomes a source of comfort, as earthly teapots are, but more so. Suppose it becomes the focus of national identities: it is especially one of our teapots, not theirs. And so on: it answers prayers, adopts babies, consecrates marriages, closes grief. The teapot was cracked, but rose again and is now whole. It has achieved mythical, legendary, even religious status. It becomes crass to ask how big it is, how its orbit is shaped, what china it is made of. These questions demean and belittle the teapot, and probably suggest sacrilegious intent on the part of those who insist upon them.

When we imagine a people recounting the now-biblical stories of the teapot, it also belittles them to imagine them asking, 'Does this story suit us, here, now?' For them, the story very probably *requires* telling as it has been told (perhaps in the very words in which it has always been told, as children often require of their stories). Suiting us is the last thing on the storyteller's mind (even atheists like me recognize that religious doctrine often does not suit people, although I also hold that in diverse ways it often does, or it would not persist).

Notice, too, that if we ask the diagnostic, 'But is it true, about the teapot?' we may meet nothing but a flat, Wittgensteinian, minimalist or disquotationalist reply. 'p is true' means that p. It is true that the teapot answers prayers if and only if it does. And according to the religious storyteller, the thing to say is: it does. He is presenting it as to be accepted—as true.

Herodotus strikes me, as a non-specialist, as much less intoxicated by myth, legend, or theology than many subsequent historians and storytellers. He nods to the times when gods walked the earth, rather than insisting on them. I am not convinced that he is gripped by these stories. But Williams cannot hear this as bringing him any closer to the contemporary fold:

There are thousands of people in classical antiquity whose names we know, and who are certainly not legendary, but about whom we can assert very little; there are others who are legendary and about whom we can assert a great deal, such as Zeus. Since these are, for us, two different matters, to run them together, as this scholar does, is, for us, a muddle. But Herodotus himself did not make this muddle, because it was not yet possible to do so. In his outlook, there was, rather, a certain kind of indeterminacy about the past.[1]

As we have seen, the same attitude would condemn the Christian mythologist to having an outlook according to which there is a certain kind of indeterminacy about space, and possibly time. My alternative suggestion is that each of them avert their eyes from some questions which, on the face of it, their stories raise. The activity of storytelling itself does not allow these questions. The response to them is not, 'We just do not know how far away, in space or time, these events are.' Nor is it that they are an indeterminate distance or time away. The response is that we just do not

---

[1] Williams 2002: 157. Williams is attacking Lateiner 1990.

ask. If someone awkward insists on asking, there may be little difference between the shrug of rejection, the shrug of indeterminacy, and the shrug of not knowing—in other words, Williams is wrong to raise it as a charge against Donald Lateiner that he 'runs these together'. They are run together in the mind of one gripped by the story, who perhaps says that it pertains to a dim and distant place in space or time, about which certain questions need not and should not be raised. The hearer, in a somewhat Russellian vein, may interpret them as *just* storytelling, even while pretending not to be. Or he may complain that what they are doing can be done better without storytelling. He may complain of 'compartmentalization', the storyteller's evident ability to keep what is to be said about the teapot free from questions that normally arise about things in space and time. But at this point, for those in the grip of the story, the shutters come down. These are the things we say, the things to be said. Listen to the story, and you may learn something about the here-and-now, for that is its point of application.

IV

I have expressed reservations about Williams's treatment of Herodotus, and mentioned the indeterminacies that affect the philosophy of religion, only as means to the very different end of trying to understand the difference between fact and fiction.

It is currently quite popular to suggest that elements of our thought involve fictions. Numbers, theoretical entities in science, possible worlds, rights and values, selves, collectives, points, sets, and many other things have been given fictional status. Some people call them inventions or constructions; others more forthright call them fictions. We make believe that things stand thus-and-so with these things, and the make-believe has a function. It enables us to get something right about the real world, or do something right in the real world, the world which is not make-believe.

I hope that the story so far alerts us to a difficulty in formulating and assessing fictionalism. Is Herodotus making believe that there was once a ruler Minos, who may have ruled the seas before the first of the human race? Is the Christian making believe that there is a better place where all differences are reconciled? In other words, were we right to see

Wittgenstein's priests as atheists in dog collars? In some respects it is as if they are. Like the purveyor of overt fairy stories, they might even use a preface like 'once upon a time . . .', as a device to ward off what would otherwise be awkward questions, such as when exactly or where exactly these events are supposed to transpire or to have transpired. But in other respects, perhaps more important, it is as if they are not. To use Austin's distinction, these are 'serious' uses of speech, as opposed to parasitical, play-acting, quotational, or other non-literal uses. We have described the storytellers as gripped by their stories. They express *conviction*.

Thus, consider a philosopher of logic insisting that there are nearby possible worlds in which there are talking donkeys. This is serious. It is a conviction. There is nothing else to think; dissent even implies failure to understand the language and its use, while attempts to reduce or analyse away the content meet the equally strong conviction that nothing else will do. There is no other equally powerful and proper way of putting it. And questions about the whereabouts of these worlds, or the temporal distance of events in them, are as inappropriate as the parallel questions about divine events. Are we to take this logician's professions of realism at face value? Or can we happily conceive of his possible worlds as fictions? Or is there even an issue?

Suppose first we try to understand our philosopher in terms of fiction-alism. According to Lewis's analysis (Lewis 1978), we understand what it is for something to be true in a fiction by employing the concept of what is true in the closest possible worlds in which it is told as known fact. But in the difficult cases, which include those of numbers, possible worlds themselves, human rights, and others, the question is whether *this*, our very own world, is a possible world in which these things are being told as known fact. There is nothing fake or less than serious about the convictions of the storytellers. And as we have already acknowledged, we make no headway by introducing the notion of truth. 'It is true that there are possible worlds in which there are talking donkeys' comes with just the same ring of conviction as, 'There are possible worlds in which there are talking donkeys.'

To put the same point another way, we know when we have make-believe just insofar as we know when we have real belief. In an ordinary case, we can pretend, for instance, to believe that Saddam has gallons of anthrax, because we know what it would be to believe that he has gallons of anthrax, and we know too of things that would verify or falsify that belief. And if it is false, we know what kind of nuisance the politician is who fantasizes that it is true. But what distinguishes make-believe from real belief in the case of possible worlds? Is it possible that this is a difference that makes no difference?

I am reluctant to believe that it is, although our discussion certainly tends that way. I should confess that I am among those who finds Wittgensteinian religiosity uncomfortable, and at least half of me wants to insist on the charge of atheism in a dog-collar. But I am also aware that this may be because of ethical, and aesthetic, reservations about religious packages, rather than an insistence on knowing the difference between fact and fiction.

Perhaps here we may be reminded of J. L. Austin's own apparent unease with the 'constantive/performative' distinction, and his inclination to 'play Old Harry' with, among other things, the true/false distinction (Austin 1962: 151). The radical note underlying much of Austin's apparently inconsequential botanizing among illocutionary acts and verbs describing what we are doing, is that the concrete reality is the whole speech act. Hacking the class of sayings into fairly coarse subsets, labelling some as 'describing' as opposed to 'theorizing', or 'saying what is literally true' as opposed to 'idealizing' or 'producing a comparison', and so on are, in his eyes, suspicious and misleading ways of concealing the textures.

Returning to our example, if we cannot bear to be so radical, two possible avenues towards finding a difference are already in front of us. The first would be to see what explanations our philosopher offers of the success of his sayings. Conviction in possible worlds, he is implying, is a good thing, and it is legitimate to ask him why he thinks this. If the answer is sufficiently distant from what I called the fundamental schema of success semantics, above, then we may incline to the make-believe diagnosis. In particular if there is no disquotation in the explanation—no continued reference to possible worlds and their nature—then we should be more inclined to talk of make-believe and useful fictions. But I do not set much store by this avenue as an empirical procedure. People's own explanations of their doings are sufficiently inchoate that it would be tendentious to take them very much at face value. A mathematician's explanation of why it is useful to think that if we set out with five and now number only three, two have got lost, is probably going to be that five is two greater than three, and there is an end of it. A true believer's explanation of why it is useful to tell the story of heaven is all too likely to repeat the story of heaven. Why is it useful, we might ask the poetry lover, to be gripped by the thought that life, like a dome of many-coloured glass, stains the white radiance of eternity? And predictably, the reply may be that it is because that is what life does.

The alternative avenue is to set store by *our own* explanation of why it is useful to be gripped by the story, if indeed we think that it is. And here there is plenty of scope to get away from the disquotational. We do not have to manifest the grip of the story as we enter our own explanations. Suppose, for instance, I explain the utility of possible world storytelling something like this. We want to know what would have happened if something else had happened, in order to fix standing dispositions to action. It is useful to know whether, if we had connected the two wires, we would have blown the circuit, because we may need to guard against the intention or chance of connecting the two wires, or two such wires, in the future. If we think we would not have, when in fact we would have, there is a good chance of things going worse in the future. When we get it right, there is a good chance of things going better. This is why being gripped by the stories of nearby possible worlds helps us.

This may sound like an emphasis on the distinction between the participant's standpoint, and that of a theorist external to the practice but offering an explanation or diagnosis of it. Such explanations often offend participants, rubbing the bloom off their fruit, although that by itself is no argument that they are false. But in cases like that of possible worlds (more readily than in optional cases like that of religion) we are all participants at least some of the time. We do not need to drop our convictions as we simultaneously offer a non-disquotational explanation of them.

If we can advance and cement such explanations, what have we done to belief in possible worlds? We have shown that being gripped by the story is every bit as good as belief. Take the case where conviction is good, since it may be inappropriate to waver about whether if we had crossed the wires, we would have blown the circuit. The cash value in terms of actual acts and omissions is just the same whether we think of it as being gripped by a story, or being under the control of fact.

We can now go in either of two ways. We might say that we have shown that it is good to be gripped by the story, but wrong to believe it.

But this is only one option, since we have left ourselves with no working distinction between what is said to be good—being gripped—and what is said to be wrong—believing. And it is useless to try to reinvent this alleged distinction with phrases like the overused 'ontological commitment'. The *commitment* part is already there in the conviction that the thing to say is that there is a possible world in which there is a talking donkey. And the *ontological* part is just that this sentence, the one to say, begins with a quantifier. You can talk of ontological commitment by all means, but only if you know what you mean by saying that Shelley is, or is not, ontologically committed to the white radiance of eternity.

Nevertheless, I confess to a residual sense that we have saved our own philosophical souls if our fullest or best explanation of why it is good to be gripped by the story avoids disquotation. Perhaps it is not clear why saving our ontological souls should be a priority, and such is the view of Richard Rorty and others who reject any such discussion. But I maintain a more conservative position. If we can find bare, pragmatic, non-committal explanations of the good our stories do us, we may be on the way to seeing how things hang together better than if we cannot do so.

POSTSCRIPT

It may not be clear how the explorations in this essay relate to my own view that it is a mistake to think of an expressivist and quasi-realist package as any kind of fictionalism. If, as this essay suggests, the border between accepting a fiction and believing is as delicate and perhaps unreliable as the examples of religious conviction, or mythological conviction, or other 'constructivisms' suggest, then why fight the suggestion that in ethics we have nothing but a valuable fiction, alongside many others? If the principal diagnostic is what we are prepared to put into explanations, and if the expressivist is not prepared to cite, in his explanation of the value of morality, any ethical fact, then isn't he in effect a fictionalist?

My own response to this, above, is that we could say this only if we had the working contrast case: real belief. This is what is brought out most starkly by the Lewisian account of fiction, in which we understand what is true in a fiction by deploying the very notion of telling the fiction as known fact. I want to say we have no such contrast in the case of ethics, whereas we do, for instance, in the case of fictions about Saddam's chemical weapons.

I am not entirely satisfied with this response, however. It sets a high bar, and one other fictionalists may well refuse to jump. Does a mathematical fictionalist, for instance, have to have a story about what it would be not only to have mathematics as an indispensable fiction, but also what it would be to tell the mathematical story as known fact? Or would he not do better to let the whole distinction, in this application, lapse and fail to apply? So perhaps a better thing to say about the expressivist versus fictionalist proposals is that if expressivism is right, the whole idea of a fiction as opposed to a told truth lapses in this context. But it is a difficult matter to handle notions like 'construction' in connection with a theory of ethics, as I try to bring out in essay 2.

Bibliography

Anderson, Elizabeth S., and Richard H. Pildes. 2000. 'Expressive Theories of Law: A General Restatement.' *University of Pennsylvania Law Review* 148: 1503 ff.

Annas, Julia. 1999. *Platonic Ethics Old and New*. Ithaca, N.Y.: Cornell University Press.

Aristotle. 1998. *Metaphysics*, trans. Hugh Lawson-Tancred. Harmondsworth: Penguin.

—— 2009. *Nicomachean Ethics*, trans. David Ross and Lesley Brown. Oxford: Oxford University Press.

Austin, J. L. 1962. *How to Do Things with Words*. Oxford: Oxford University Press.

Baier, Annette. 1986. 'Trust and Antitrust.' *Ethics* 96.3: 231–60.

Bain, Alexander. 1859. *The Emotions and the Will*. London: Parker.

Bateson, M., D. Nettle, and G. Roberts. 2006. 'Cues of Being Watched Enhance Cooperation in a Real-World Setting.' *Biology Letters* 2: 412–14.

Bayle, Pierre. 1965. *Historical and Critical Dictionary*, trans. Richard H. Popkin. Indianapolis: Bobbs Merrill.

Bennett, Jonathan. 1965. 'Substance, Reality, and Primary Qualities.' *American Philosophical Quarterly* 2: 1–17.

—— 1974. 'The Conscience of Huckleberry Finn.' *Philosophy* 49.188: 123–34.

Berkeley, George. 1988. *Principles of Human Knowledge* and *Three Dialogues between Hylas and Philonous*, ed. R. S. Woolhouse. London: Penguin.

Binmore, Ken. 1994. *Game Theory and the Social Contract*, vol. 1. Cambridge, Mass.: MIT Press.

Blackburn, Simon. 1981. 'Reply: Rule-Following and Moral Realism.' In S. Holtzman and C. Leich, eds., *Wittgenstein: To Follow a Rule*, 163–87 (a reply to McDowell 1981). London: Routledge.

—— 1984a. 'The Individual Strikes Back.' *Synthèse* 58: 281–301. Reprinted in Blackburn 1993: 213–28.

—— 1984b. 'Knowledge, Truth, and Reliability'. Henrietta Hertz Lecture to the British Academy. *Proceedings of the British Academy* 70: 167–87. Reprinted in Blackburn 1993: 35–51.

—— 1984c. *Spreading the Word*. Oxford: Oxford University Press.

—— 1987. 'Morals and Modals.' In C. Wright and G. Macdonald, eds., *Fact, Science, and Value: Essays in Honour of A. J. Ayer's Language, Truth, and Logic*. Oxford: Blackwell, 1987. Reprinted in Blackburn 1993: 52–74.

——1990. 'Filling in Space.' *Analysis* 50.2: 62–5. Reprinted in Blackburn 1993: 255–8.

——1993. *Essays in Quasi-Realism*. New York: Oxford University Press.

——1998. *Ruling Passions*. Oxford: Clarendon Press.

——2002. 'How Emotional is the Virtuous Person?' In Peter Goldie, ed., *Understanding Emotions: Mind and Morals*. Aldershot: Ashgate Publishing.

——2005a. 'Quasi-Realism No Fictionalism' (a reply to Lewis 2005). In Kalderon 2005. Oxford: Oxford University Press.

——2005b. 'Success Semantics.' In Hallvard Lillehammer and D. H. Mellor, eds., *Ramsey's Legacy*, 22–36. Mind Association Occasional Series. Oxford: Oxford University Press.

——2009. 'Truth and A Priori Possibility: Egan's Charge against Quasi-Realism.' *Australasian Journal of Philosophy* 87.2: 201–13.

Boghossian, Paul. 1989. 'The Rule-Following Considerations.' *Mind* 98: 507–49.

Bonevac, D. 1998. 'Against Conditional Obligation.' *Noûs* 32.1: 37–53.

Braithwaite, J., and T. Makkai. 1993. *Trust and Compliance*. Canberra: ANU Working Papers.

Brandom, R. 1994. *Making it Explicit*. Cambridge, Mass.: Harvard University Press.

——2008. *Between Doing and Saying*. Oxford: Oxford University Press.

Bratman, M. 1987. *Intention, Plans, and Practical Reason*. Cambridge, Mass.: Harvard University Press.

Brest, Paul. 1976. 'The Supreme Court, 1975 Term. Foreword: In Defense of the Antidiscrimination Principle.' *Harvard Law Review* 90.1: 8 ff.

Broome, John. 2004. 'Reasons.' In R. Jay Wallace et al., eds., *Reason and Value: Themes from the Moral Philosophy of Joseph Raz*, 28–55. Oxford: Clarendon Press.

Butler, Bishop Joseph. 1953. *Fifteen Sermons*. London: G. Bell & Sons.

Carnap, R. 1958. 'Empiricism, Semantics and Ontology.' In *Meaning and Necessity: A Study in Semantics and Modal Logic* Chicago: University of Chicago Press.

Carroll, Lewis (Charles Dodgson). 1895. 'What the Tortoise Said to Achilles.' *Mind* 4: 278–80.

Cavell, Stanley. 1969. *Must We Mean What We Say?* New York: Charles Scribner.

Coady, A. J. 1992. *Testimony*. Oxford: Oxford University Press.

Cohon, Rachel. 1997. 'The Common Point of View in Hume's Ethics.' *Philosophy and Phenomenological Research* 57.4: 827–50.

Cowley, Christopher. 2005. 'A New Defence of Williams's Reasons-Internalism.' *Philosophical Investigations* 28.4: 346–68.

Cruttenden, Alan. 1986. *Intonation*. Cambridge: Cambridge University Press.

Dancy, J. 2000. *Practical Reality*. New York: Oxford University Press.

Davidson, Donald. 1968. 'On Saying That.' *Synthèse* 19: 130–46. Reprinted in Davidson, *Inquiries into Truth and Interpretation*. Oxford: Clarendon Press, 2nd edn 2001.

Dawes, Robyn M. 1988. *Rational Choice in an Uncertain World*. Orlando, Fla.: Harcourt Brace.

Dawkins, Richard. 1976. *The Selfish Gene*. Oxford: Oxford University Press.

Dokic, Jérôme, and Pascal Engel. 2002. *Frank Ramsey: Truth and Success*. London: Routledge.

Dreier, J. 2002. 'Meta-Ethics and Normative Commitment.' *Noûs* 36: 241–63.

—— 2004. 'Metaethics and the Problem of Creeping Minimalism.' *Philosophical Perspectives* 18: 23–44.

Drury, M. O'C. 1981. 'Conversations with Wittgenstein.' In Rush Rhees, ed., *Recollections of Wittgenstein*. Oxford: Oxford University Press.

Edwards, Jim. 1992. 'Secondary Qualities and the A Priori.' *Mind* 101: 263–72.

Field, H. 1994. 'Deflationist Views of Meaning and Content.' *Mind* 103: 249–85. Reprinted in Simon Blackburn and Keith Simmons, eds., *Truth*, 351–91. Oxford Readings in Philosophy. Oxford: Oxford University Press, 1999.

Fitzpatrick, W. 2004. 'Reasons, Value, and Particular Agents: Normative Relevance without Motivational Internalism.' *Mind* 113: 285–318.

Foot, P. R. 1978. 'Reasons for Action and Desires.' In Joseph Raz, ed., *Practical Reasoning*, 178–84. Oxford Readings in Philosophy. Oxford: Oxford University Press.

Gauthier, David. 1986. *Morals by Agreement*. Oxford: Oxford University Press.

Gibbard, Allan. 1990. *Wise Choices, Apt Feelings*. Cambridge, Mass.: Harvard University Press.

Gilbert, Margaret. 1989. *On Social Facts*. London: Routledge.

Green, T. H. 1874. Introduction to David Hume, *A Treatise of Human Nature*, ed. T. H. Green and T. H. Grose. London: Longmans, Green.

Grice, G. R. 1978. 'Motive and Reason.' In Joseph Raz, ed., *Practical Reasoning*, 168–77. Oxford Readings in Philosophy. Oxford: Oxford University Press.

Grice, H. P. 1957. 'Meaning.' *Philosophical Review* 66: 377–88.

Grover, D., J. Camp, and N. Belnap. 1975. 'A Prosentential Theory of Truth.' *Philosophical Studies* 27: 73–125.

Haldane, John, and Crispin Wright, eds. 1993. *Reality, Representation, and Projection*. Mind Association Occasional Series. New York: Oxford University Press.

Hampton, Jean. 1995. 'Does Hume Have an Instrumental Conception of Practical Reason?' *Hume Studies* 21: 57–74.

Hankinson, R. J. 1995. *The Sceptics*. London: Routledge.

Hardin, C. L. 1988. *Colour for Philosophers*. Bloomington, Ind.: Hackett.

Hardin, Russell. 1982. *Collective Action*. Baltimore, Md.: Johns Hopkins University Press.

Harman, G. 1977. *The Nature of Morality*. New York: Oxford University Press.

Harsanyi, John. 1977. *Rational Behaviour and Bargaining Equilibrium in Games and Social Situations*. Cambridge: Cambridge University Press.

Holton, Richard. 1993. 'Intentions, Response-Dependence and Immunity from Error', in Menzies 1993: 83–121.

—— 1994. 'Deciding to Trust, Coming to Believe.' *Australasian Journal of Philosophy* 72.1: 63–76.

—— 1996. 'Reason, Value, and the Muggletonians.' *Australasian Journal of Philosophy* 74.3: 484–7.

—— 1999. 'Intention and Weakness of Will.' *Journal of Philosophy* 96: 241–62.

Horwich, P. 1990. *Truth*. Oxford: Blackwell.

—— 1995. 'Meaning, Use and Truth.' *Mind* 104: 355–68.

—— 1998. *Meaning*. Oxford: Oxford University Press.

Hume, David. 1978. *A Treatise of Human Nature*, ed. L. A. Selby-Bigge, 3rd edn. rev. P. H. Nidditch. Oxford: Oxford University Press.

—— 1998. *An Enquiry Concerning the Principles of Morals*, ed. Tom Beauchamp. Oxford: Oxford University Press.

Johnston, Mark. 1989. 'Dispositional Theories of Value' (part of a symposium with Lewis 1989 and Smith 1989). *Proceedings of the Aristotelian Society Supplementary Volume* 63: 139–74.

—— 1993. 'Explanation, Response Dependence and Judgement Dependence.' In Menzies 1993.

—— 1994. 'Objectivity Refigured: Pragmatism without Verificationism.' In Haldane and Wright 1994: 85–130.

Jones, Karen. 1996. 'Trust as an Affective Attitude.' *Ethics* 107.1: 4–25.

Kalderon, M., ed. 2005. *Fictionalism in Metaphysics*. Oxford: Oxford University Press.

Kant, Immanuel. 1952. *The Critique of Judgement*, trans. James Meredith. Oxford: Clarendon Press.

—— 1963. *Critique of Pure Reason*, trans. Norman Kemp Smith. London: Macmillan.

—— 1997. *Groundwork of the Metaphysics of Morals*, in Kant, *Practical Philosophy*, ed. and trans. Mary J. Gregor, 37–108. Cambridge: Cambridge University Press.

Kaplan, D. 1978. 'Dthat.' Repr. in A. P. Martinich, ed., *Philosophy of Language*. New York: Oxford University Press.

Kerstein, Samuel. 2006. 'Reason, Sentiment and Categorical Imperatives.' In J. Dreier, ed., *Contemporary Debates in Moral Theory*. Oxford: Blackwell.

Korsgaard, Christine. 1986. 'Skepticism about Practical Reason.' *Journal of Philosophy* 83: 5–25.

—— 1996. *The Sources of Normativity*. Cambridge: Cambridge University Press.

—— 1999. 'The General Point of View: Love and Moral Approval in Hume's Ethics.' *Hume Studies* 25: 3–41.

Kraus, Jody. 1993. *The Limits of Hobbesian Contractarianism*. Cambridge: Cambridge University Press.

Kraut, Robert. 1990. 'Varieties of Pragmatism.' *Mind* 99.394: 157–83.

Kreps, David M. 1990. *Game Theory and Economic Modelling*. Oxford: Oxford University Press.

Kuehn, Manfred. 2001. *Kant*. Cambridge: Cambridge University Press.

Langton, Rae. 2007. 'Objective and Unconditioned Value.' *Philosophical Review* 116.2: 157–85.

Lateiner, Donald. 1990. *The Historical Method of Herodotus*. Toronto: University of Toronto Press.

Lewis, David. 1969. *Convention*. Cambridge, Mass.: Harvard University Press.

—— 1978. 'Truth in Fiction.' *American Philosophical Quarterly* 15: 37–46.

—— 1983. 'New Work for a Theory of Universals.' *Australasian Journal of Philosophy* 61: 343–77.

—— 1984. 'Putnam's Paradox.' *Australasian Journal of Philosophy* 62: 221–36.

—— 1989. 'Dispositional Theories of Value' (part of a symposium with Johnston 1989 and Smith 1989). *Proceedings of the Aristotelian Society Supplementary Volume* 63: 89–174.

—— 1996. 'Elusive Knowledge.' *Australasian Journal of Philosophy* 74: 549–67.

—— 2005. 'Quasi-Realism is Fictionalism.' In Kalderon 2005: 312–21. Oxford: Oxford University Press.

Lovibond, Sabina. 1983. *Realism and Imagination in Ethics*. Oxford: Blackwell.

McDowell, John. 1981. 'Non-Cognitivism and Rule-Following.' In S. Holtzman and C. Leich, eds., *Wittgenstein: To Follow a Rule*, 141–62. London: Routledge.

—— 1985. 'Values and Secondary Qualities.' In Ted Honderich, ed., *Morality and Objectivity*. London: Routledge & Kegan Paul.

—— 1996. *Mind and World*. Cambridge, Mass.: Harvard University Press.

McGinn, Colin. 1983. *The Subjective View*. Oxford: Clarendon Press.

Mackie, John. 1977. *Ethics: Inventing Right and Wrong*. Harmondsworth: Penguin.

Mann, Thomas. 1996. *The Magic Mountain*, trans. John E. Woods. New York: Vintage.

Menzies, Peter, ed. 1993. *Response-Dependent Concepts*. Working Papers in Philosophy, 1. Canberra: Australian National University, Research School of Social Sciences.

Milgram, Elijah. 1995. 'Was Hume a Humean?' *Hume Studies* 21: 75–93.

Monroe, Kresten Renwick, with Kristen Hill Marher. 1995. 'Psychology and Rational Actor Theory.' *Political Psychology* 16.1: 1–21.

Moore, G. E. 1903. *Principia Ethica*. Cambridge: Cambridge University Press.

Nagel, T. 1970. *The Possibility of Altruism*. Princeton: Princeton University Press; repr. 1978.

Nietzsche, Friedrich. 1968. *Twilight of the Idols*, trans. R. J. Hollingdale. Harmondsworth: Penguin Books.

—— 1969. *The Genealogy of Morals*, trans. Walter Kaufmann and R. J. Hollingdale. New York: Vintage Books.

—— 1974. *The Gay Science*, trans. Walter Kaufmann. New York: Vintage Books.

—— 1997. *Beyond Good and Evil*, trans. Helen Zimmern. Mineola, N.Y.: Dover.

Olson, M. 1963. *The Logic of Collective Action*. Cambridge, Mass.: Harvard University Press.

Papineau, David. 1987. *Reality and Representation*. Oxford: Blackwell.

—— 1993. *Philosophical Naturalism*. Oxford: Blackwell.

Parfit, Derek. 1984. *Reasons and Persons*. Oxford: Oxford University Press.

—— 1997. 'Reason and Motivation.' *Proceedings of the Aristotelian Society Supplementary Volume* 71: 99–130.

Peacocke, Christopher. 2004. *The Realm of Reason*. Oxford: Oxford University Press.

Pettit, Philip. 1991. 'Realism and Response Dependence.' *Mind* 100: 588.

—— and Wlodek Rabinowicz. 2001. 'Deliberative Democracy and the Discursive Dilemma.' *Noûs* 35, supplement: *Philosophical Issues*, no. 11, *Social, Political, and Legal Philosophy*, 268–99.

Plato. 2008. *Republic*, trans. R. Waterfield. Oxford: Oxford University Press.

Postema, J. 1995. 'Morality in the First Person Plural.' *Law and Philosophy* 14.1: 35–64.

Price, Huw. 1993. 'Two Paths to Pragmatism.' In Menzies 1993.

—— 2004. 'Naturalism Without Representationalism.' In David Macarthur and Mario De Caro, eds., *Naturalism in Question*, 71–88. Cambridge, Mass.: Harvard University Press.

—— 2010. *Naturalism Without Mirrors*. Oxford: Oxford University Press.

Price, Huw, and David Macarthur. 2007. 'Pragmatism, Quasi-Realism and the Global Challenge.' In Cheryl Misak, ed., *The New Pragmatists*, 91–120. Oxford: Oxford University Press.

Putnam Hilary. 1983. 'Models and Reality.' In his *Realism and Reason*, 1–26. Cambridge: Cambridge University Press.

—— 1992. *Renewing Philosophy*. Cambridge, Mass.: Harvard University Press.

—— 2000. *The Threefold Cord: Mind, Body, and World*. New York: Columbia University Press.

Putnam, Hilary. 2001. 'Reply to Bernard Williams's Philosophy as a Humanistic Discipline.' *Philosophy* 76: 605–14.

—— 2002. *The Collapse of the Fact/Value Dichotomy and Other Essays.* Cambridge, Mass.: Harvard University Press.

Quine, W. V. 1960. 'Carnap and Logical Truth.' *Synthèse* 12: 350–74.

—— 1969. 'Epistemology Naturalised.' In *Ontological Relativity and Other Essays.* New York: Columbia University Press.

Quinn, W. 1995. 'Putting Rationality in its Place.' In R. Hursthouse, G. Lawrence, and W. Quinn, eds., *Virtues and Reasons: Philippa Foot and Moral Theory.* Oxford: Oxford University Press.

Radcliffe, E. 1994. 'Hume on Motivating Sentiments, the General Point of View, and the Inculcation of Morality.' *Hume Studies* 20: 37–58.

Ramsey, F. P. 1990. 'Facts and Propositions.' Reprinted in Ramsey, *Foundations: Essays in Philosophy, Logic, Mathematics and Economics,* ed. D. H. Mellor. London: Routledge & Kegan Paul.

Raz, Joseph. 1975. *Practical Reason and Norms.* London: Hutchinson & Co. Ltd.

—— ed. 1978. *Practical Reasoning.* Oxford Readings in Philosophy. Oxford: Oxford University Press.

—— 2003. *The Practice of Value.* Oxford: Clarendon Press.

Regan, Donald H. 1986. 'The Supreme Court and State Protectionism: Making Sense of the Dormant Commerce Clause.' *Michigan Law Review* 84: 1091 ff.

Rhees, Rush. 1965. 'Some Developments in Wittgenstein's View of Ethics.' *Philosophical Review* 74: 17–26.

Robinson, H. 2009. 'Vagueness, Realism, Language and Thought.' *Proceedings of the Aristotelian Society* 109: 83–101.

Rorty, Richard. 1982. *Consequences of Pragmatism.* Brighton: Harvester Press.

Rosen, Gideon. 1994. 'Objectivity and Modern Idealism.' In Michaelis Michael and John O'Leary Hawthorne, eds., *Philosophy in Mind.* Dordrecht: Kluwer.

Russell, Bertrand. 1980. *Problems of Philosophy.* Oxford: Oxford University Press.

Samuelson, P. A. 1947. *Foundations of Economic Analysis.* Cambridge, Mass: Harvard University Press.

Sartre, J.-P. 1946. 'Existentialism is a Humanism', trans. Philip Mairet. In Walter Kaufman, ed., *Existentialism from Dostoevsky to Sartre,* 287–311. New York: Meridian.

Sayre-McCord, Geoff. 1994. 'On Why Hume's "General Point of View" isn't Ideal—and Shouldn't Be.' *Social Philosophy and Policy* 11: 202–28.

Scanlon, T. M. 1998. *What We Owe to Each Other.* Cambridge, Mass.: Belknap Press.

Schiller, F. C. S. 1907. *Studies in Humanism*. London: Macmillan.

Sellars, Wilfred. 1997. *Empiricism and the Philosophy of Mind*. Cambridge, Mass.: Harvard University Press.

Sen, Amartya. 1982. *Choice, Welfare, and Measurement*. Cambridge, Mass.: MIT Press.

Setiya, K. 2004. 'Against Internalism.' *Noûs* 38: 266–98.

—— 2007. 'Cognitivism about Instrumental Reason.' *Ethics* 117: 649–73.

Shafer-Landau, R. 2003. *Moral Realism: A Defence*. New York: Oxford University Press.

Shaw, Patrick. 1996. 'The Tortoise and the Prisoners' Dilemma.' *Mind* 105: 475–83.

Sidgwick, Henry. 1874. *Methods of Ethics*. London: Macmillan.

Sinclair, N. 2006. 'The Moral Belief Problem.' *Ratio* 19: 249–60.

—— 2007. 'Propositional Clothing and Belief.' *Philosophical Quarterly* 57: 342–62.

Sinnott-Armstrong, Walter. 1988. *Moral Dilemmas*. Oxford: Blackwell.

Skinner, Quentin. 2002. *Visions of Politics*. Cambridge: Cambridge University Press.

Smith, A. D. 1990. 'Of Primary and Secondary Qualities.' *Philosophical Review* 99: 221–54.

Smith, Adam. 1976. *The Theory of Moral Sentiments*, ed. D. D. Raphael and A. M. Macfie. Oxford: Oxford University Press.

Smith, Michael. 1989. 'Dispositional Theories of Value' (part of a symposium with Johnston 1989 and Lewis 1989). *Proceedings of the Aristotelian Society Supplementary Volume* 63: 89–111.

—— 1994. *The Moral Problem*. Oxford: Blackwell.

Snowdon, Paul. 1990. 'The Objects of Perceptual Appearance.' *Proceedings of the Aristotelian Society Supplementary Volume* 64: 121–50.

Suikkanen, Jussi. 2004. 'Reasons and Value: In Defence of the Buck-Passing Account.' *Ethical Theory and Moral Practice* 7: 513–35.

Suits, Bernard. 1978. *The Grasshopper: Games, Life and Utopia*. Toronto: University of Toronto Press.

Taylor, Barry. 1991. ' "Just More Theory": A Manoeuvre in Putnam's Model-Theoretic Argument for Antirealism.' *Australasian Journal of Philosophy* 69: 152–66.

Thomason, R. 1981. 'Deontic Logic and the Role of Freedom in Moral Deliberation.' In R. Hilpinen, ed., *New Studies in Deontic Logic*, 177–86. Dordrecht: Reidel.

Von Neumann, J., and O. Morgenstern. 1944. *The Theory of Games and Economic Behavior*. Princeton: Princeton University Press.

Wallace, R. Jay. 1999. 'Three Conceptions of Rational Agency.' *Ethical Theory and Moral Practice* 2: 21–42.

—— 2002. 'Scanlon's Contractualism.' *Ethics* 112.3: 429–70.

—— et al., eds. 2004. *Reason and Value: Themes from the Moral Philosophy of Joseph Raz*. Oxford: Clarendon Press.

Westphal, Jonathan. 1991. *Colour: A Philosophical Introduction*. Oxford: Blackwell.

Whyte, Jamie. 1990. 'Success Semantics.' *Analysis* 50: 149–57.

Williams, Bernard. 1966. 'Consistency and Realism.' *Proceedings of the Aristotelian Society Supplementary Volume* 40: 1–22.

—— 1978. *Descartes: The Project of Pure Inquiry*. Harmondsworth: Penguin Books.

—— 1979. 'Internal and External Reasons.' Reprinted in Williams, *Moral Luck*, 101–13. Cambridge: Cambridge University Press, 1981.

—— 1985. *Ethics and the Limits of Philosophy*. London: Fontana.

—— 1993. *Shame and Necessity*. Berkeley and Los Angeles: University of California Press.

—— 1995. 'Internal Reasons and the Obscurity of Blame.' In Williams, *Making Sense of Humanity*. Cambridge: Cambridge University Press.

—— 2002. *Truth and Truthfulness*. Princeton: Princeton University Press.

Wilson, Margaret. 1992. 'History of Philosophy in Philosophy Today, and the Case of Secondary Qualities.' *Philosophical Review* 101.1: 191–243.

Wisdom, John. 1936–7. 'Philosophical Perplexity.' *Proceedings of the Aristotelian Society* 37.

Wittgenstein, Ludwig. 1953. *Philosophical Investigations*, trans. G. E. M. Anscombe. Oxford: Blackwell.

—— 1965. 'A Lecture on Ethics.' *Philosophical Review* 74.1: 3–12.

—— 1966. *Lectures and Conversations on Aesthetics, Psychology, and Religious Belief*, ed. Cyril Barrett. Oxford: Blackwell.

—— 1967. *Zettel*, ed. G. E. M. Anscombe and G. H. von Wright, trans. G. E. M. Anscombe. Oxford: Blackwell.

—— 1969. *On Certainty*, ed. G. E. M. Anscombe and G. H. von Wright, trans. Denis Paul and G. E. M. Anscombe. Oxford: Blackwell.

—— 1978. *Remarks on the Foundations of Mathematics*, 3rd edn., ed. G. H. von Wright, R. Rhees, and G. E. M. Anscombe, trans. G. E. M. Anscombe. Oxford: Blackwell.

—— 1980a. *Culture and Value*, ed. G. H. von Wright, trans. Peter Winch. Oxford: Blackwell. [1977 date given in 'Witt's Irrealism', n. 1]

—— 1980b. *Remarks on the Philosophy of Psychology*, ed. G. E. M. Anscombe, G. H. von Wright, and Heikki Nyman, trans. G. E. M. Anscombe. Oxford: Blackwell.

Wong, D. 2006. 'Moral Reasons: Internal and External.' *Philosophy and Phenomenological Research* 72: 536–58.

Wright, Crispin. 1988. 'Moral Values, Projection and Secondary Qualities.' *Proceedings of the Aristotelian Society Supplementary Volume* 62: 1–26.

—— 1989. 'Wittgenstein's Rule-Following Considerations and the Central Project of Theoretical Linguistics.' In A. George, ed., *Reflections on Chomsky*. Oxford: Blackwell.

Index